NOT JUST PARIS
SCENES FROM FRANCE

Other Books by Liz Scotta:

My Sketchbook of San Miguel de Allende | Mi cuaderno de dibujo de San Miguel de Allende

Travels with a Sketchbook

ISBN: 978-0-9906102-4-3

CREDITS
Cover: Honfleur by Liz Scotta
Author Photo: Martin Jennings
Book Design: Patricia García Arreola

NOT JUST PARIS
SCENES FROM FRANCE

LIZ SCOTTA

FOR MARTIN

"It's really a drag to sit around when you're old, and think,
'Ah, gee, I never went to France.' Go to France. Life is very
short; you've got to pack it all in there."

— Grace Slick

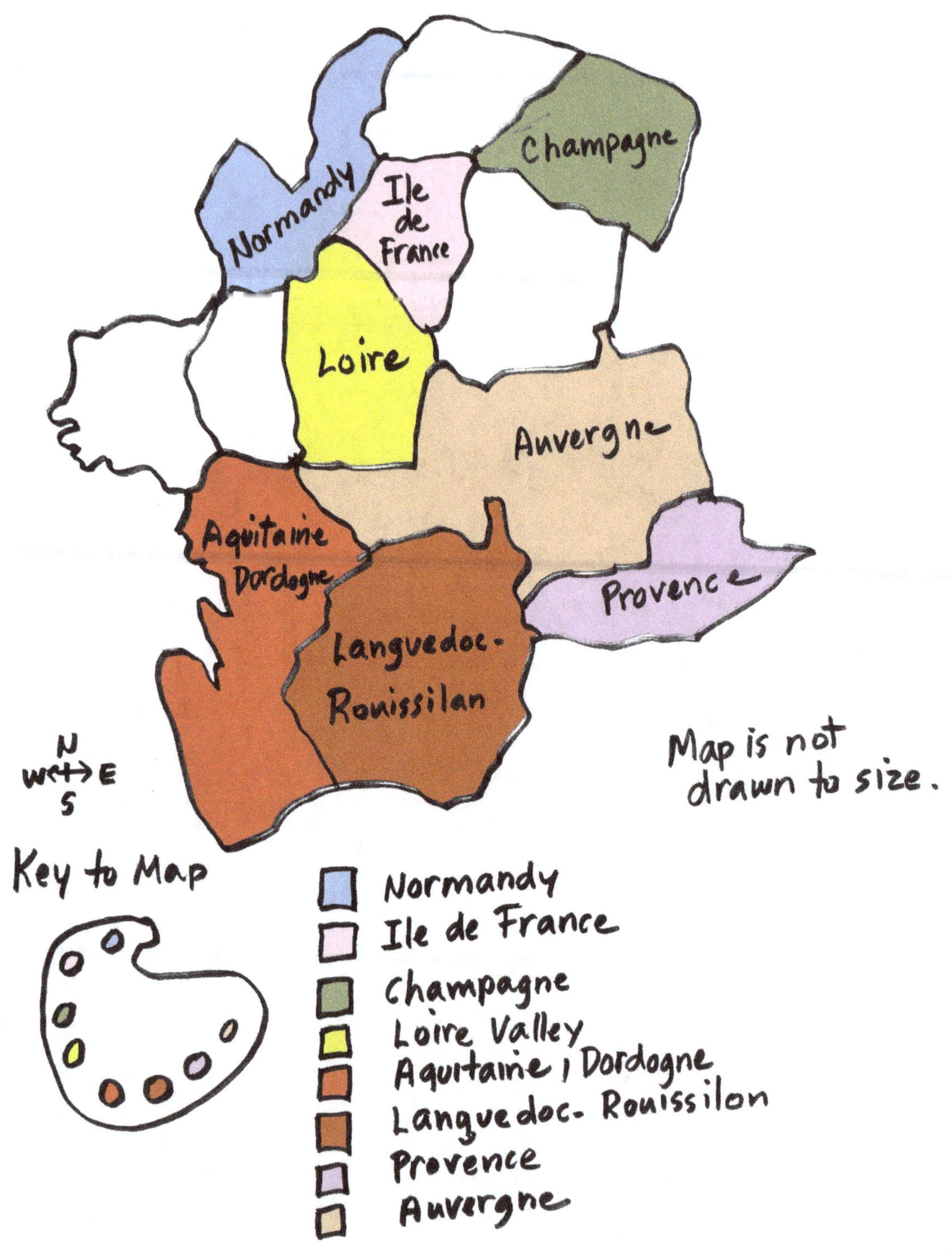

Champagne
Normandy
Ile de France
Loire
Auvergne
Aquitaine / Dordogne
Provence
Languedoc-Rouissilan
N
W E
S
Map is not drawn to size.
Key to Map
Normandy
Ile de France
Champagne
Loire Valley
Aquitaine / Dordogne
Languedoc- Rouissilon
Provence
Auvergne

TABLE OF CONTENTS

FOREWORD

It's our pleasure to write a foreword to Liz Scotta's new book of sketches, *Not Just Paris*. We've been getting glimpses of her work over the past several years and are delighted to see it all come together in this lovely portfolio that reminds us of so many of our favorite places in France.

Liz is a great woman and a talented artist. She devoted herself to teaching the children of San Francisco and other civic endeavors before her retirement a few years ago. But retirement is hardly the word for Liz: she is always occupied in drawing, traveling the world and expanding her mind and skills.

After extensive travels in Latin America, Liz started French courses at City College of San Francisco and enrolled in our European Studies Paris July program. That experience fueled her desires to visit other parts of France, from Normandy and the Loire to Provence and the Southwest. She is passionate about drawing and had published her drawings of Latin America.

Now she brings her artistic abilities to many picturesque regions of France. She presents the vivid colors of the Midi and the castles and cathedrals of the Loire. Her enthusiasm for drawing and painting has inspired us to add a "Landscapes with Liz" class to our summer program—a new favorite activity for everyone.

As Paris has been her temporary home for many months over the last years, her sketches encompass both the famous monuments like Notre Dame and St. Sulpice, as well as more personal perspectives like the view from her dorm room near the Luxembourg Gardens. Alternating with the famous spots, Liz's artwork gives you the flavor of French life in cafés and restaurants, markets and residential streets. She clearly brings a fresh eye to her multiple subjects.

This book of sketches is both a reminder to those who have also been to France and a visual guide to those who wish to continue their exploration. If you are a budding artist, the book provides encouragement to your work; and if you are a visitor to la belle France, it invites you to follow in Liz's footsteps. "Bon Voyage!" says Liz whether you are sketching or sitting in your armchair.

Dr. Tom Blair & Dr. Terri Nelson

INTRODUCTION

This book is a tribute to Dr. Tom Blair. He's a wonderful educator, who has introduced students of all ages to Paris, through a French language study program, the European Studies Association ("ESA"). At the age of 67, I became one of those students and documented my experiences and sensations in pen and ink, watercolor, and collage. ESA placed us in the heart of Paris for the entire month of July.

My dormitory was built in 1755 by the Real Estate Lawyer of the Royal Family, King Louis XVI, and would be my home for the entire month. I squealed in delight that I would be "living like a local" and made the decision there and then to document my experiences in a book I would publish in roughly five years. As that first month progressed, I decided, like attempting to eat "just one Lay's potato chip", I couldn't do with just one summer. So, I returned in 2018 and then in 2019. In 2020, Covid forced me to stay home and dream of going to Paris and France, shown in this book by the Virtual Vacation I created with scissors, glue and fashion magazine pages. I returned for a short visit in 2021, followed by 3 months studying French and fashion that fall when I lived in a dormitory with French university students.

The goal and catalyst of this book was to celebrate this program that allowed me to be enthralled by, and capture, all things Parisian. The book is divided into seven chapters of images selected from 20 of the sketchbooks I completed between the pre-Covid and post- Pandemic years of 2017–2022.

Through ESA, Dr. Blair has shared his love of France with community college students from both Northern and Southern California for 45 years. He opens the ears of students to hear the music of Vivaldi in concert at the medieval Sainte-Chapelle, Opera at the Palais Garnier built for Napoleon, street musicians on the Port Neuf, oldest bridge in Paris, and even to the sounds of Parisian ambulances. Students experience an unforgettable séjour, including visits to Musee d'Orsay to view early Modern and Impressionist art and the Louvre to see Leonardo da Vinci's Mona Lisa. He invites students to smell the flowers of Monet's garden at Giverny and taste the fresh baguettes at breakfast, and has taught them the near touch of the bisou "kisses" with which the charming French greet one another. All students have the opportunity to learn the French language and to learn about Parisian culture, including the etiquette of how to eat a banana with a fork and knife.

In 2021, during the pandemic, I left San Francisco for France on two occasions. The last trip I've included in this book is a trip with Dr. Blair & Dr. Nelson to the Dordogne in June and Paris, in July 2022. I joined Urban Sketchers Paris drawing at the horse track of Hippodrome-St. Cloud, not betting on the horses like Hemingway. I enjoyed the jitterbug dancers along the River Seine. Then crowned it all with my two watercolors of Mont St. Michel.

In addition to Paris, I've taken and recorded day and weekend trips to Auvers-sur-Oise, Chartres, Reims, Mont St. Michelle, and weekend trips to the Loire Valley and Normandy; side trips to Reims, Rouen, and included are my renderings of art workshops in southern France.

I especially like painting at both Honfleur (watercolor on the cover of this book) and Étretat where students visited on a weekend excursion. As part of ESA, I have endeavored to draw all major museums, churches, markets, train stations, stores, and opera houses in Paris as well as the castles in the surrounding areas. Imagine having drawn Notre Dame both before and after the 2019 fire, or sketching the interior and exteriors of the Louvre. With great pleasure I taught watercolor to Milton, a nephew of I.M. Pei.

Reflecting back over the years, I have drawn cabaret by candle light at the Moulin Rouge, in the dark at Lombard Le Luc Jazz Club, and in the grandeur of Sainte-Chapelle for concerts. My drawings occurred on top of the Pompidou museum, at the Arc de Triomphe where 40 degree winds blew for hours, and at Place de l'Horloge, Avignon in the sultry heatwave. I have often irritated waiters with my sketchbook on the table while drawing in cafes and restaurants, but then delighted them when finished. My drawings include documenting my boyfriend's hair cut, washing clothes in a laundromat (right down the street from Gertrude Stein's home), visiting Père-Lachaise Cemetery in the rain, and capturing caricature artists at Montmartre as well as enjoying a plethora of water fountains.   I even drew a Priest performing a Catholic service. When I showed him the sketch afterwards, he asked me if he could take a photo of my drawing for his mother. I drew during classes, lectures, in book stores, at a Messy Nessy blogger's book opening, and at the magnificent Parisian Bibliothèque Richelieu-Louvois (the national library).

As a former Art History major, I have walked in the footsteps of French impressionist artists and collaged my version of the church at Auvers-sur-Oise, made famous by Van Gogh, and the cliffs of Étretat. I've drawn on boats down the Seine, and on trains observing the countryside.

My advice to travelers - don't go anywhere without a sketchbook. Unlike an iPhone it doesn't run out of juice. Take photos for color reference—in case a truck parks in front of your view as you sit in an adorable café but draw, draw, draw. Even if you don't consider yourself an "artist", drawing will help you to experience the sites more profoundly and intimately as you explore the contours of the shapes, noticing details like 2 different temperatures on the same building. Drawing helps to imprint these moments in a very personal and permanent way.

While the drawings in this book are a record of my experiences, the true subject of this book is delight—delight found in the subject, surroundings, and circumstances presented to me each day in France. It was a curious pleasure for all my senses. In 2017 when I asked myself, "do you want to wake up in Paris for 30 consecutive mornings or stroll along the Seine under a full moon?" This book is my answer—oui! Bien sûr et avec plaisir!

Veni, vidi, illustravi
I came, I saw, I drew.

Liz Scotta
San Francisco

2017

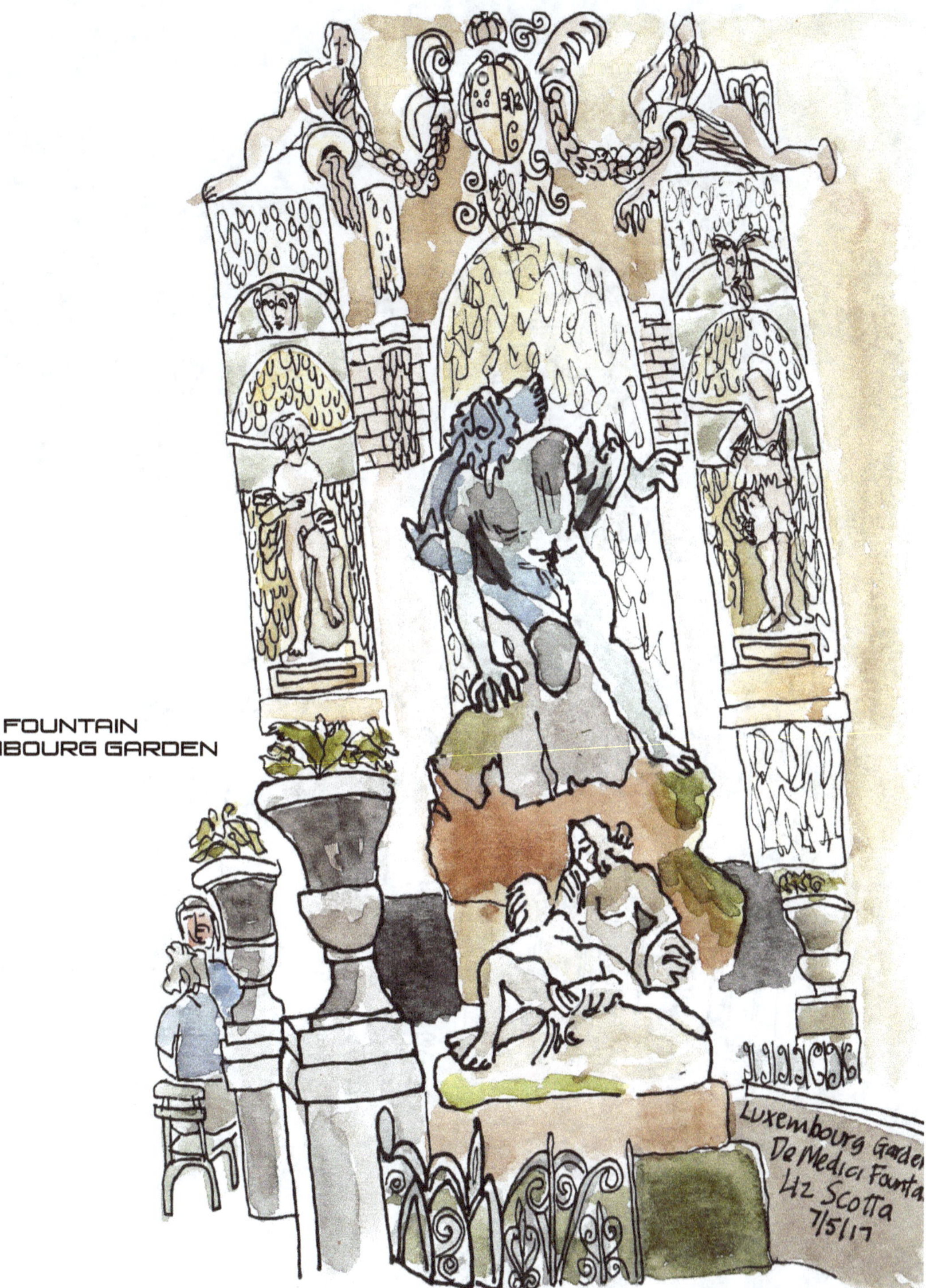

MEDICI FOUNTAIN
LUXEMBOURG GARDEN
PARIS

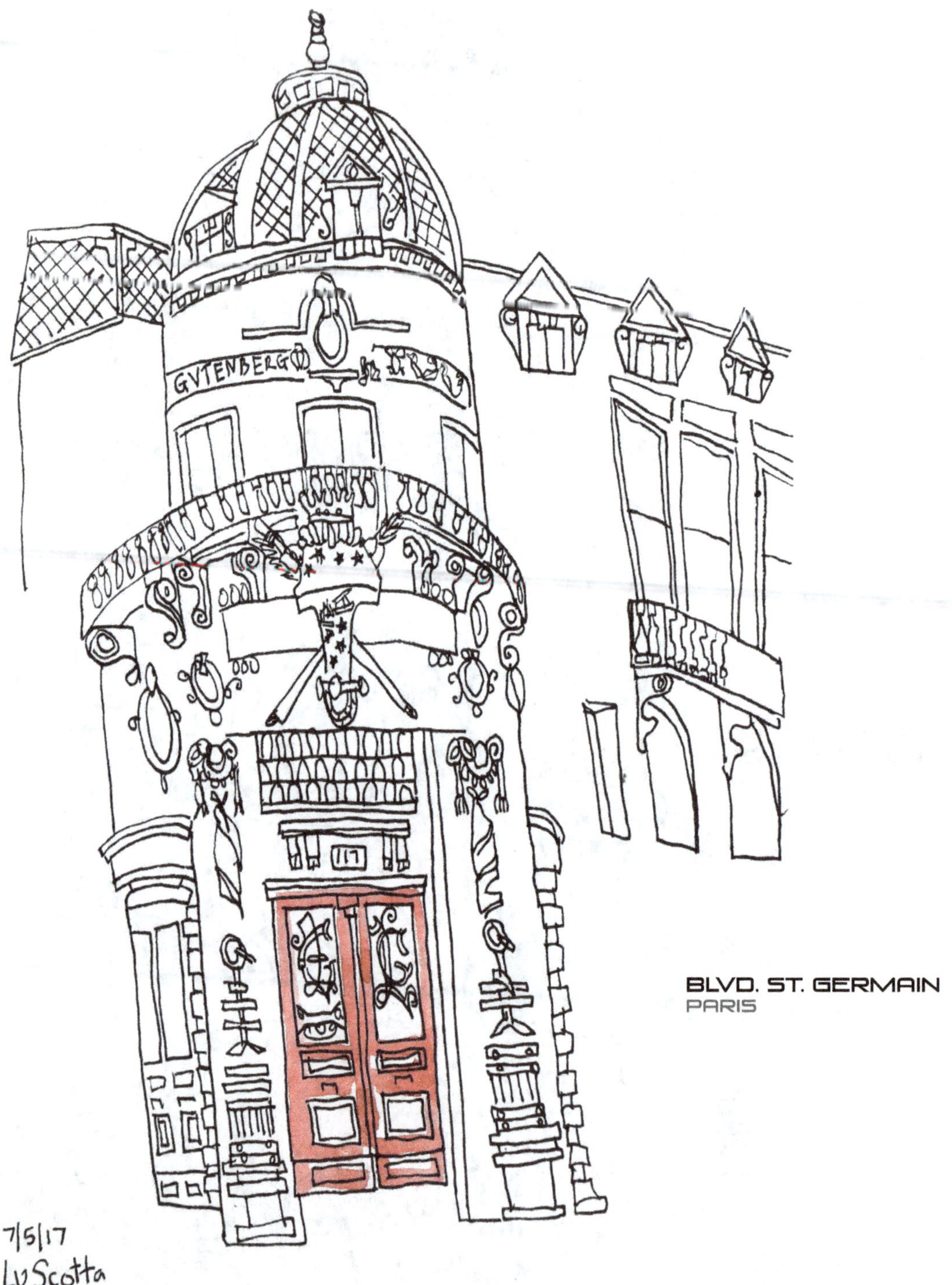

BLVD. ST. GERMAIN
PARIS

7/5/17
Le Scotta

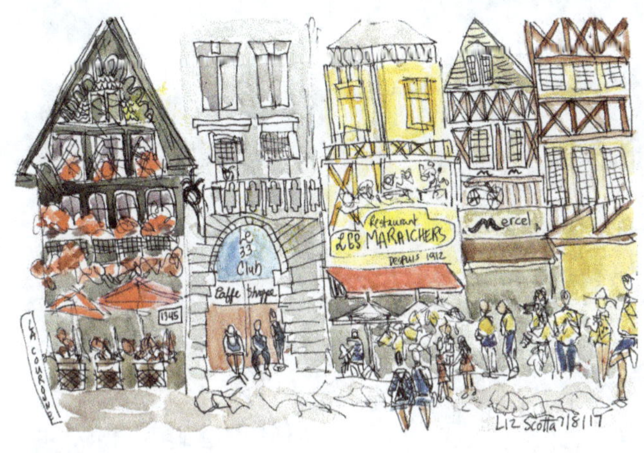

HALF-TIMBERED ARCHITECTURE
ROUEN

RUE D'ASSAS
PARIS

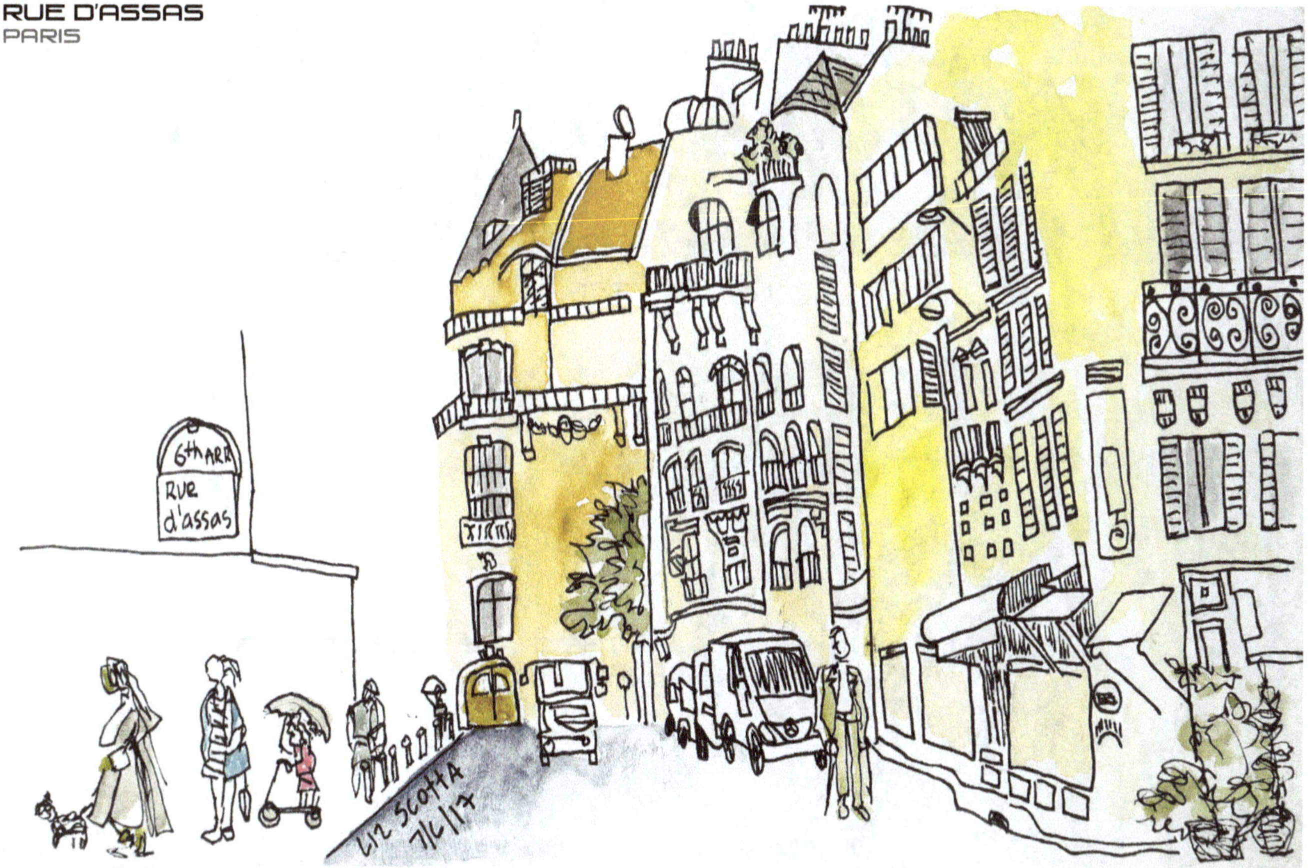

2017

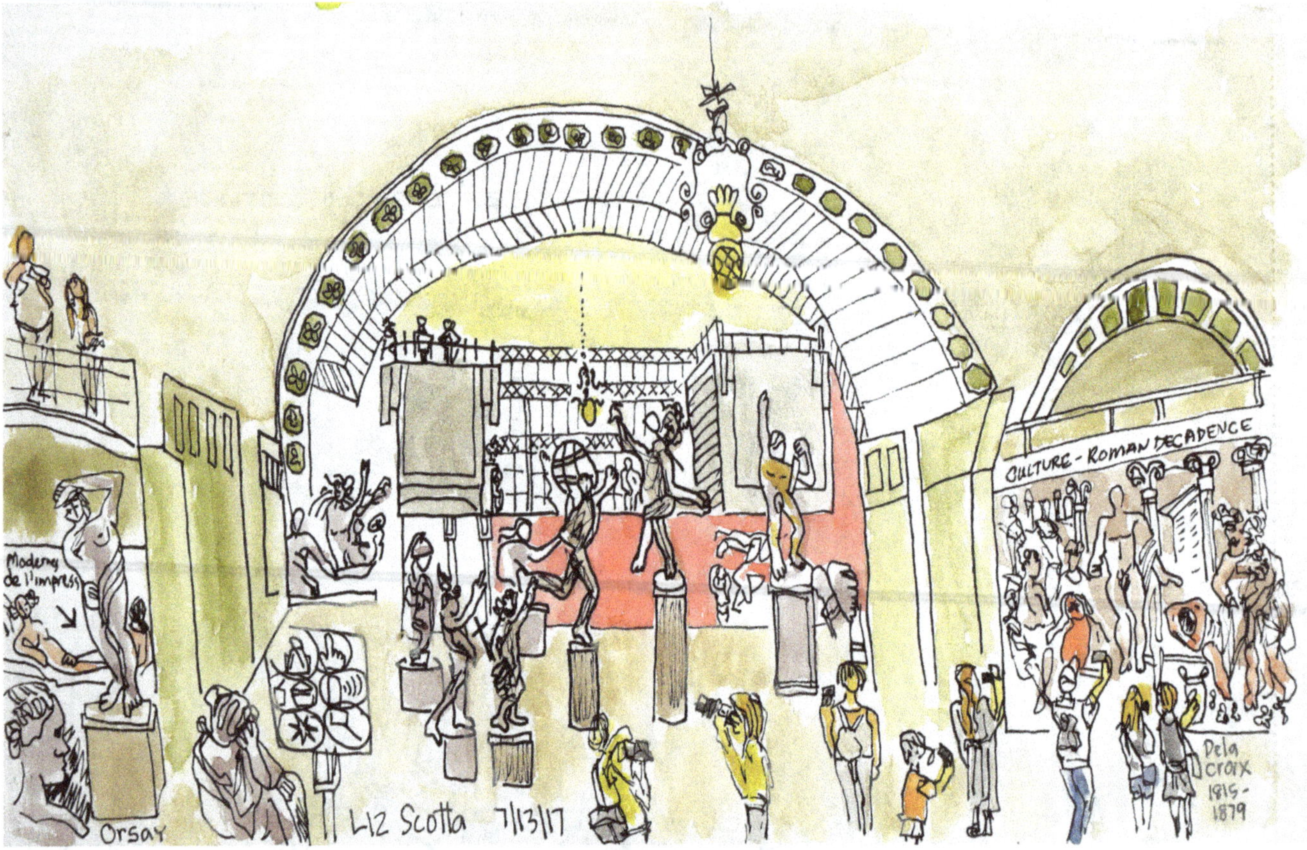

MUSÉE ORSAY
PARIS

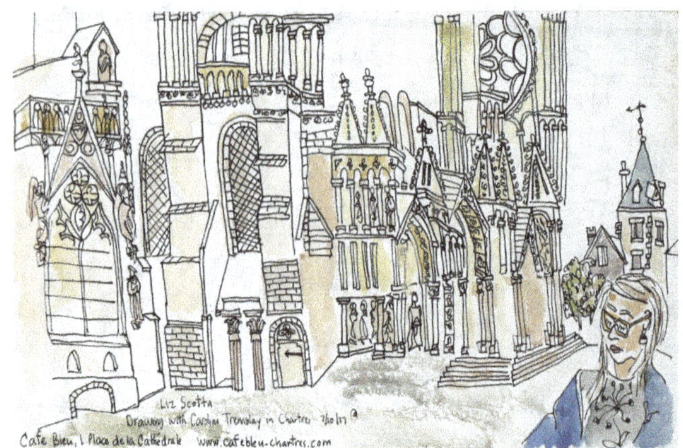

CATHÉDRALE DE CHARTRES
CHARTRES

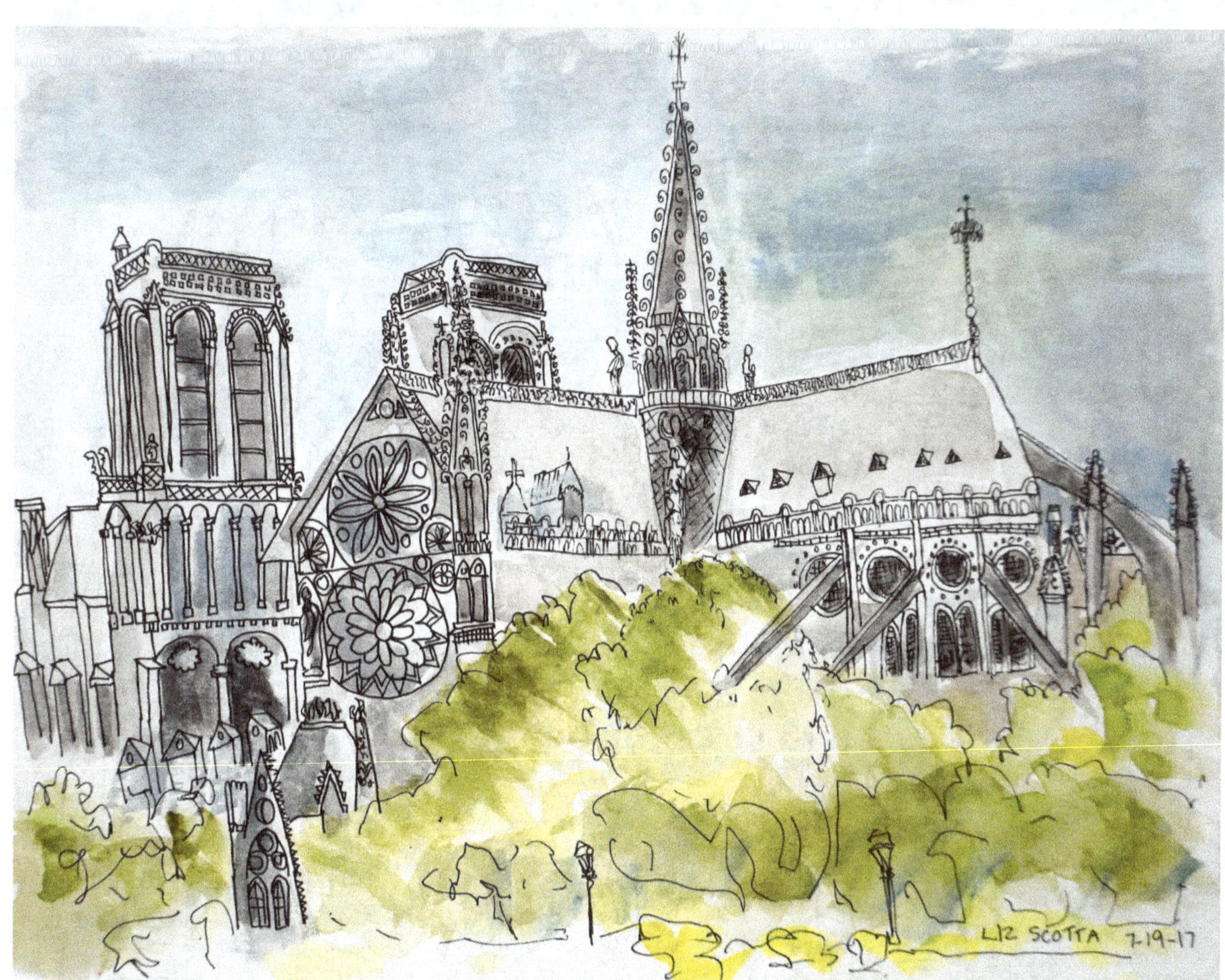

CATHÉDRALE DE NOTRE DAME
PARIS

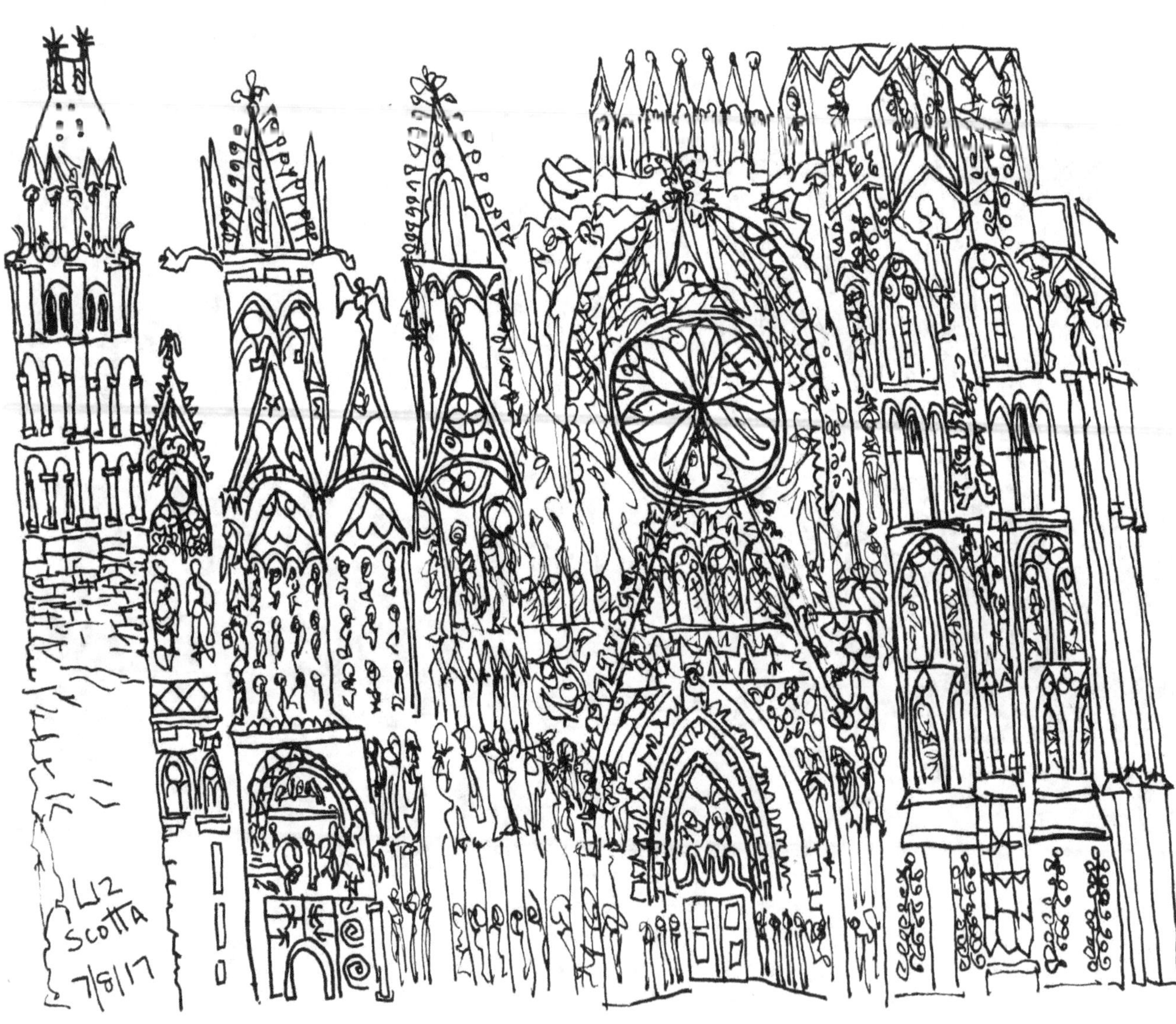

CATHÉDRALE DE ROUEN
ROUEN

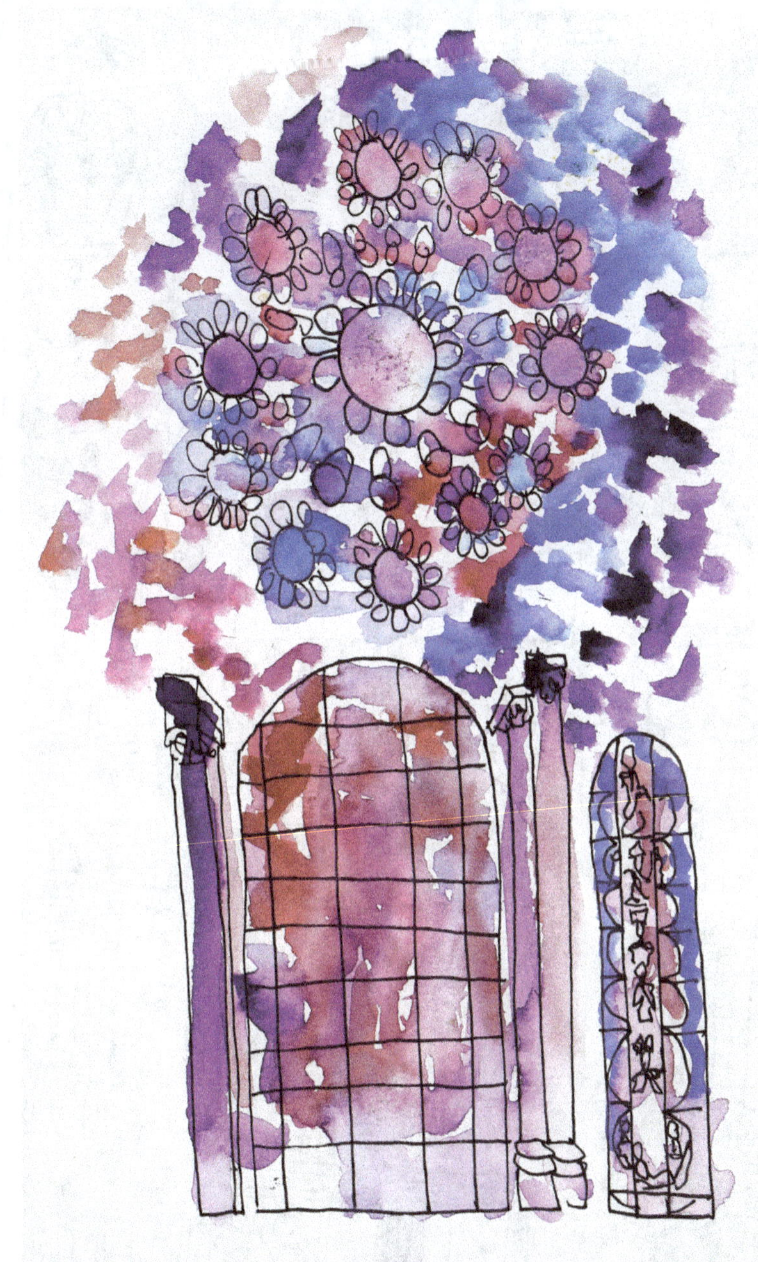

ROSE WINDOW CHARTRES
CHARTRES

2017

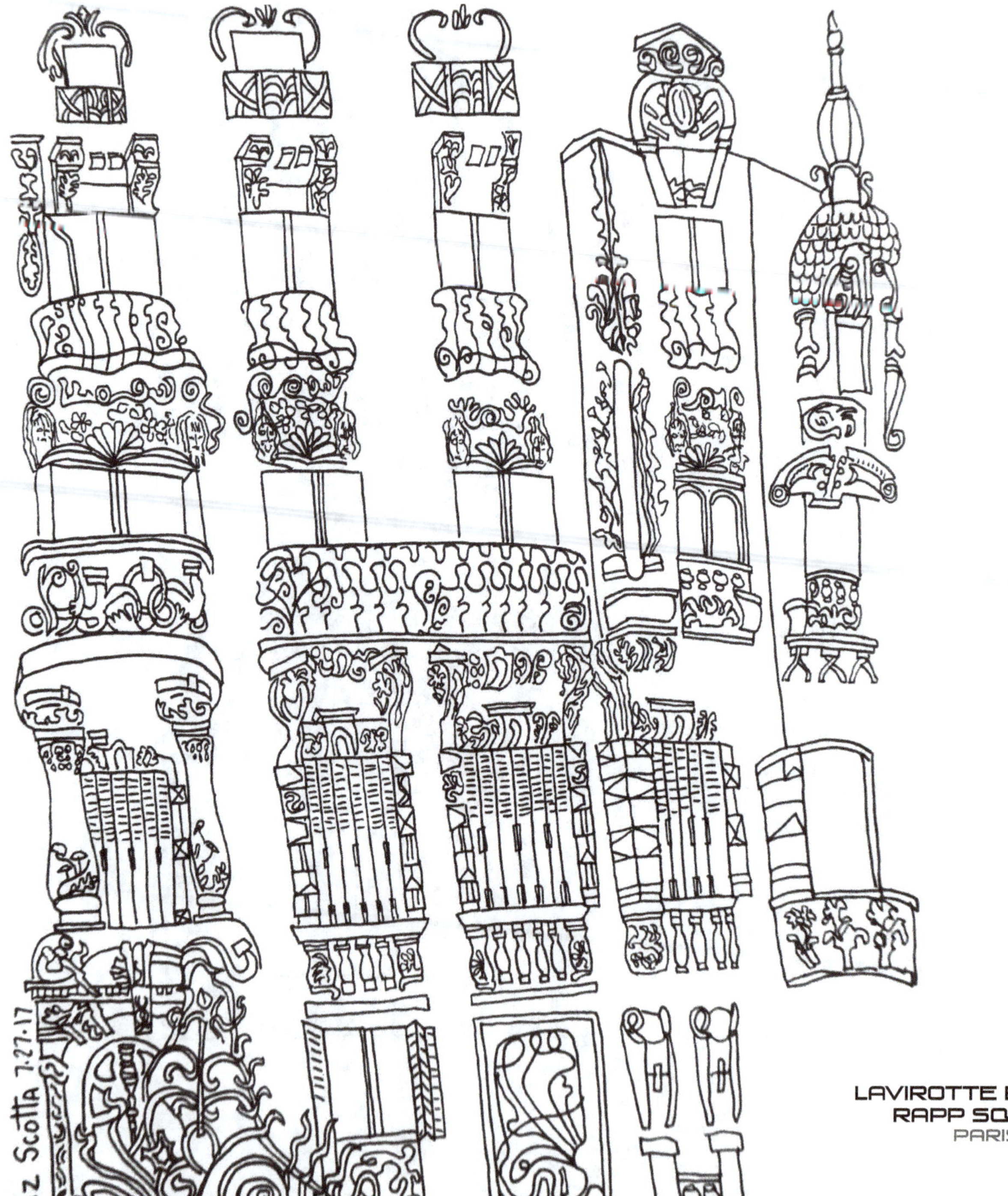

2017

Liz Scotia 7.27.17

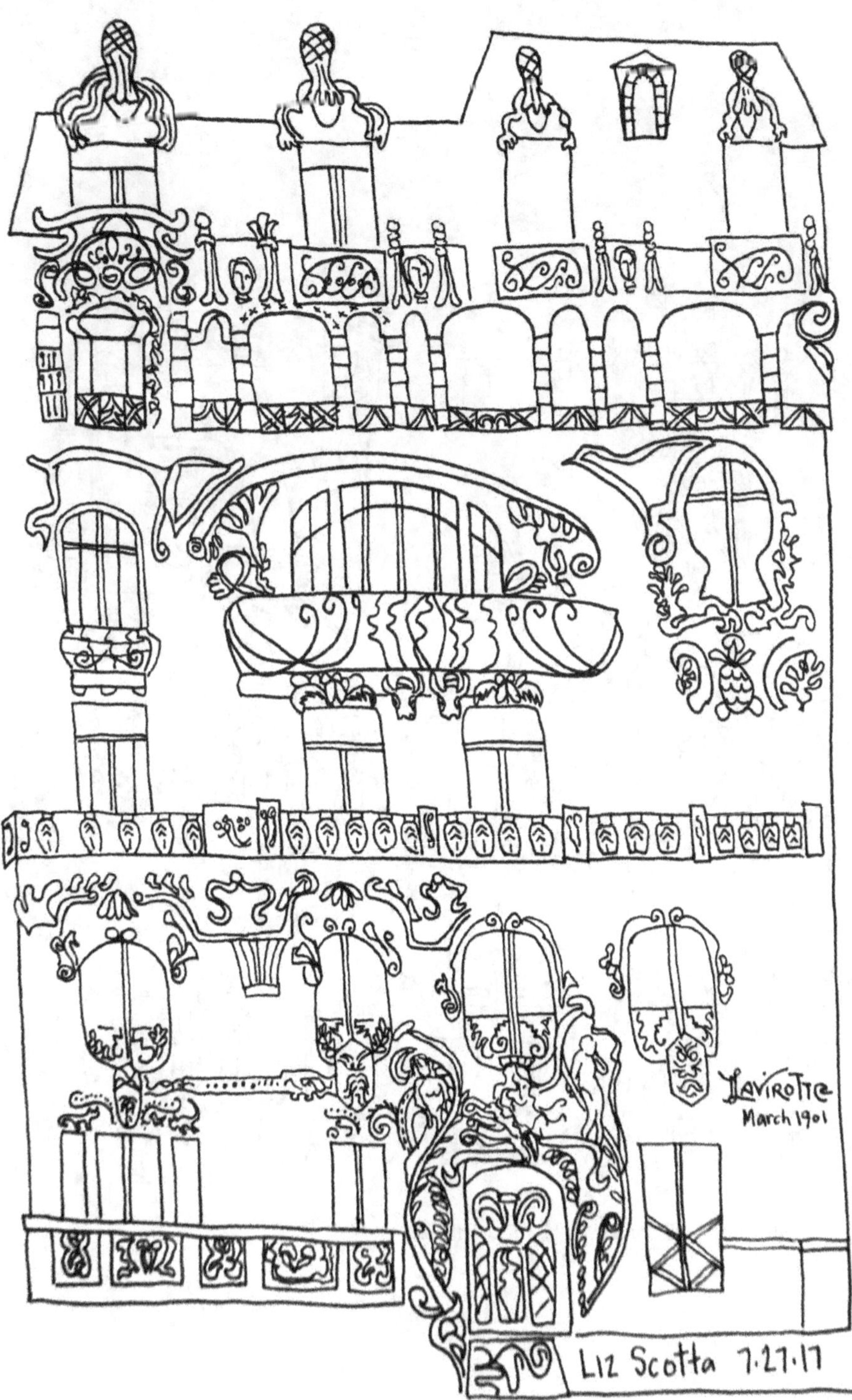

**LAVIROTTE BUILDING
AVENUE RAPP**
PARIS

2017

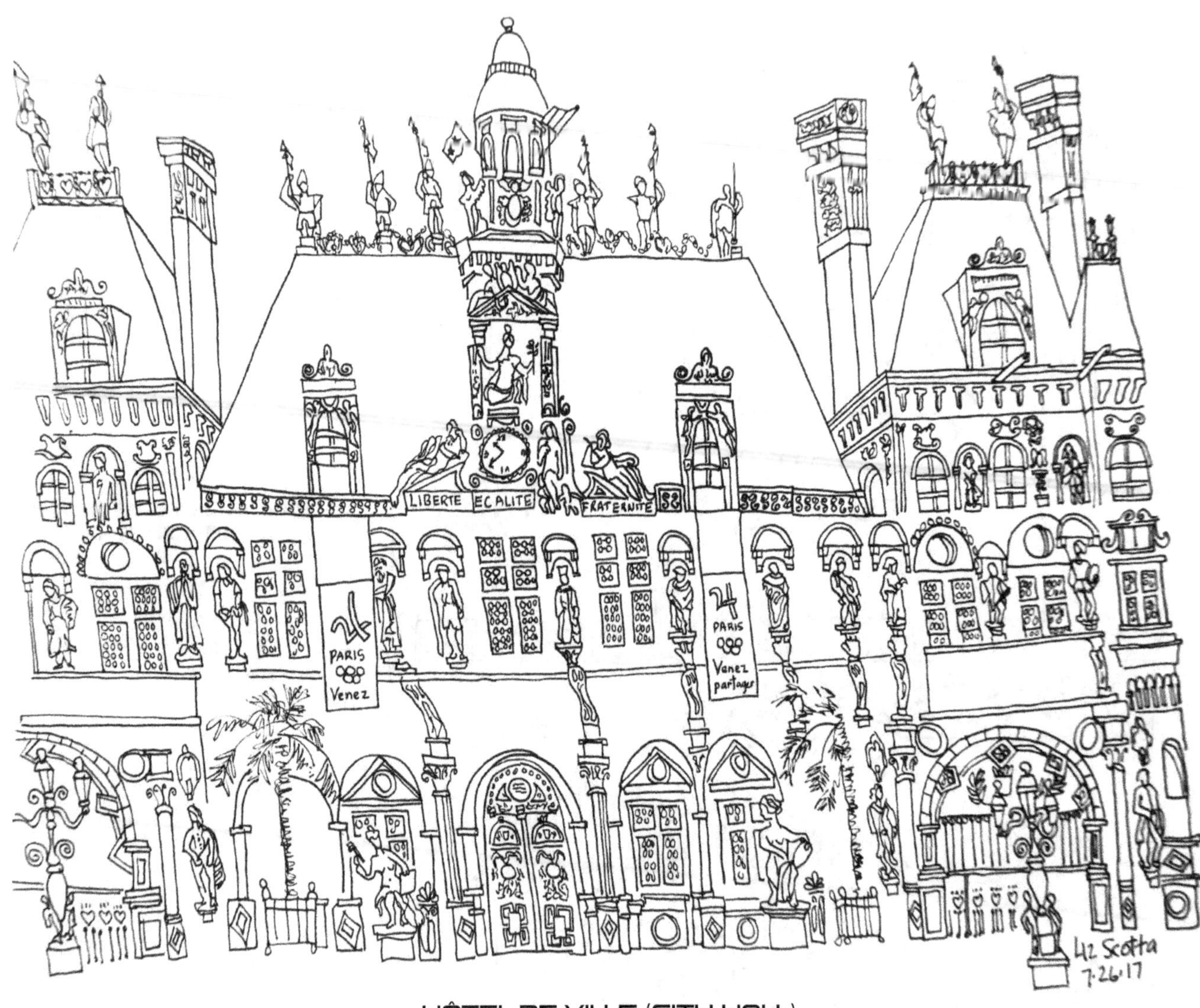

HÔTEL DE VILLE (CITY HALL)
PARIS

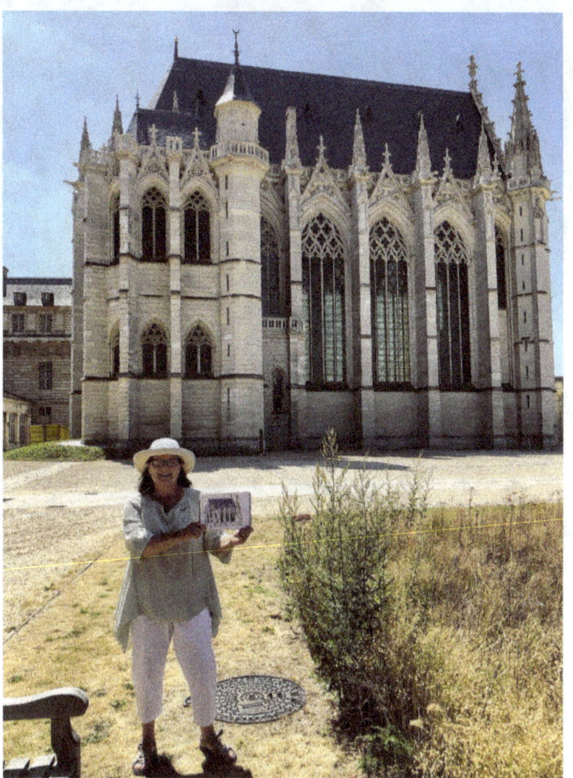
SAINTE-CHAPELLE AT
VINCENNES CHÂTEAU
PARIS

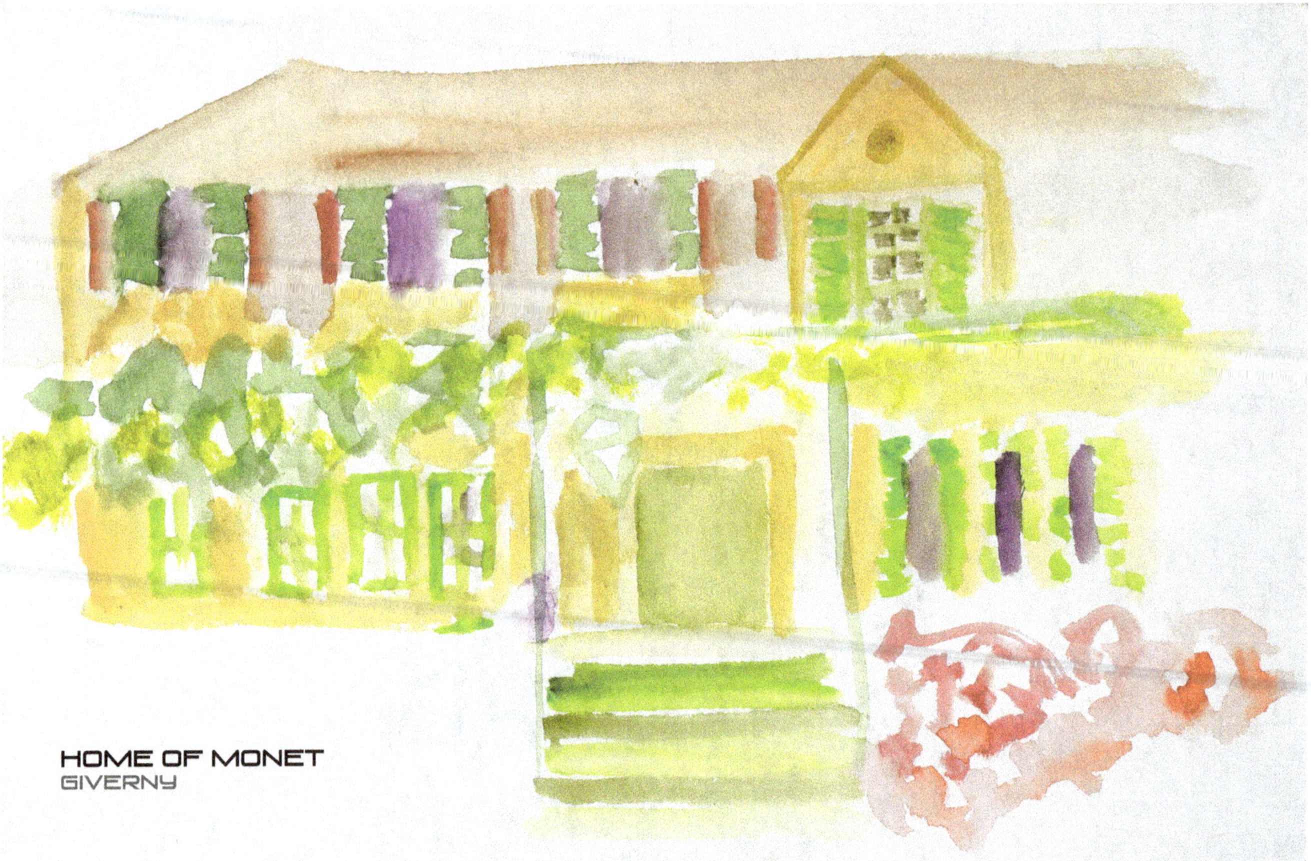

HOME OF MONET
GIVERNY

BRIDGE
GIVERNY

GARDEN
GIVERNY

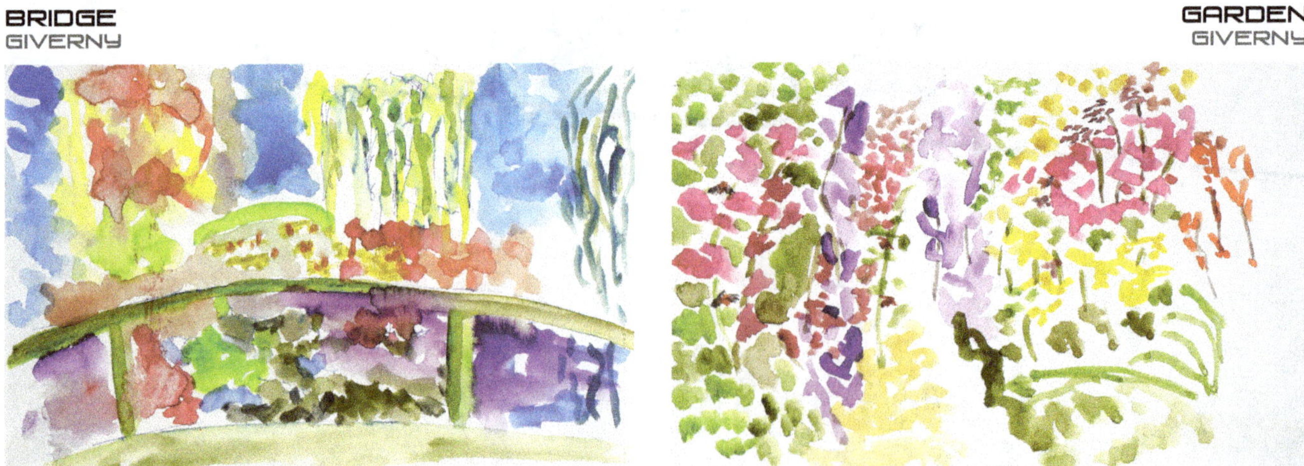

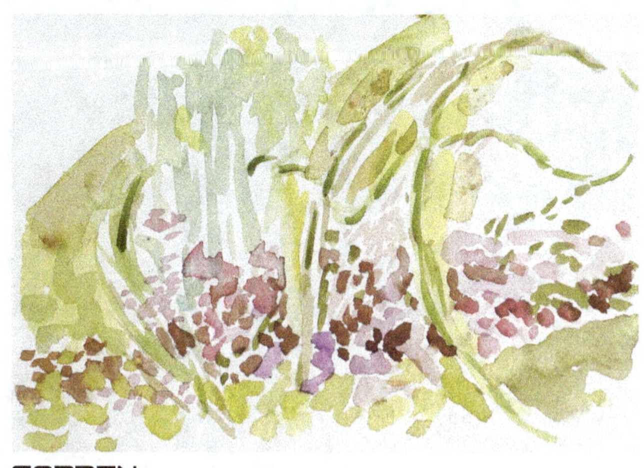

GARDEN
GIVERNY

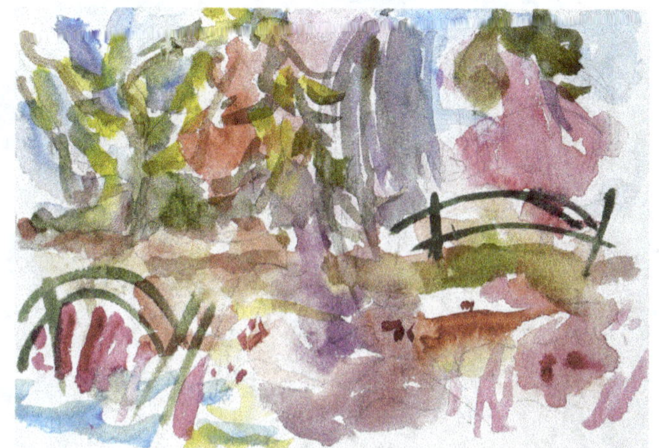

BRIDGE
GIVERNY

HOME OF MONET
GIVERNY

2017

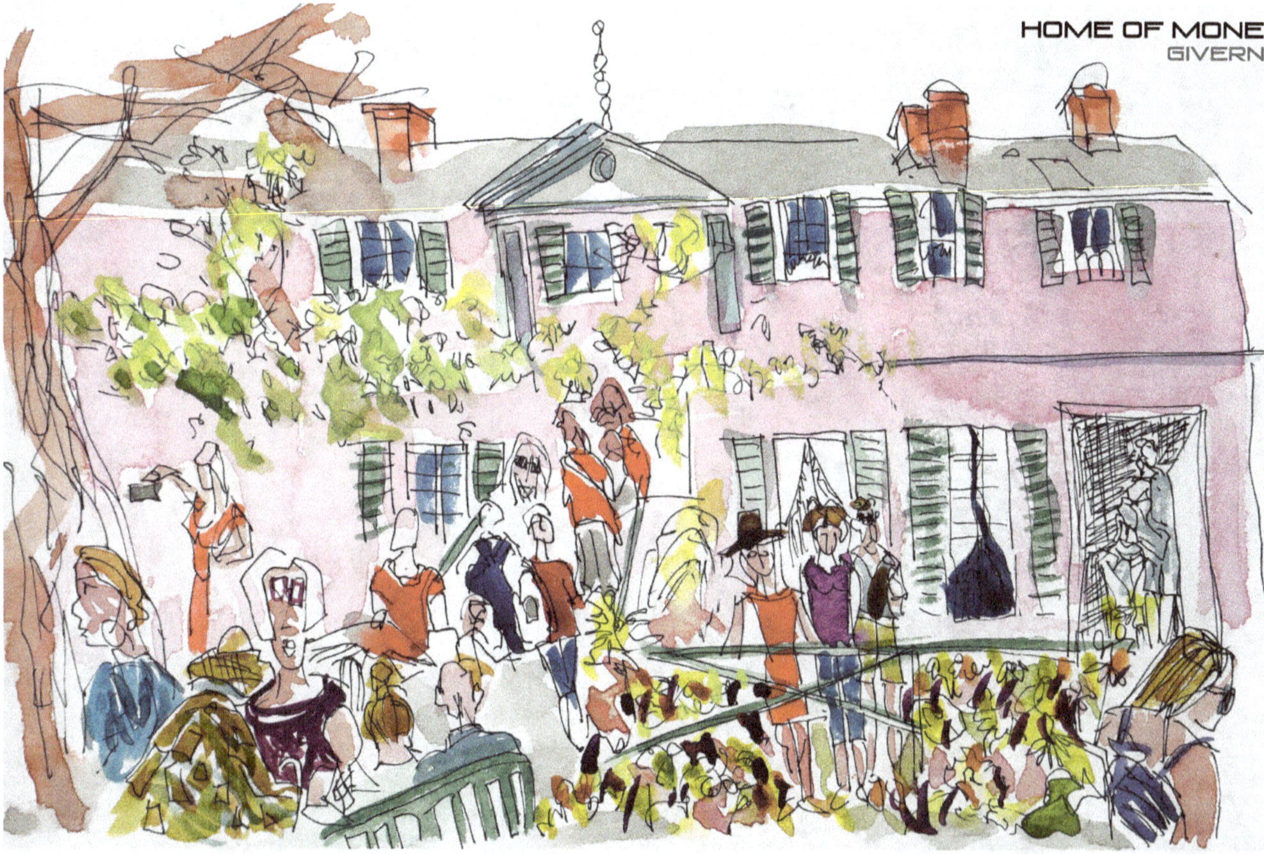

2017

LOCHES
LOIRE VALLEY

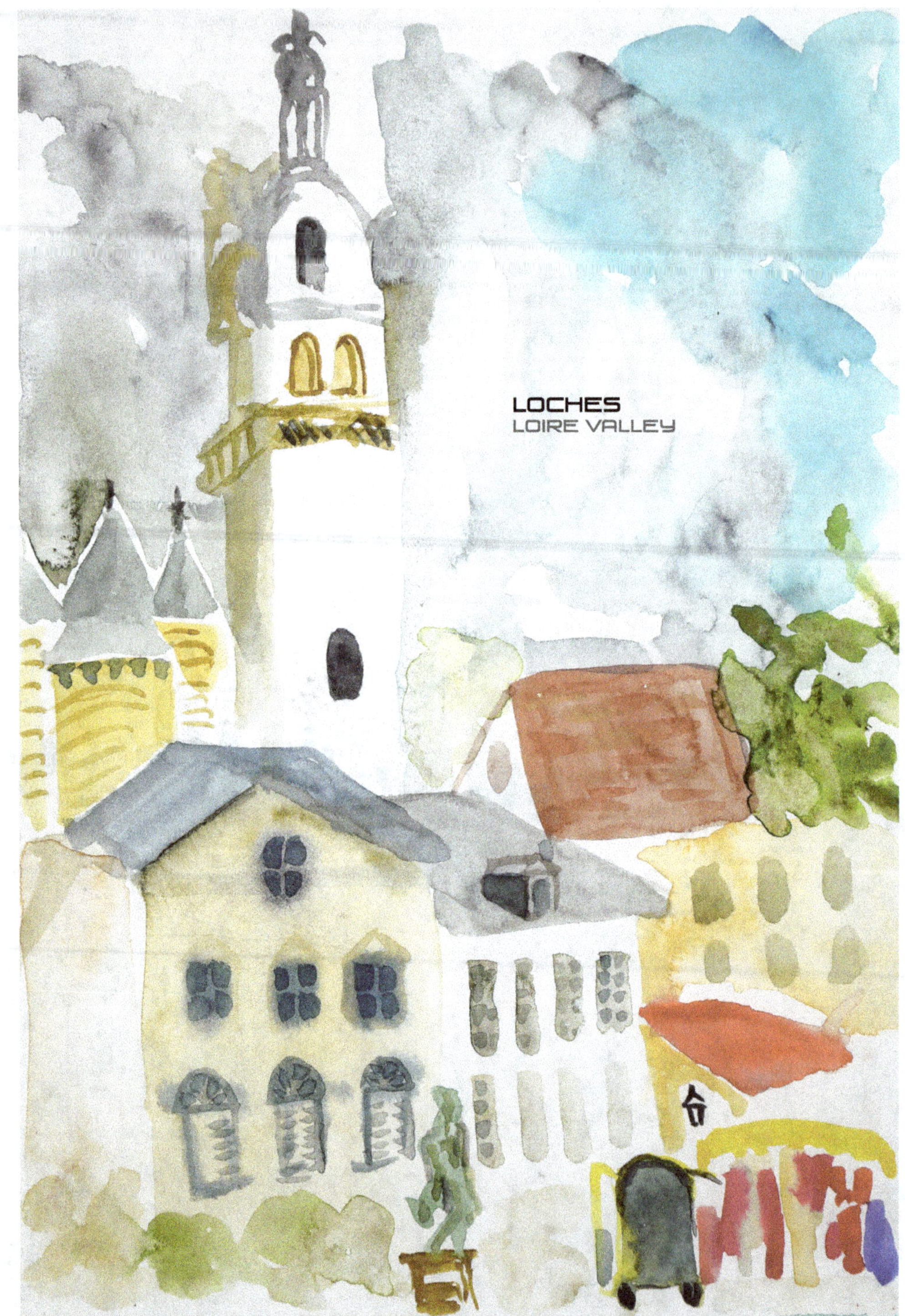

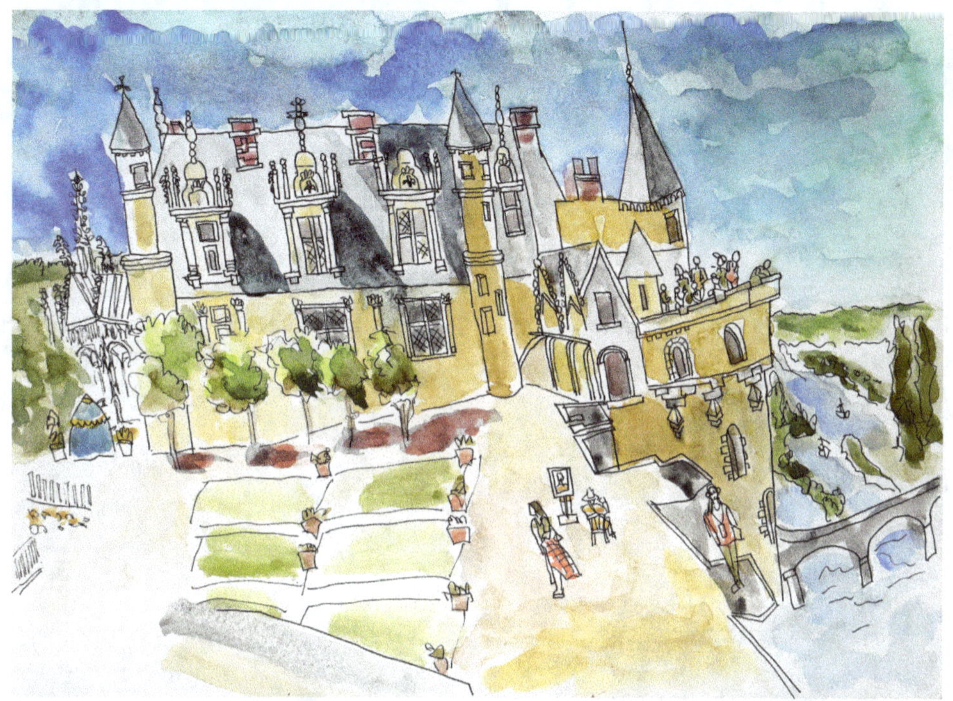

CHÂTEAU D'AMBOISE
LOIRE VALLEY

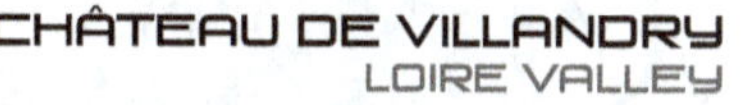

CHÂTEAU DE VILLANDRY
LOIRE VALLEY

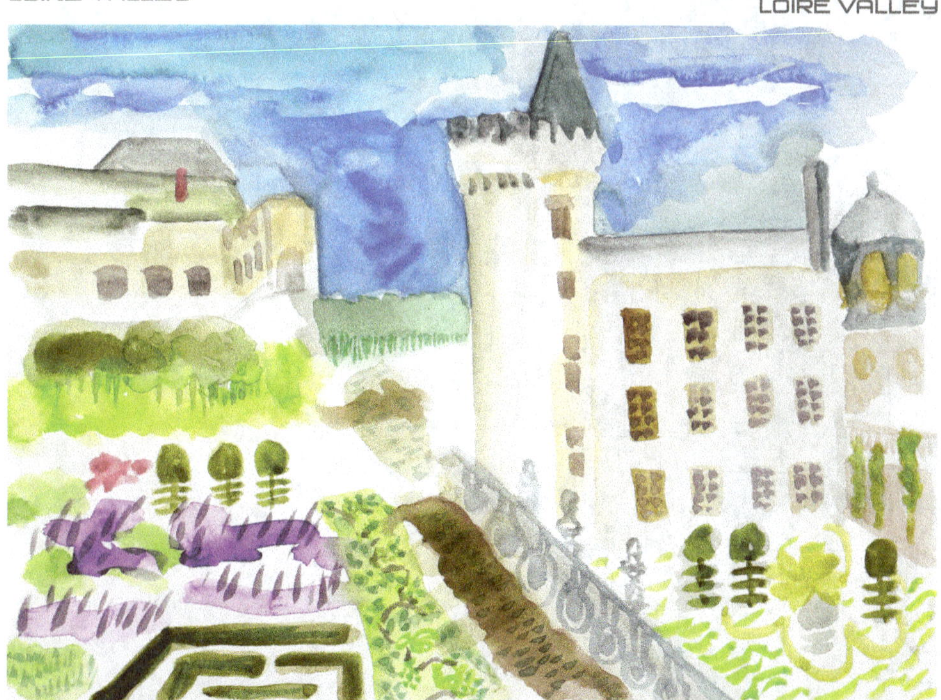

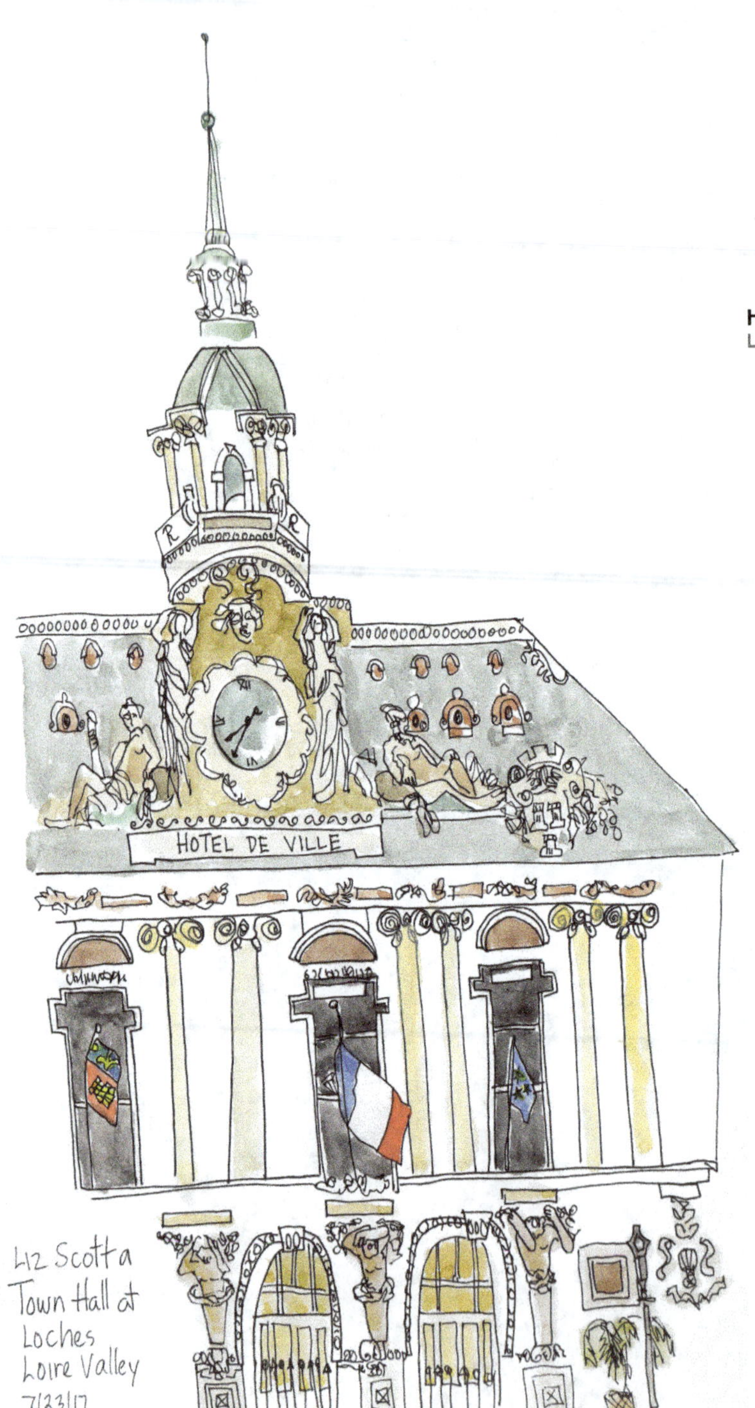

HÔTEL DE VILLE (TOWN HALL)
LOCHES, LOIRE VALLEY

2017

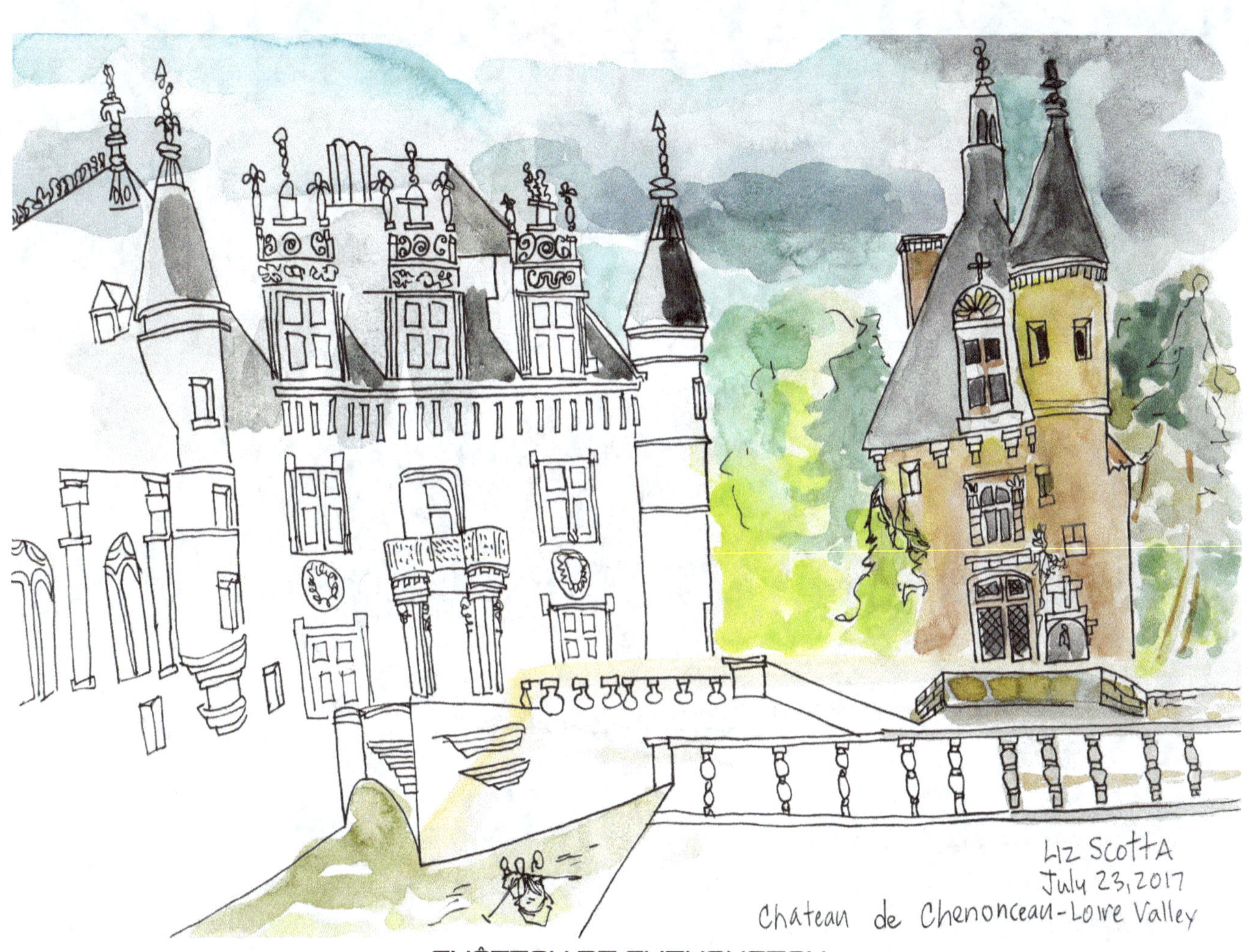

CHÂTEAU DE CHENONCEAU
LOIRE VALLEY

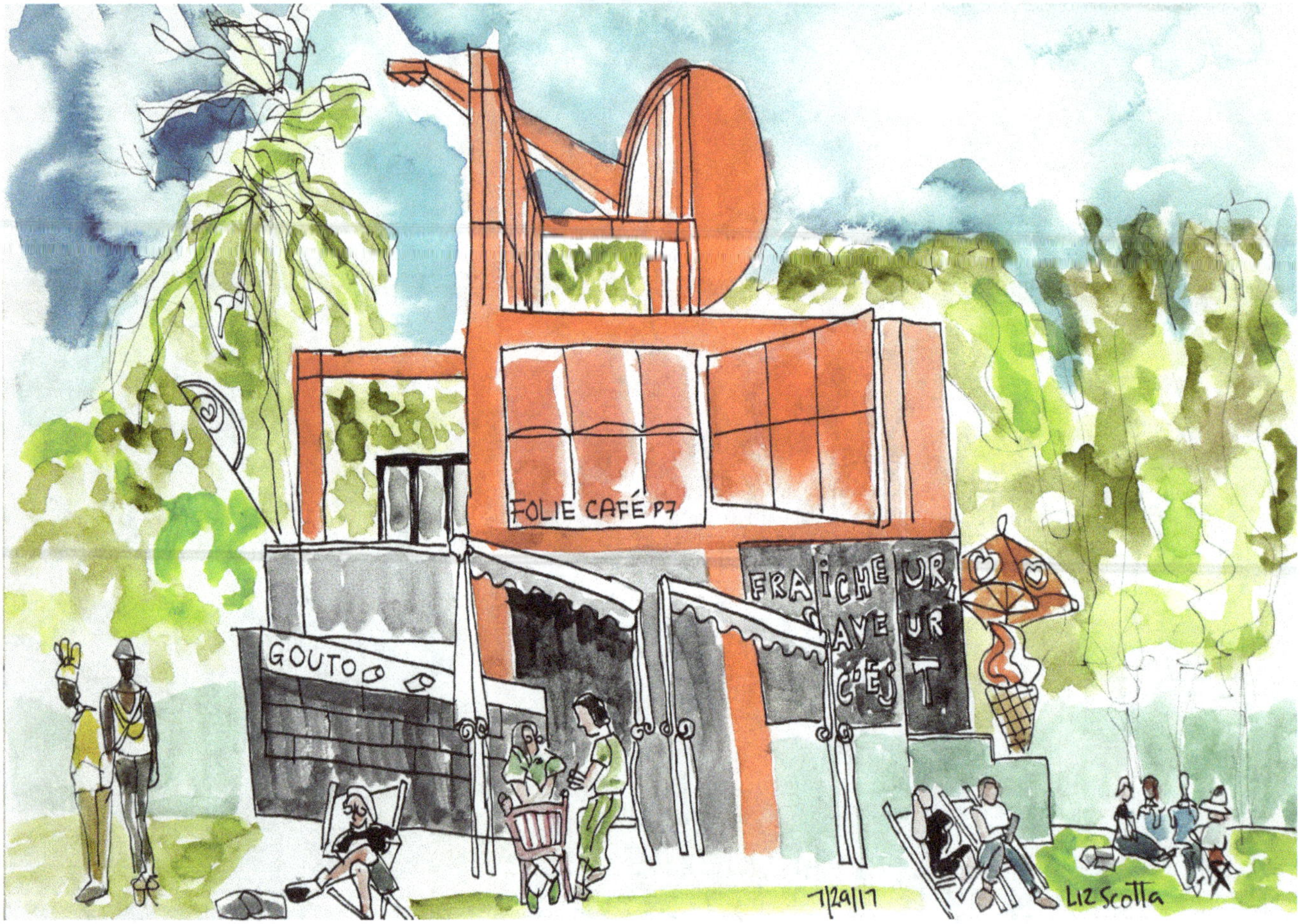

PARC DE LA VILLETTE
PARIS

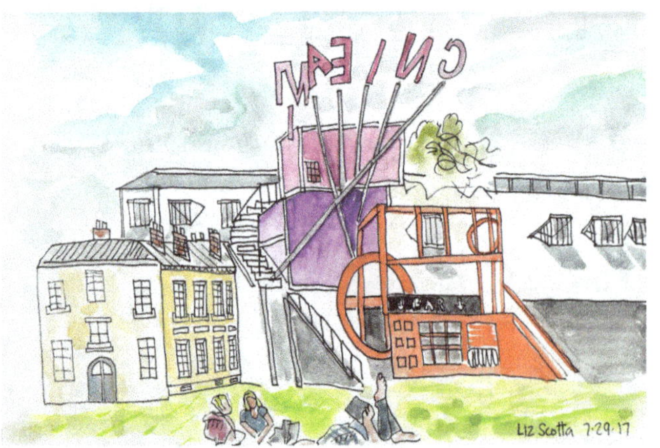

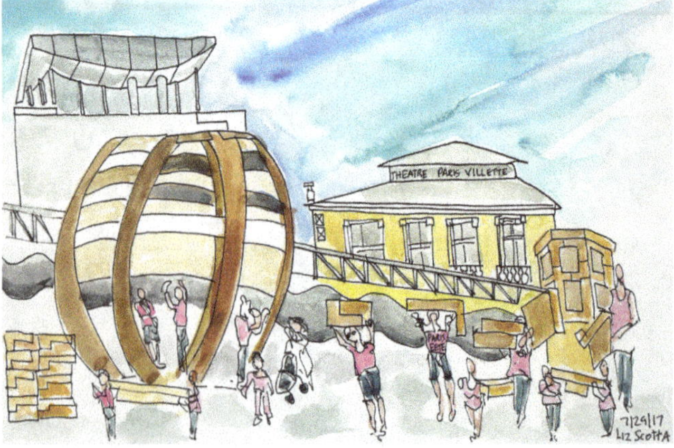

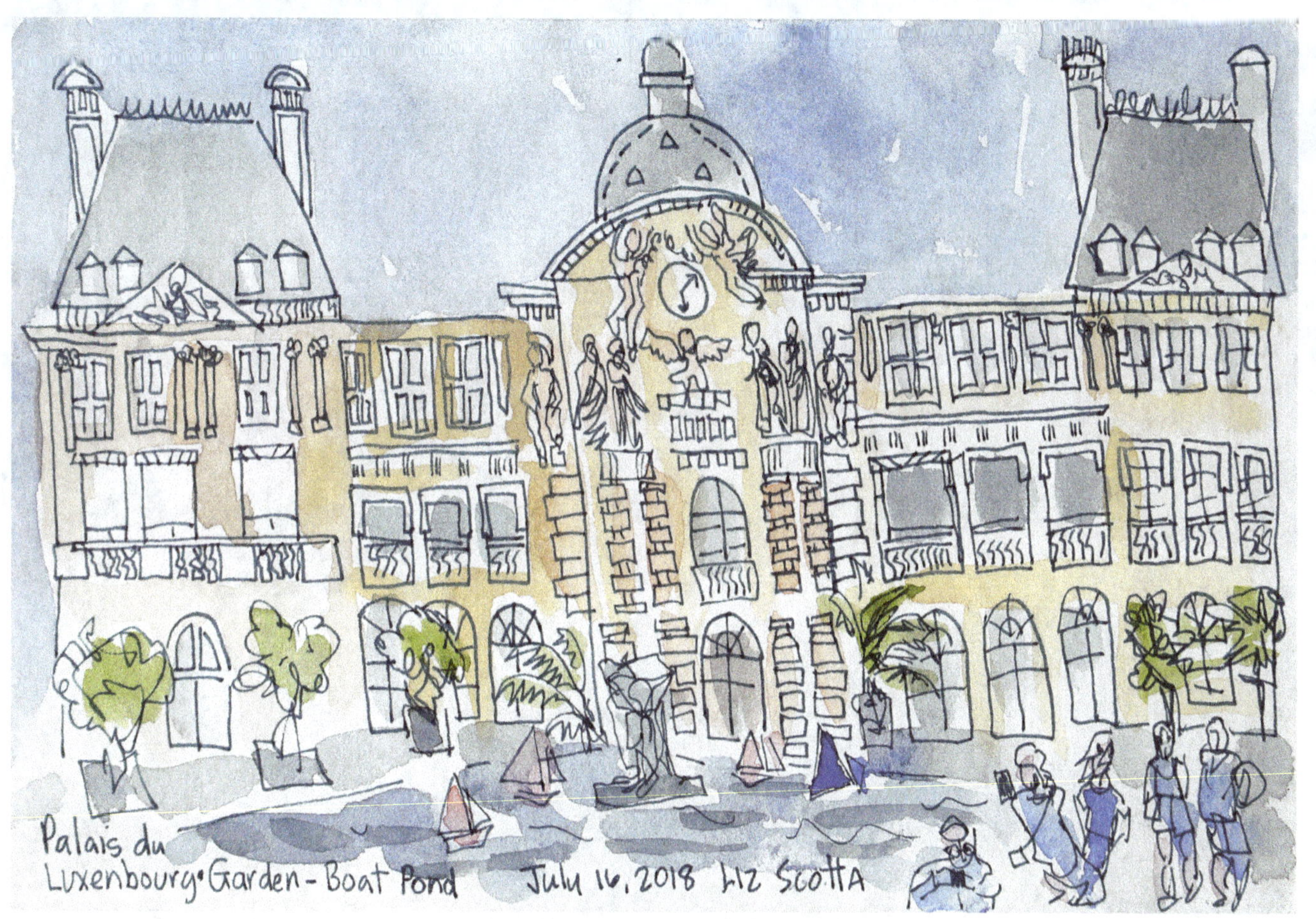

PALAIS DE LUXEMBOURG
PARIS

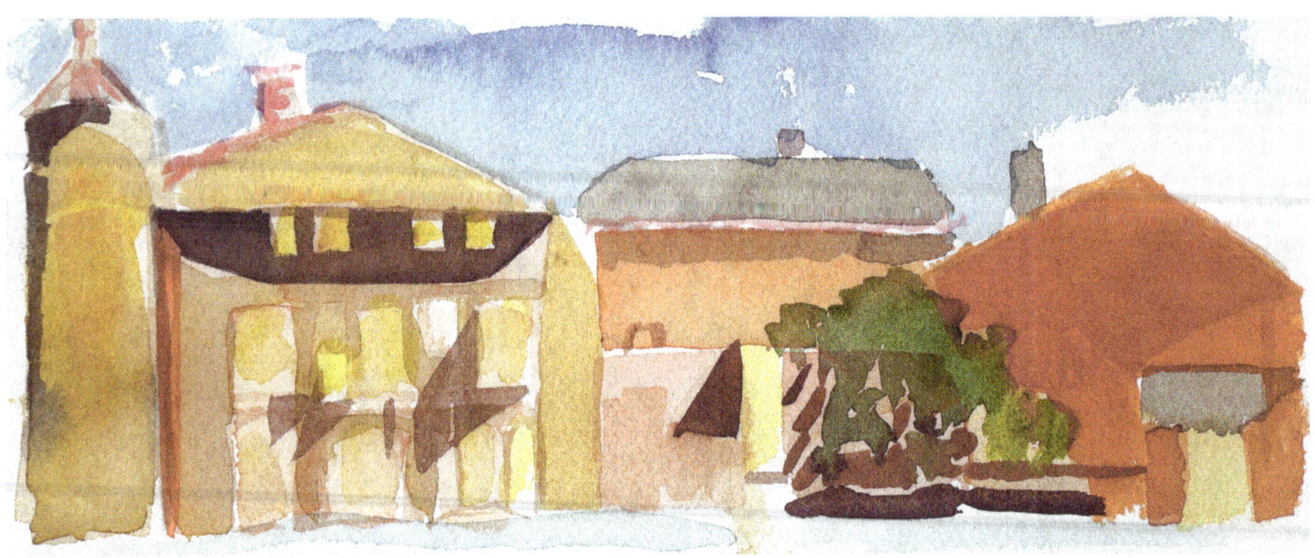

LES BASACS
LUBERON VALLEY, PROVENCE

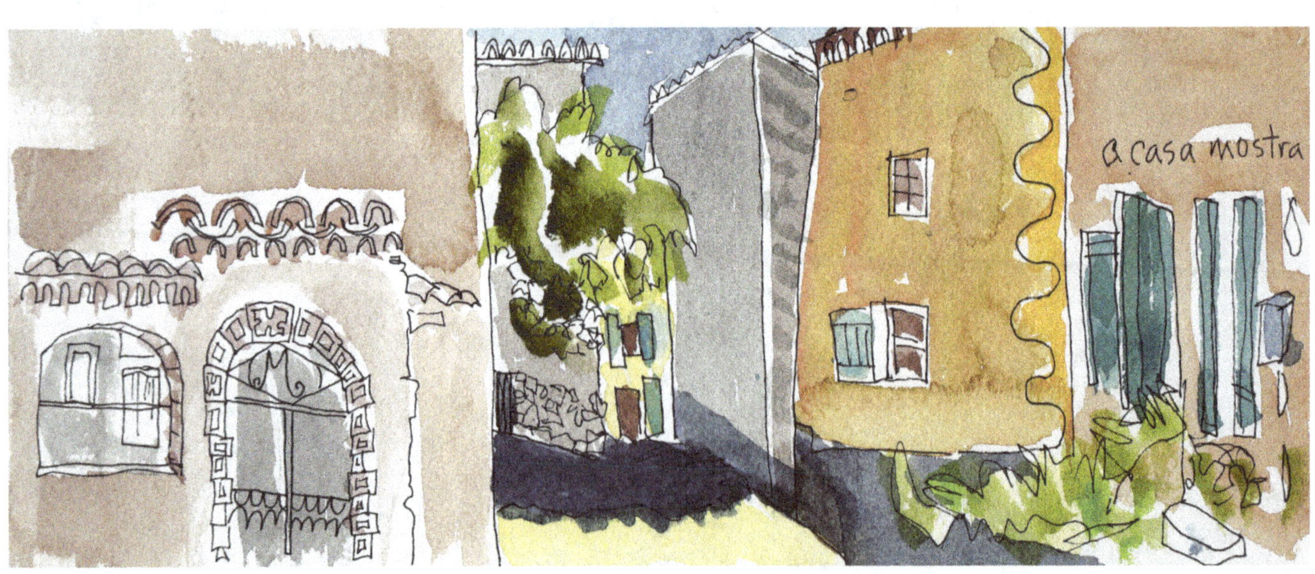

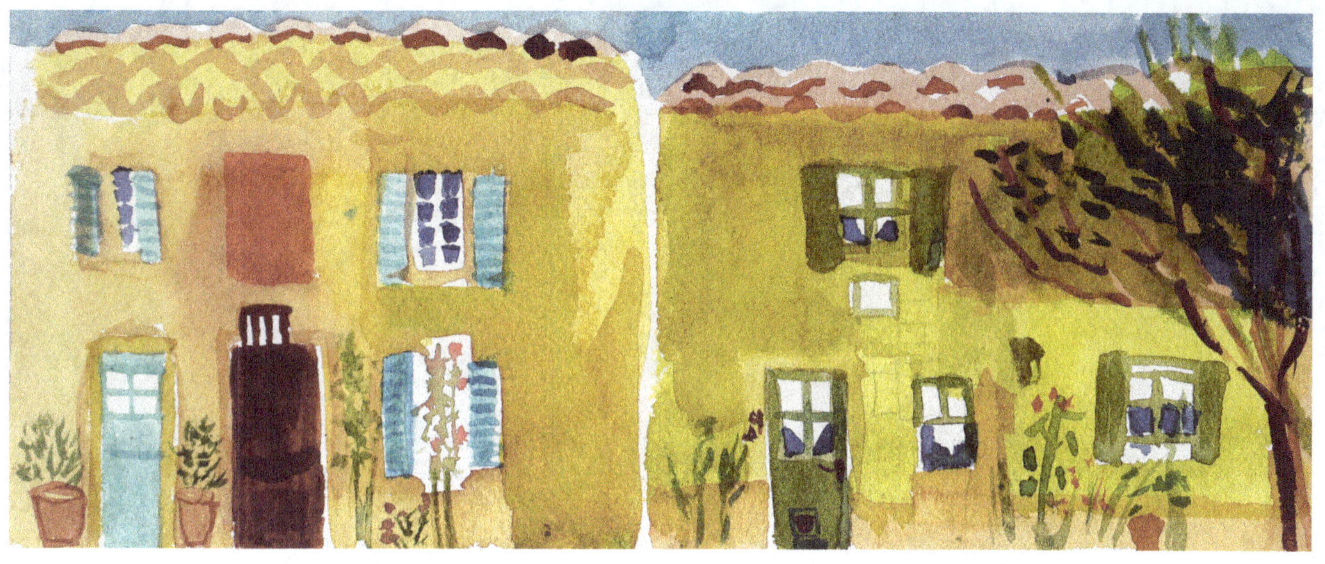

LES BASACS
LUBERON VALLEY, PROVENCE

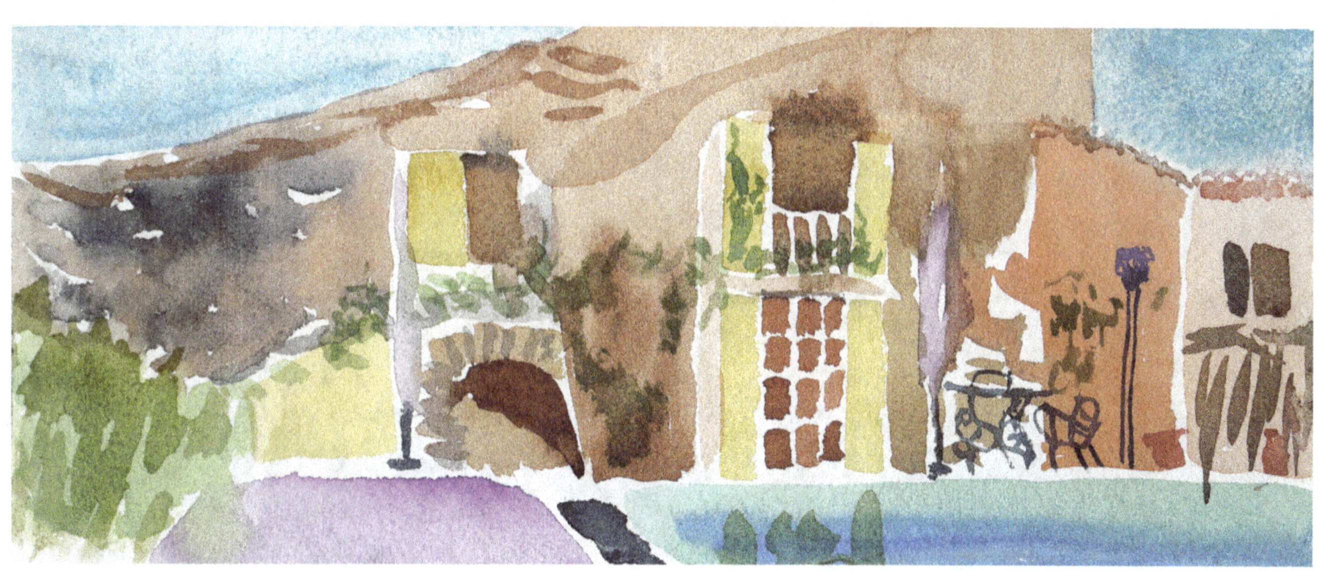

2018

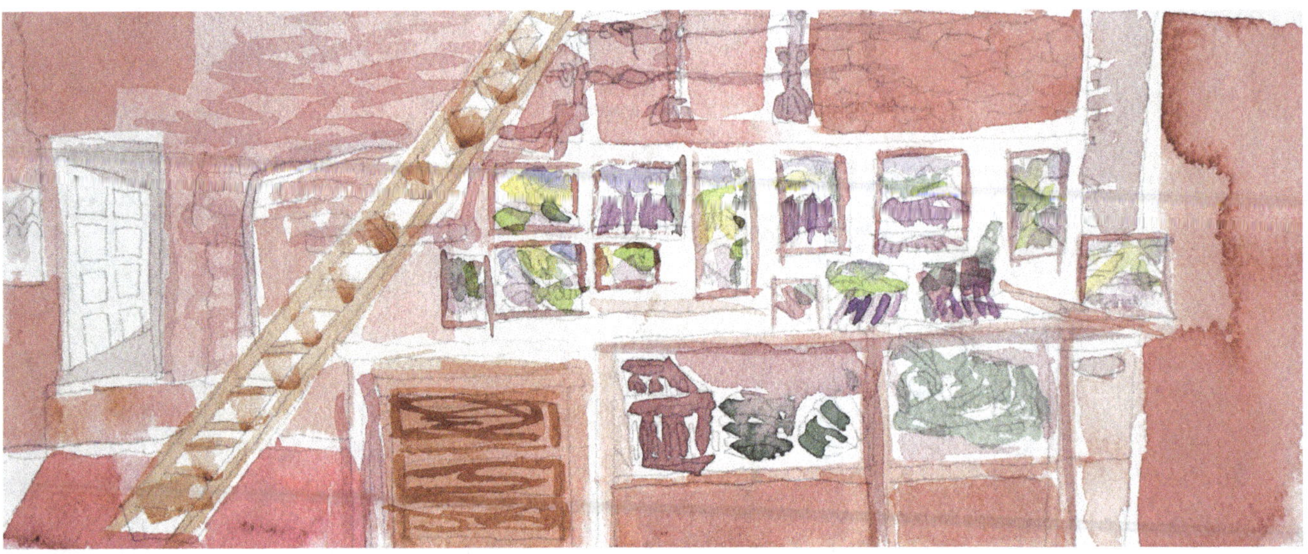

LES BASACS
LUBERON VALLEY, PROVENCE

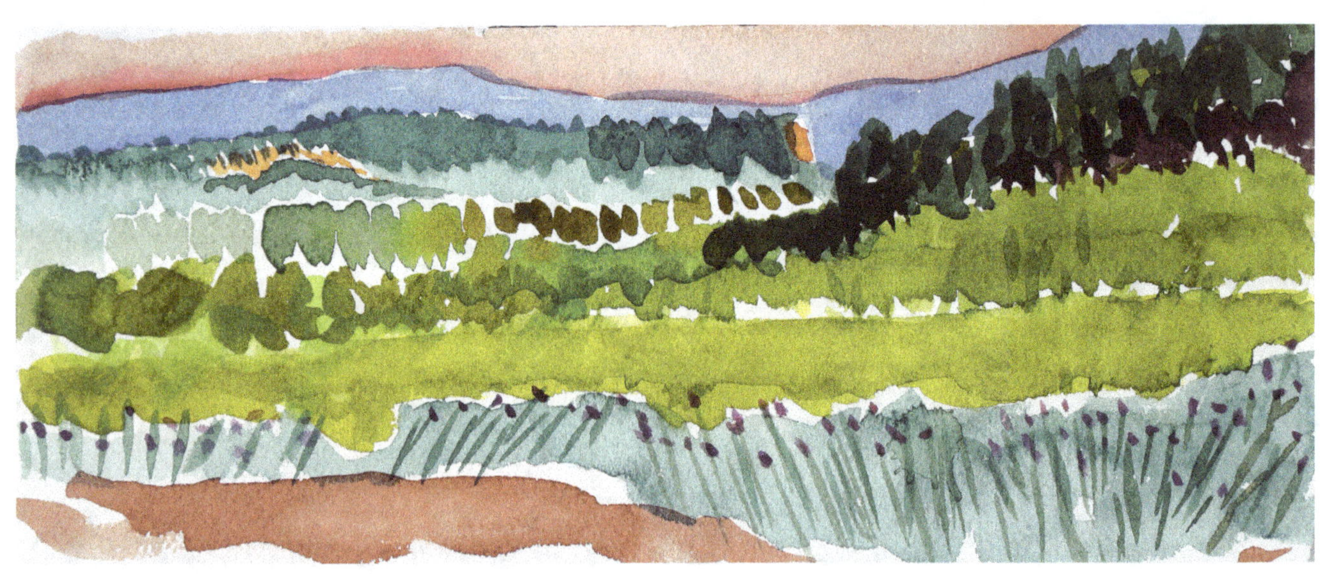

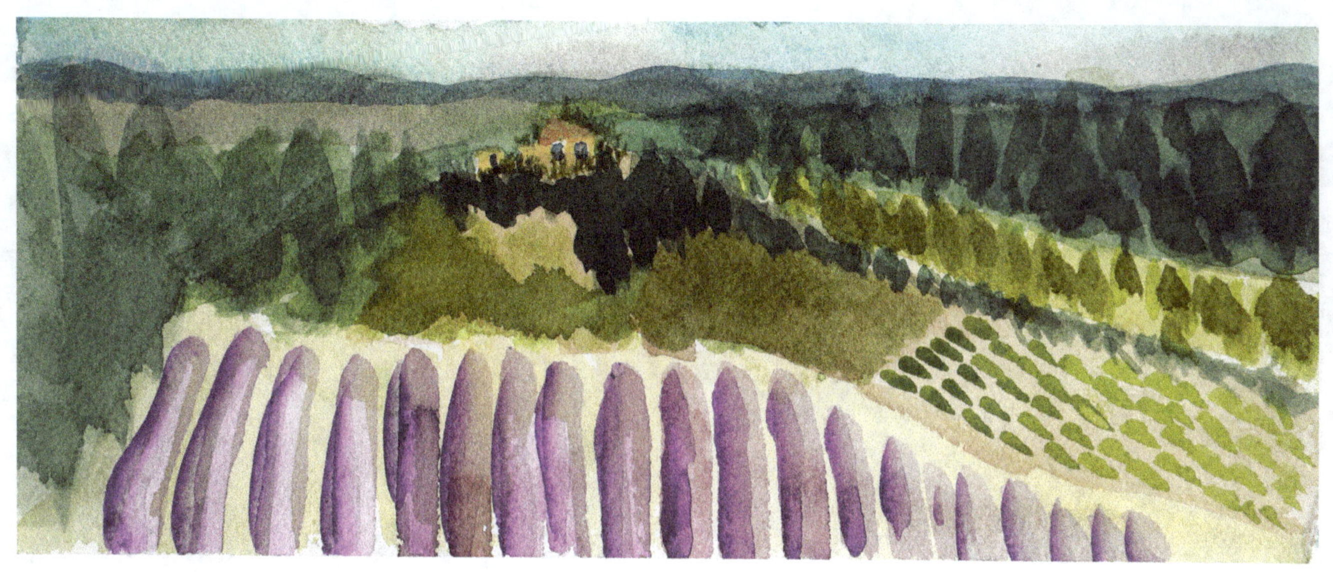

LES BASACS
LUBERON VALLEY, PROVENCE

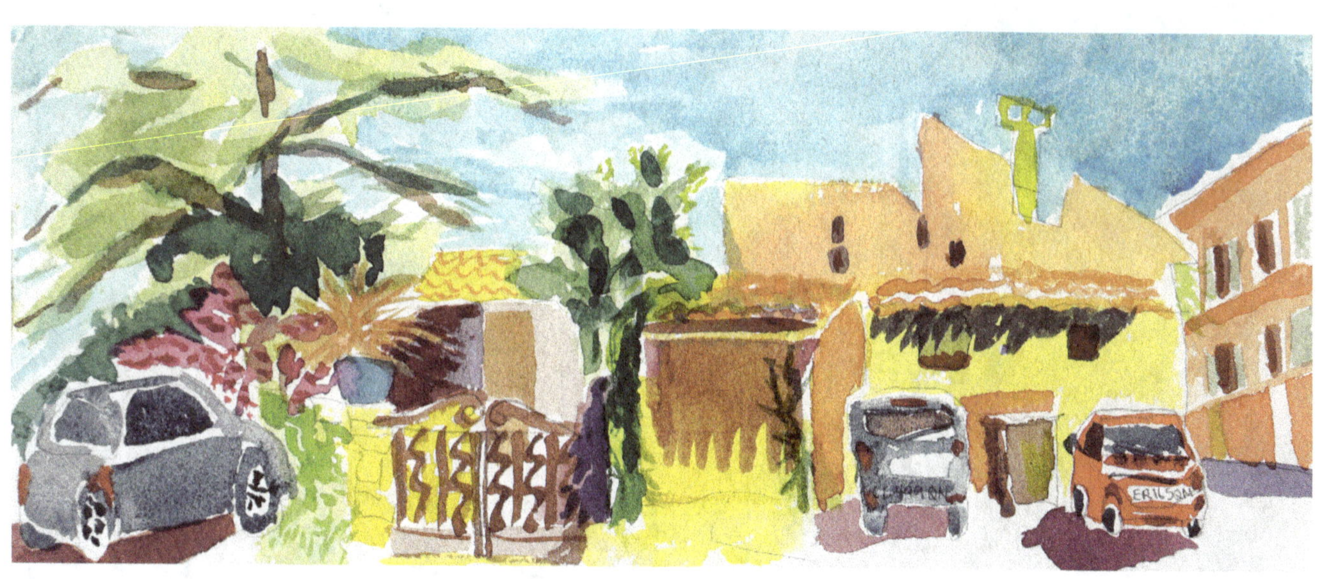

2018

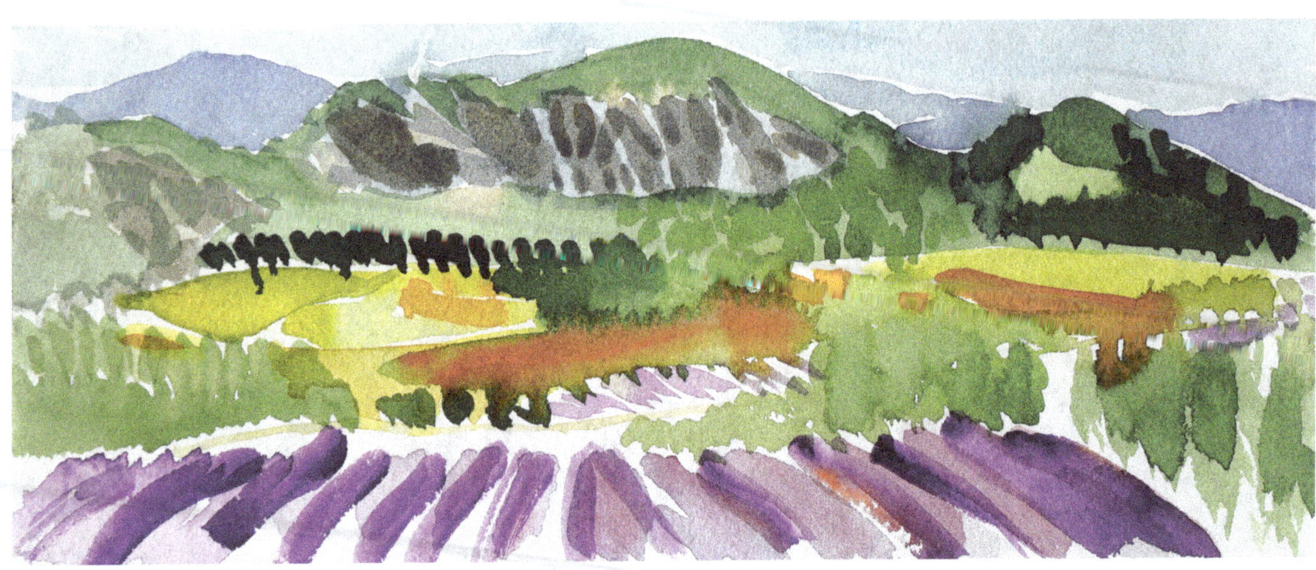

LES BASACS
LUBERON VALLEY, PROVENCE

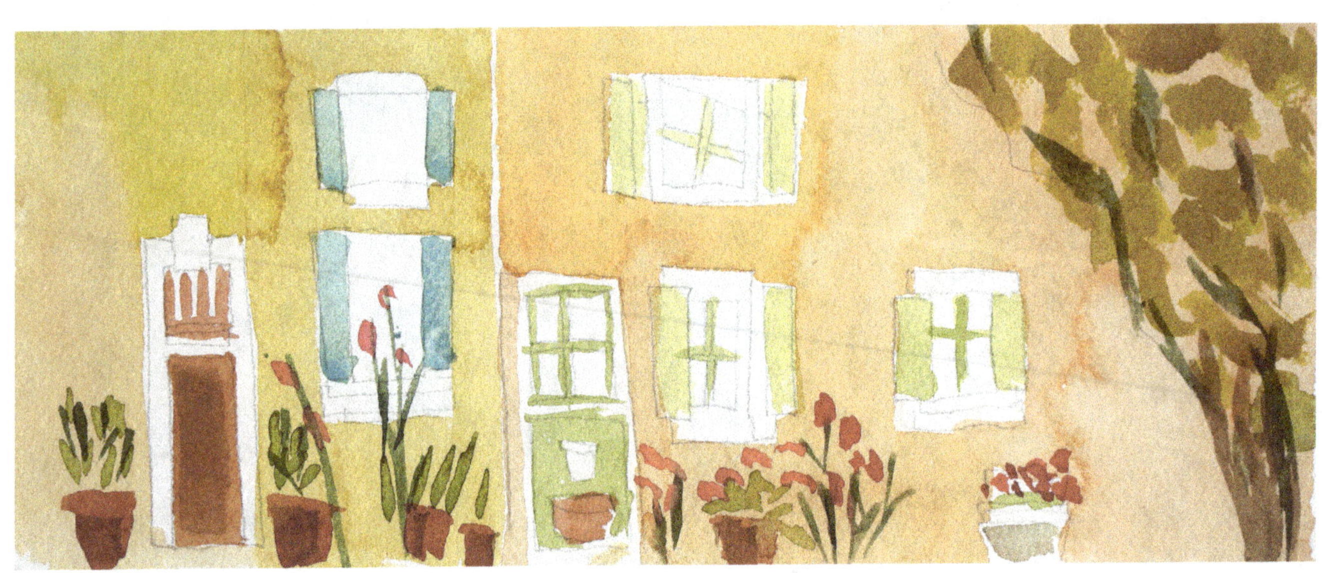

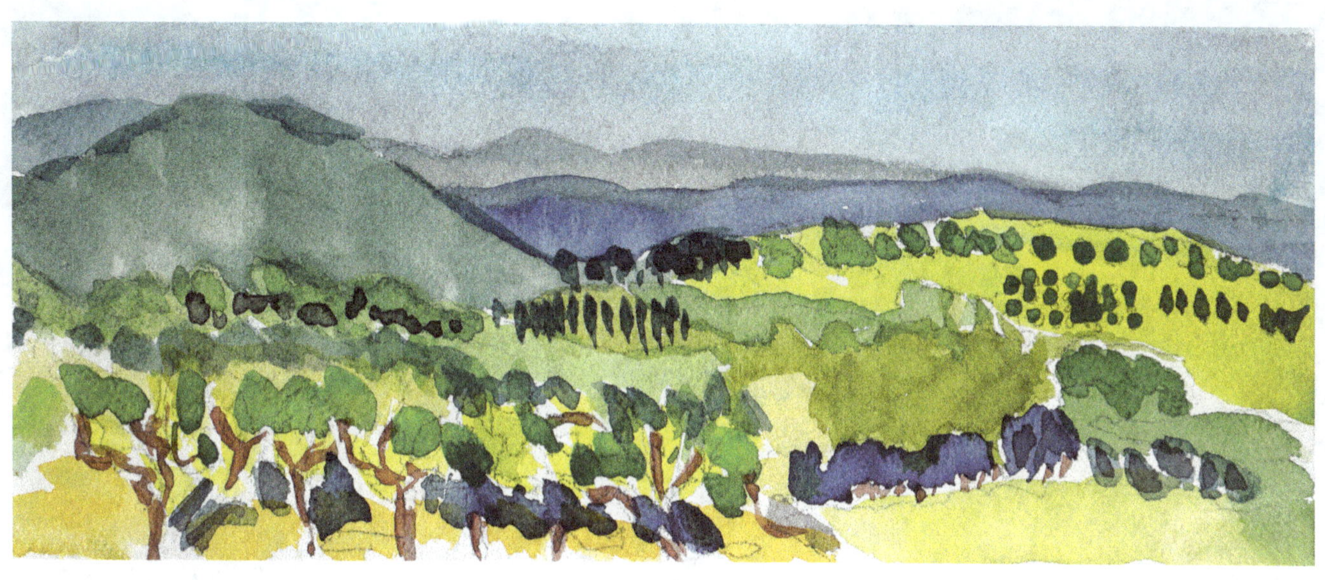

LES BASACS
LUBERON VALLEY, PROVENCE

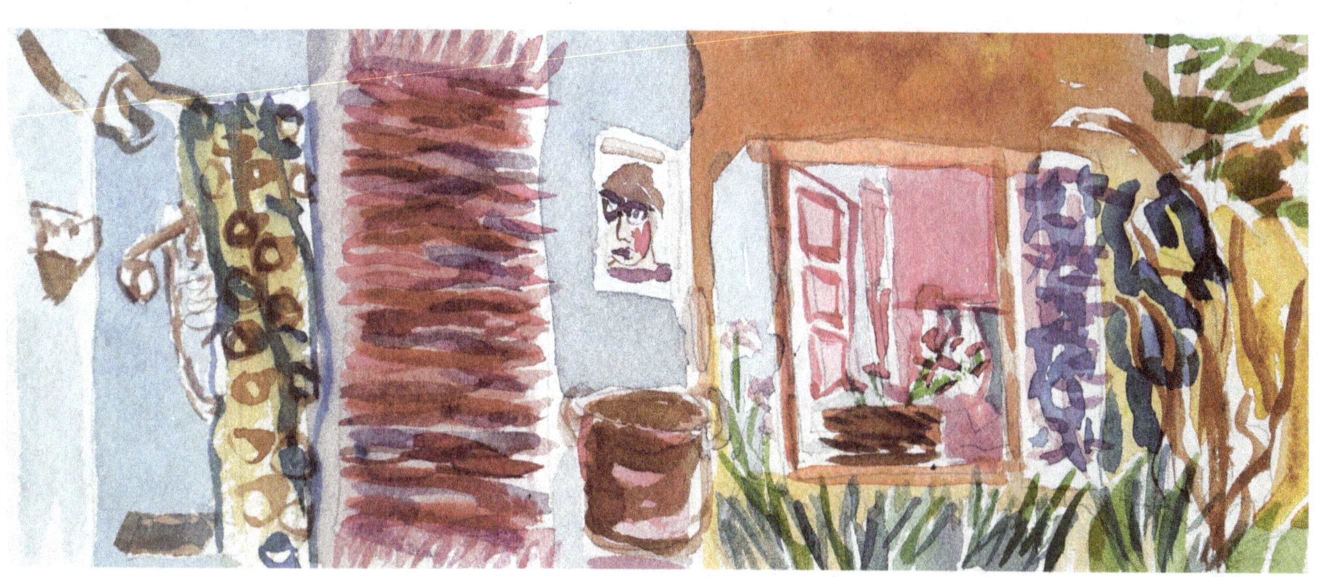

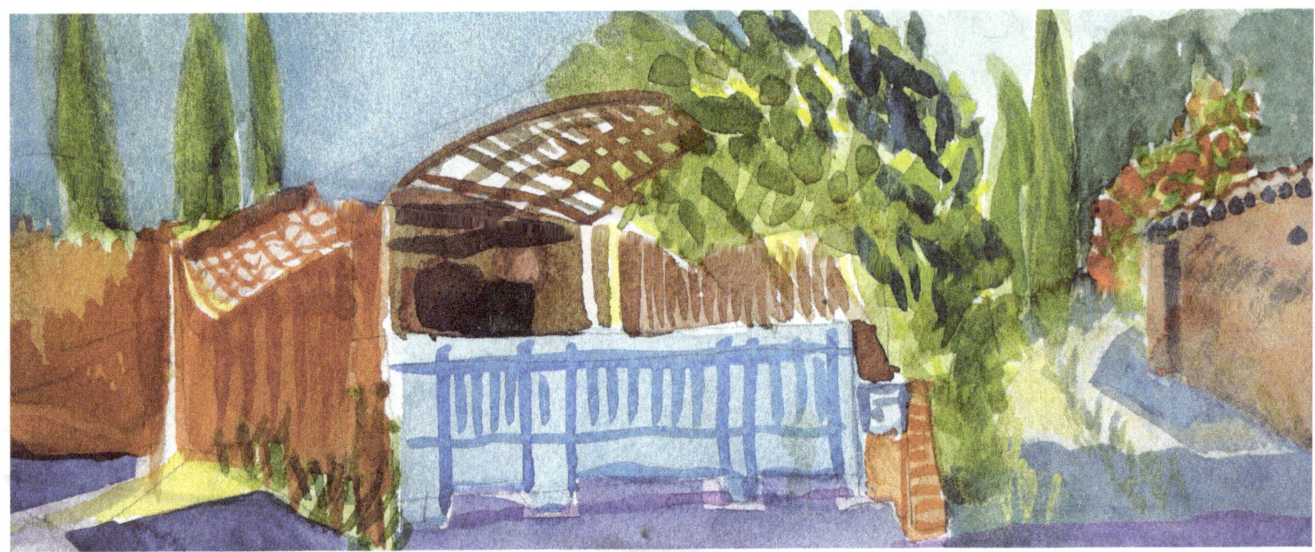

LES BASACS
LUBERON VALLEY, PROVENCE

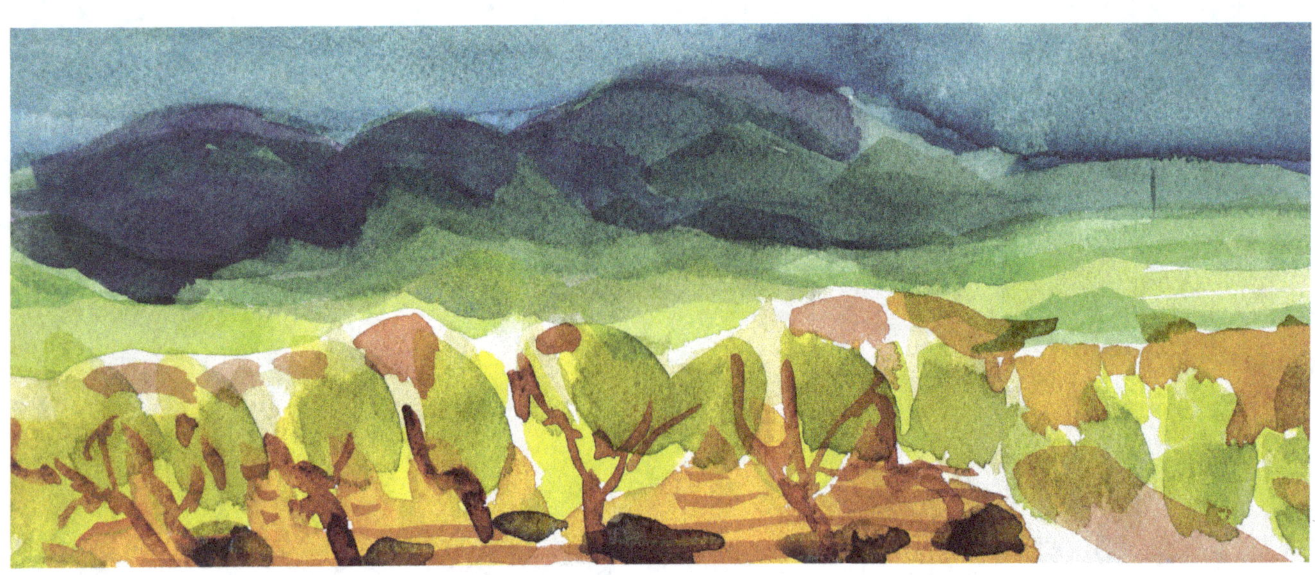

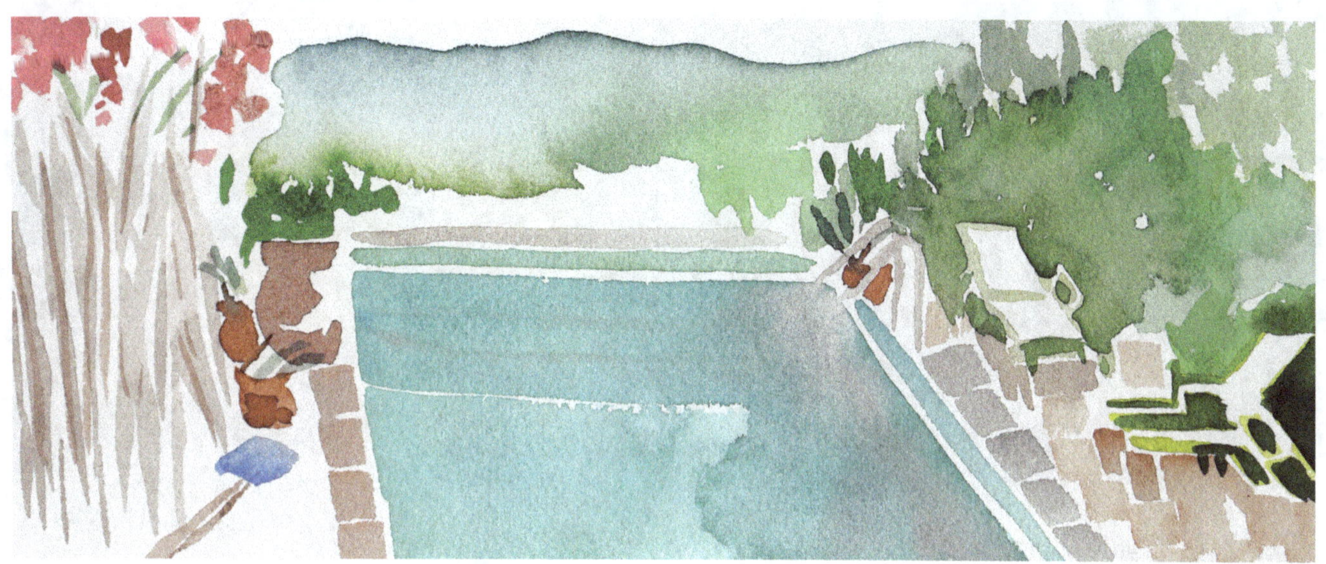

LES BASACS
LUBERON VALLEY, PROVENCE

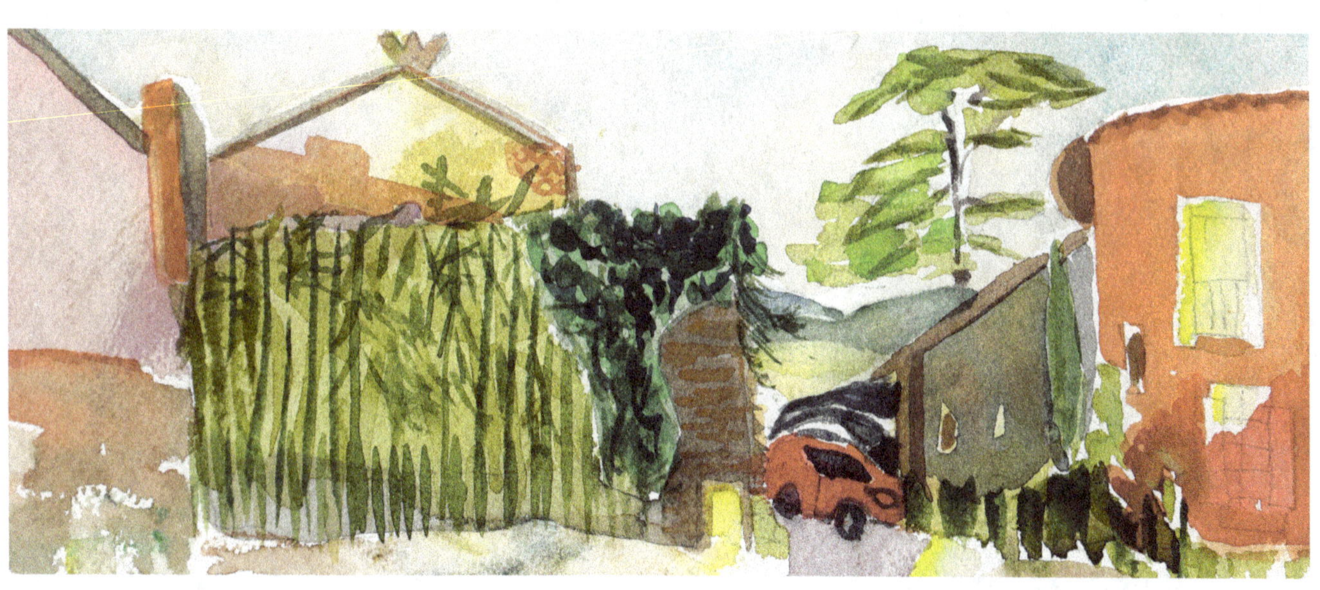

2018

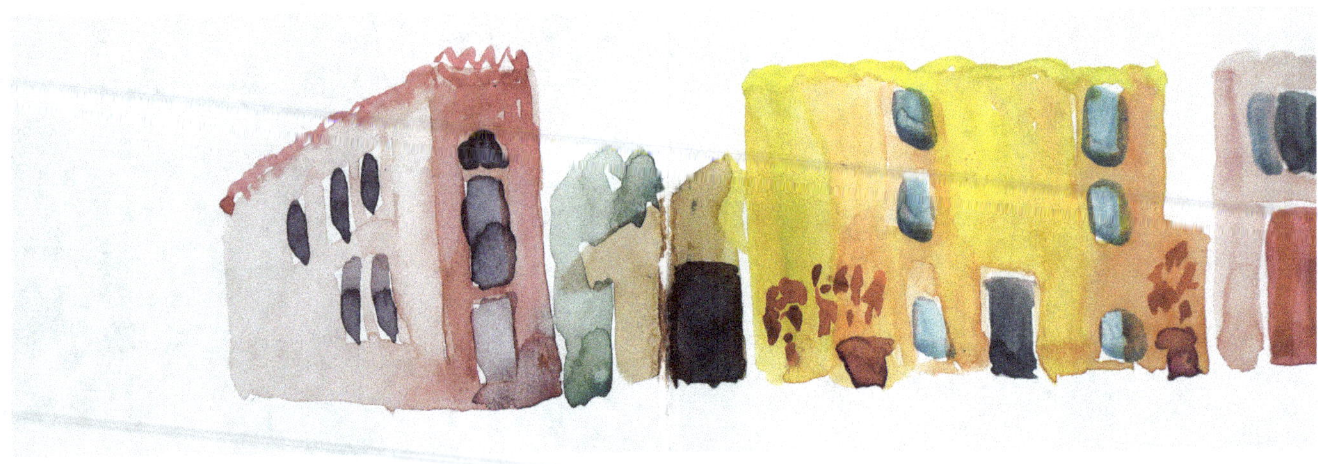

LES BASACS
LUBERON VALLEY, PROVENCE

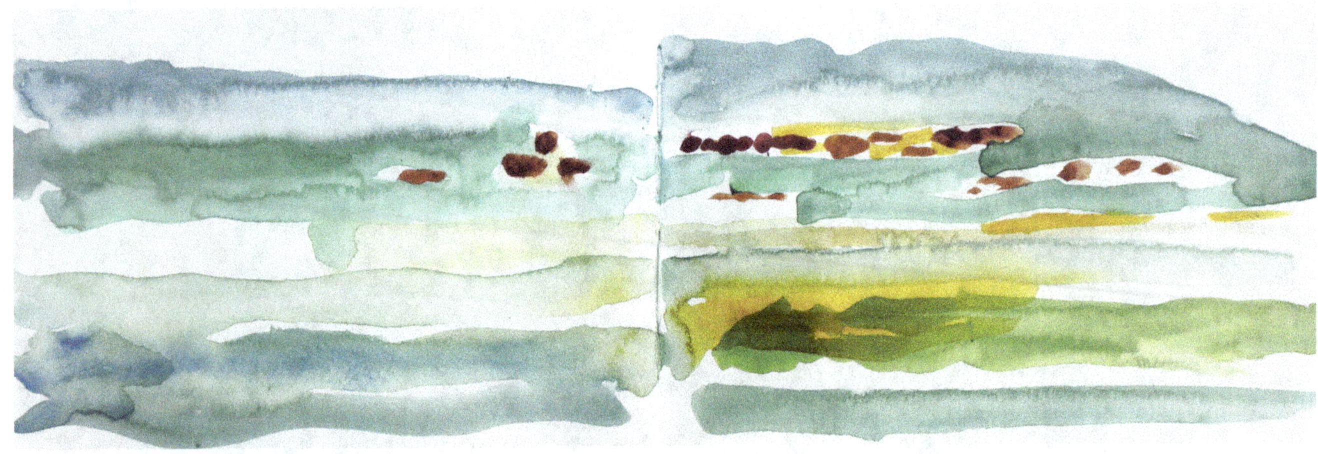

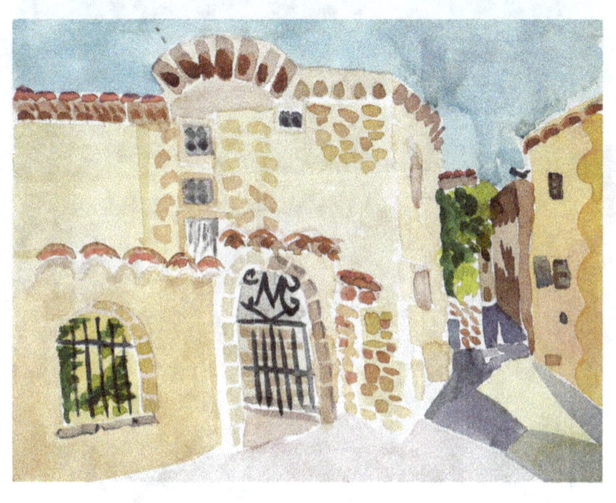
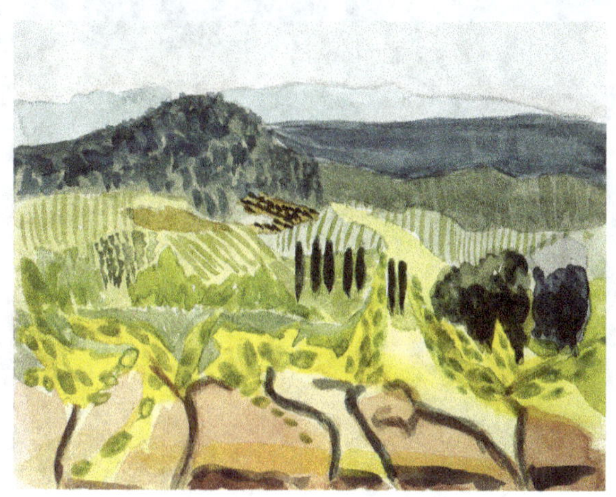

LUBERON VALLEY
PROVENCE

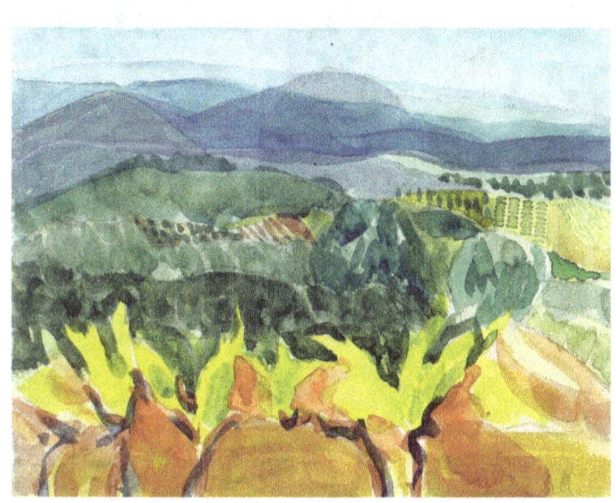
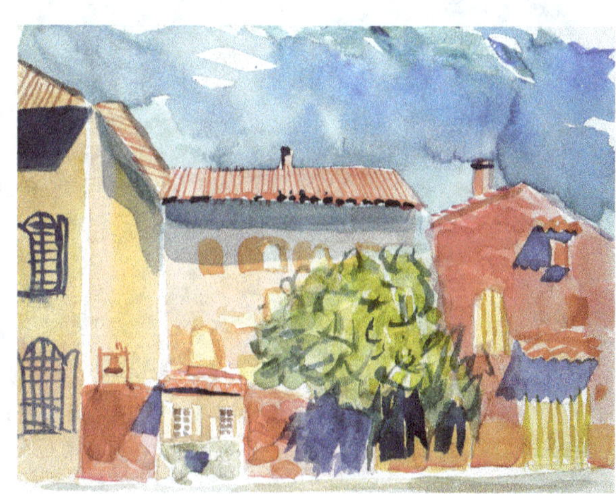

2018

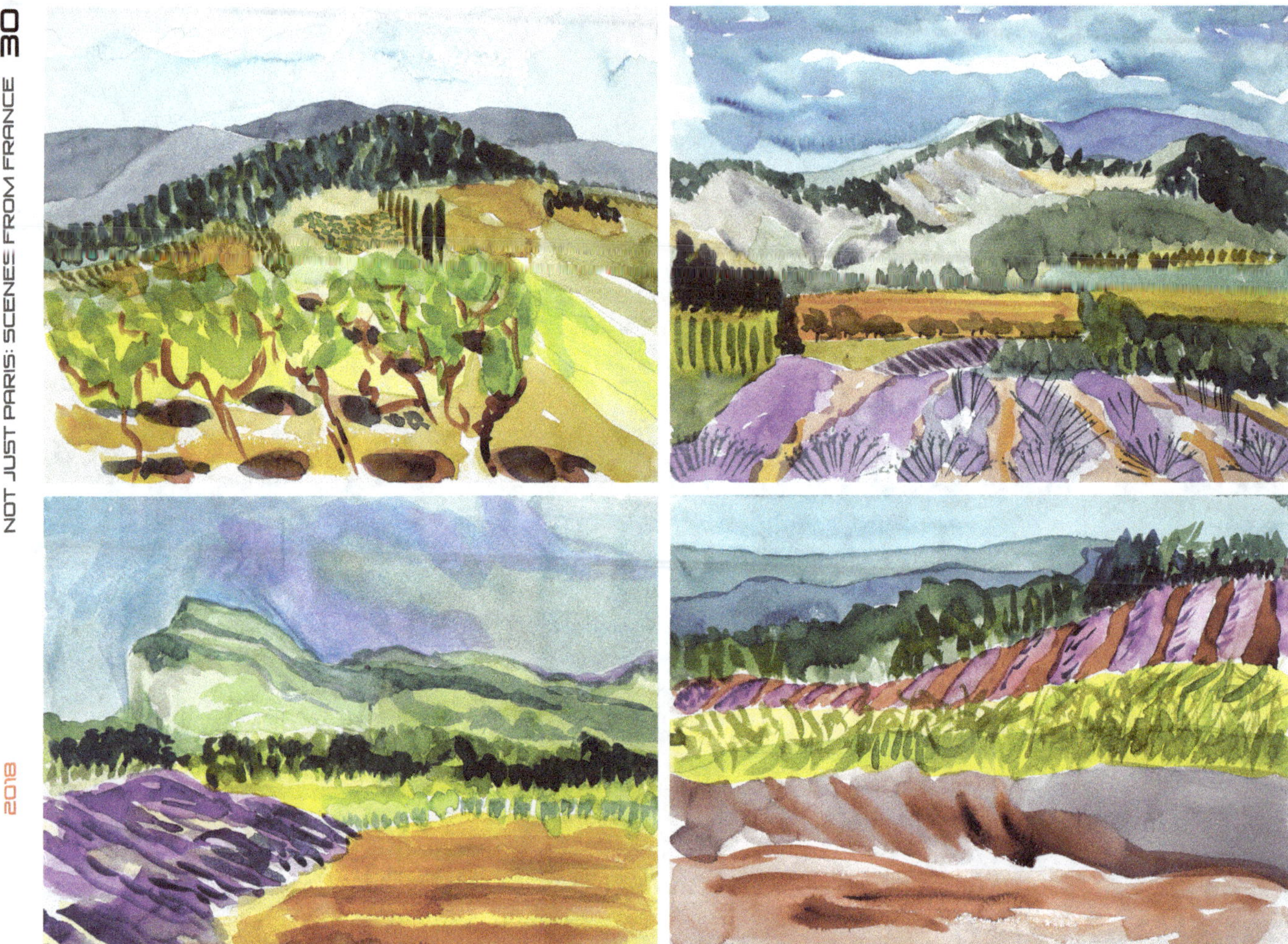

LUBERON VALLEY
PROVENCE

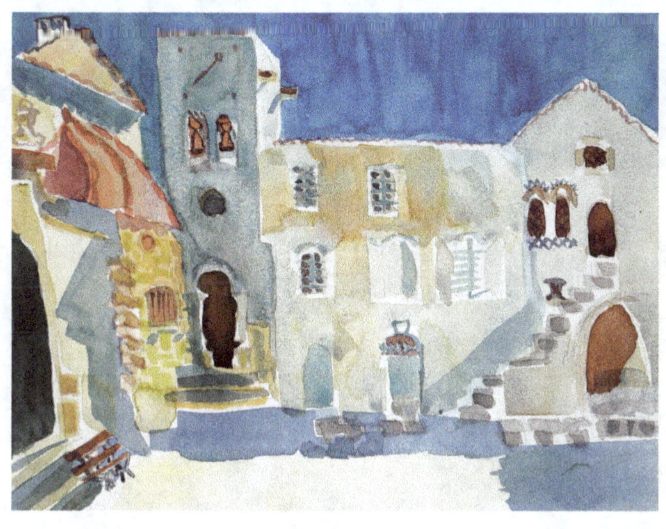

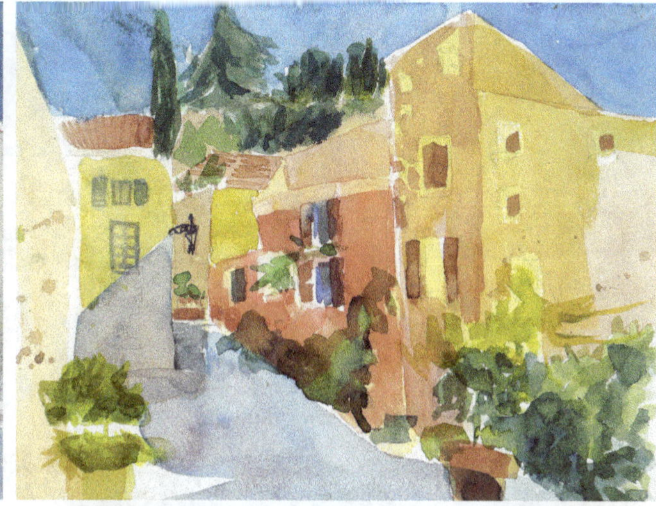

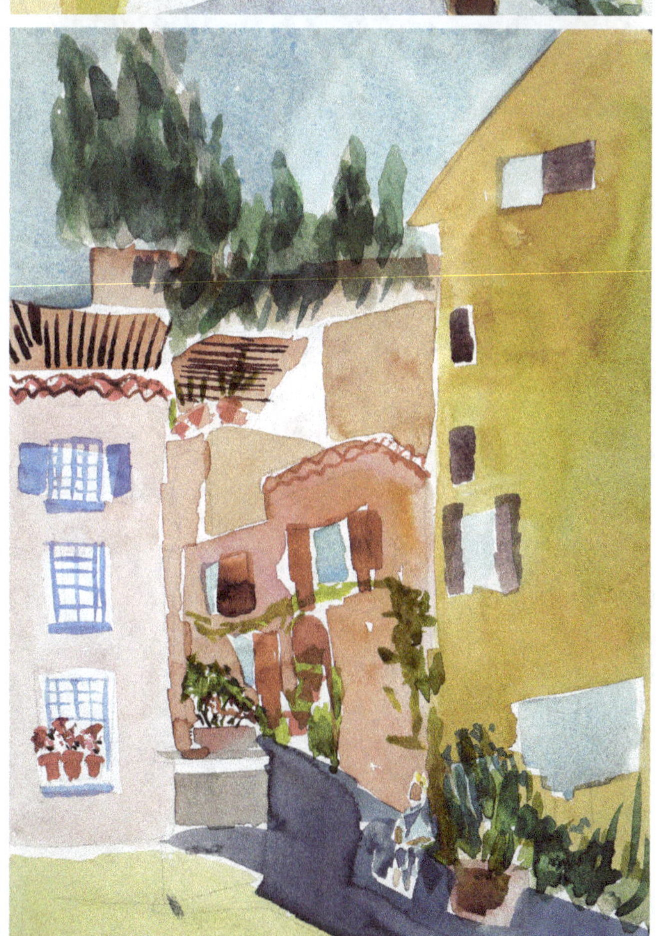

2018

LUBERON VALLEY
PROVENCE

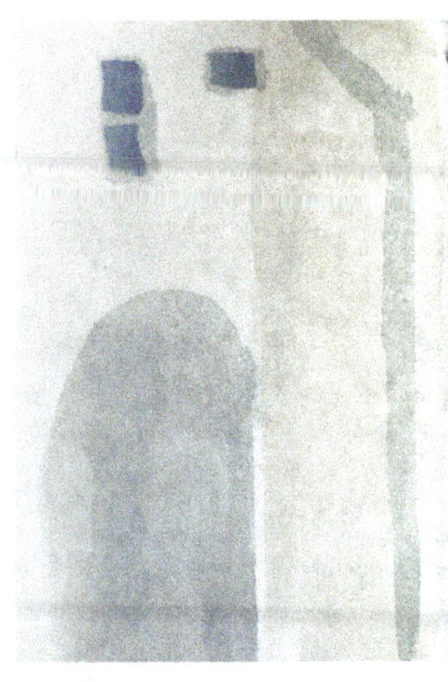
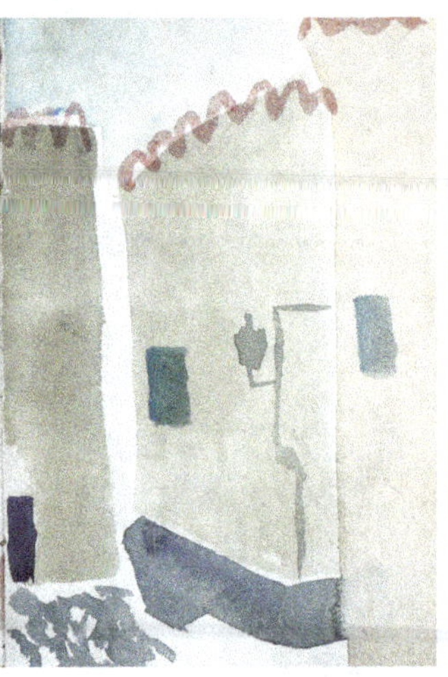
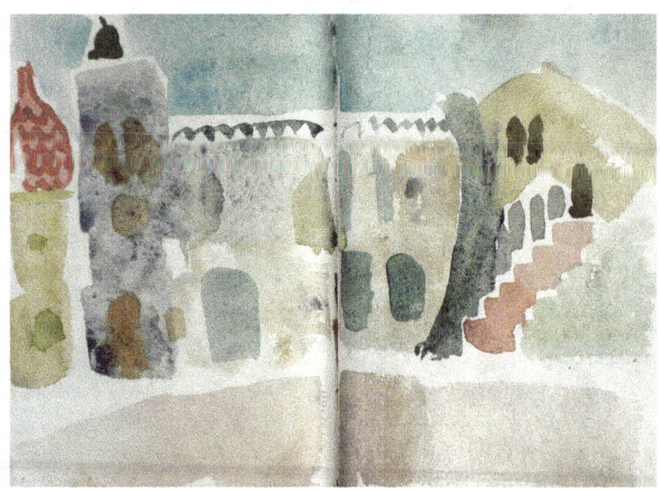

VIENS
LUBERON VALLEY, PROVENCE

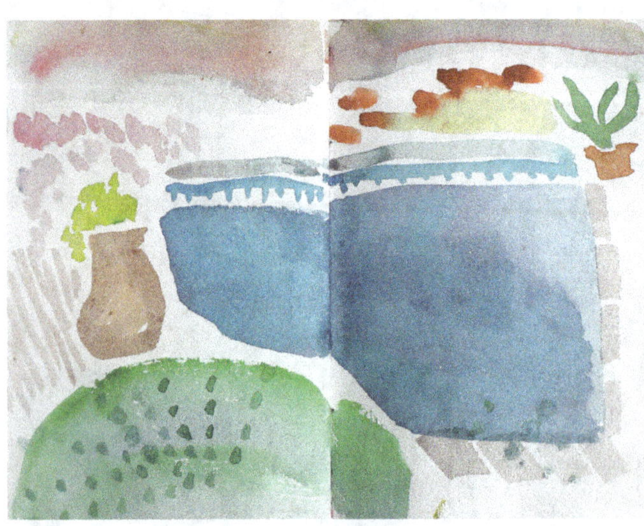
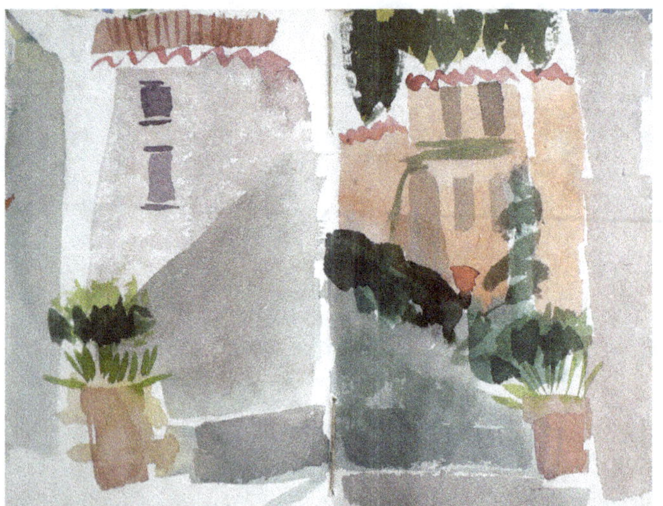

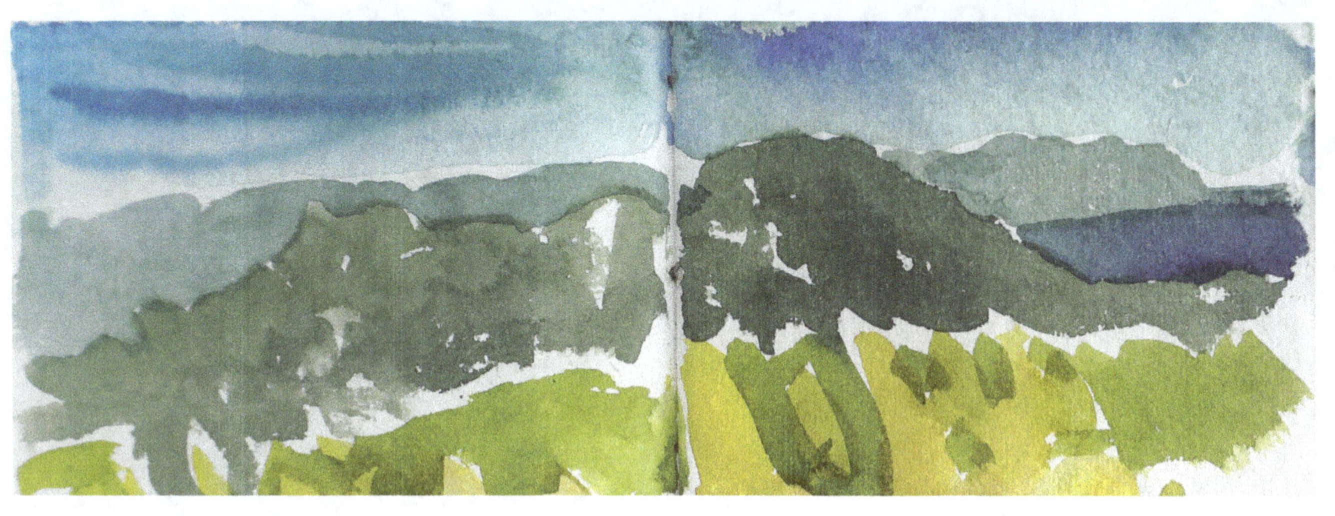

LUBERON VALLEY
PROVENCE

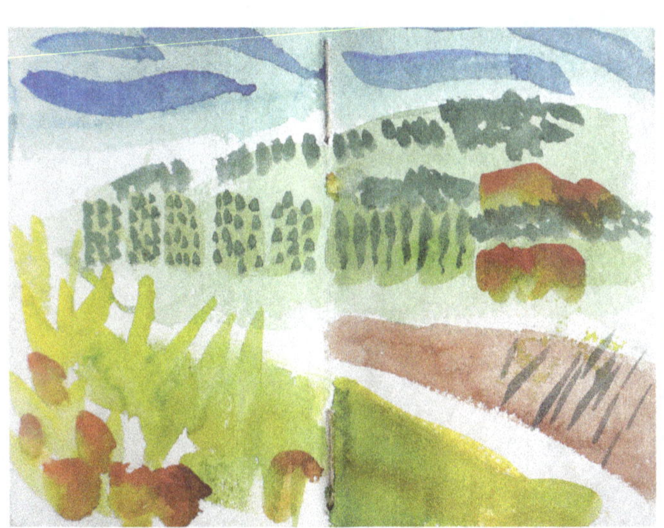
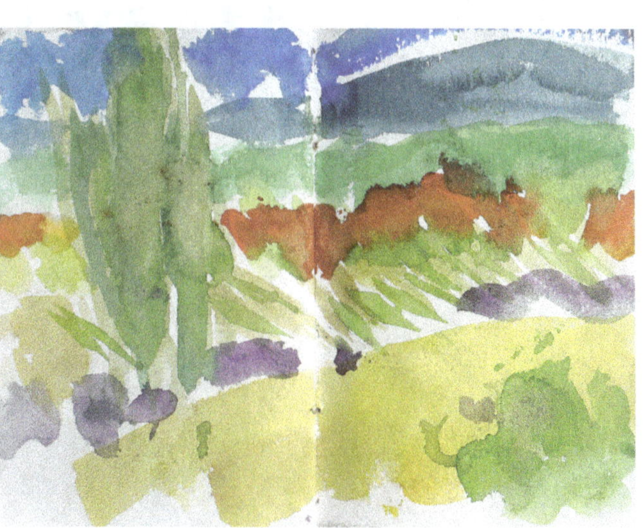

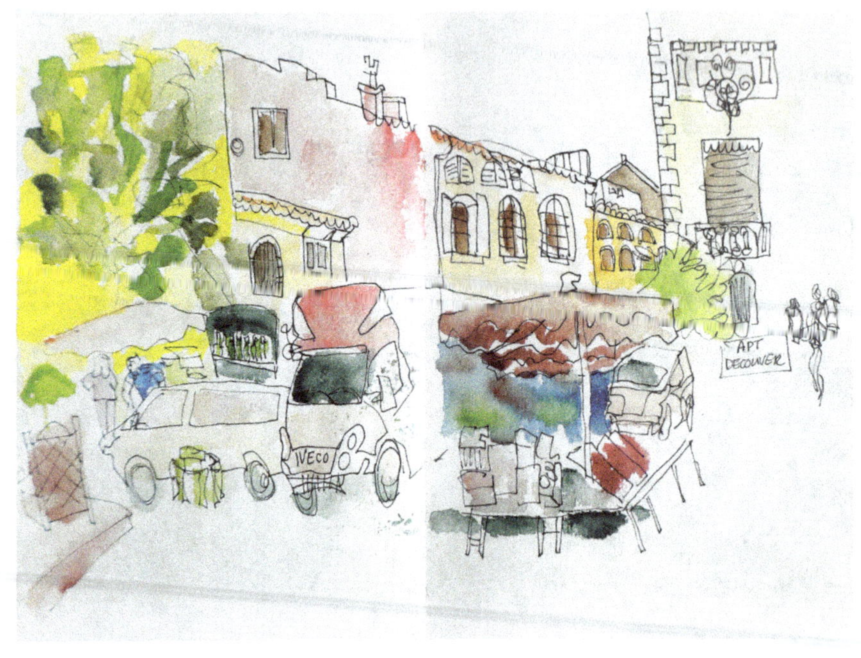

SAINT-SATURNIN-LÈS-APT
LUBERON VALLEY, PROVENCE

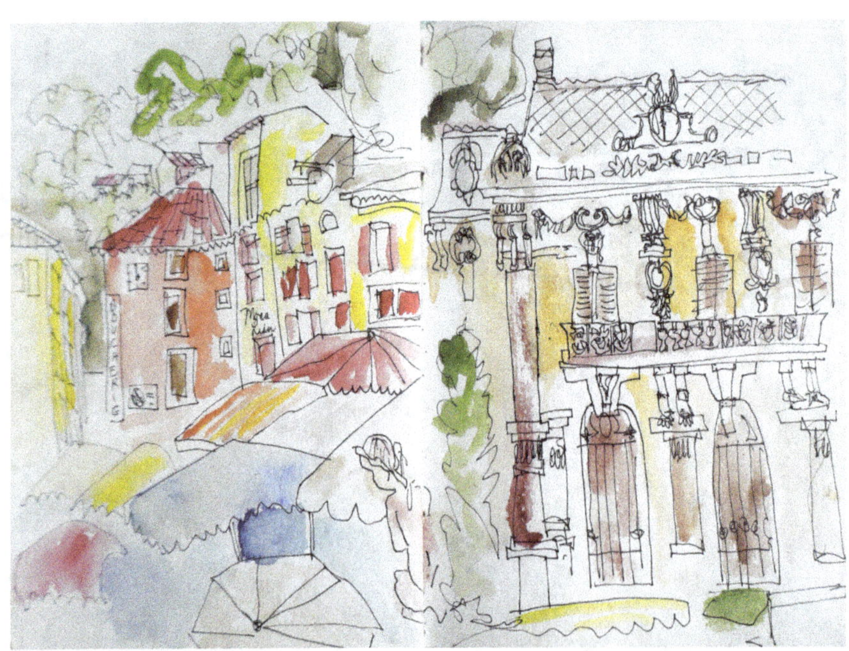

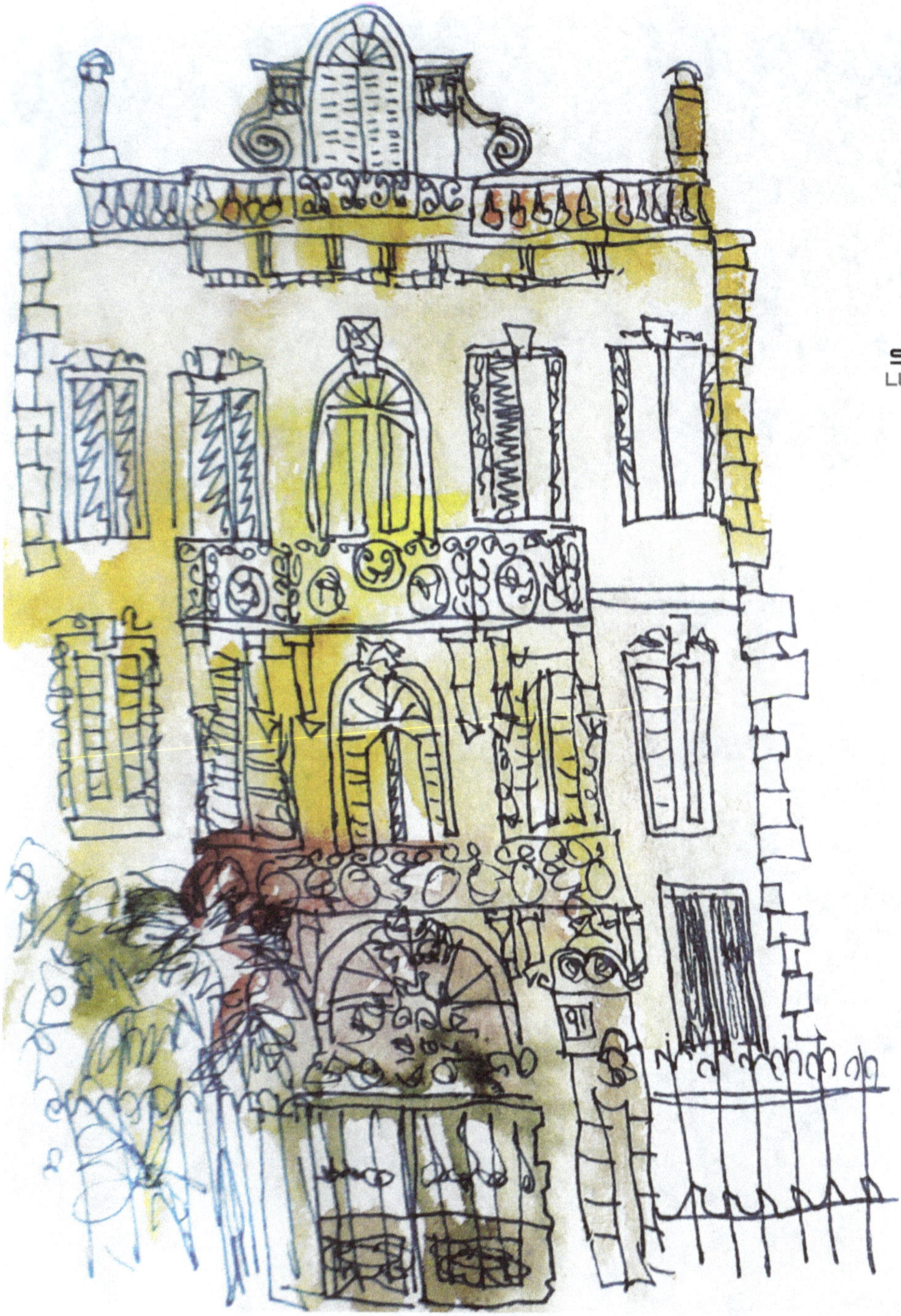

SAINT-SATURNIN-LÈS-APT
LUBERON VALLEY, PROVENCE

2018

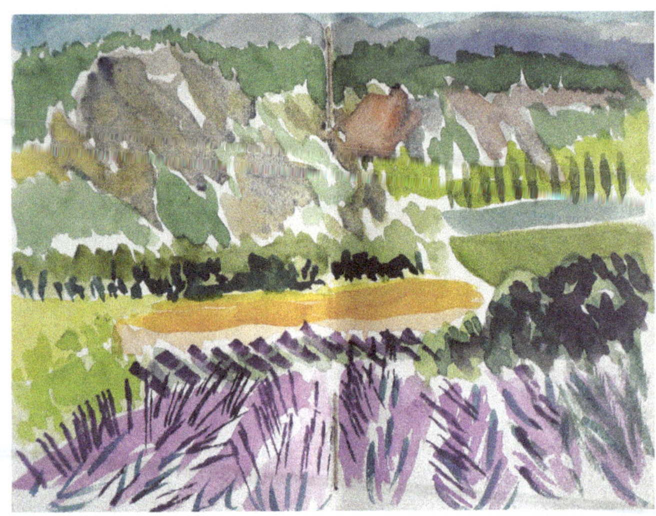

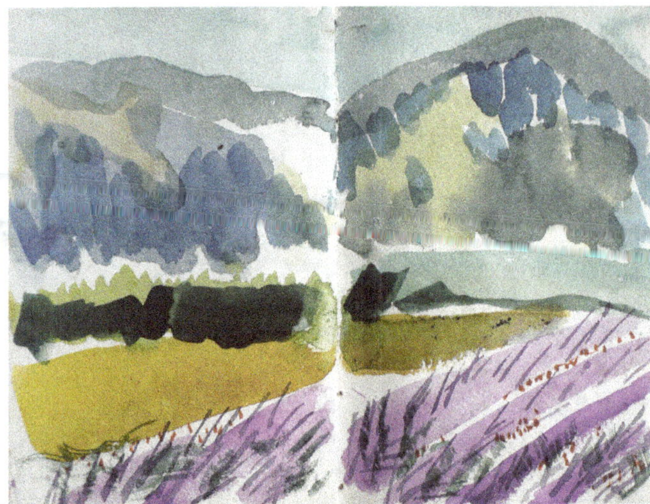

LUBERON VALLEY
PROVENCE

2018

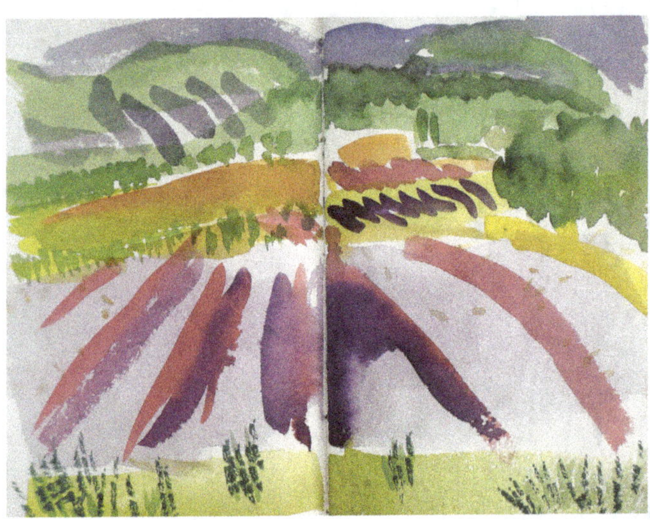

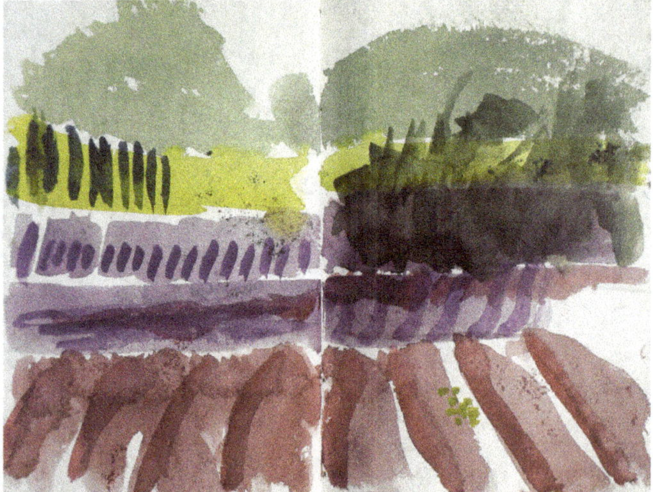

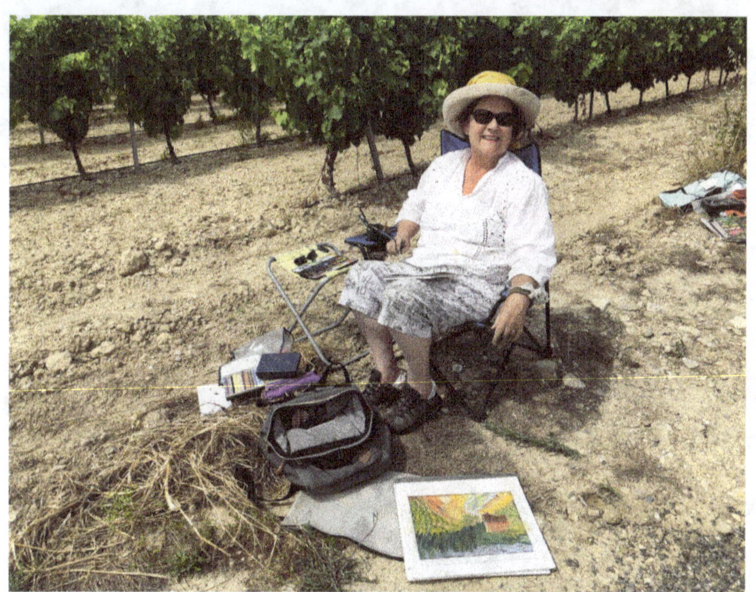

LUBERON VALLEY
PROVENCE

2018

LES ROUSILLONS
LUBERON VALLEY, PROVENCE

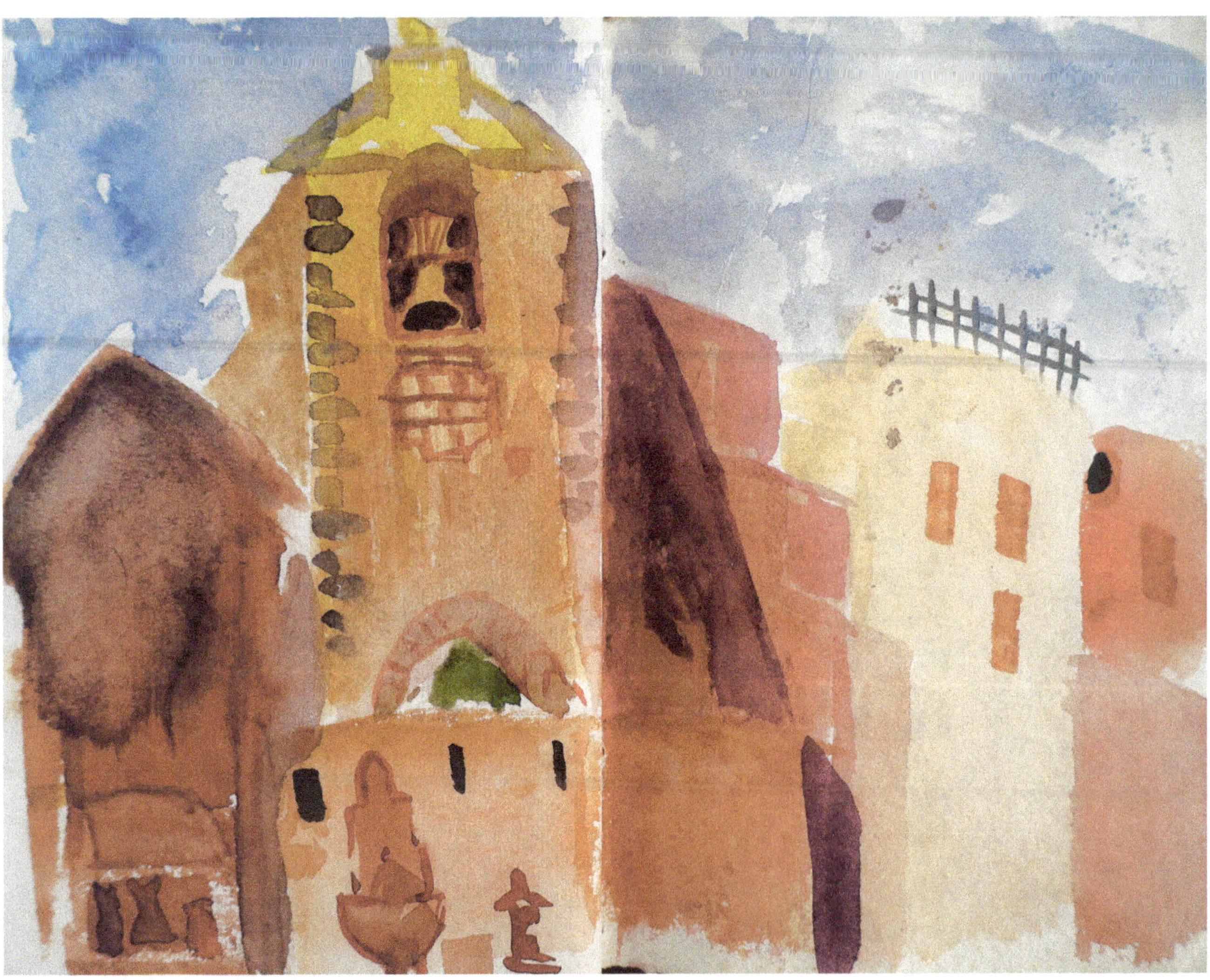

LES ROUSILLONS
LUBERON VALLEY, PROVENCE

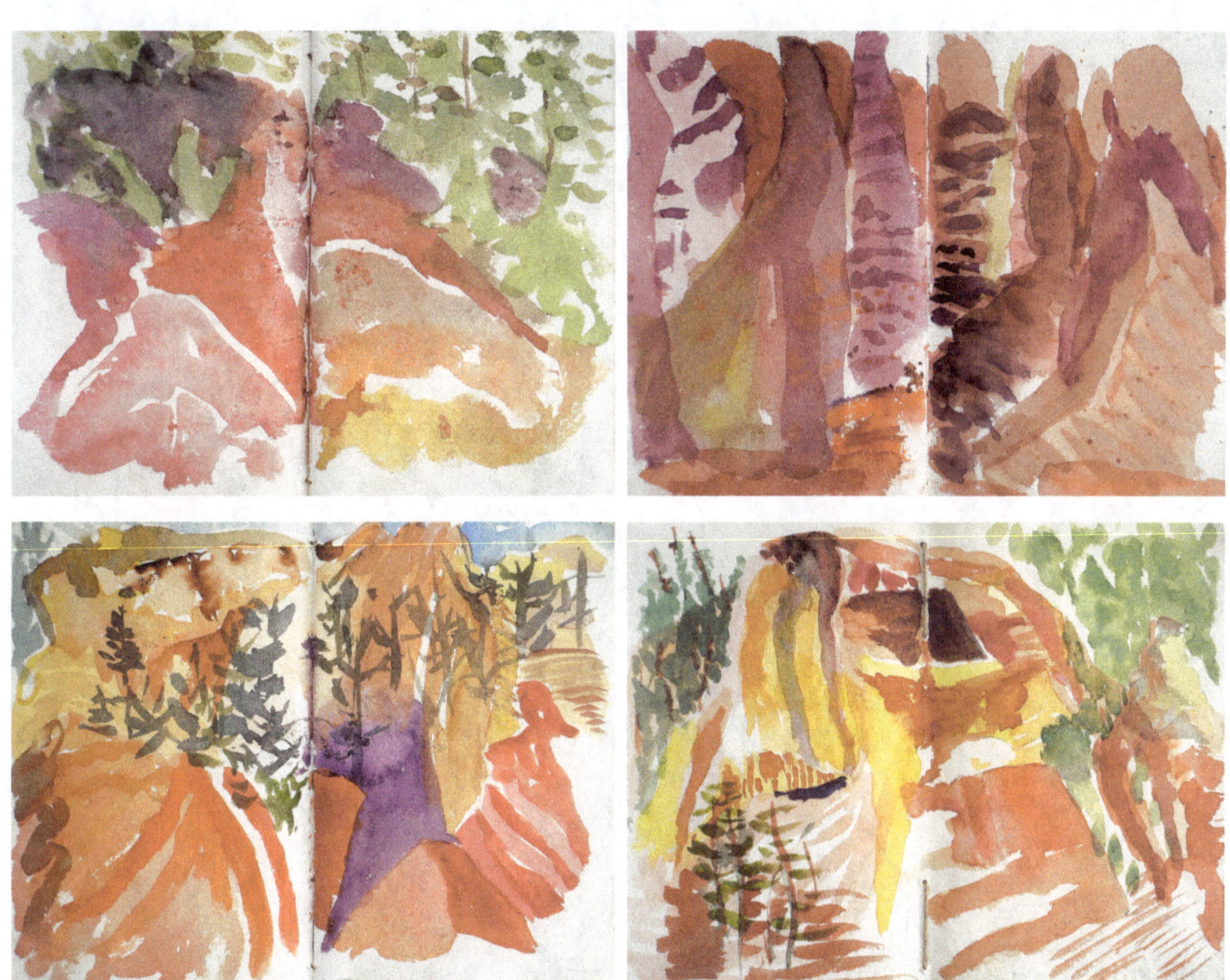

2018

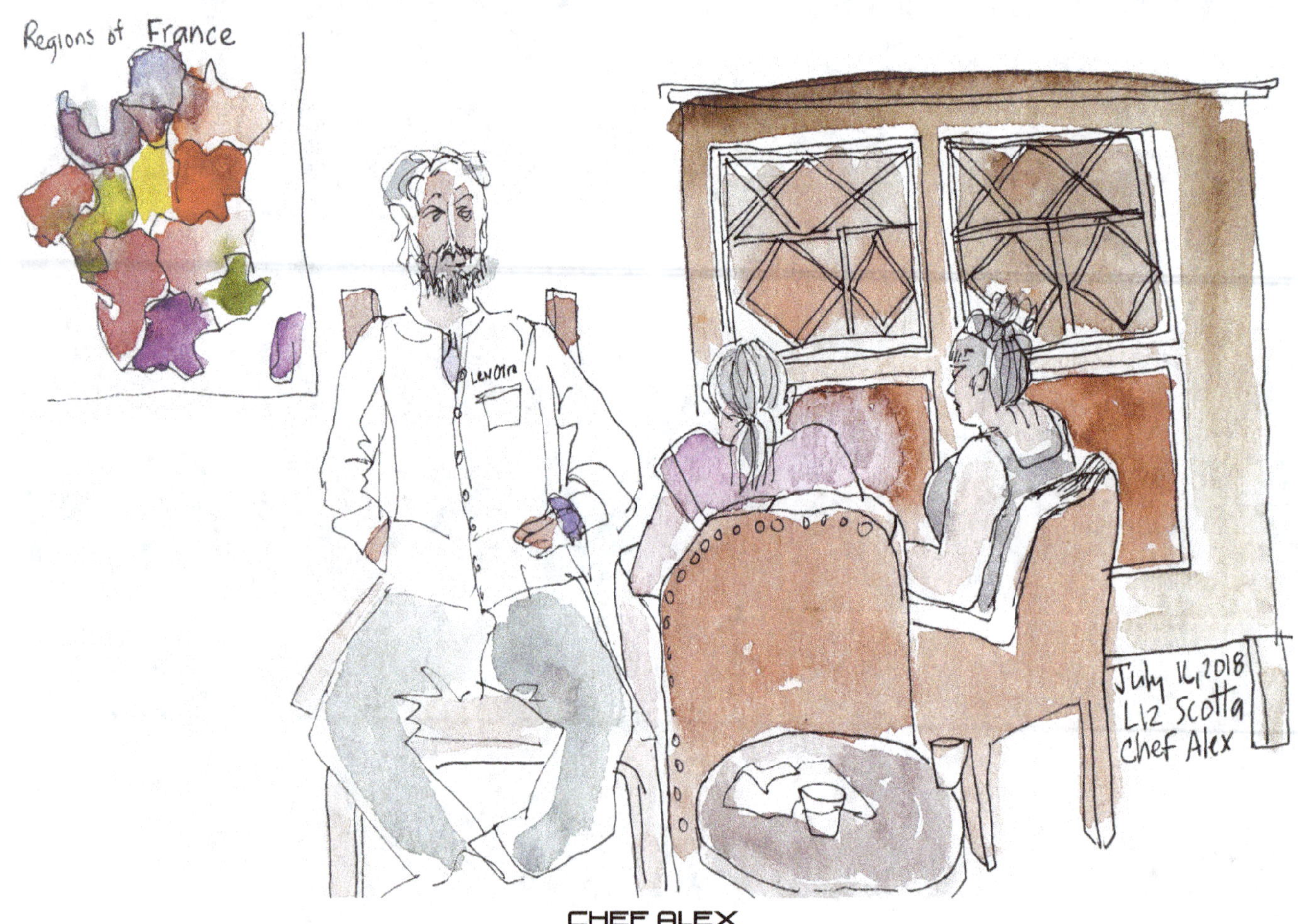

CHEF ALEX
PARIS

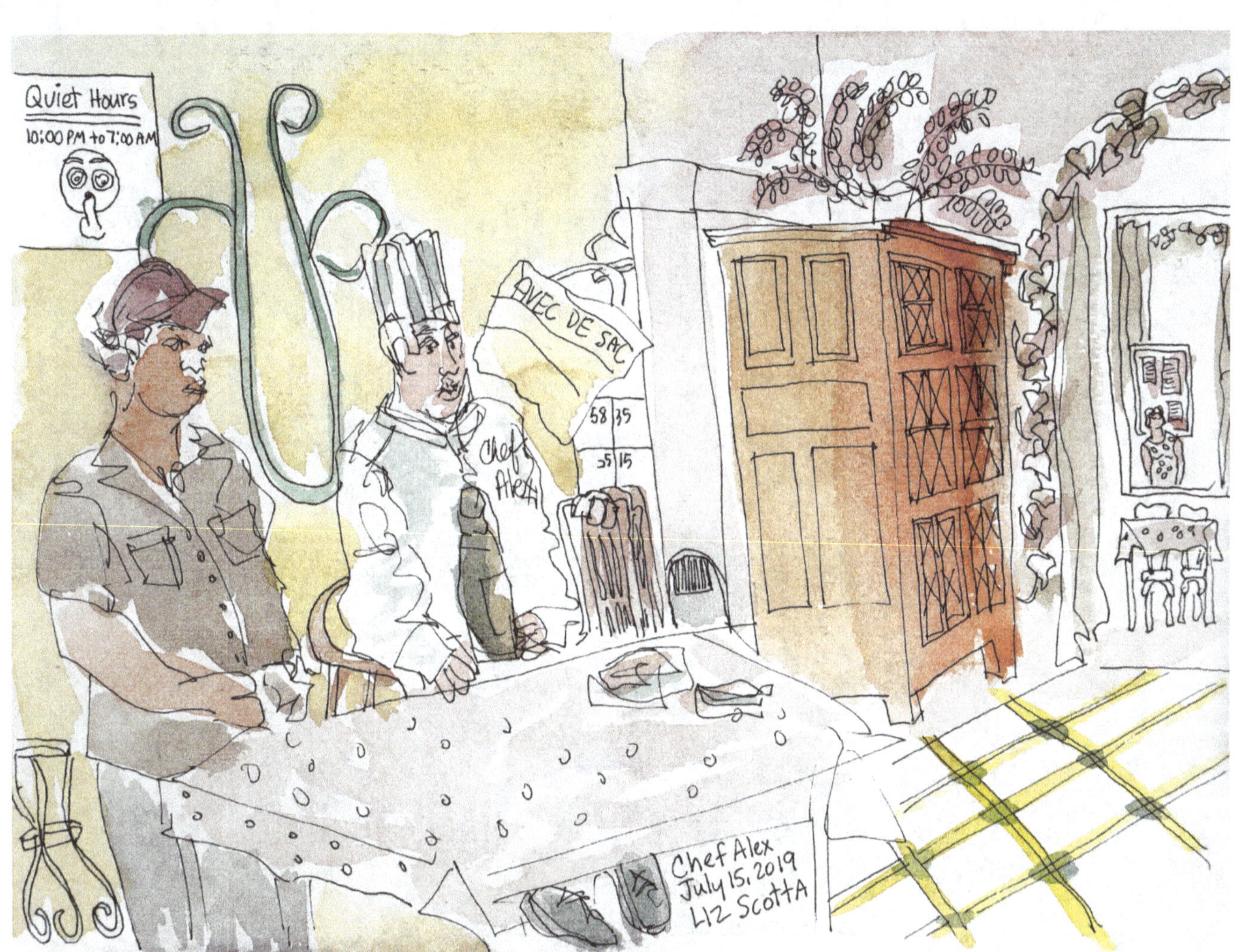

MAX AND CHEF ALEX
PARIS

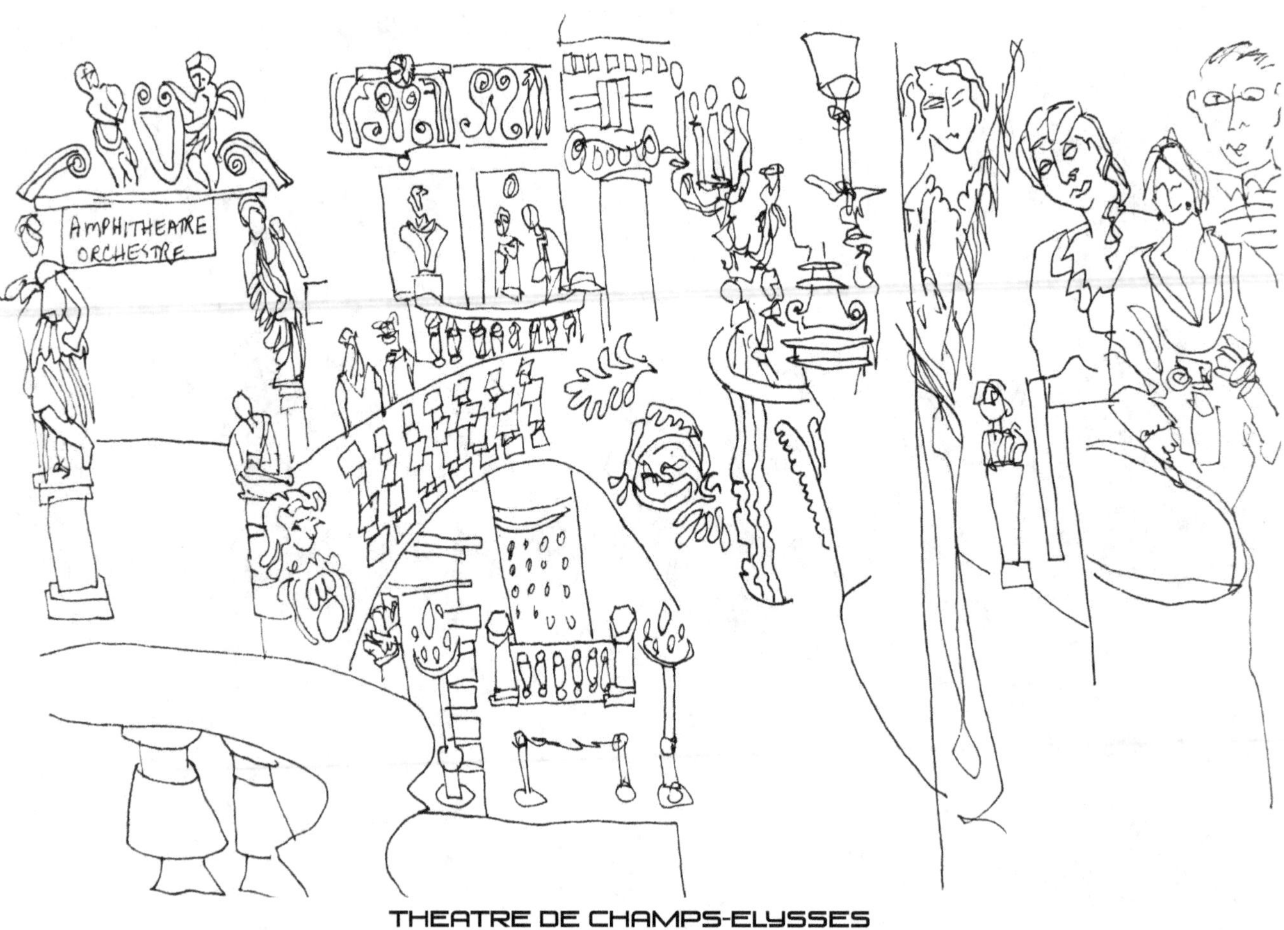

THEATRE DE CHAMPS-ELYSSES
PARIS

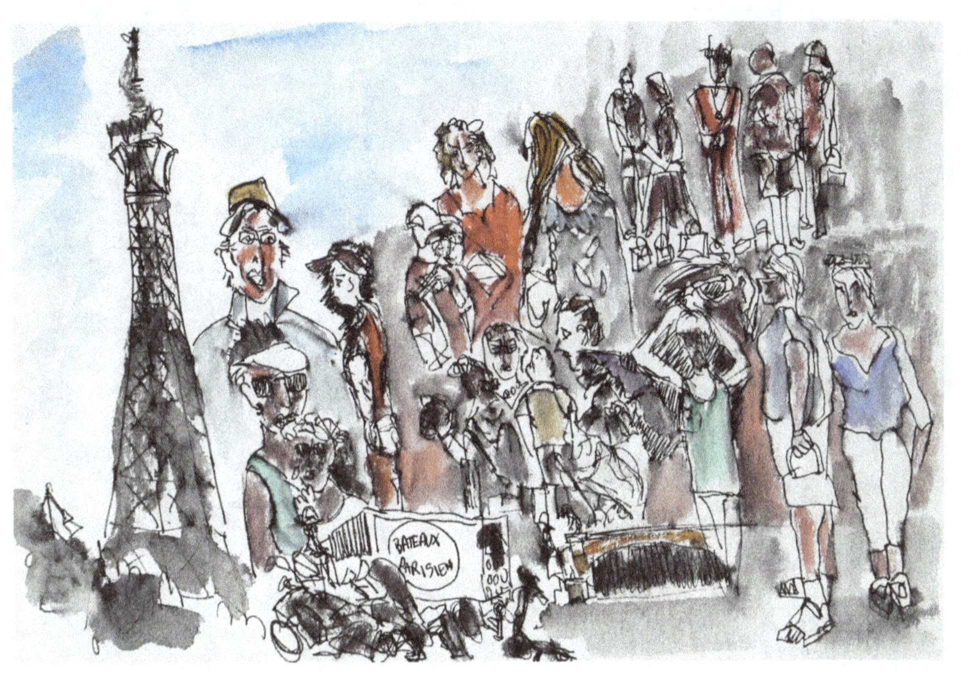

BATEAUX PARISIENS ON THE SEINE
PARIS

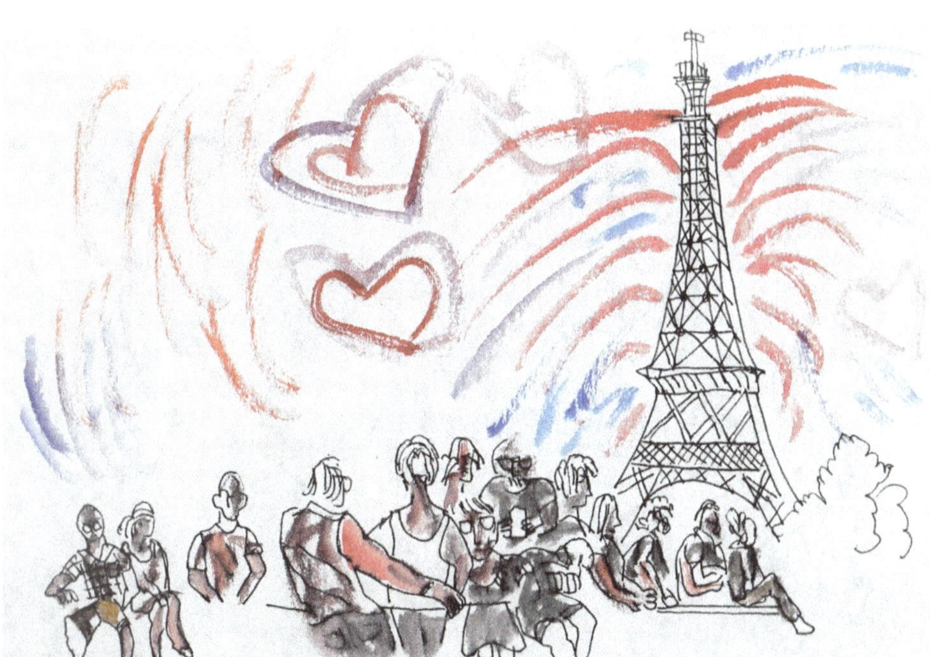

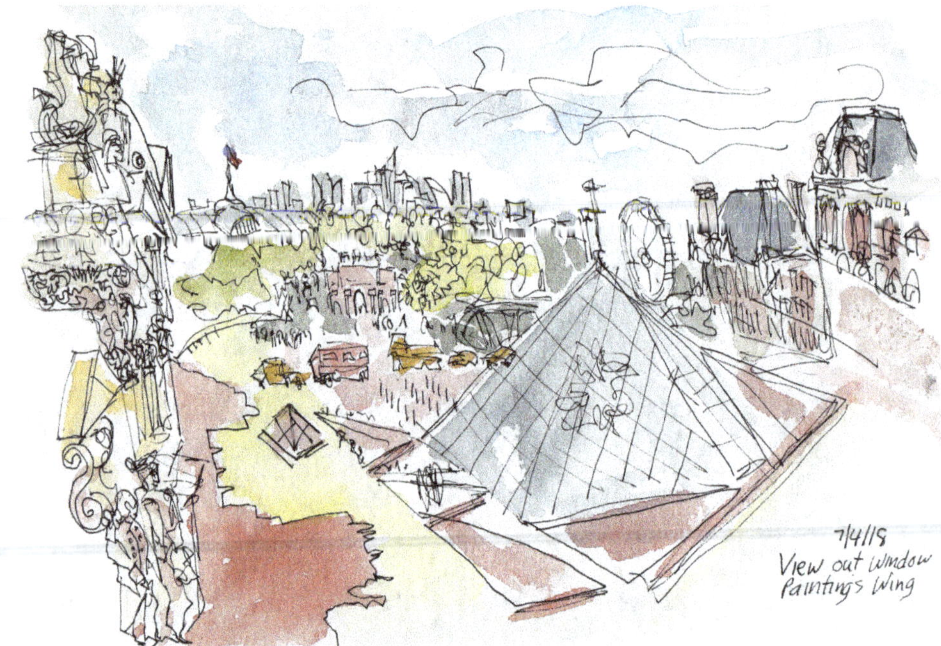

LOUVRE
PARIS

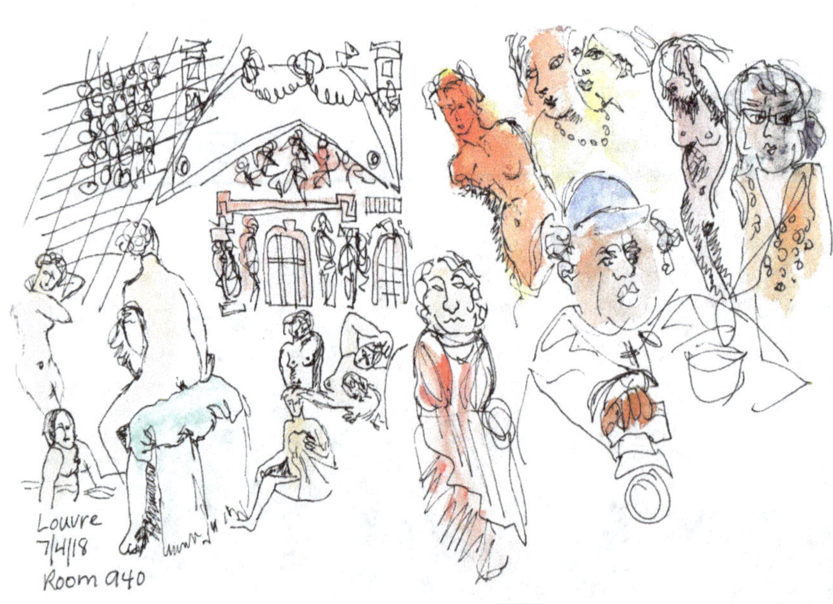

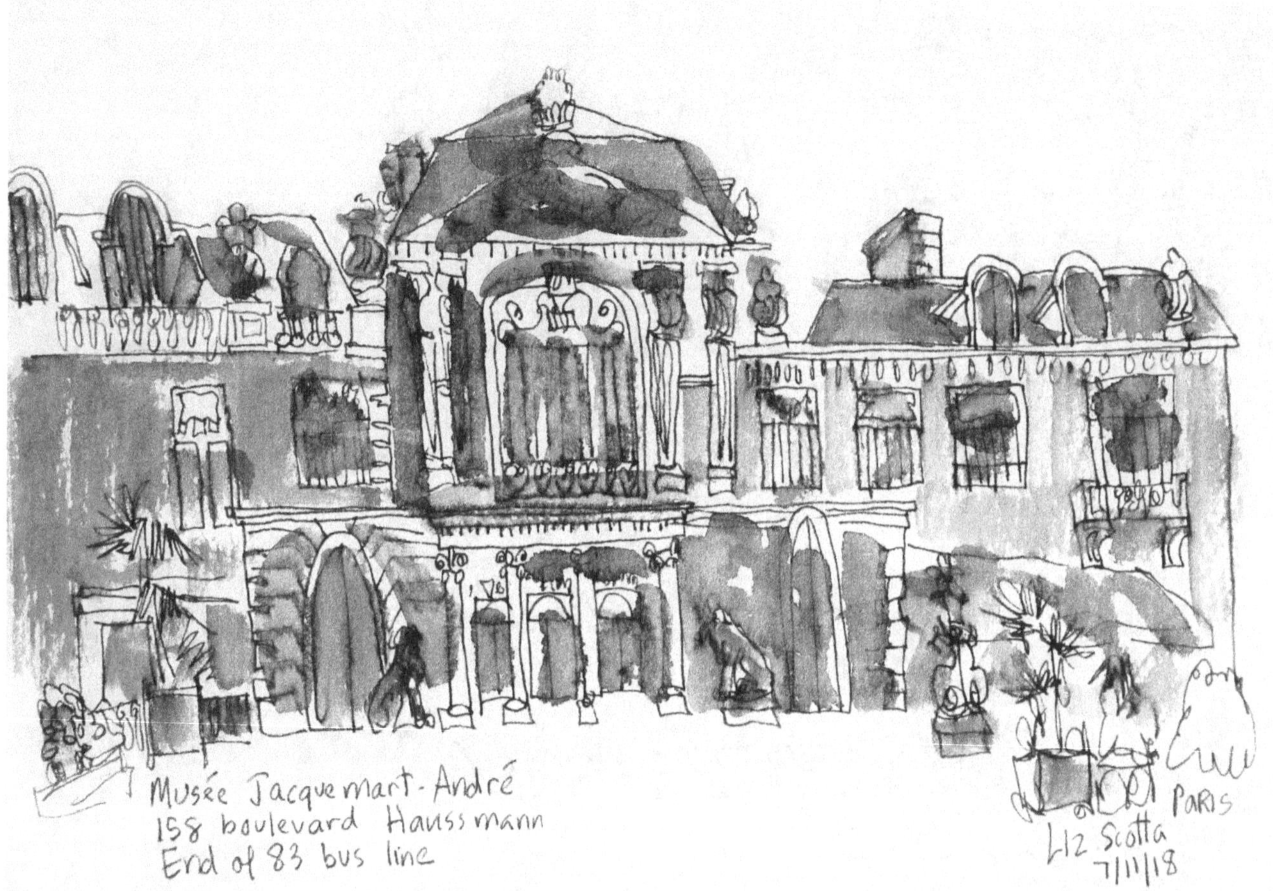

MUSÉE JACQUEMART ANDRÉ
PARIS

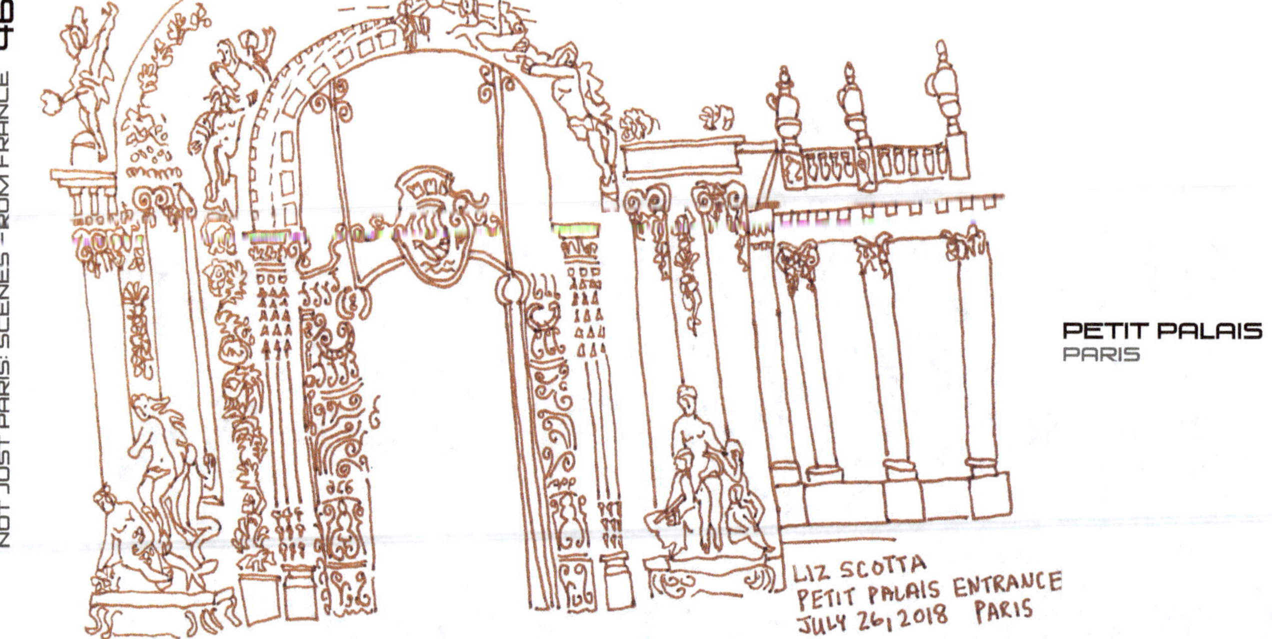

PETIT PALAIS
PARIS

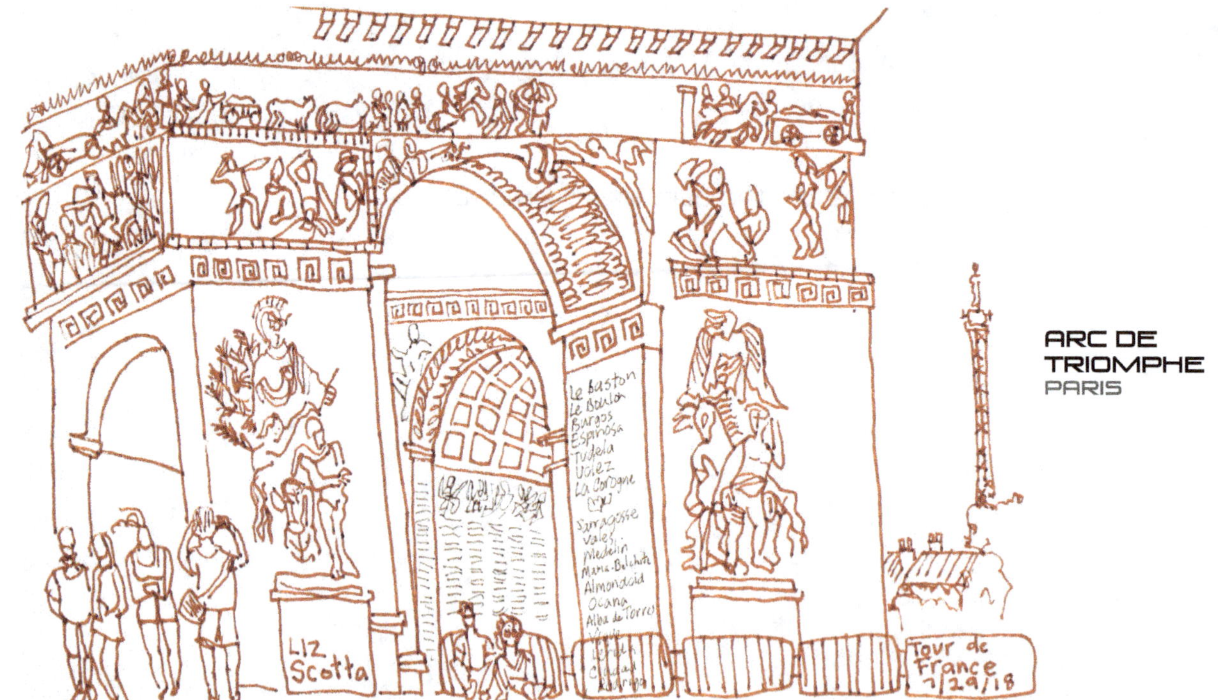

**ARC DE
TRIOMPHE**
PARIS

MUSÉE DES ARTS ET MÉTIERS
PARIS

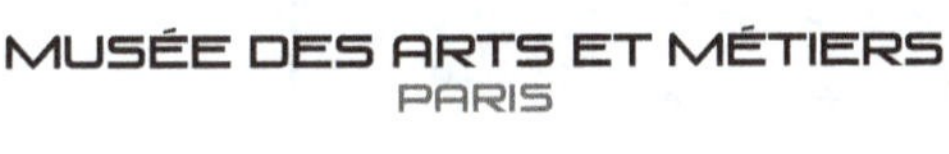

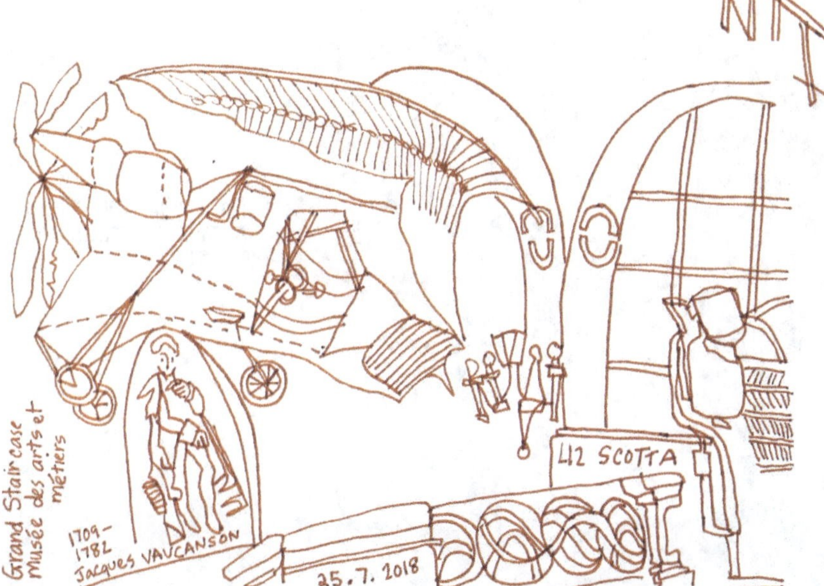

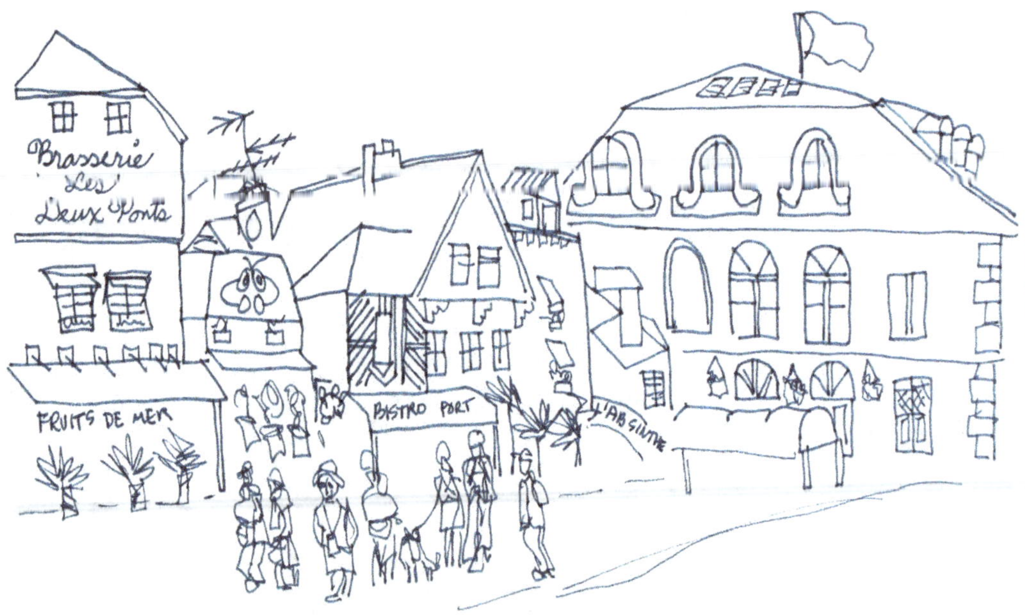

**LES DEUX PONTS
RESTAURANT
AND OFFICE
OF TOURISM**
HONFLEUR

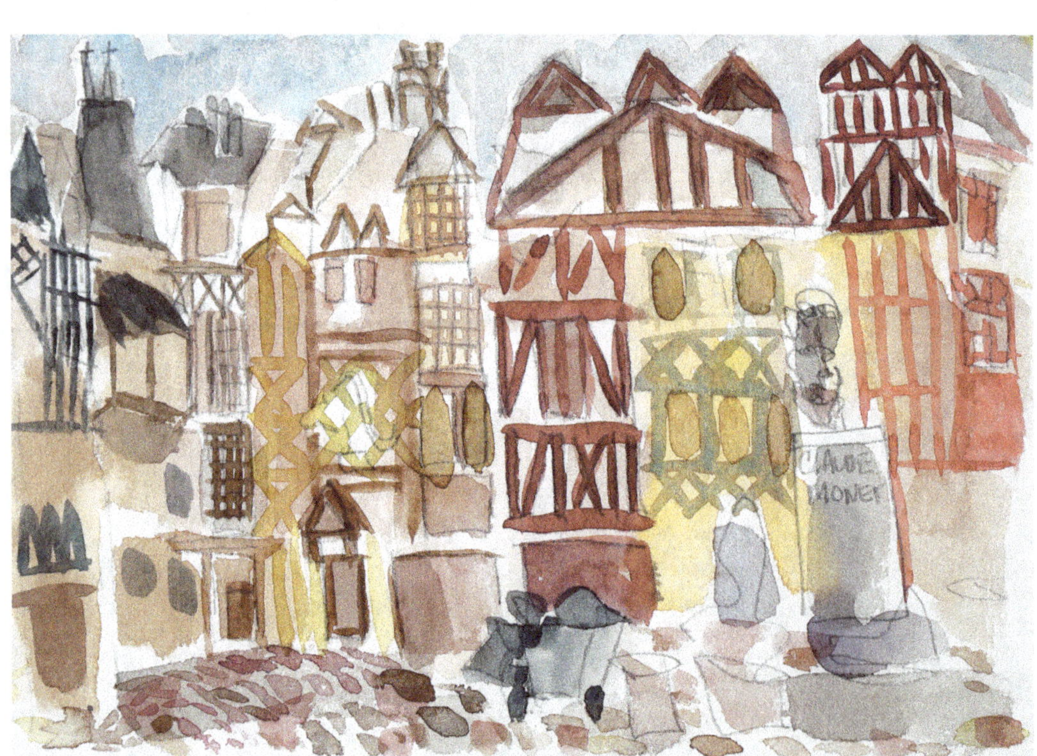

**HALF-TIMBERED
ARCHITECTURE**
ROUEN

CATHÉDRALE DE BAYEUX
BAYEUX

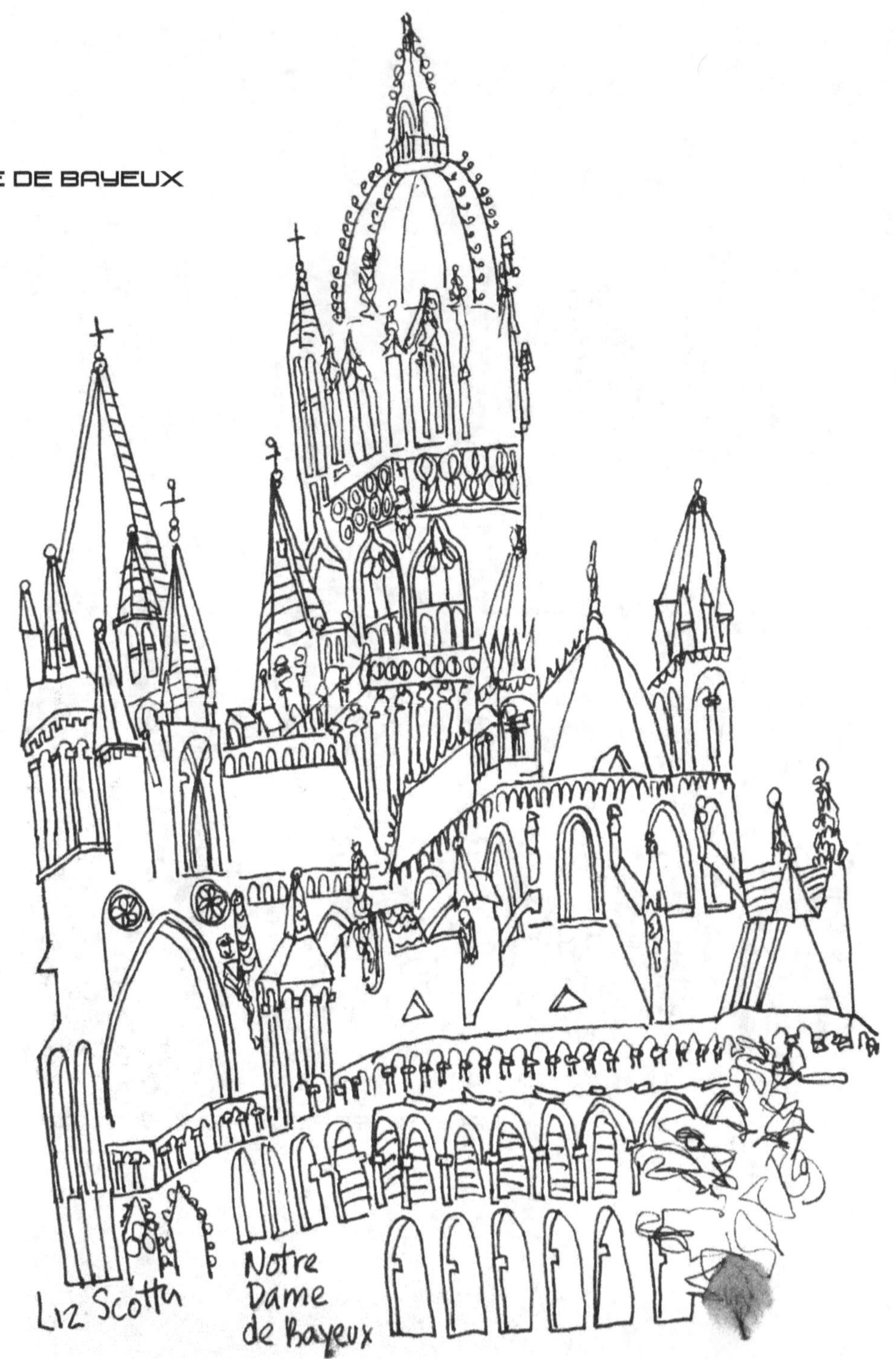

2018

2018

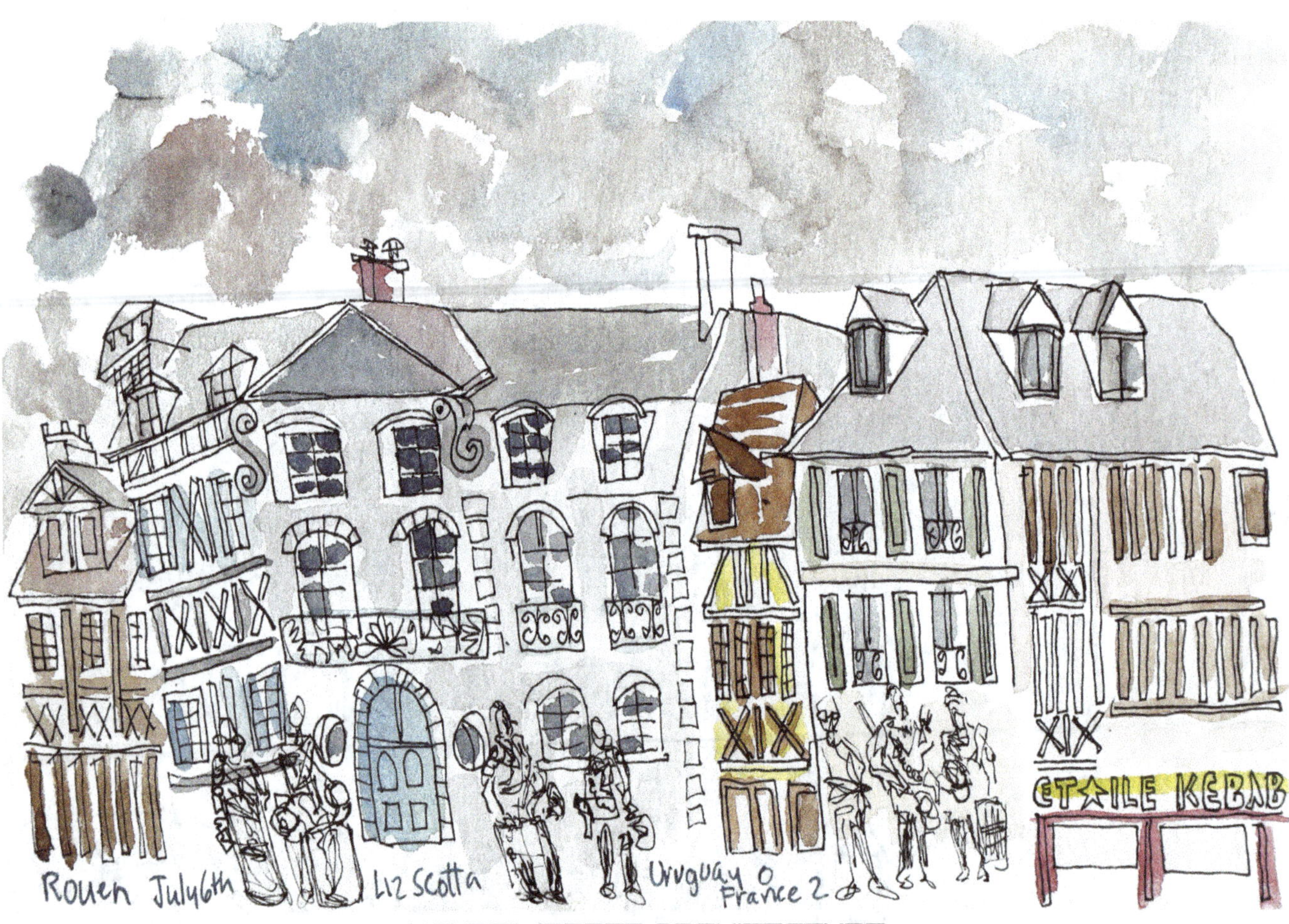

HALF-TIMBERED ARCHITECTURE
ROUEN

2018

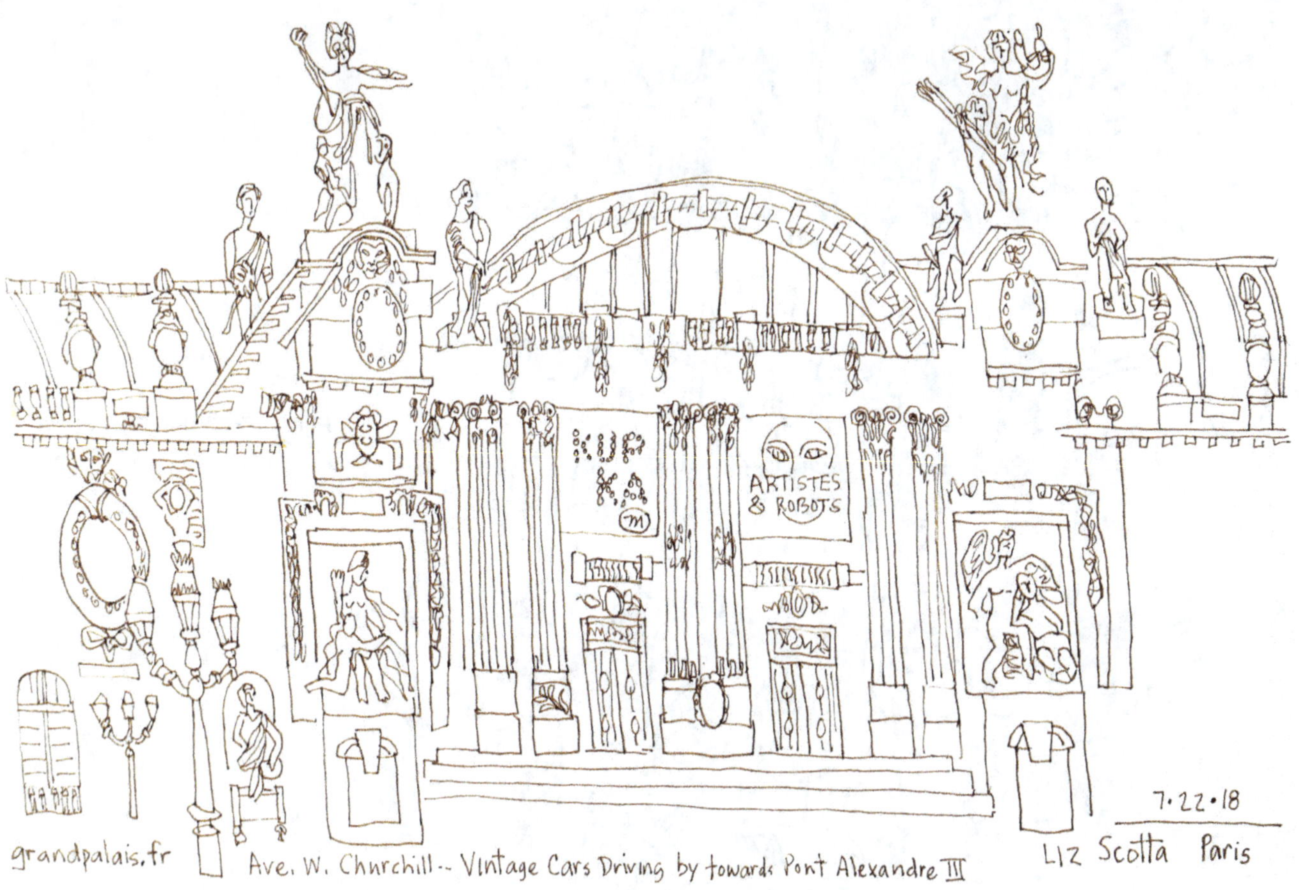

grandpalais.fr   Ave. W. Churchill -- Vintage Cars Driving by towards Pont Alexandre III

7·22·18

Liz Scotta Paris

GRAND PALAIS
PARIS

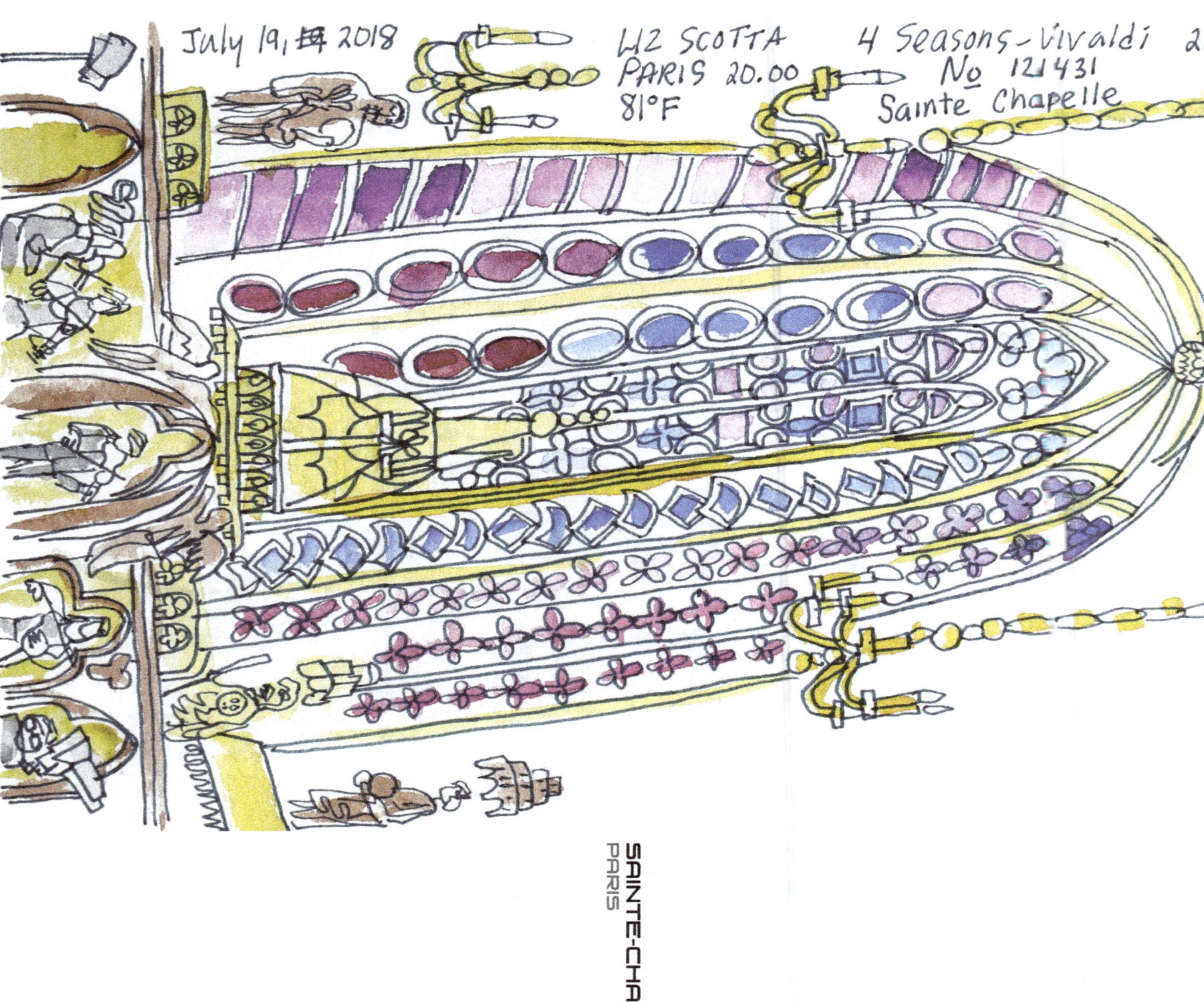

SAINTE-CHAPELLE
PARIS

SAINT-SULPICE
PARIS

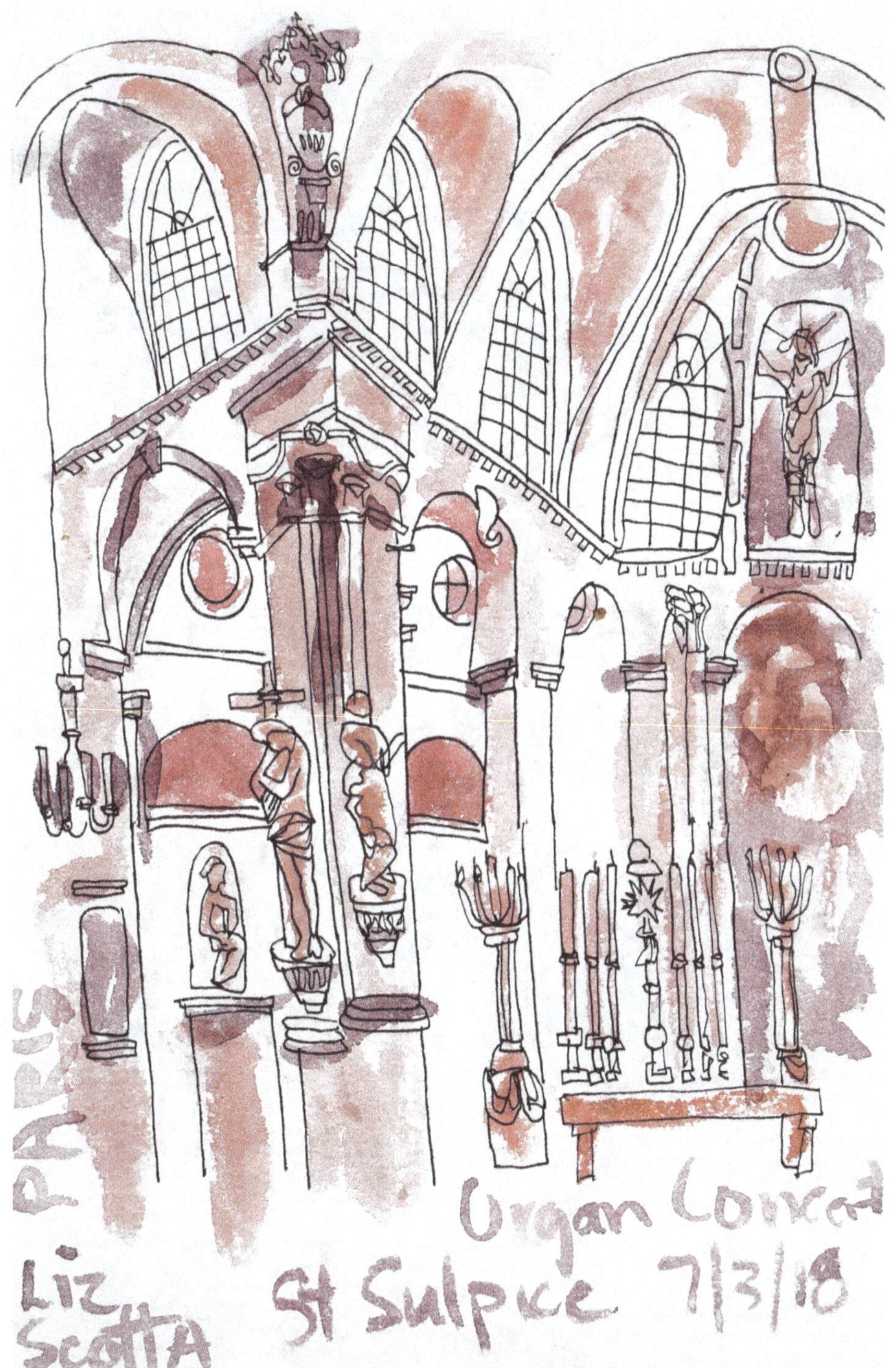

2018

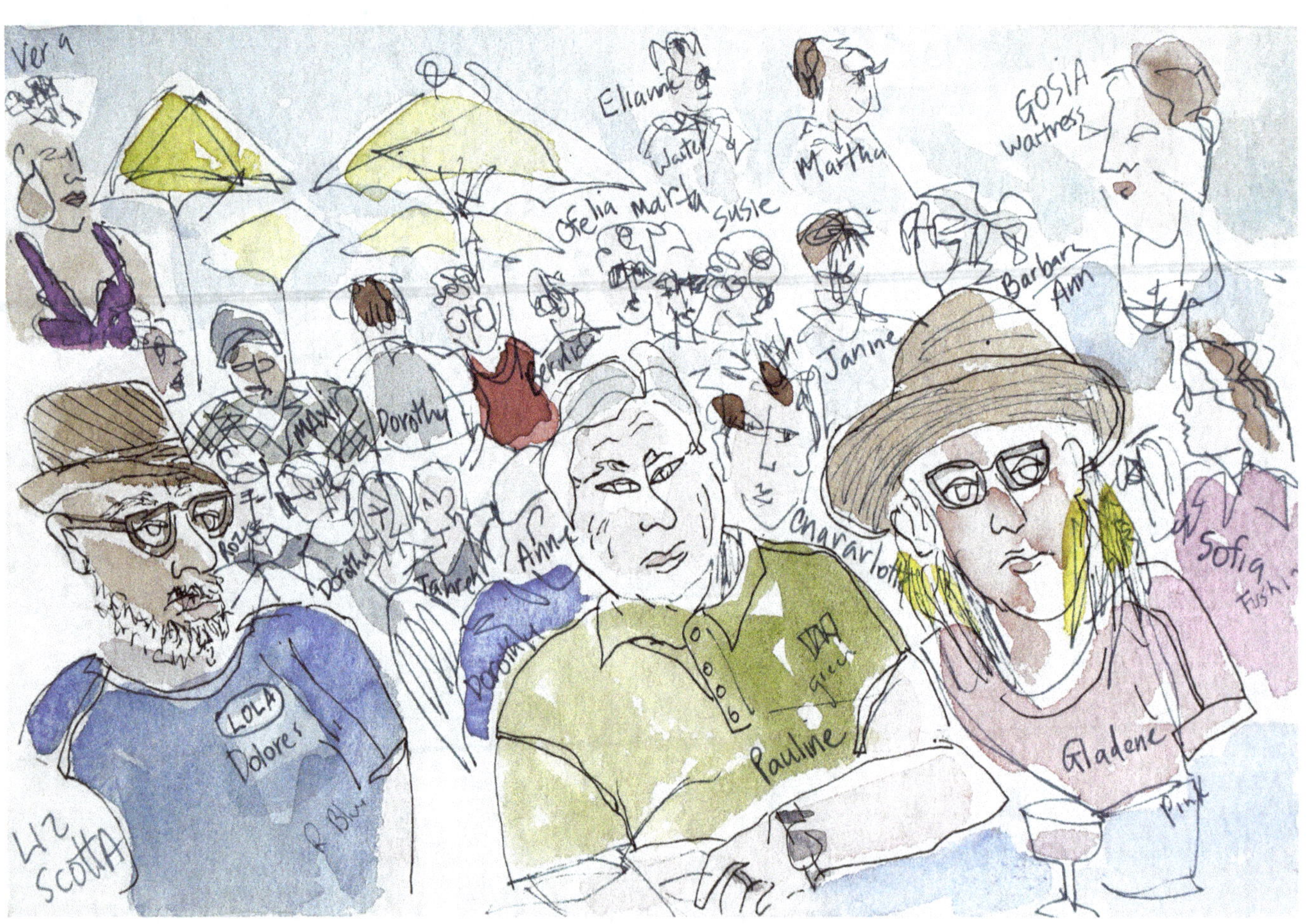

LUNCH WITH FRIENDS

2018

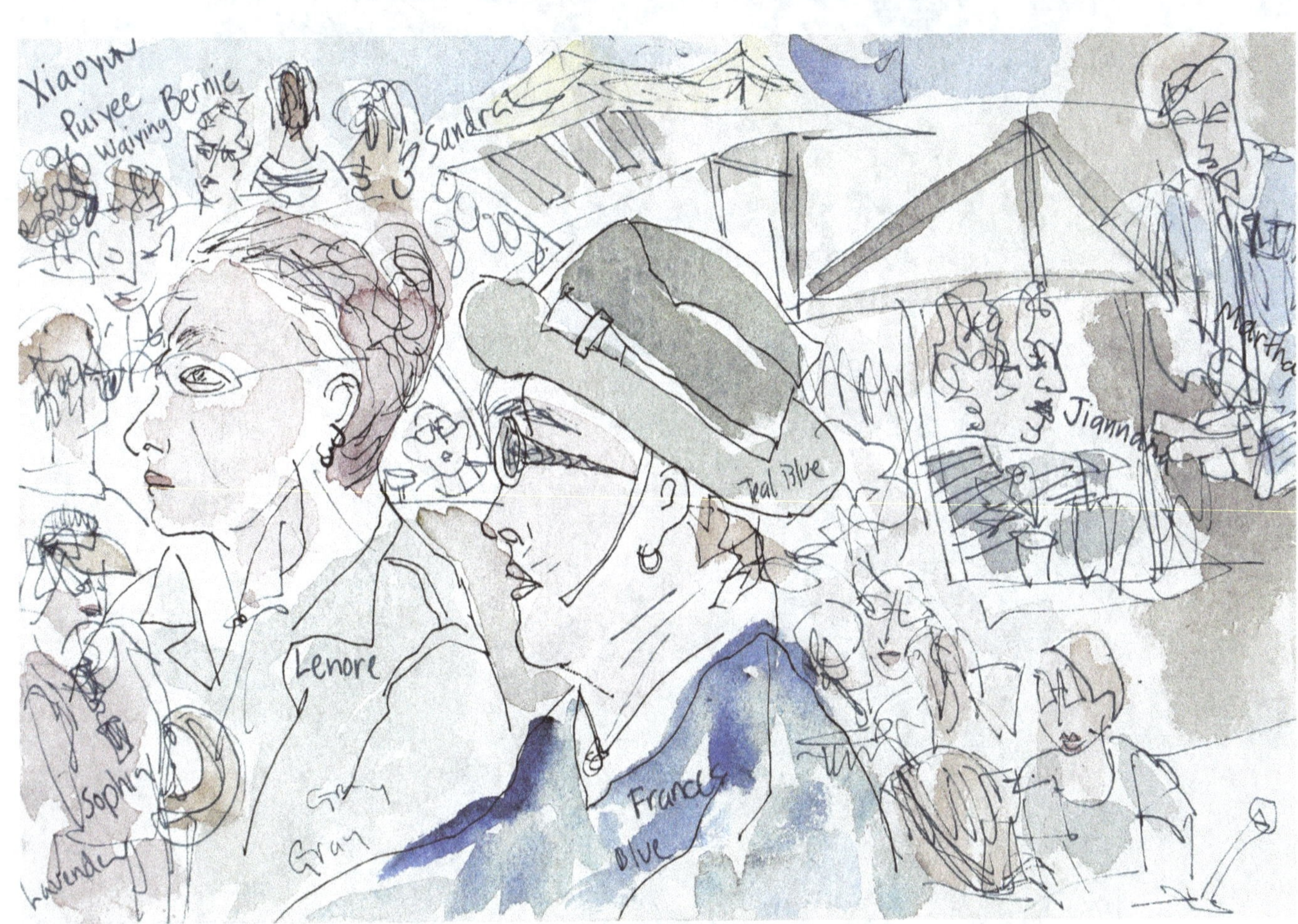

LUNCH WITH FRIENDS

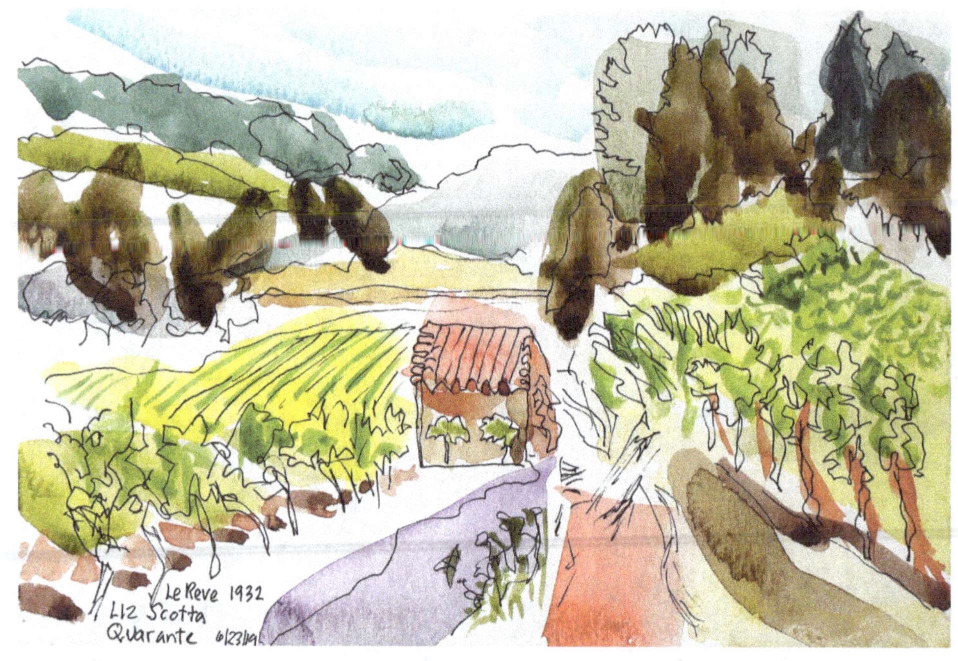

QUARANTE VINEYARD
LANGUEDOC-ROUSSILLON

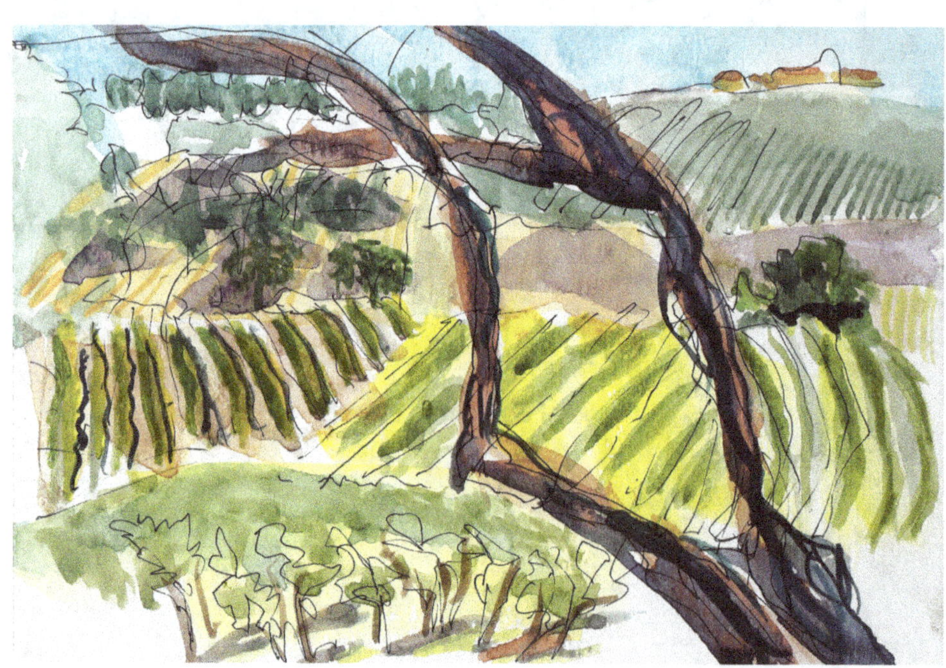

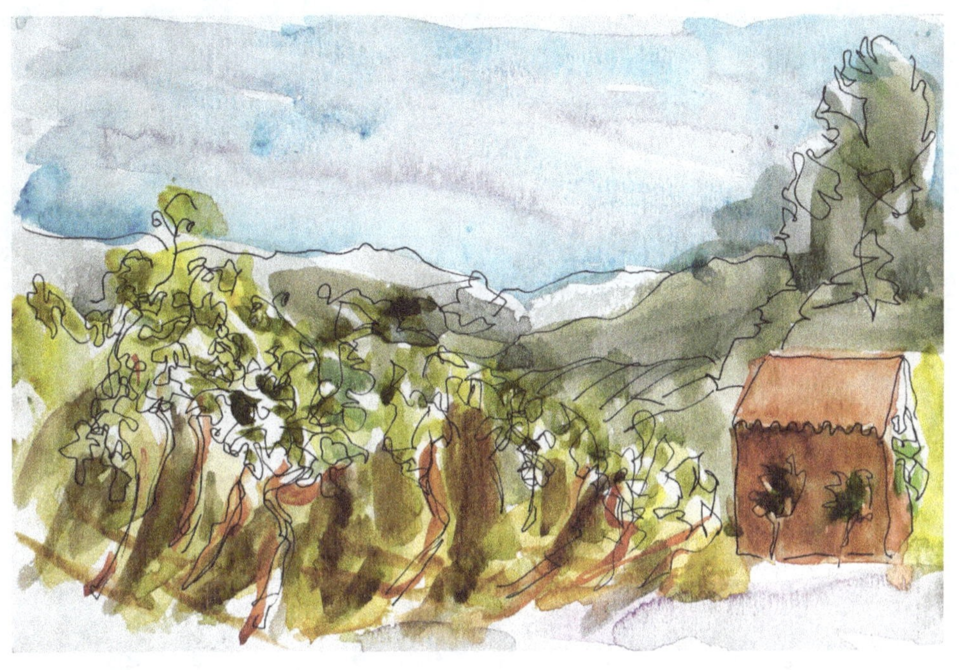

QUARANTE VINEYARD
LANGUEDOC-ROUSSILLON

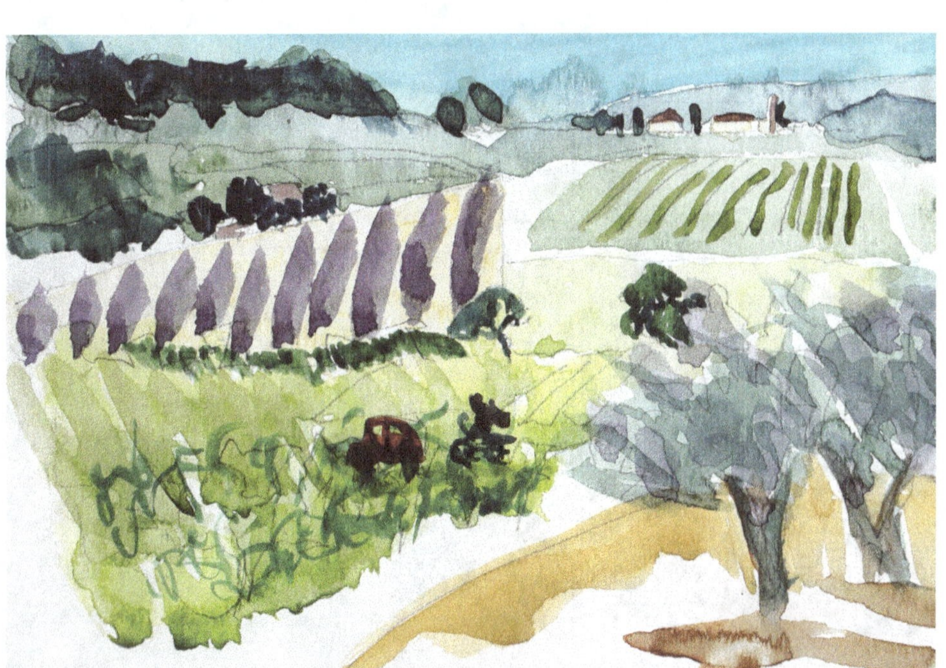

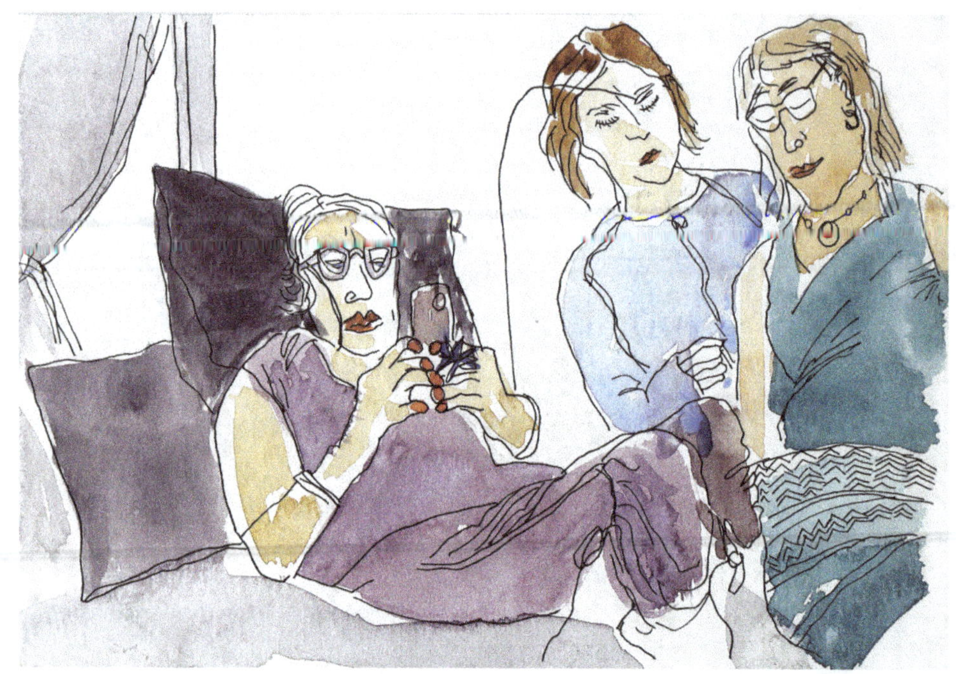

RELAXING AFTER PAINTING

QUARANTE
LANGUEDOC-ROUSSILLON

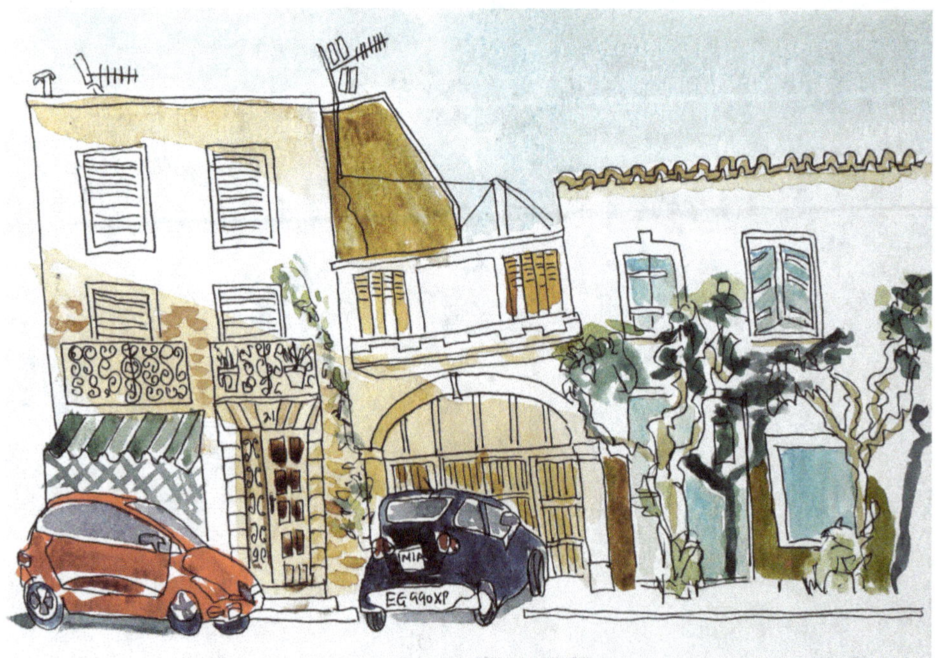

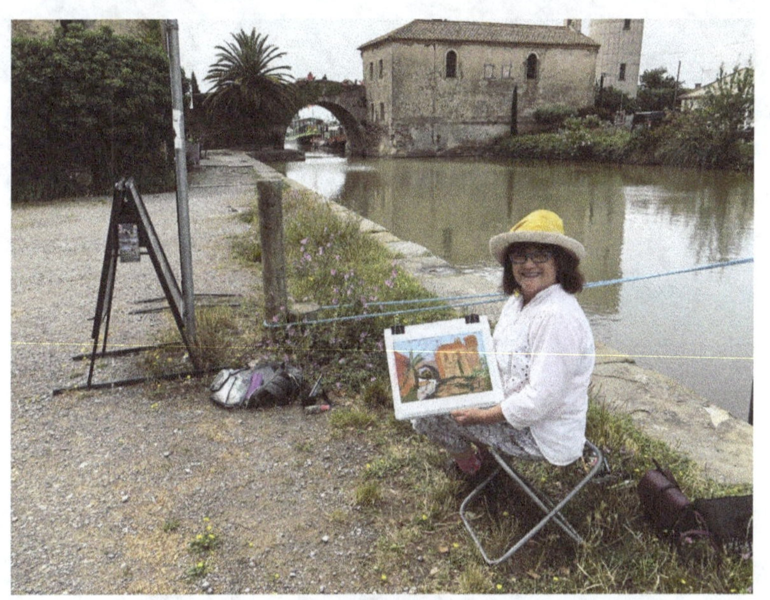

LANGUEDOC
FRANCE

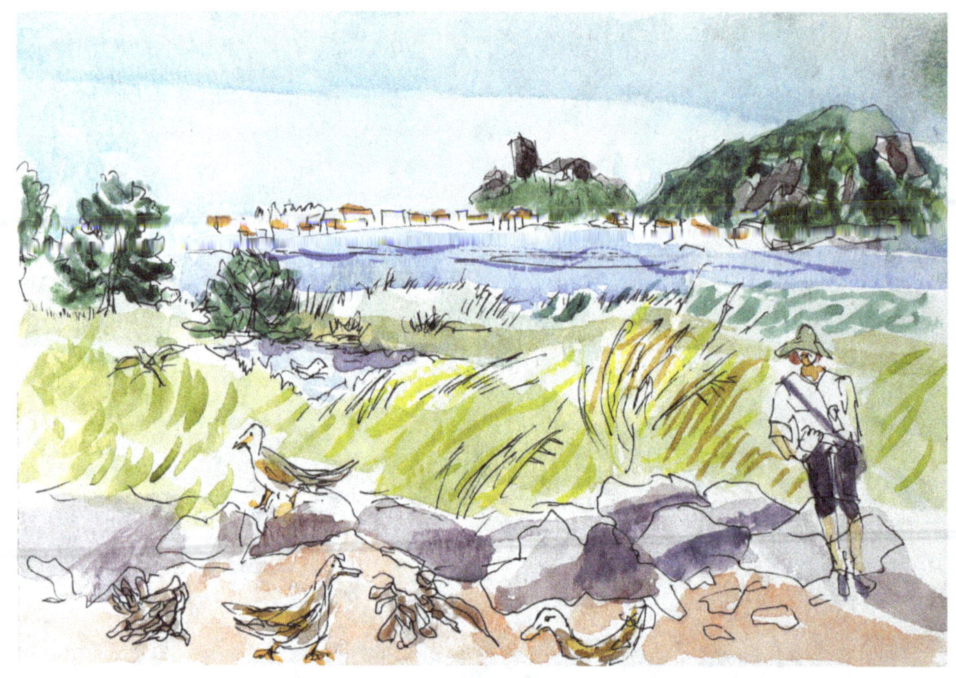

GRUISSAN
LANGUEDOC-ROUSSILLON

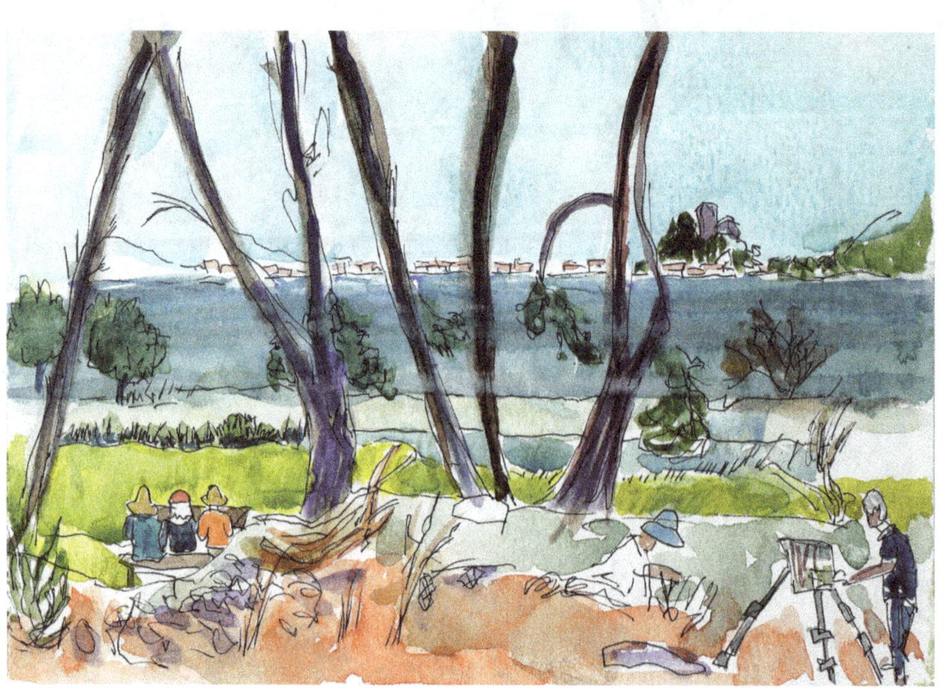

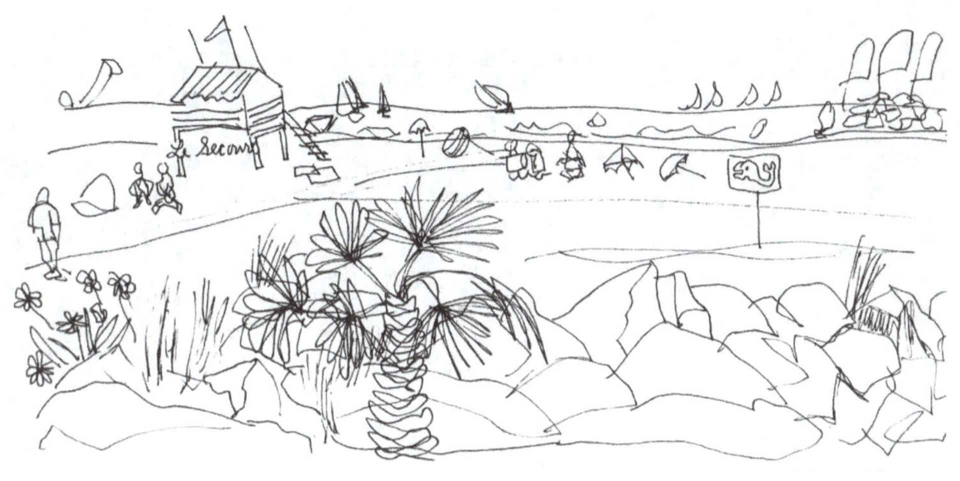

GRUISSAN
LANGUEDOC-ROUSSILLON

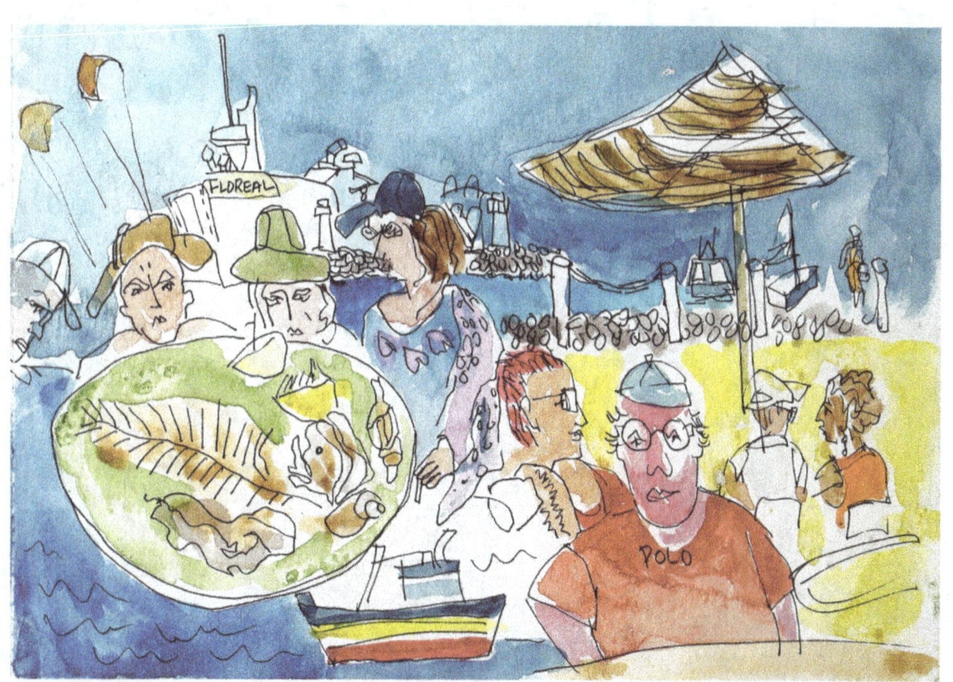

2019

TOWN SQUARE
ARLES

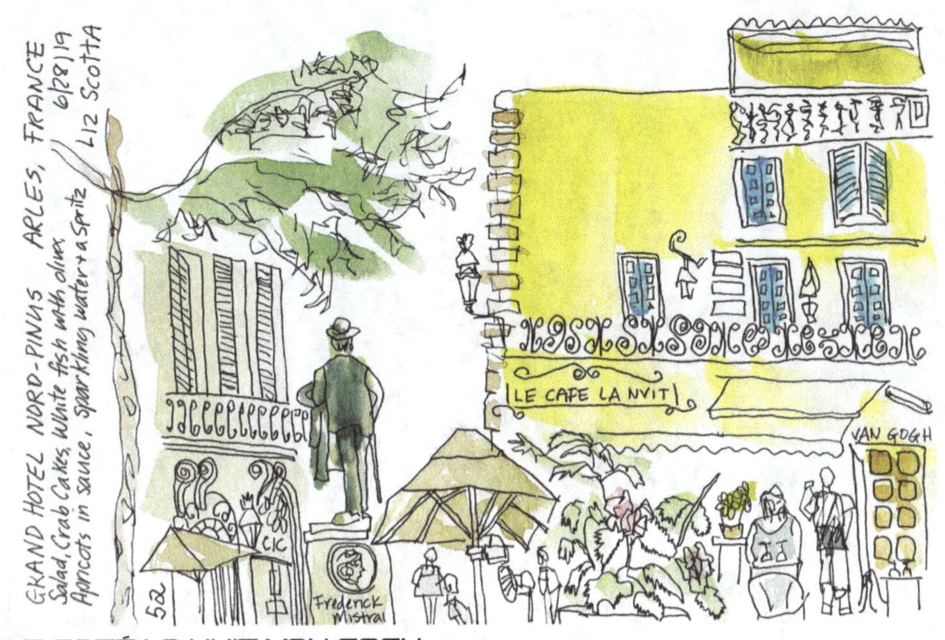

LE CAFÉ LA NUIT VAN GOGH
ARLES

ARLES

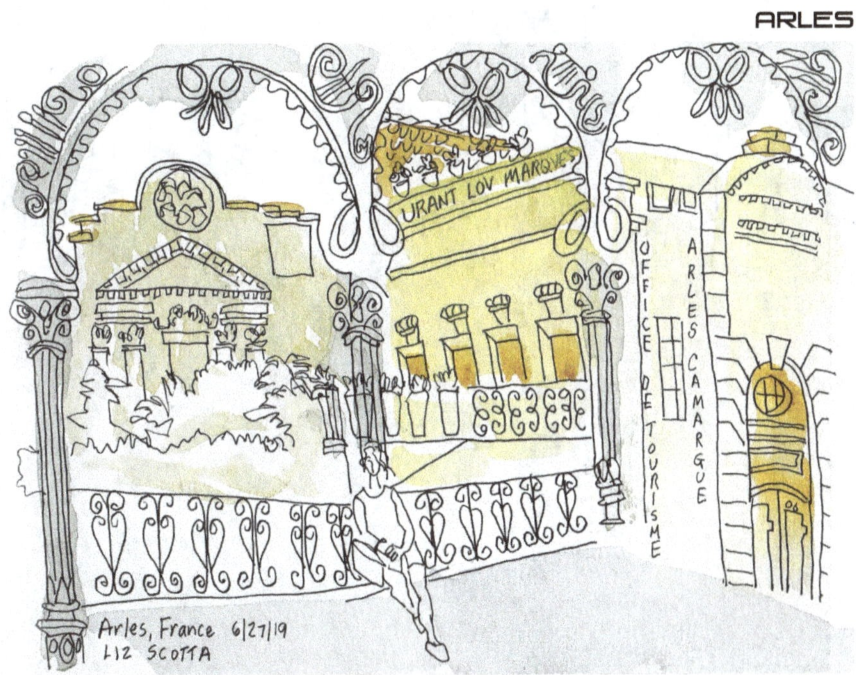

2019

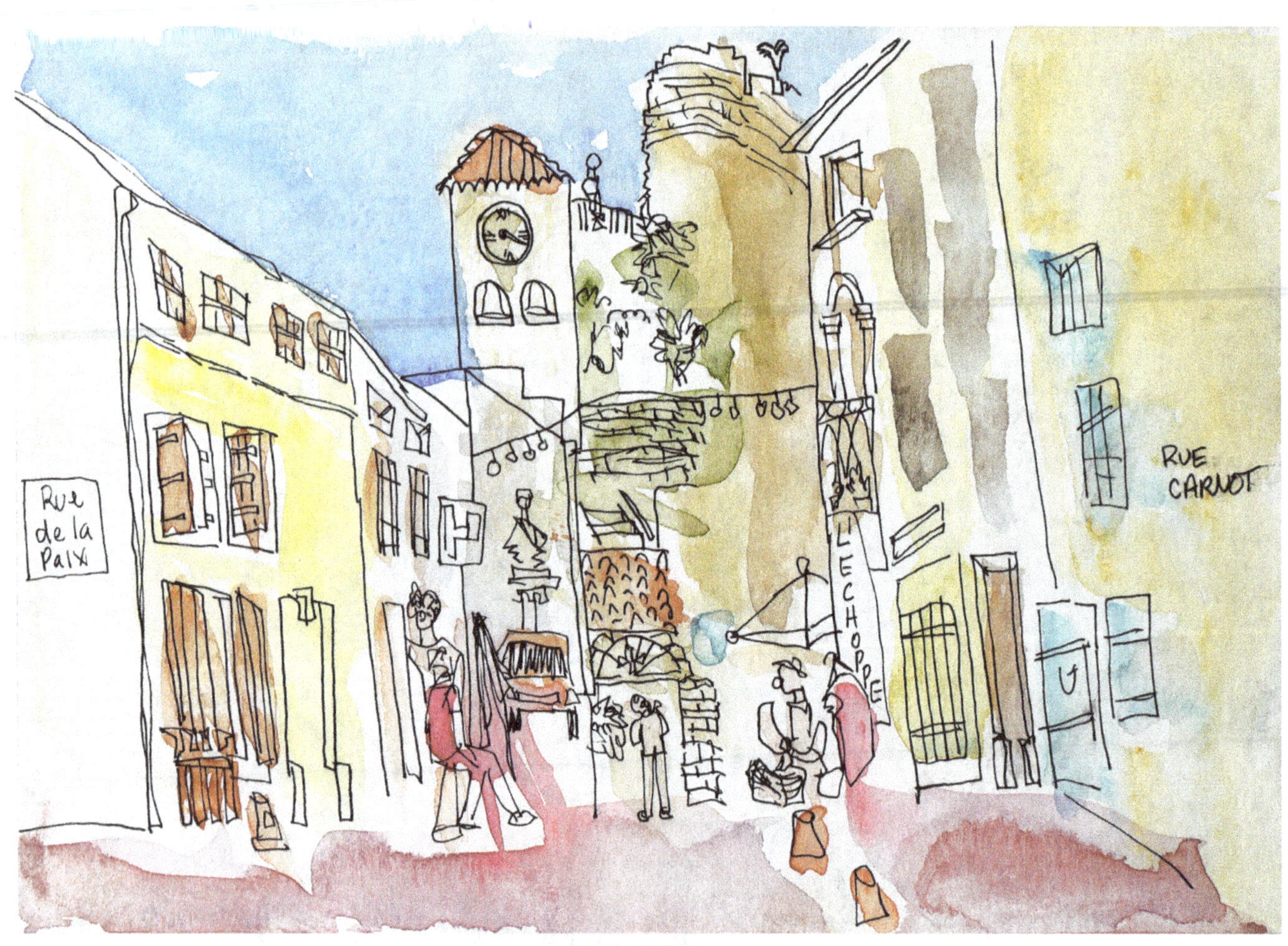

GRUISSAN
LANGUEDOC-ROUSSILLON

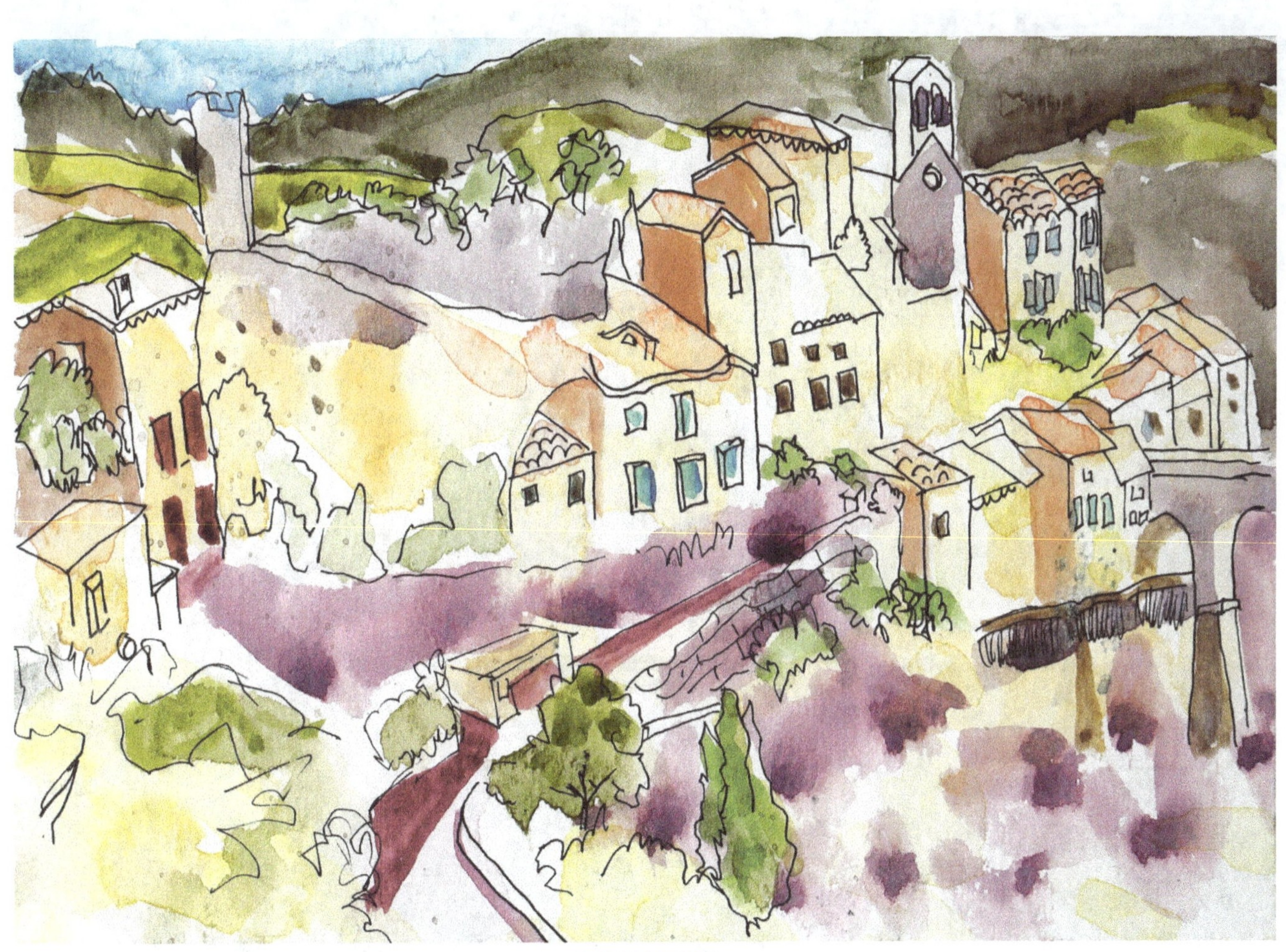

2019

MINERVE
LANGUEDOC-ROUSSILLON

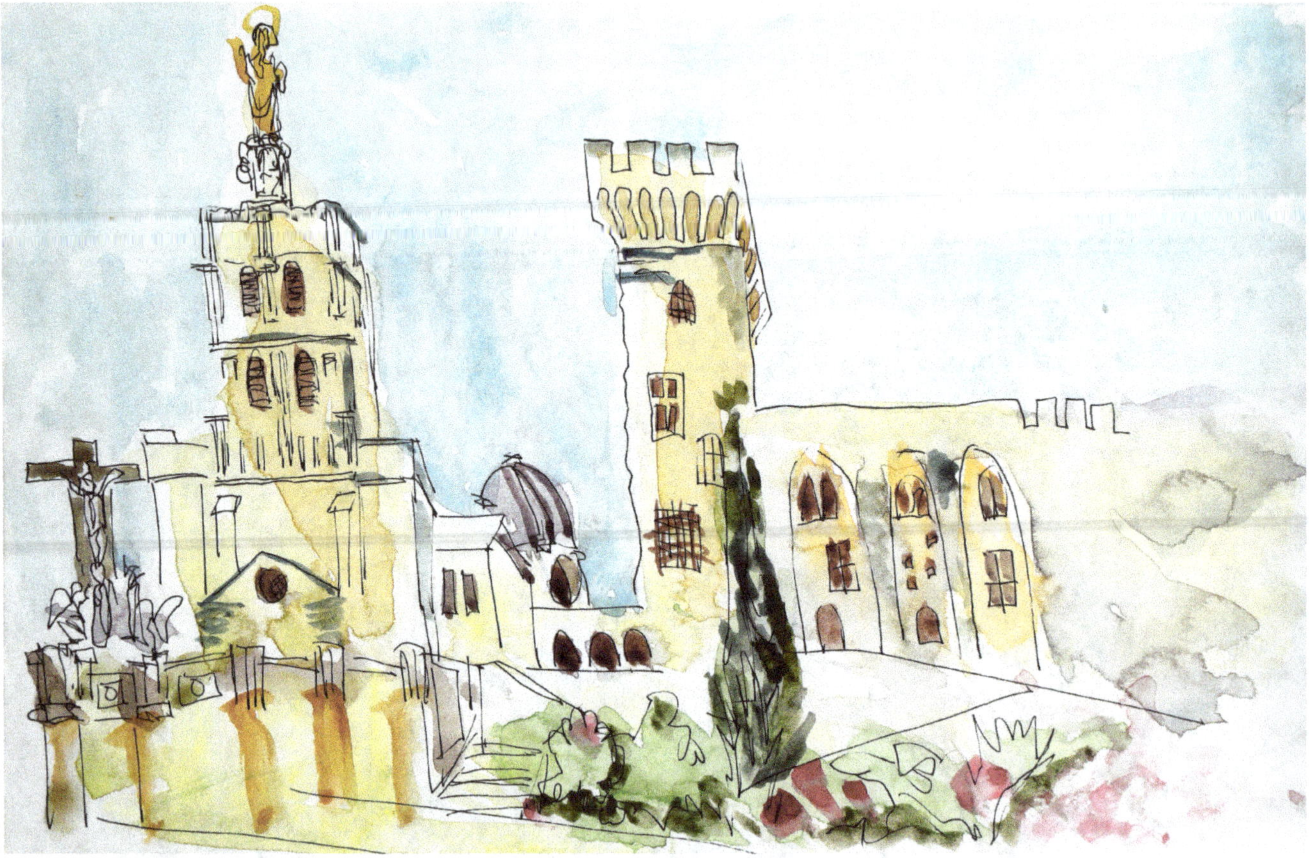

PALAIS DES PAPES
AVIGNON

2019

PALAIS DES PAPES
AVIGNON

AVIGNON

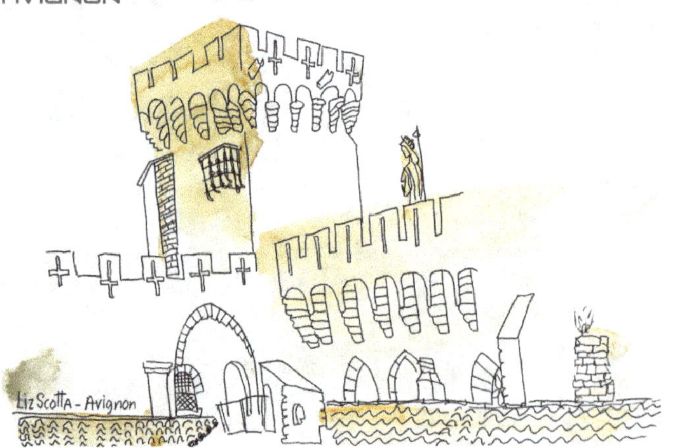

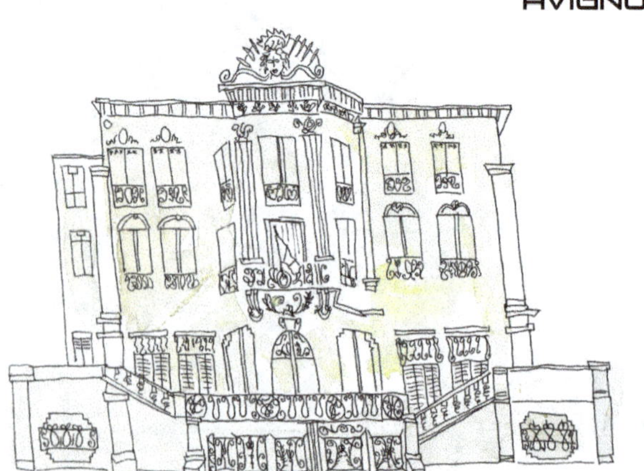

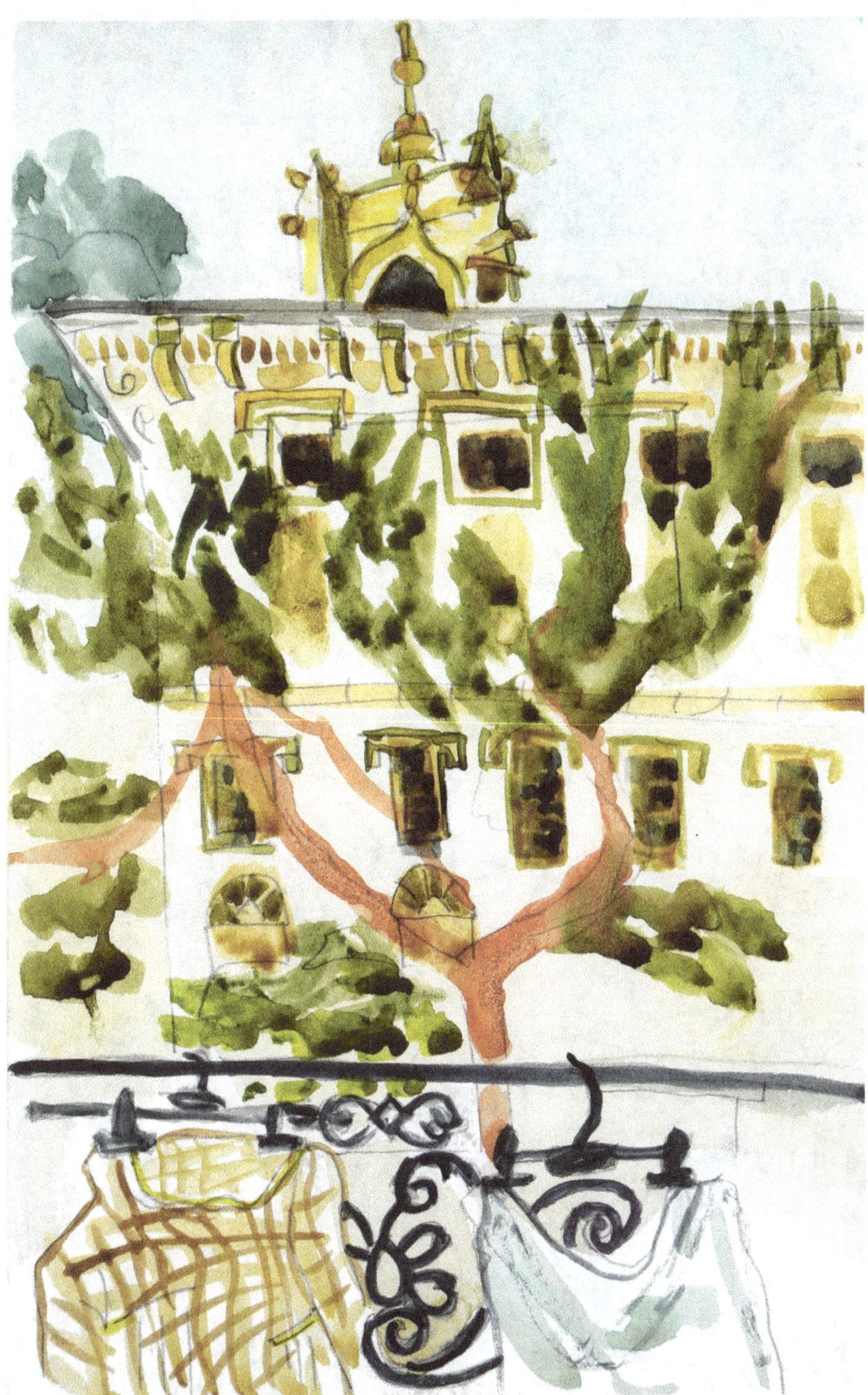

VIEW FROM
HOTEL ROOM
AVIGNON

2019

Do
your
shopping.
- Buy it!
- Bring it!
We cook it!
10€
Le
Halle
Avignon
6/30/19
Liz & Scott

AVIGNON

DEPART HERE
PETIT TRAIN

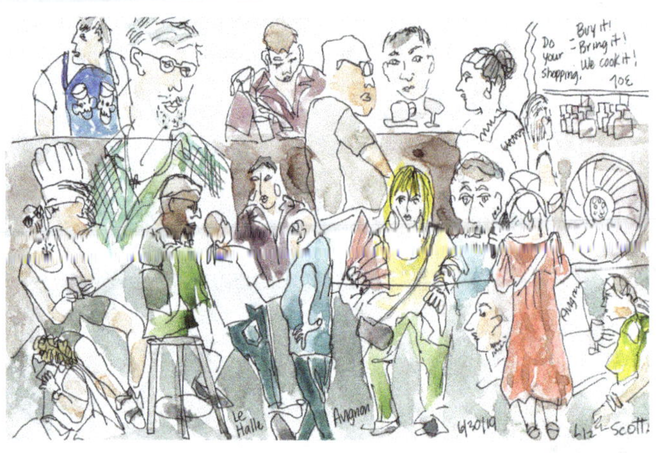

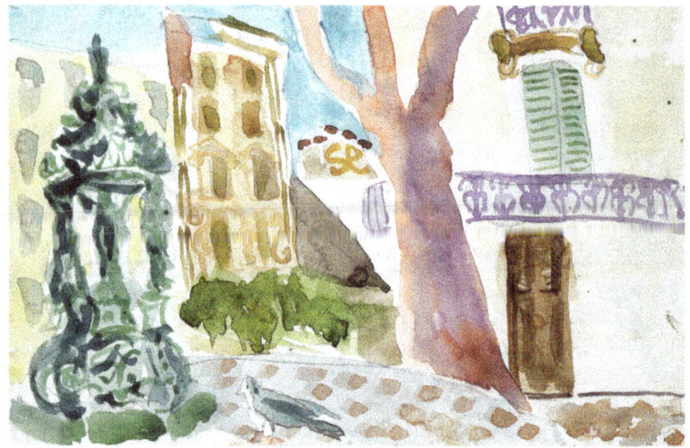

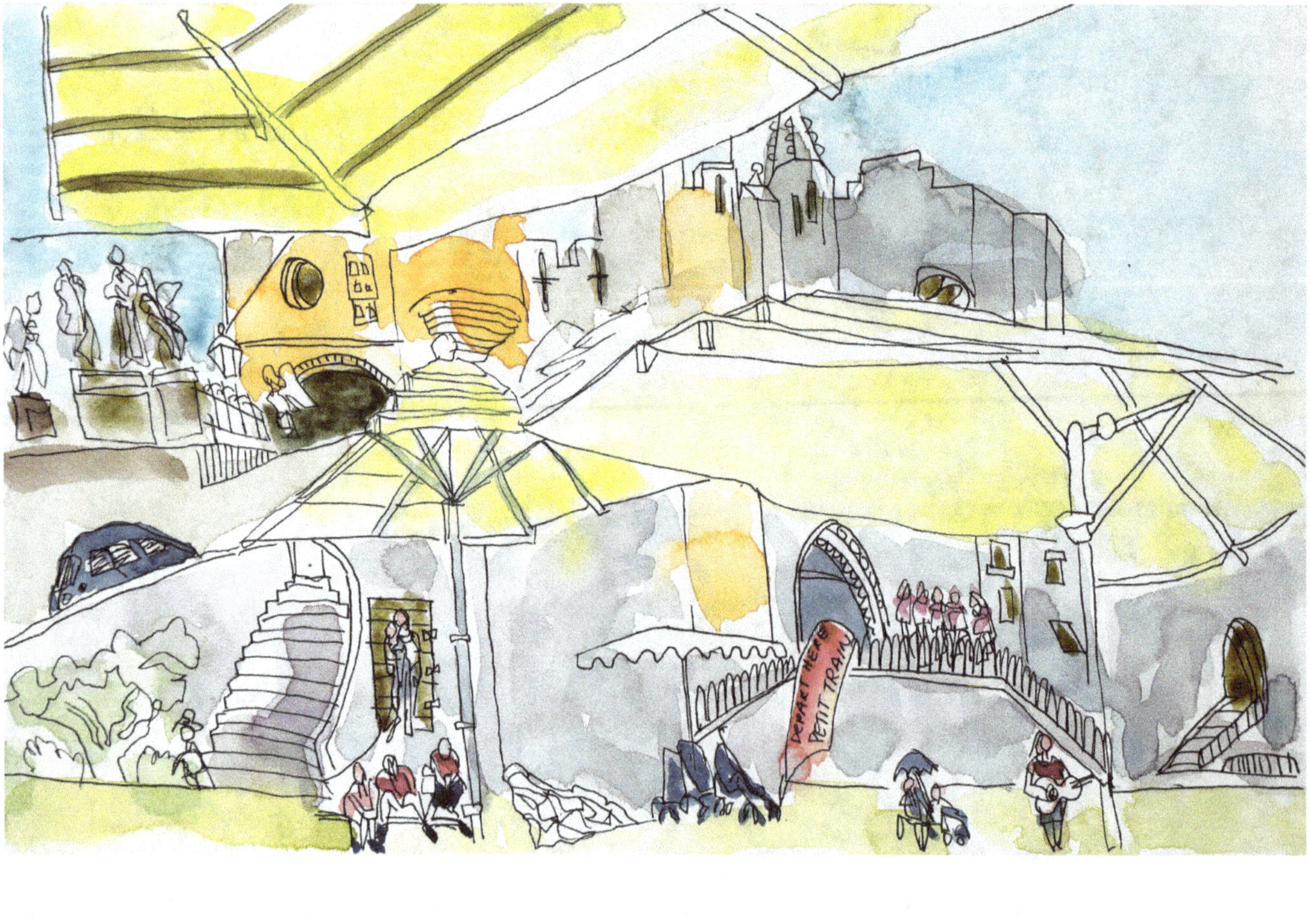

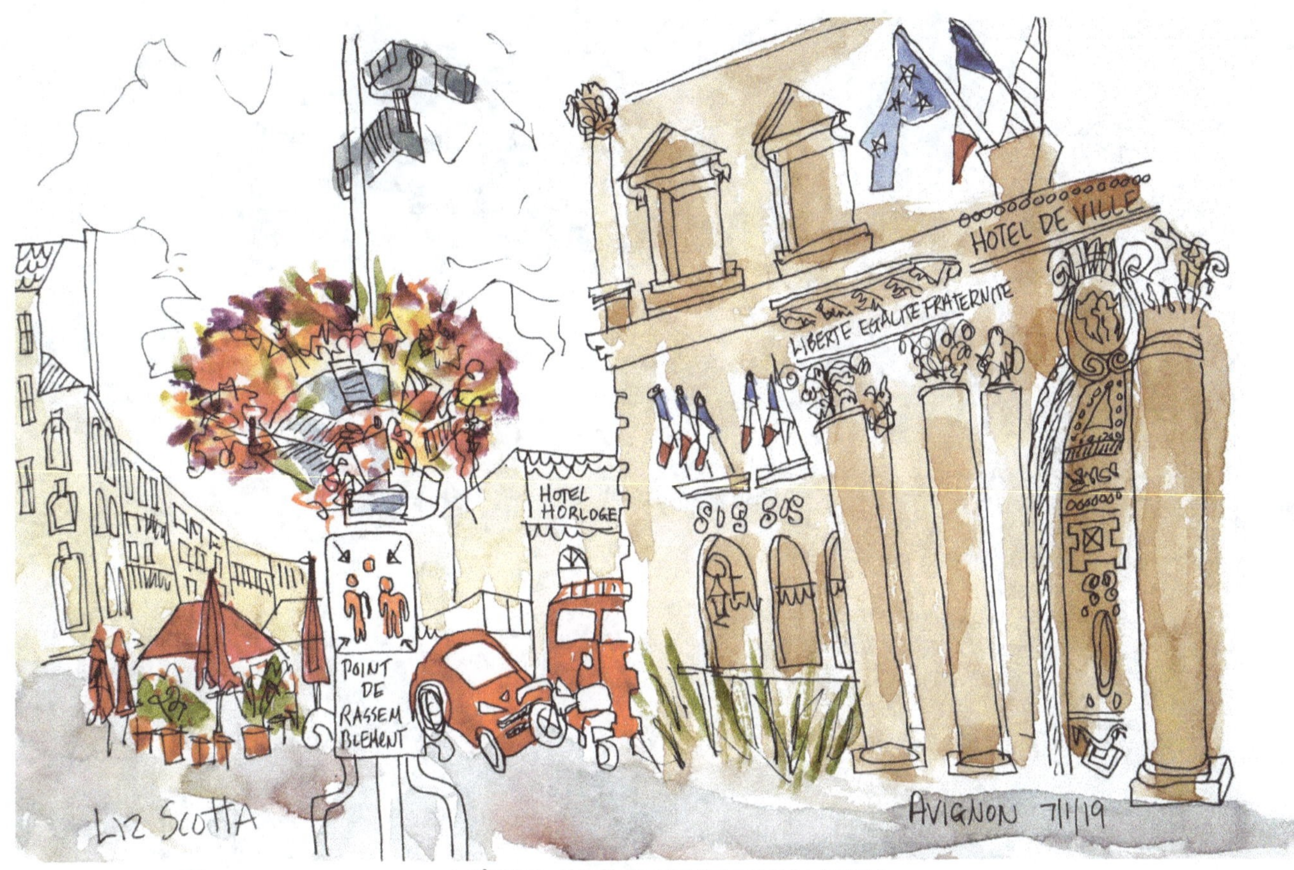

HÔTEL DE VILLE (TOWN HALL)
AVIGNON

2019

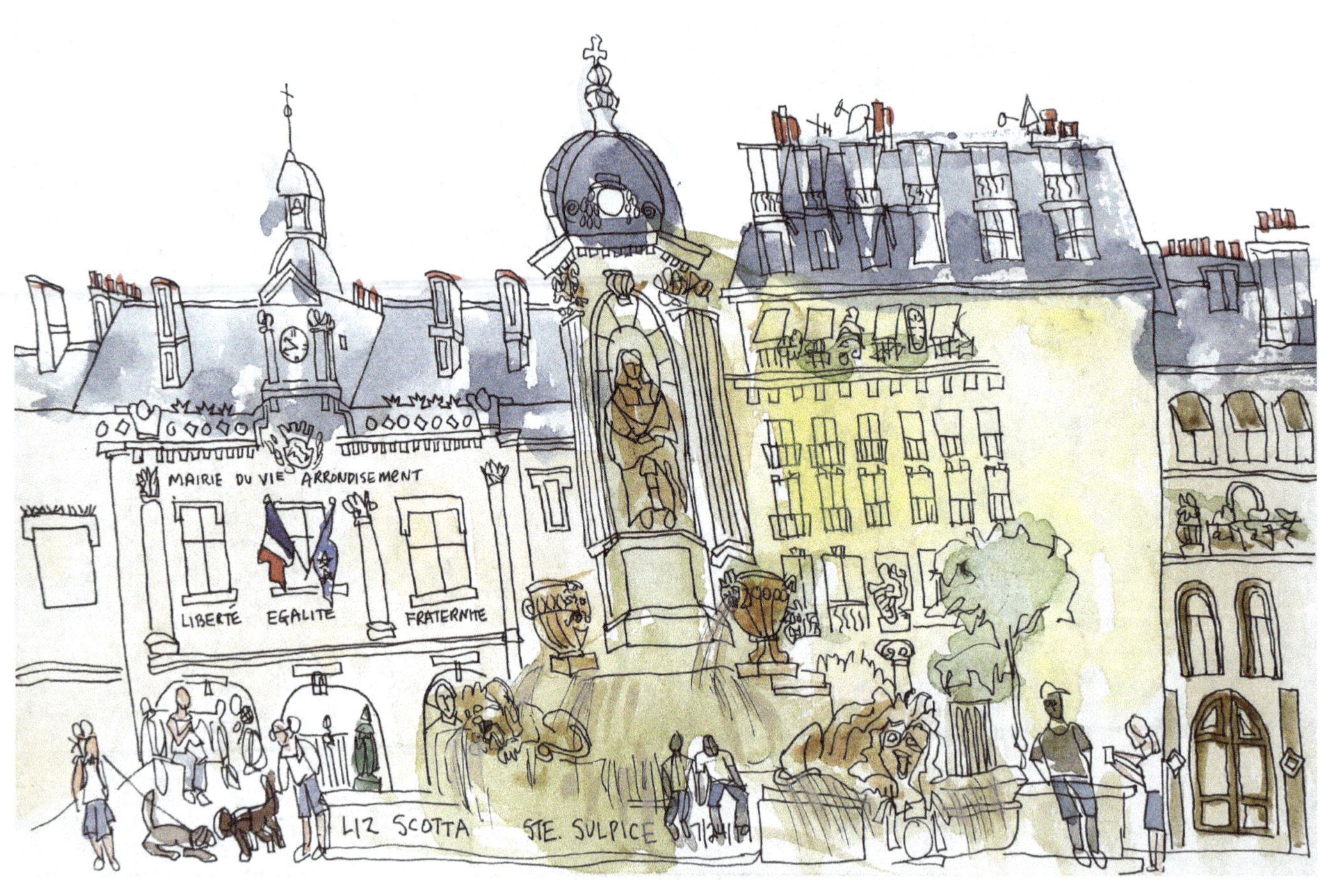

SAINT-SULPICE
PARIS

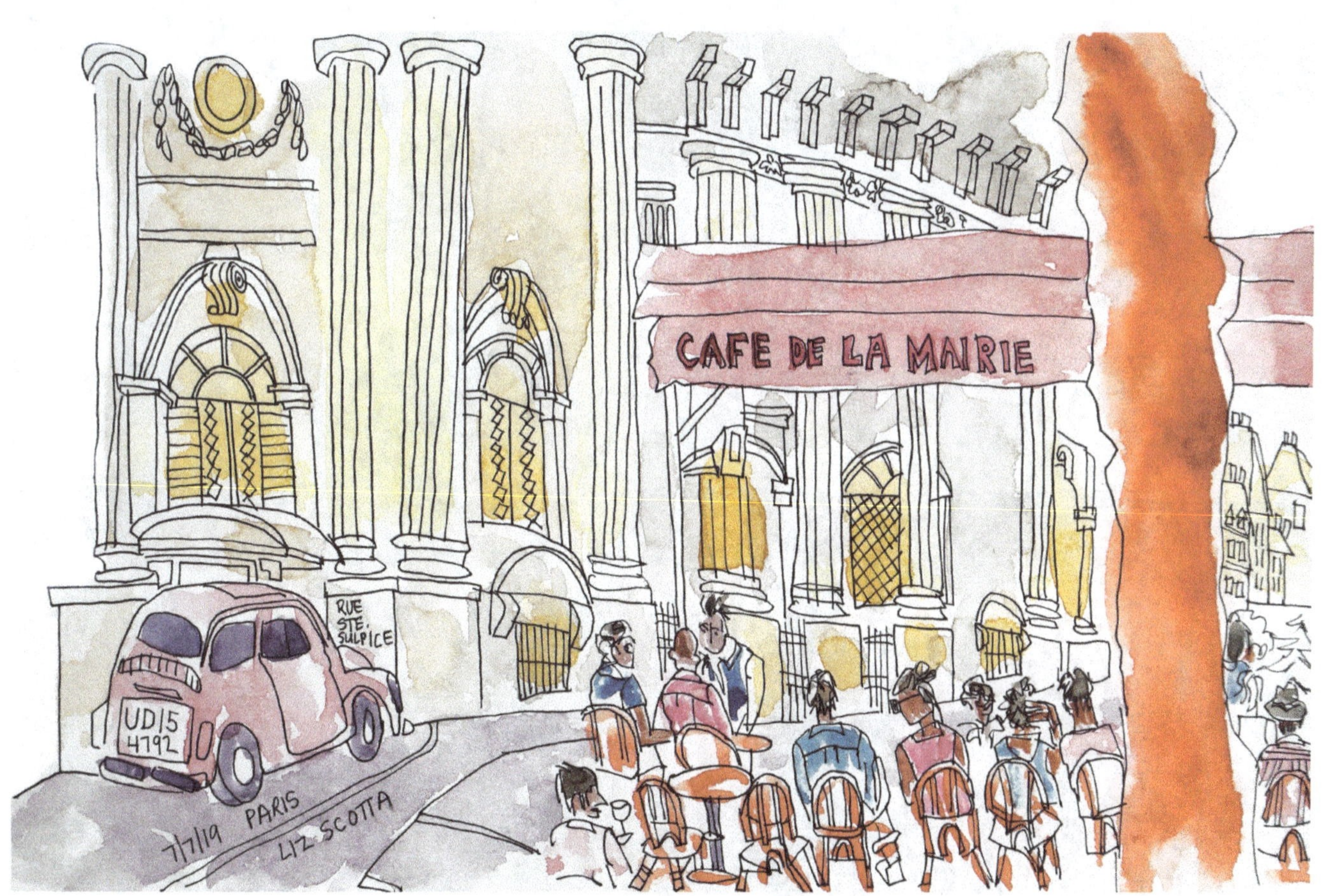

CAFE DE LA MAIRIE
PARIS

HONFLEUR

OFFICE DE TOURISME
Mon installion a   Honfleur a toujours été
le plus cher de mes rêves.
Galerie
Via
ARTE

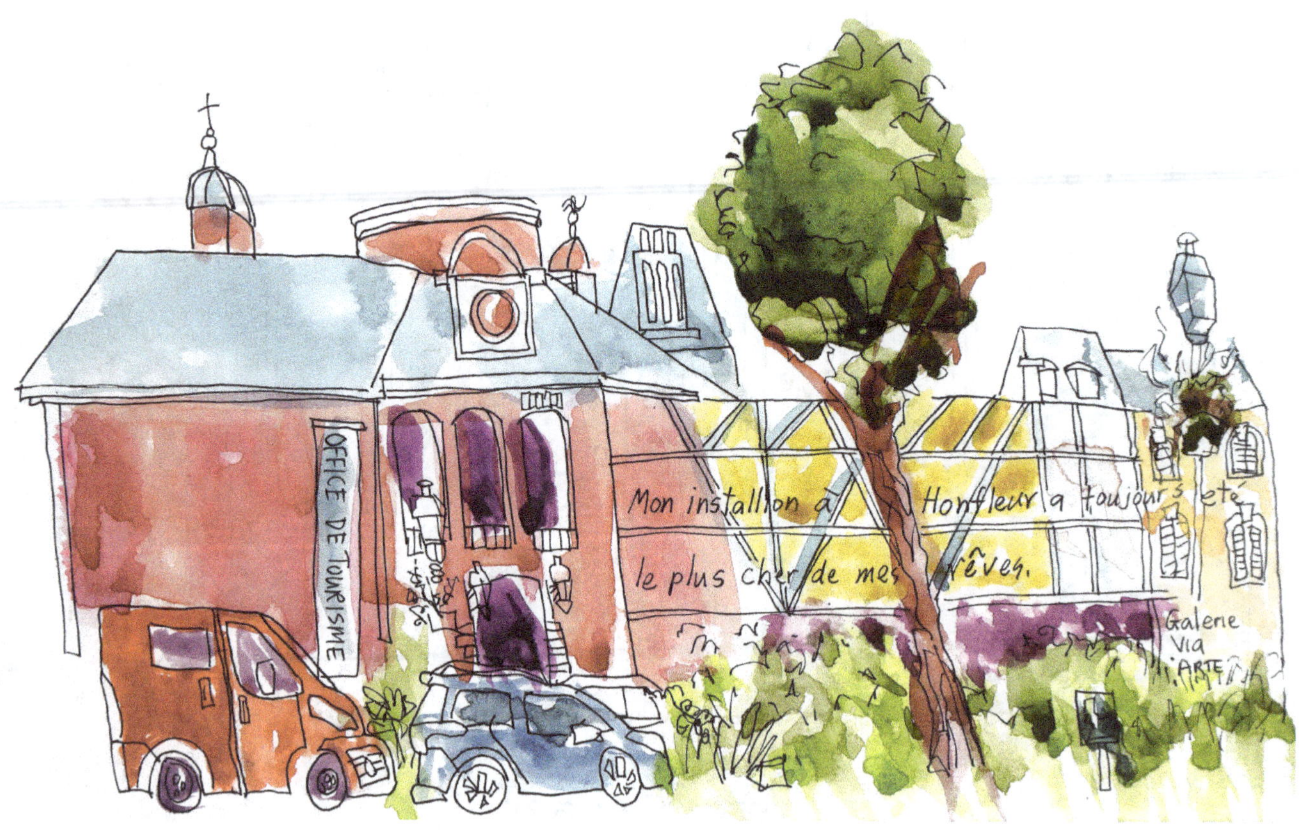

ROUEN

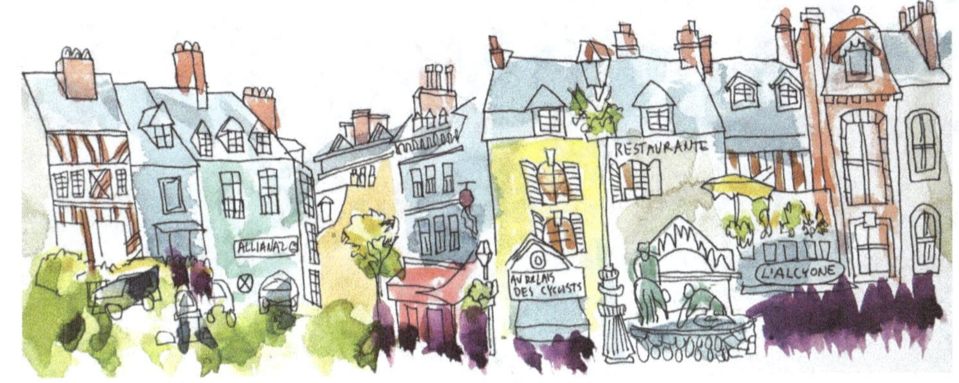

JOAN OF ARC MUSEUM
ROUEN

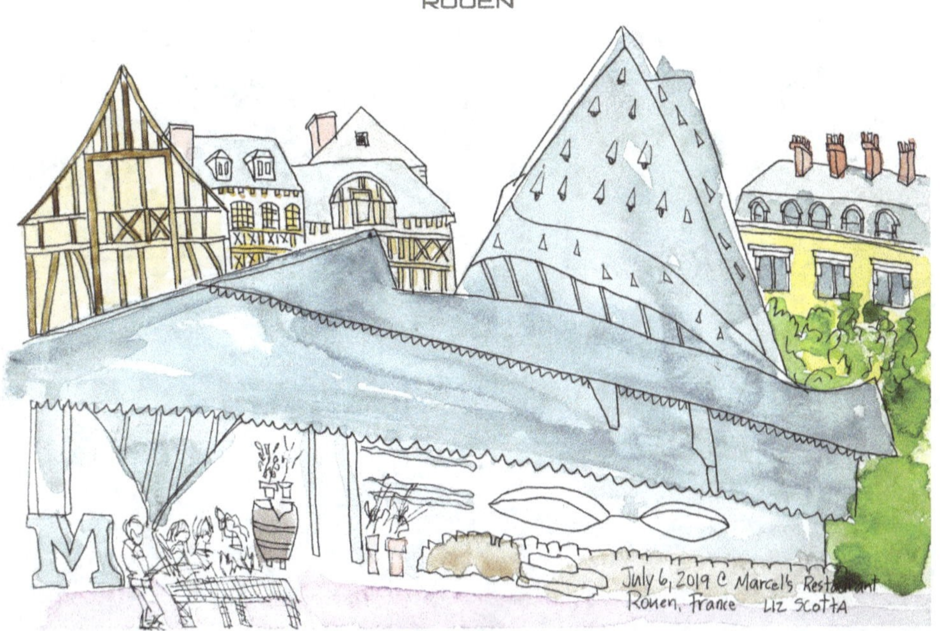

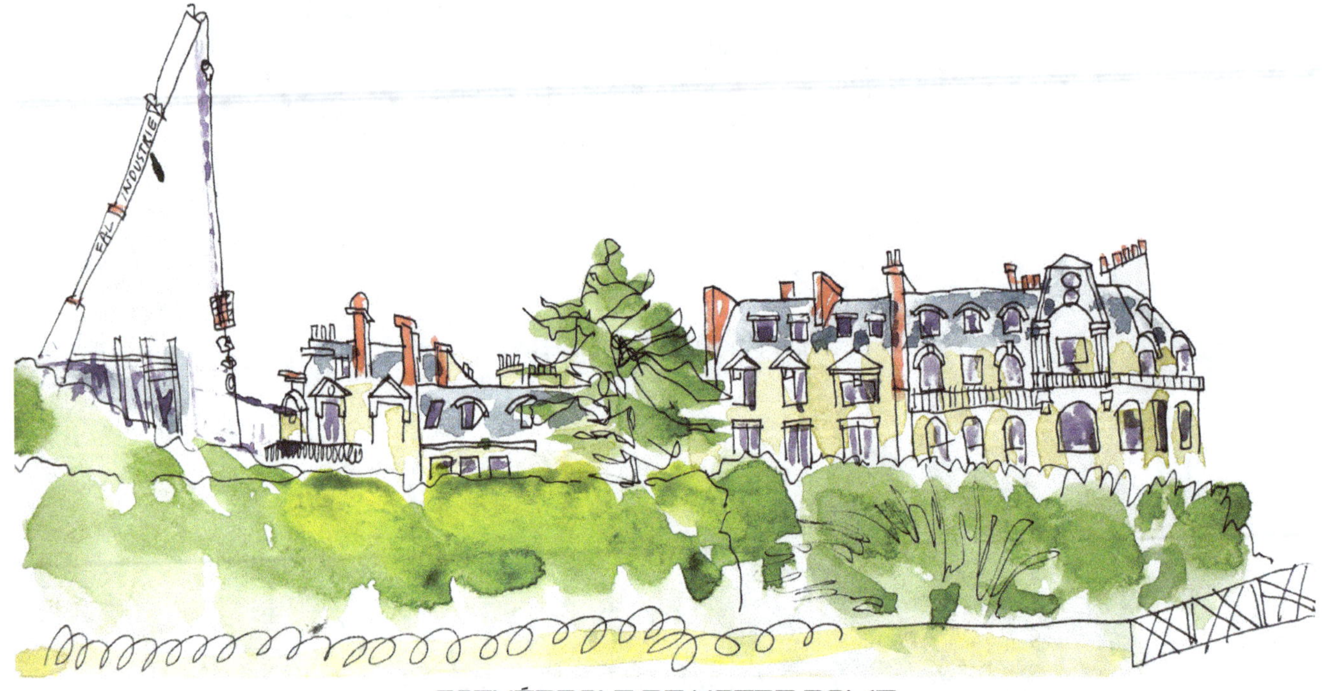

CATHÉDRALE DE NOTRE DAME
PARIS

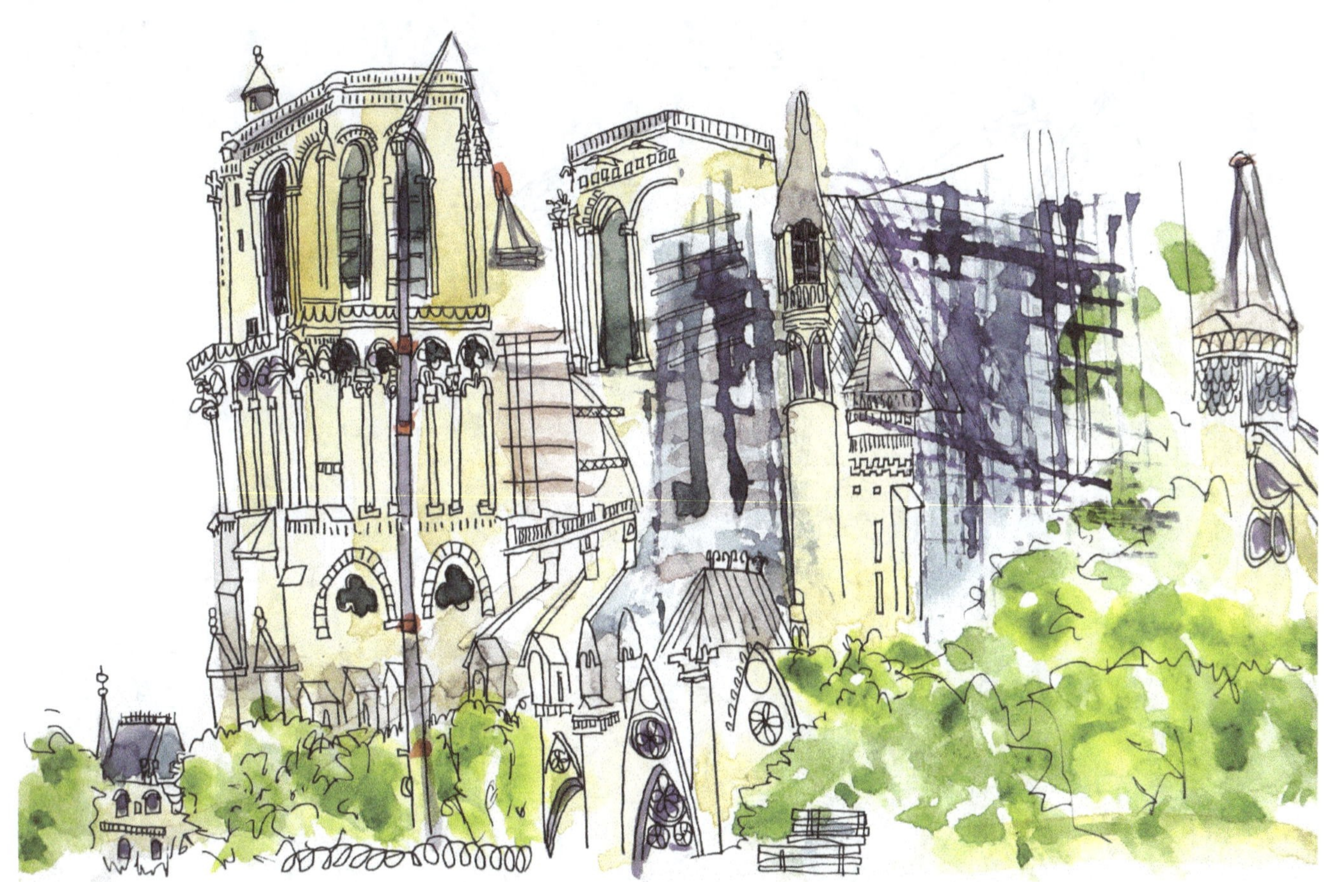

CATHÉDRALE DE NOTRE DAME
PARIS

2019

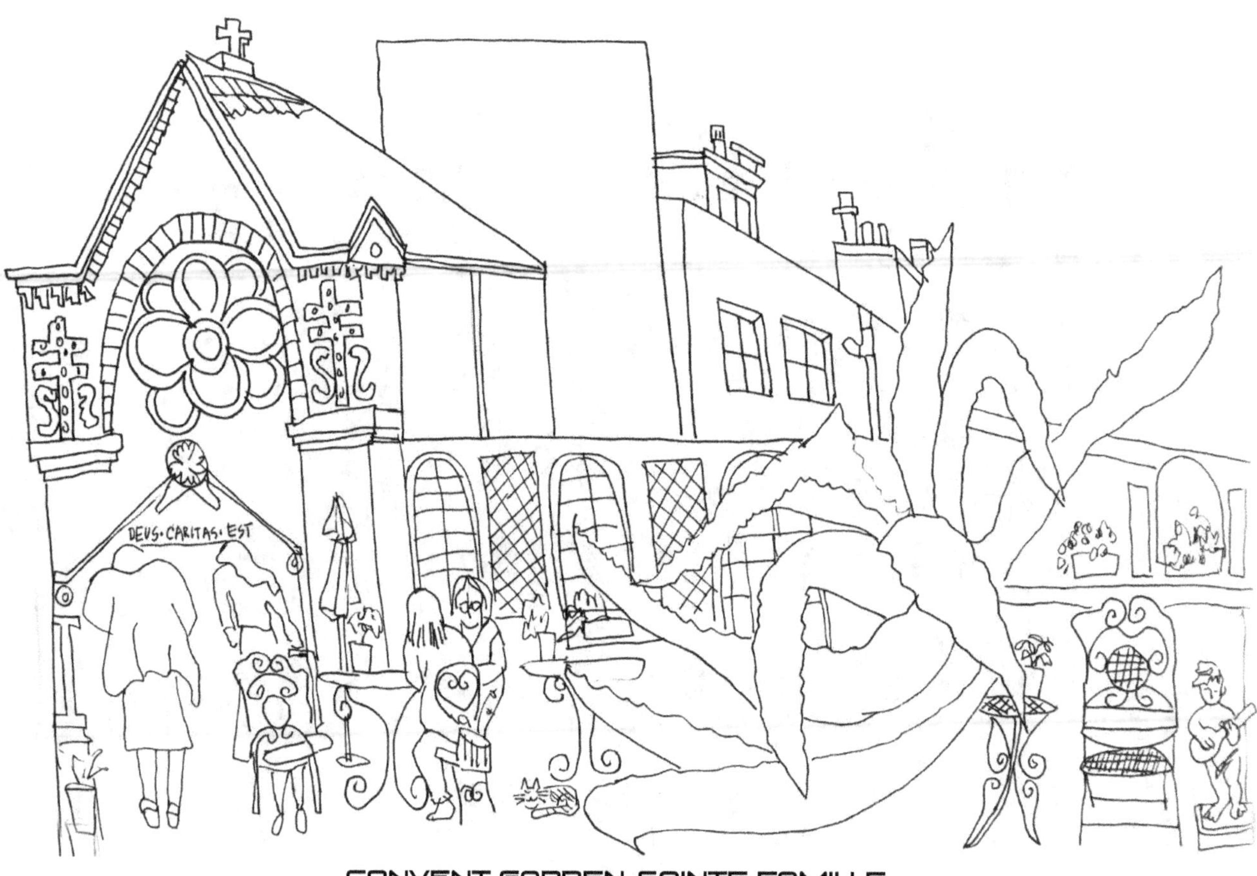

CONVENT GARDEN, SAINTE-FAMILLE
PARIS

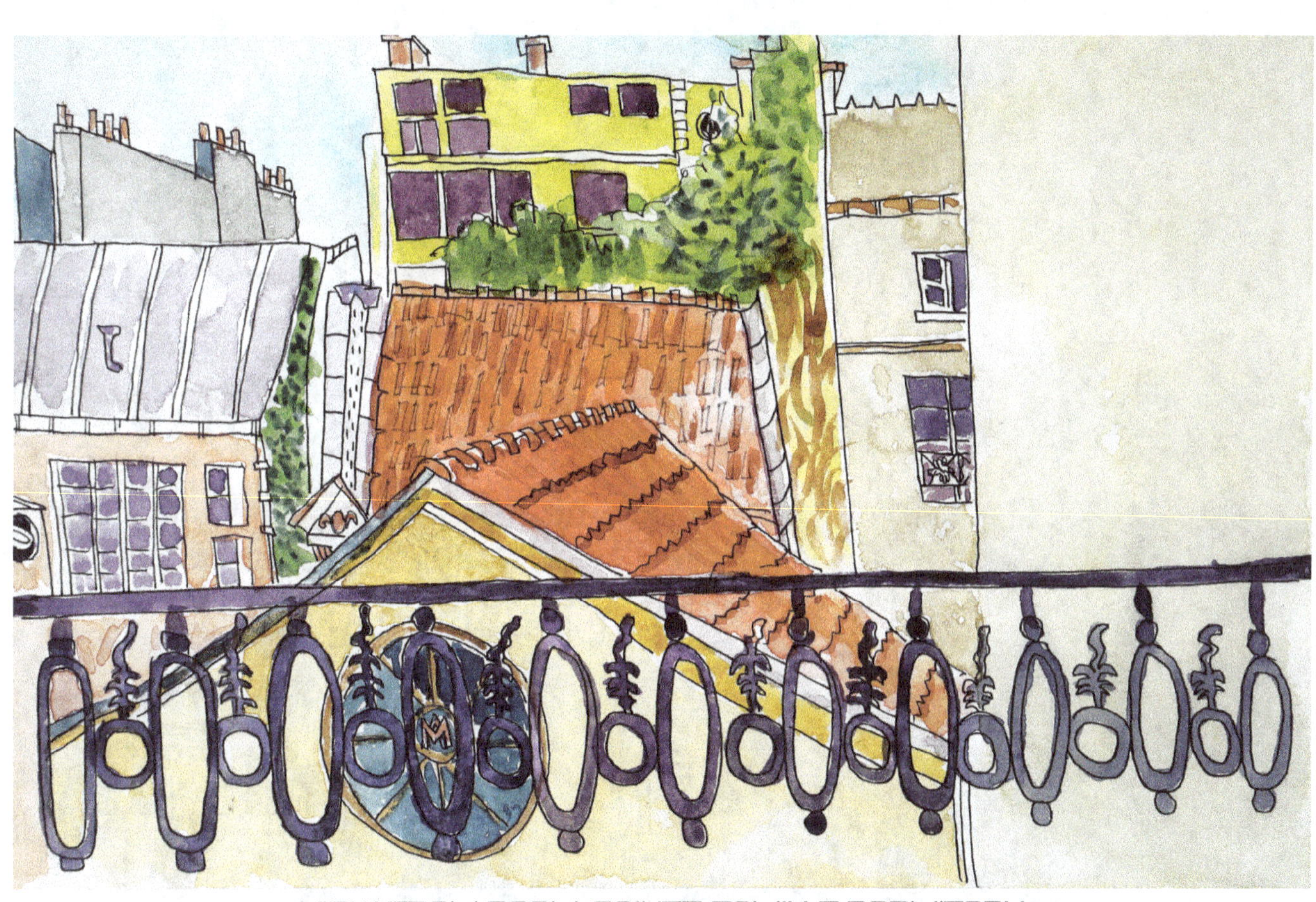

VIEW FROM ROOM, SAINTE-FAMILLE DORMITORY
PARIS

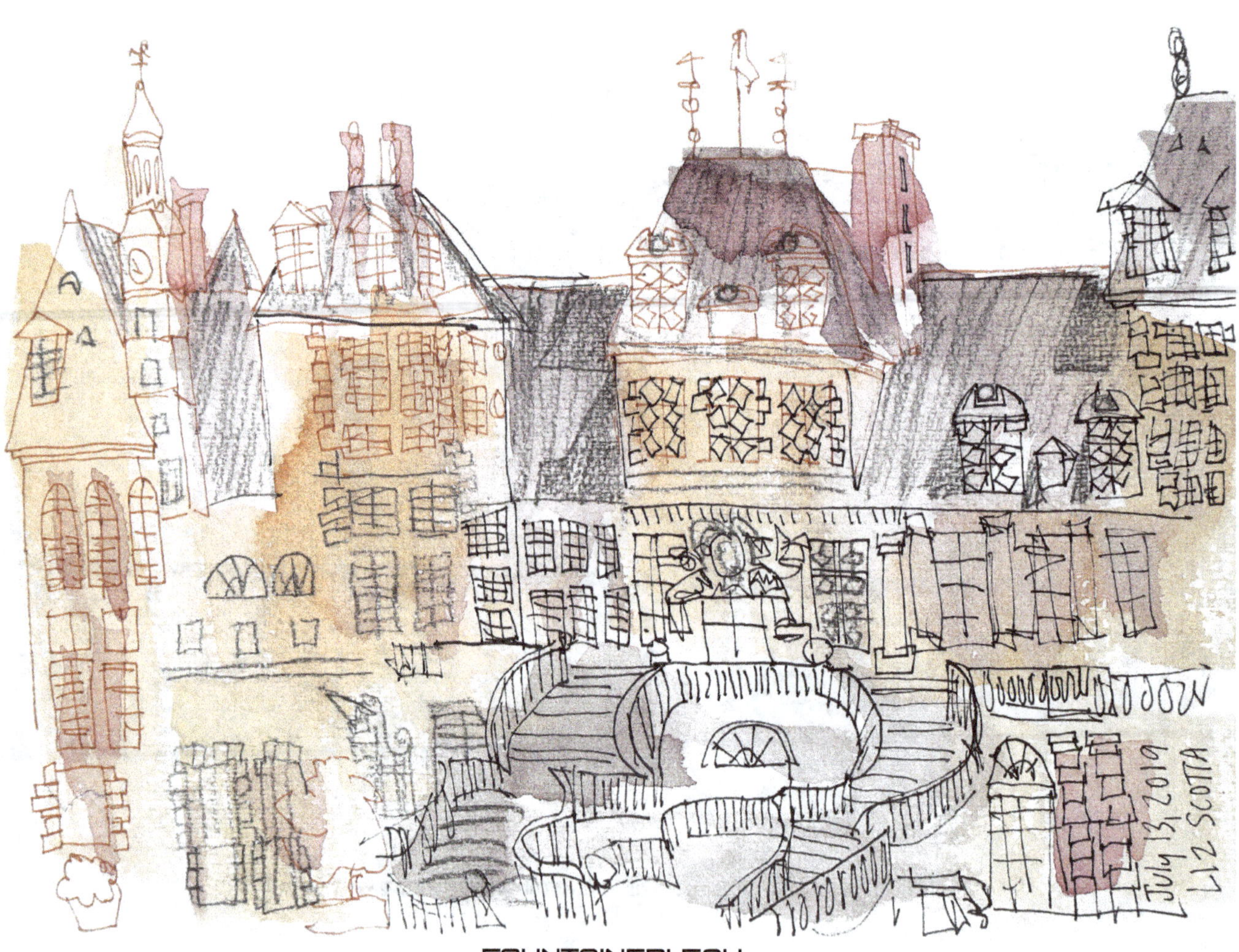

FOUNTAINEBLEAU
LOIRE VALLEY

2019

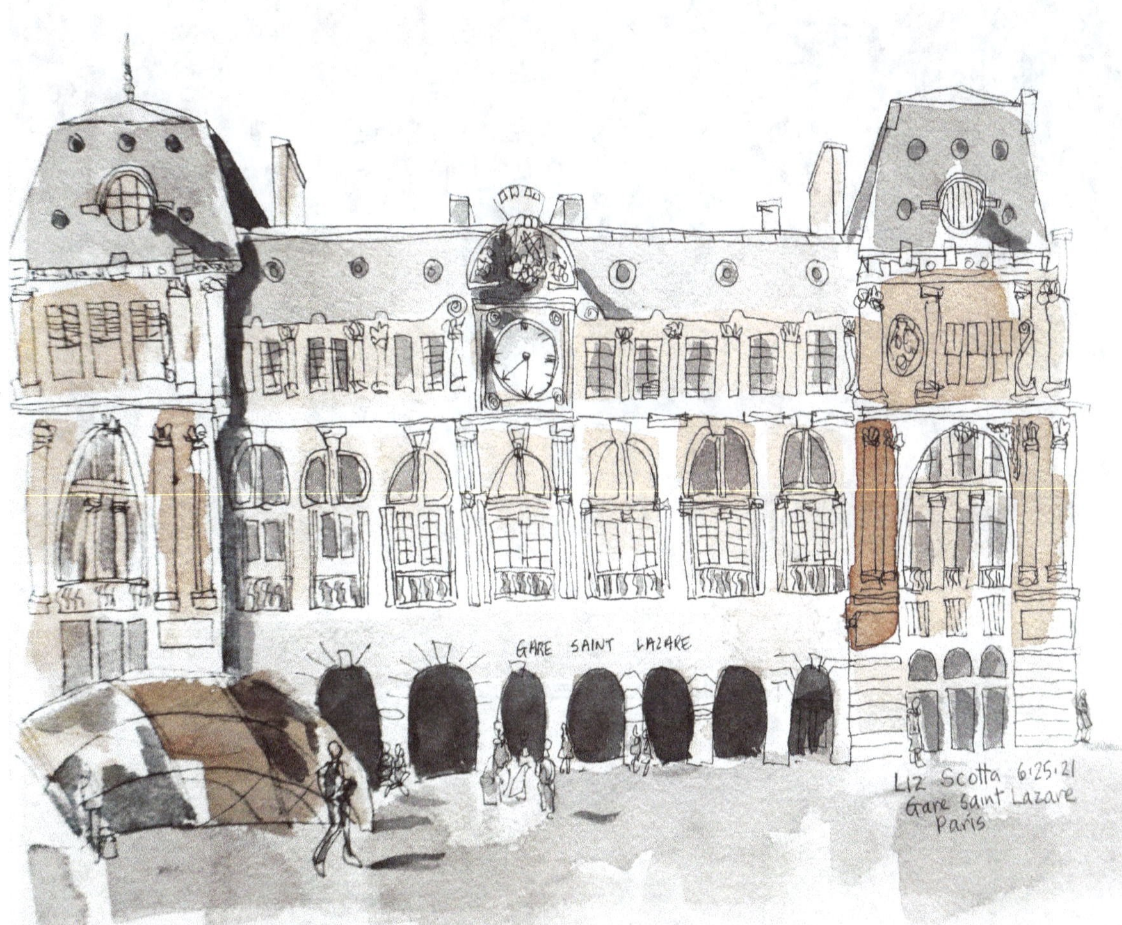

GARE SAINT-LAZARE
PARIS

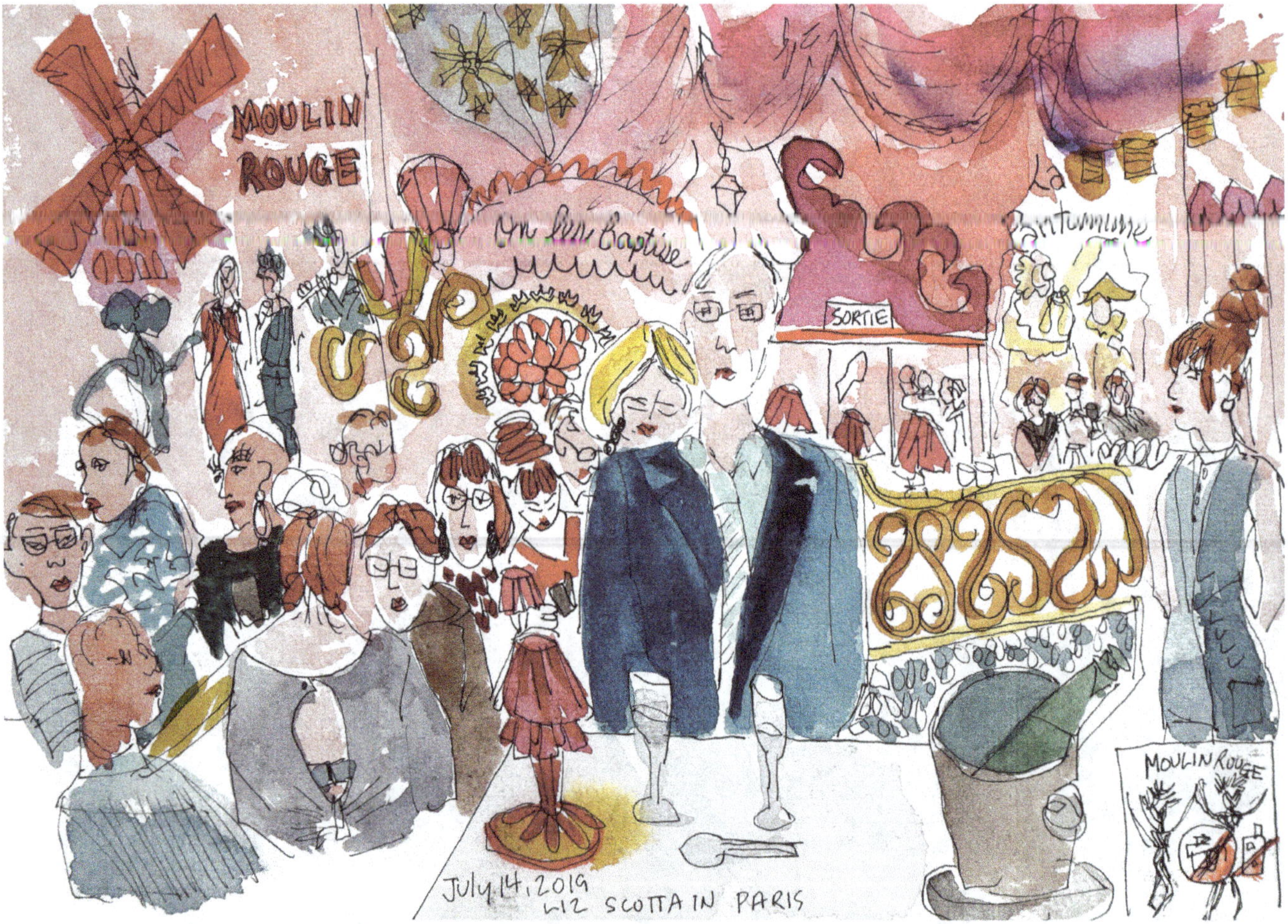

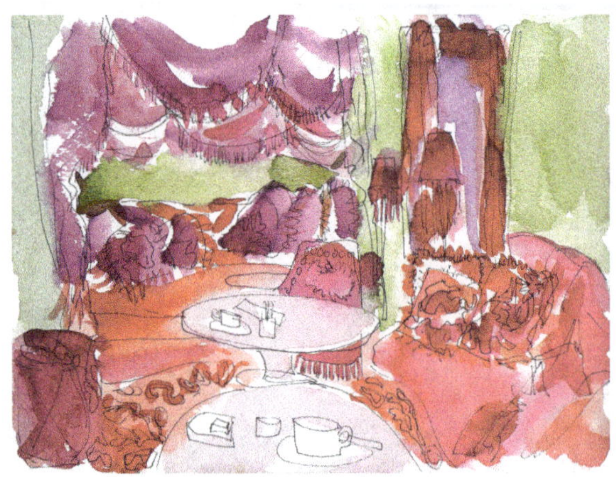

MOULIN ROUGE
PARIS

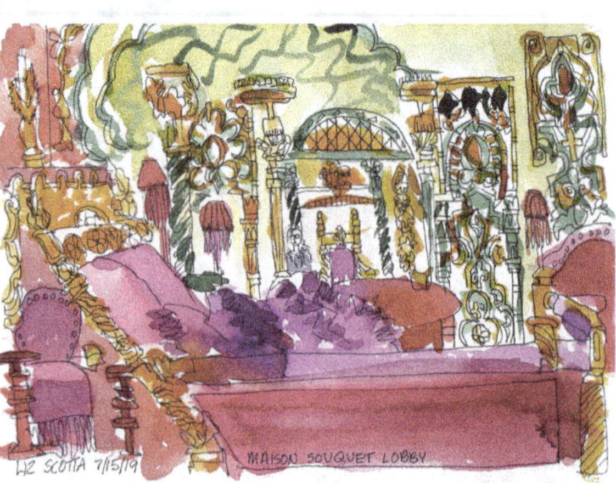

HÔTEL
MAISON
SOUQUET
PARIS

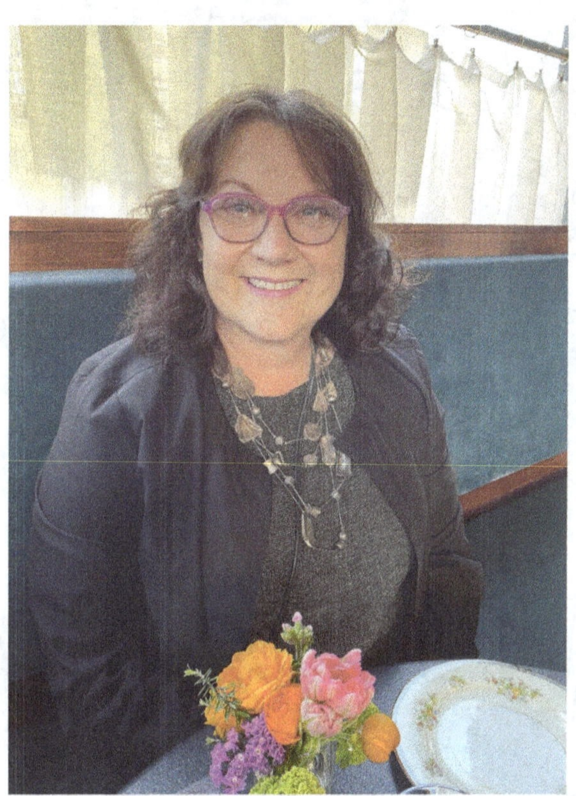

BIRTHDAY CELEBRATION
WITH GILET MARCO

2019

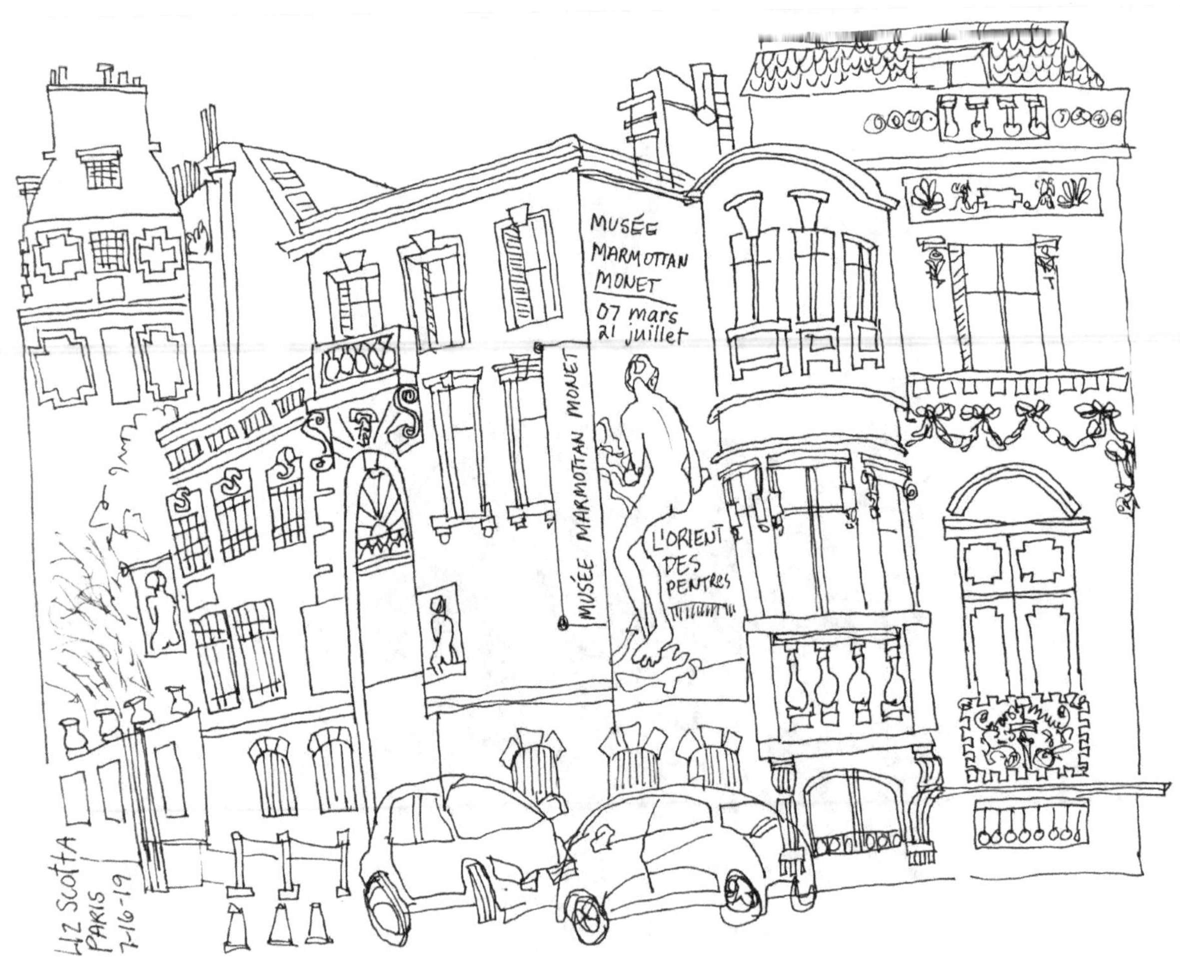

MUSÉE MARMOTTAN MONET
PARIS

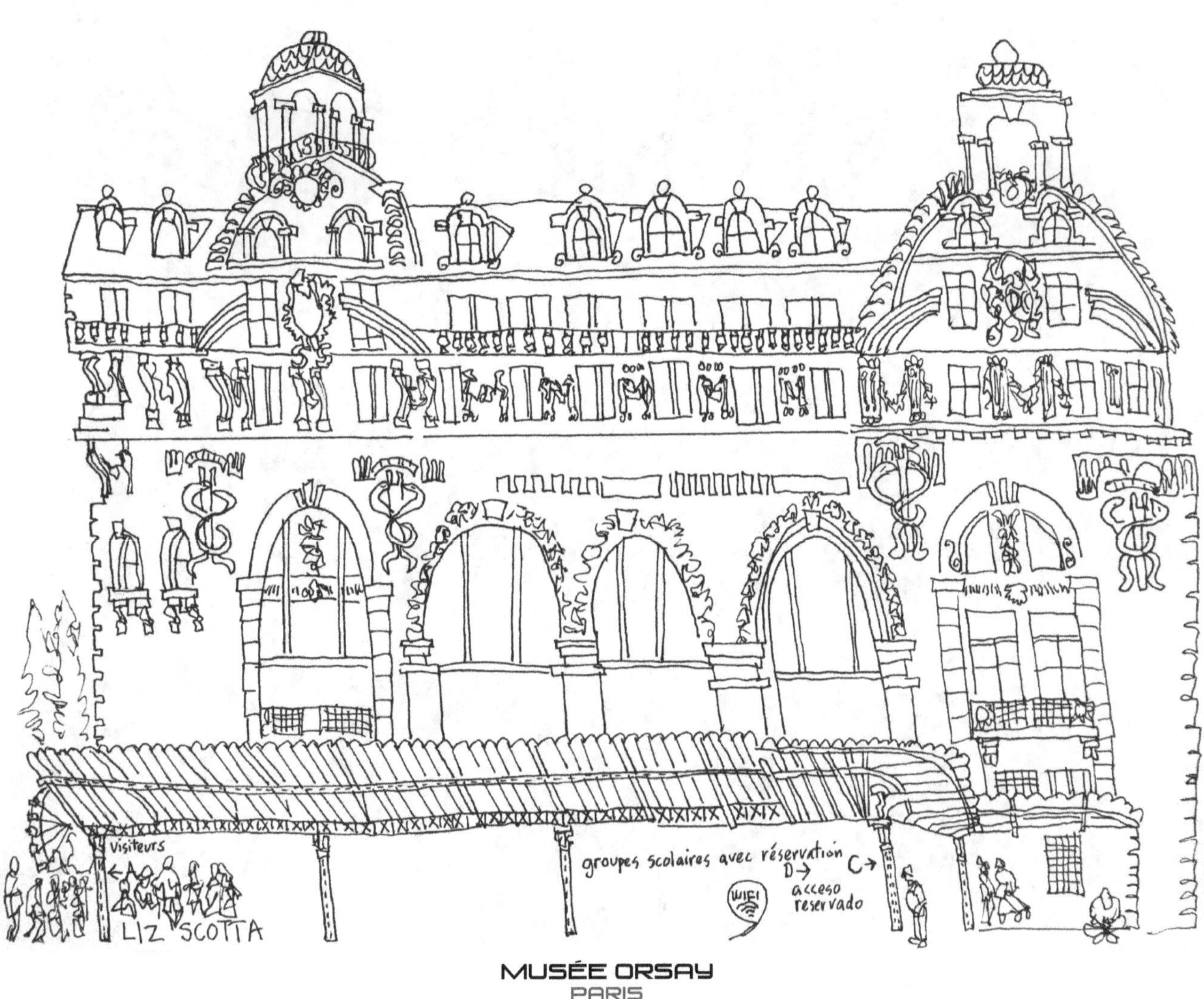

MUSÉE ORSAY
PARIS

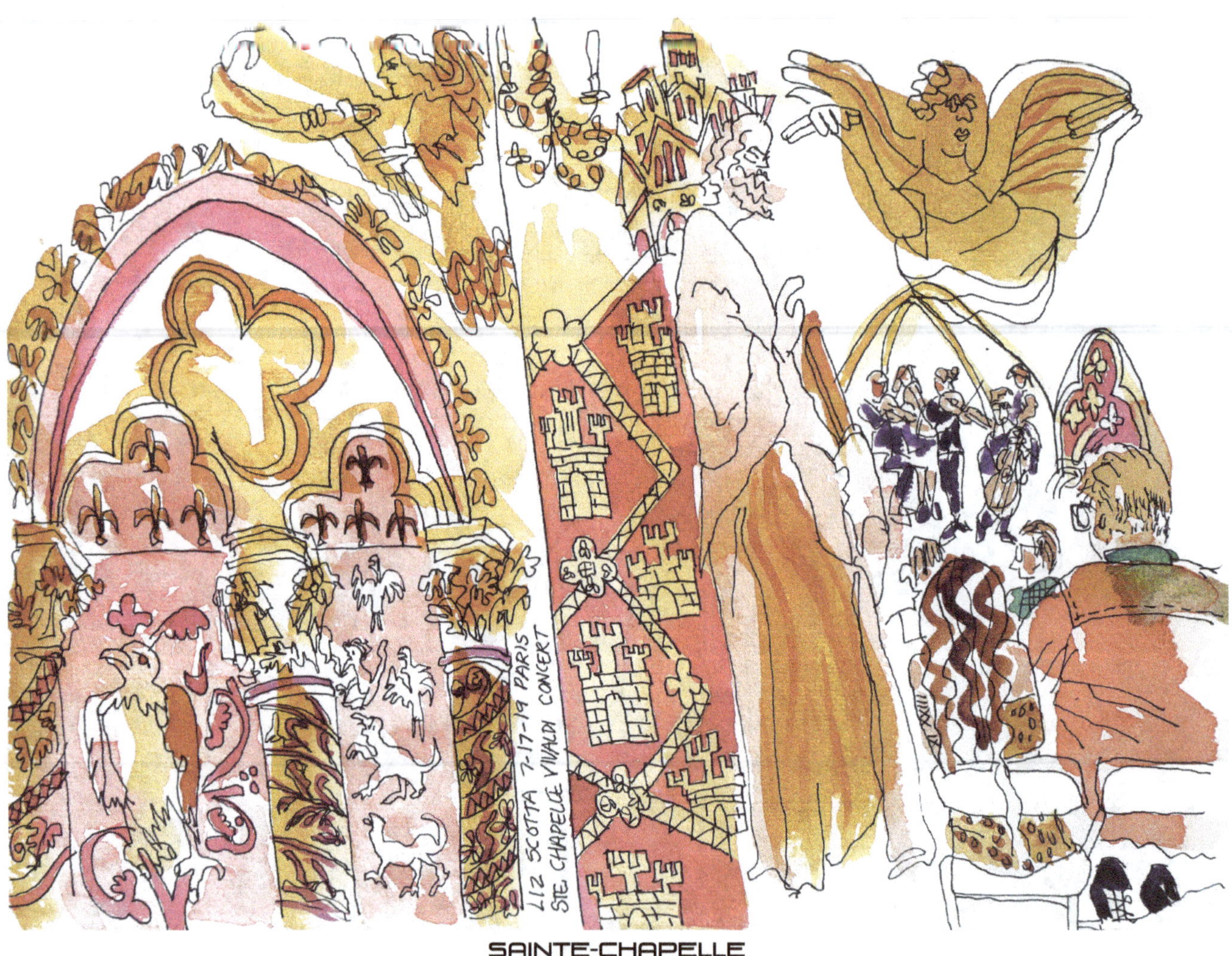

SAINTE-CHAPELLE
PARIS

2019

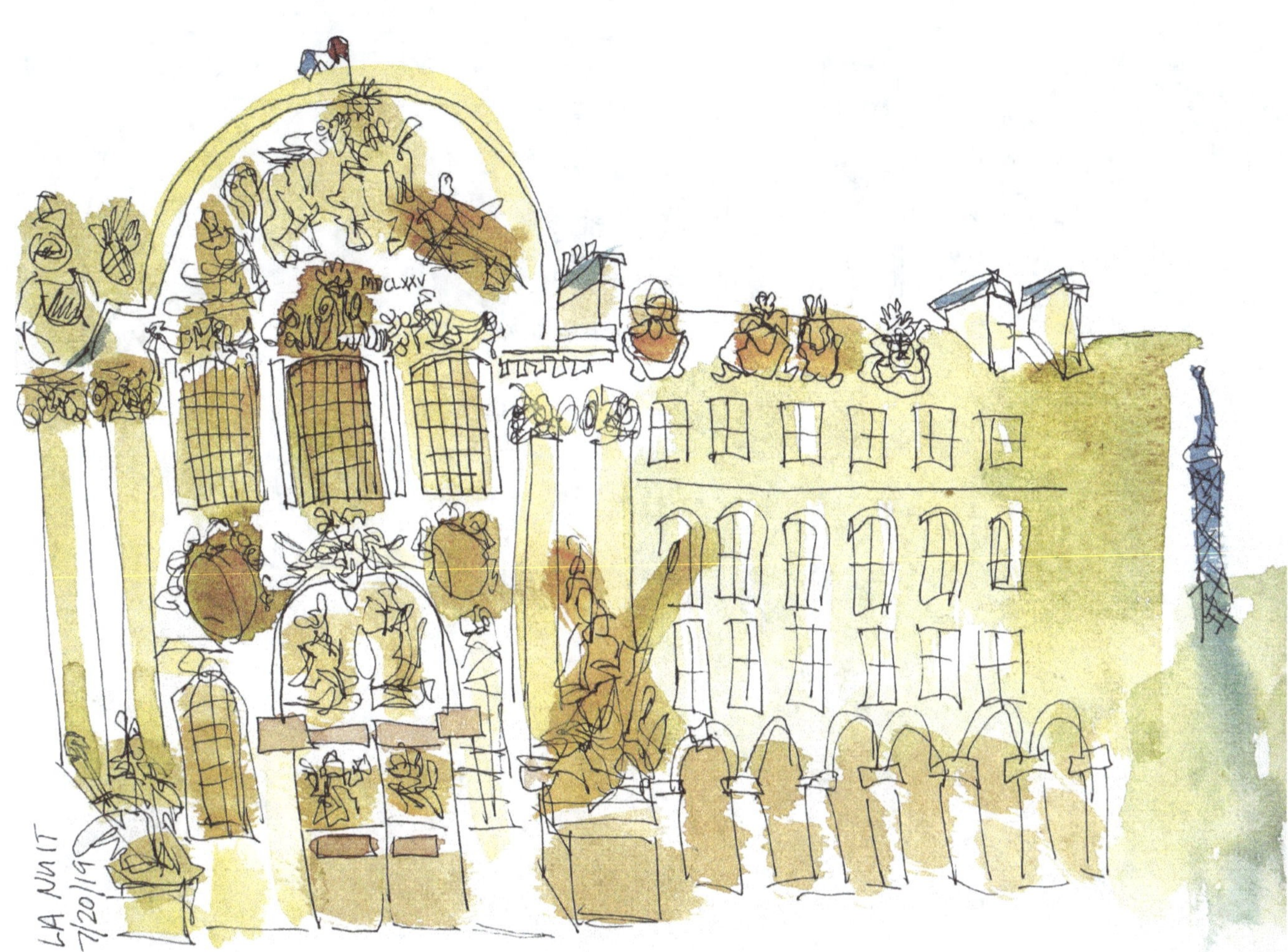

CATHÉDRALE DE REIMS
REIMS

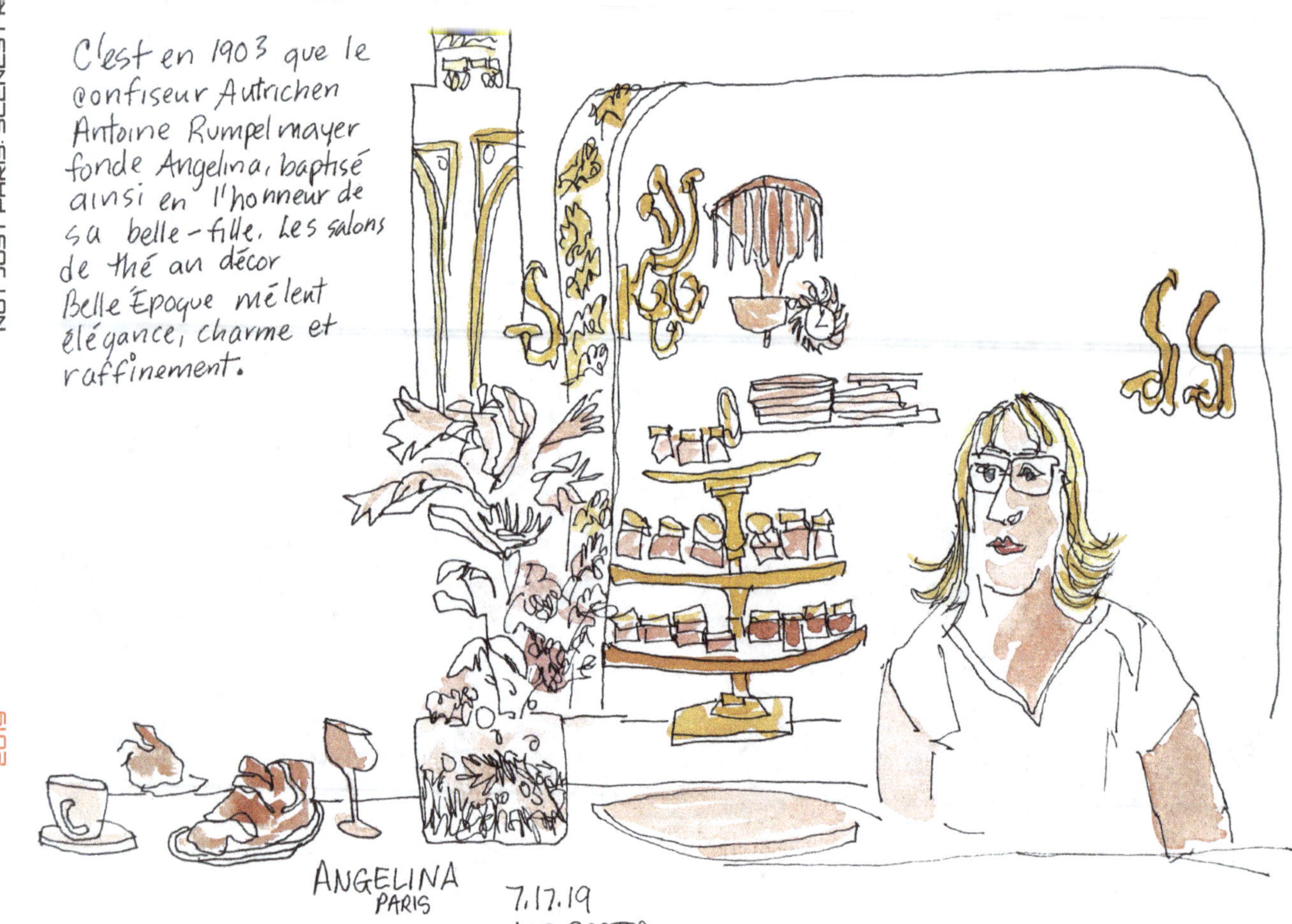

ANGELINA'S HOT CHOCOLATE & PASTRY
PARIS

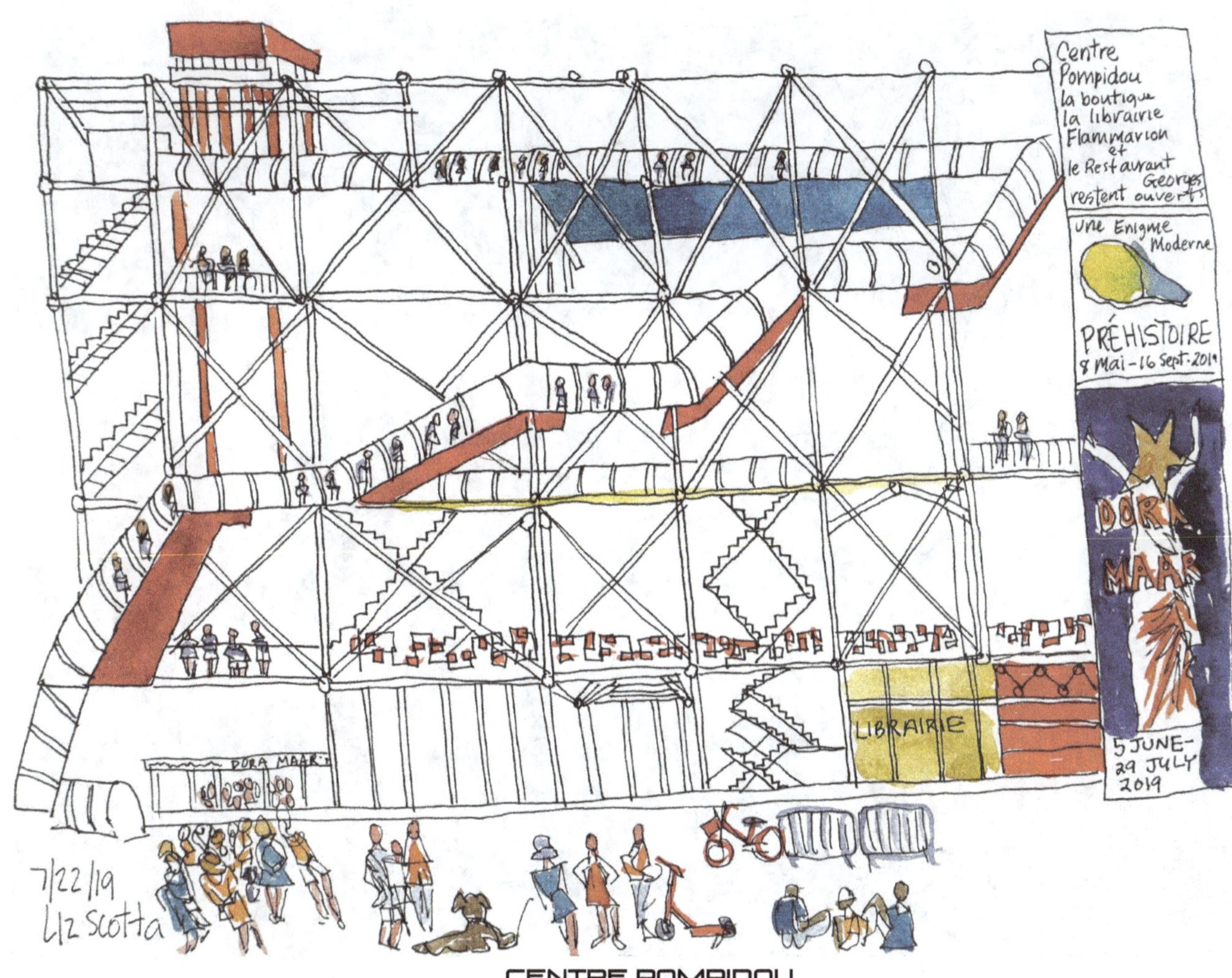

CENTRE POMPIDOU
PARIS

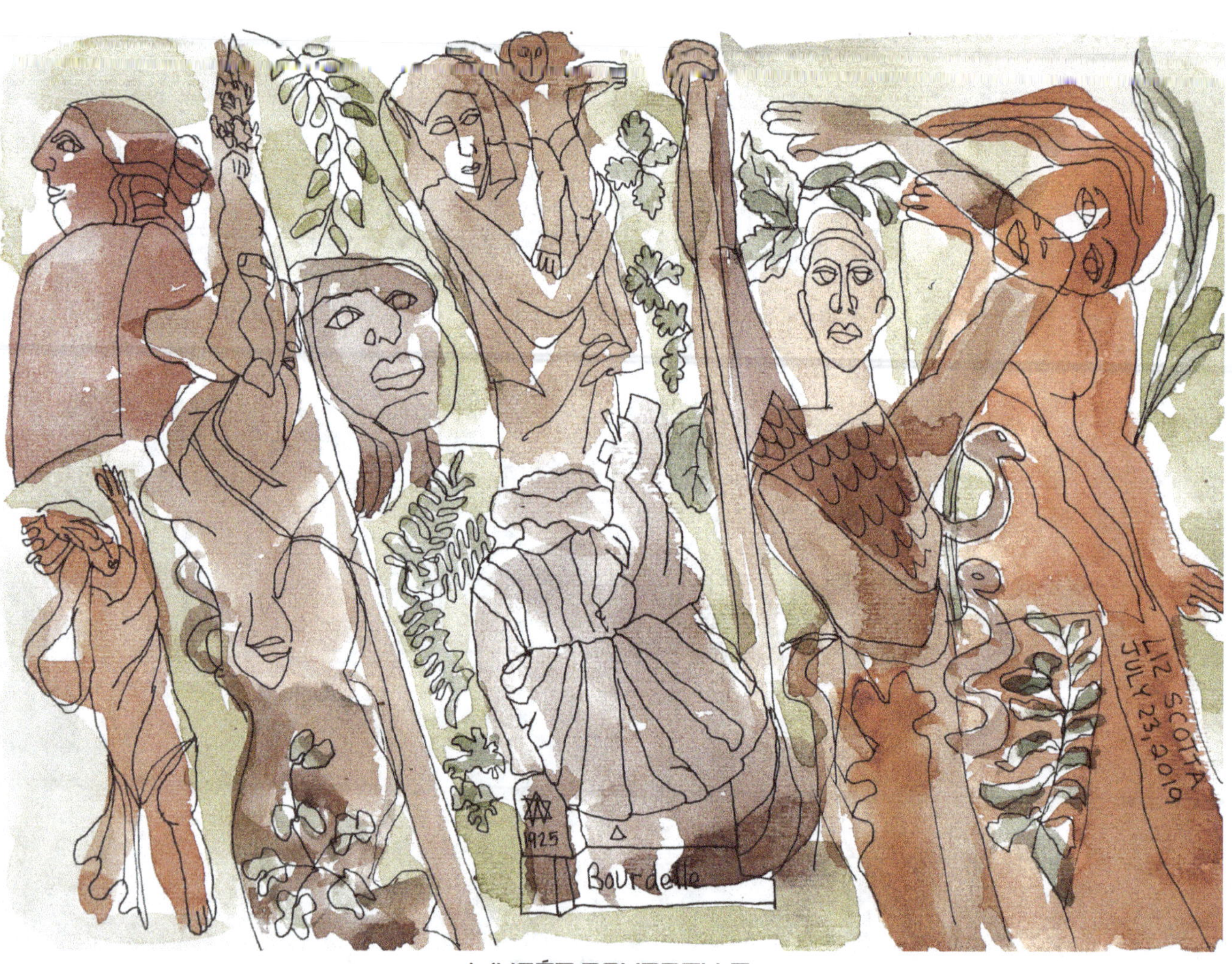

MUSÉE BOURDELLE
PARIS

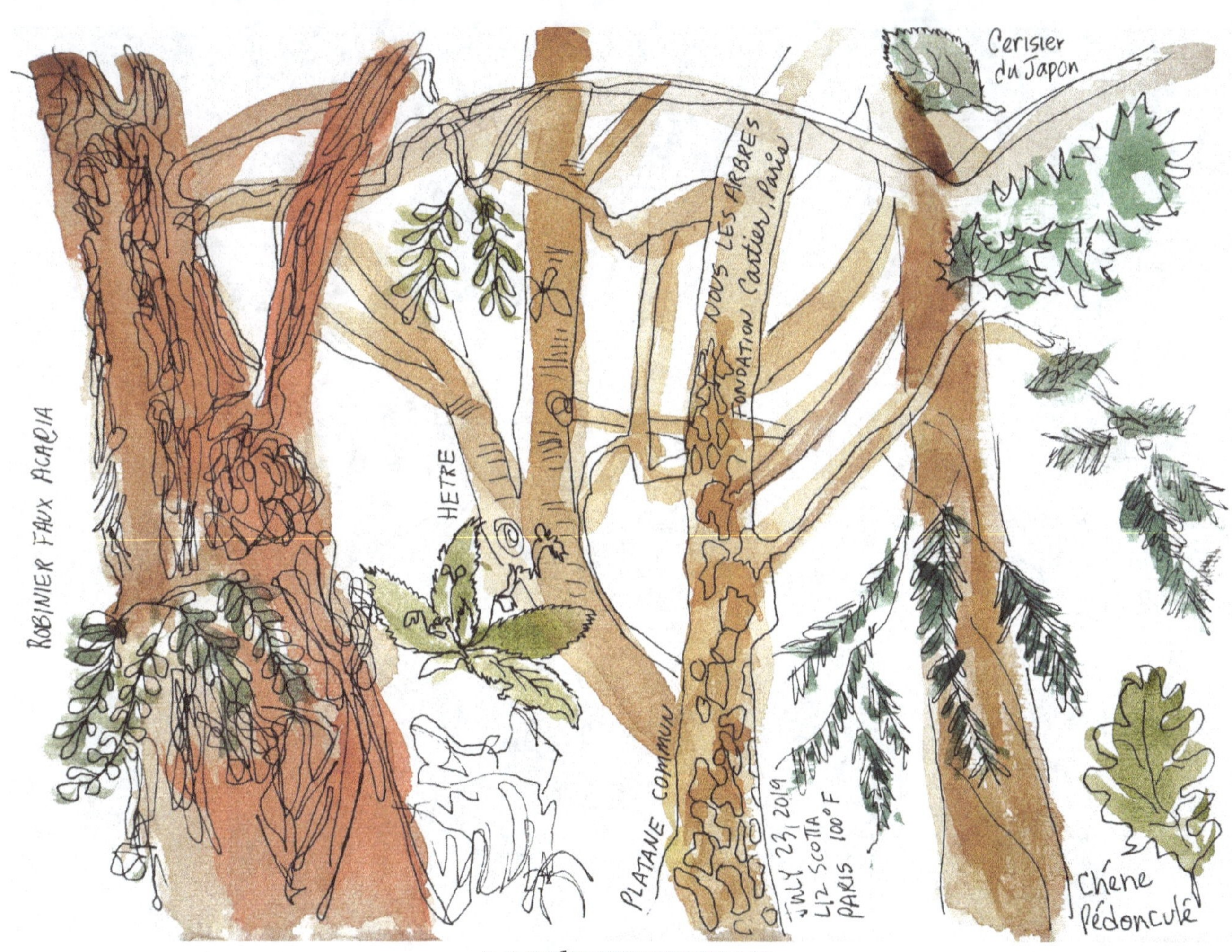

MUSÉE BOURDELLE
PARIS

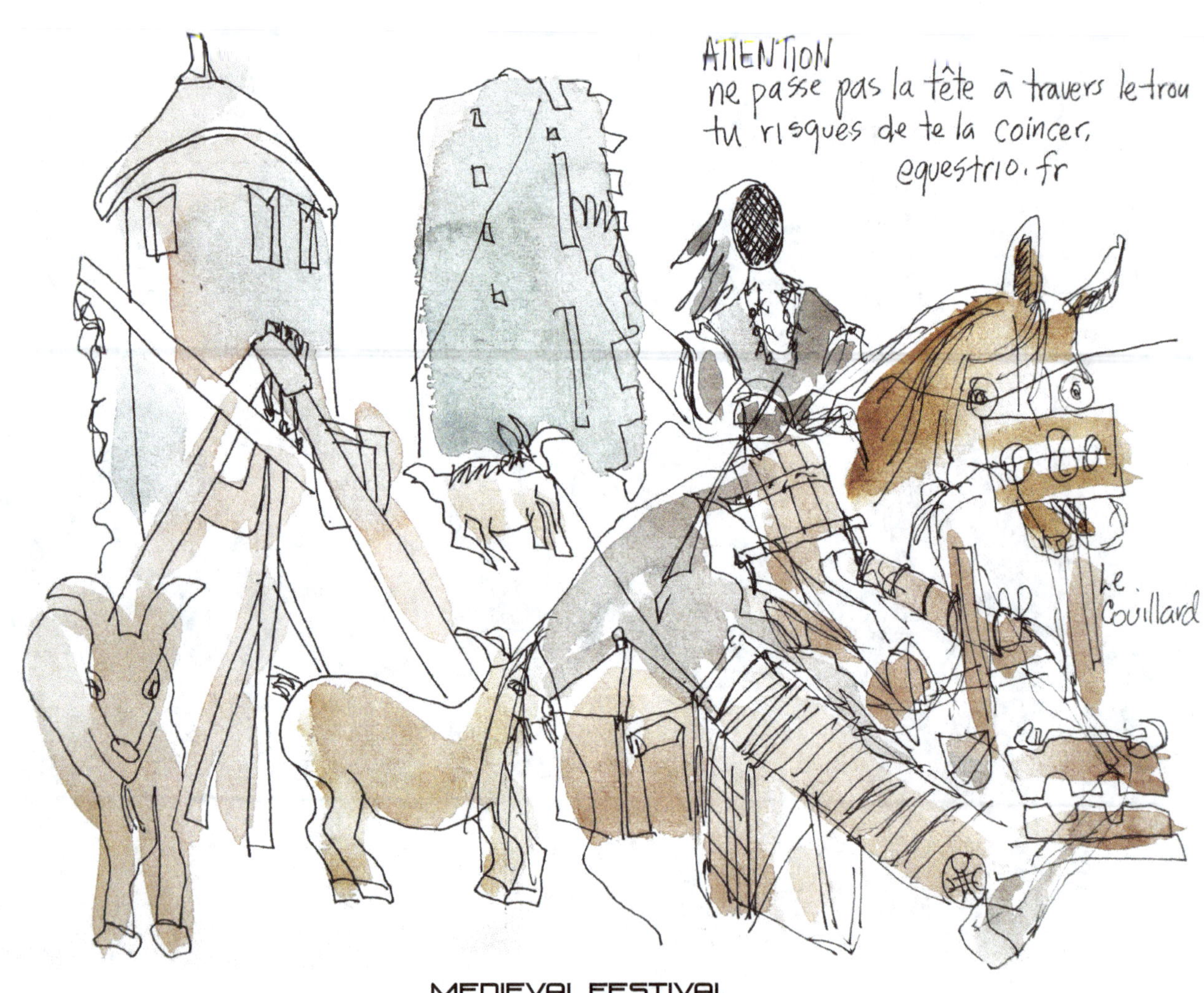

MEDIEVAL FESTIVAL
PROVINS

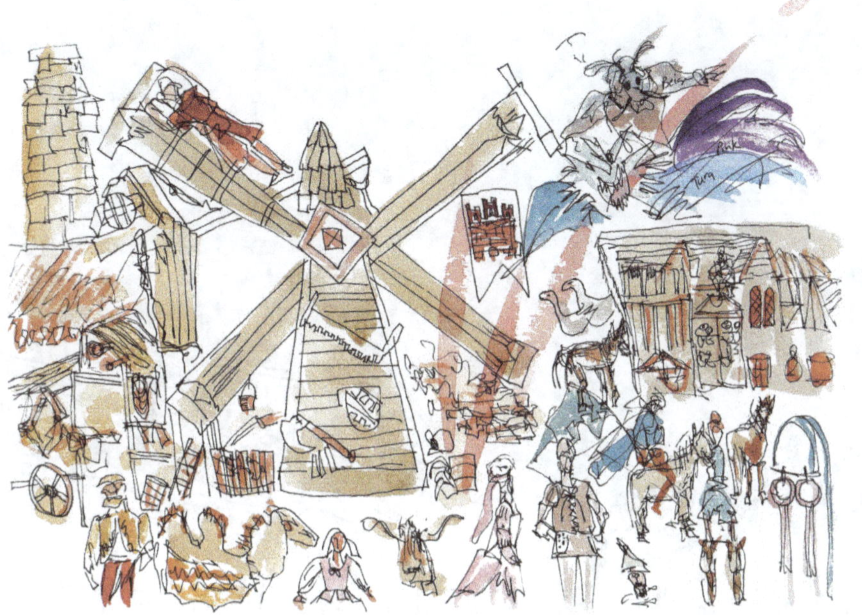

MEDIEVAL FESTIVAL
PROVINS

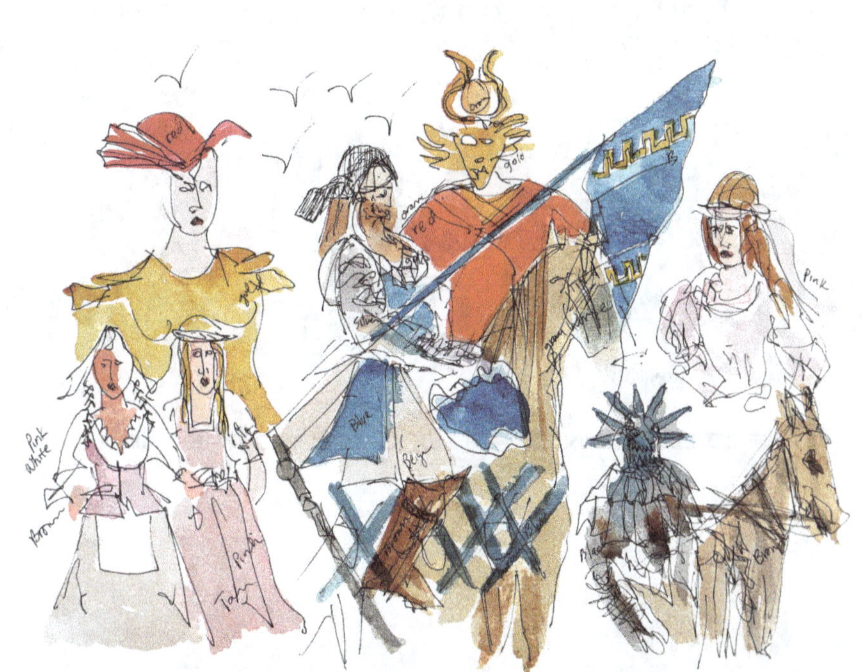

2019

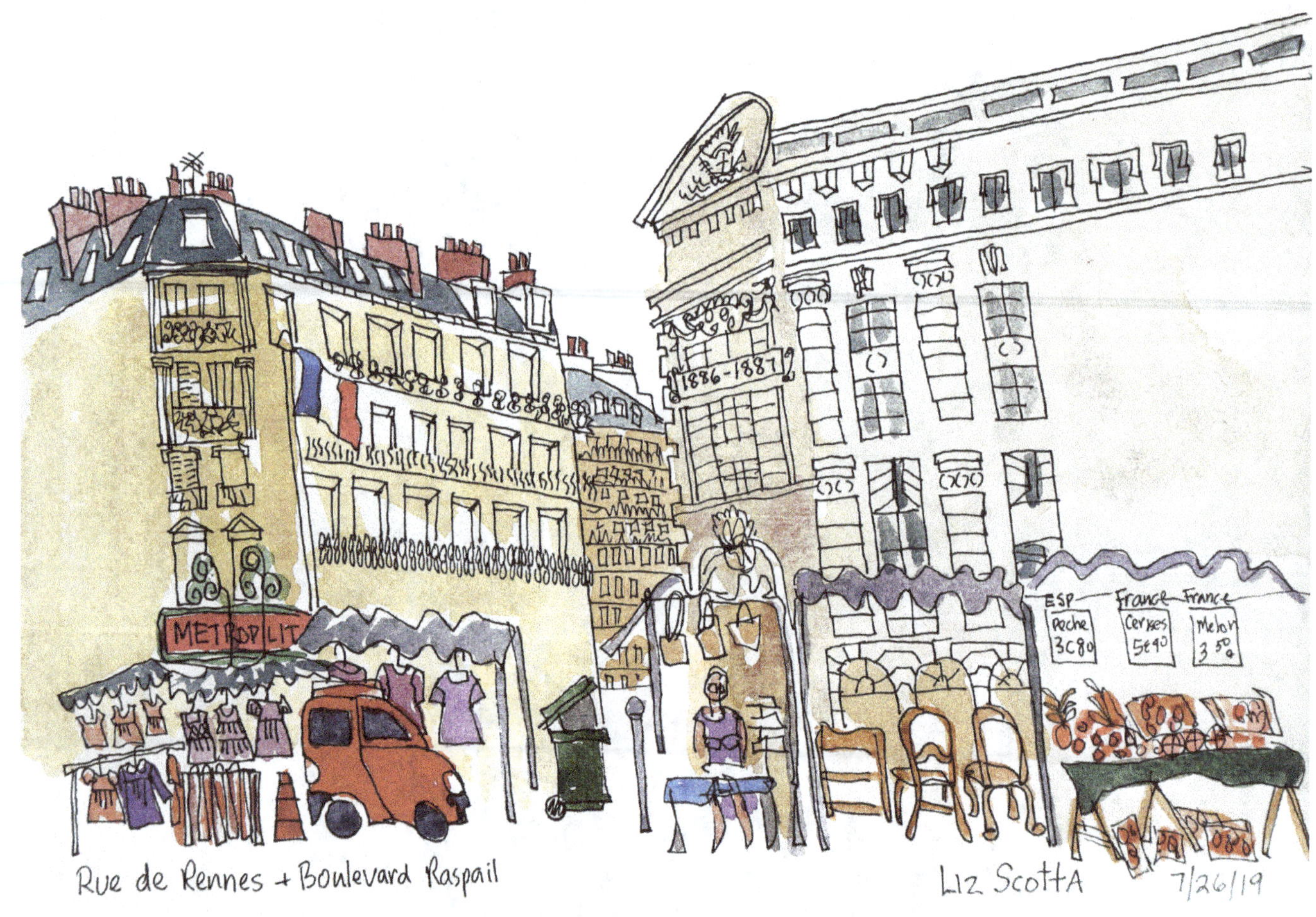

RUE DE RENNES AND BOULEVARD RASPAIL
PARIS

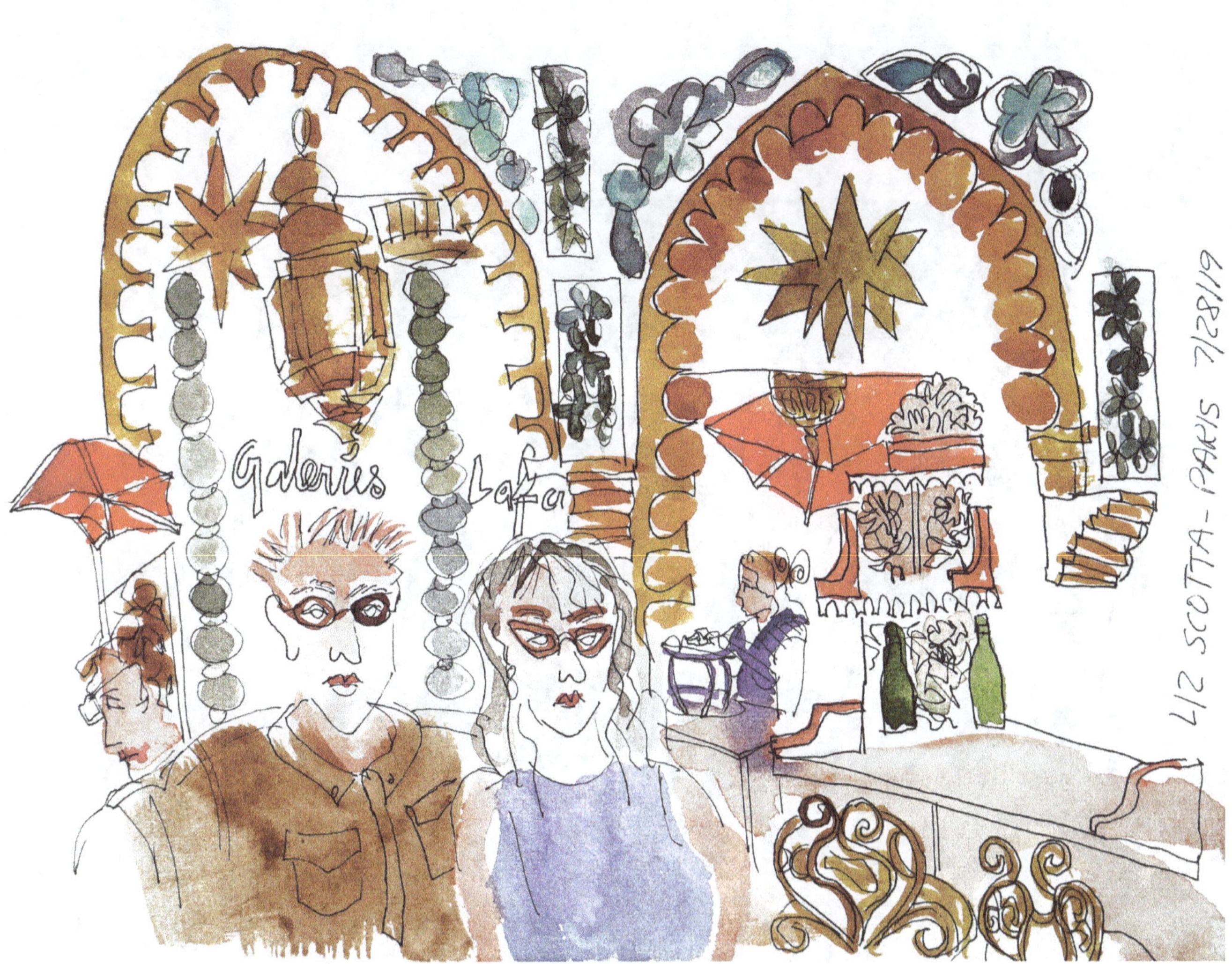

DINNER WITH BARBARA AND GORDON
PARIS

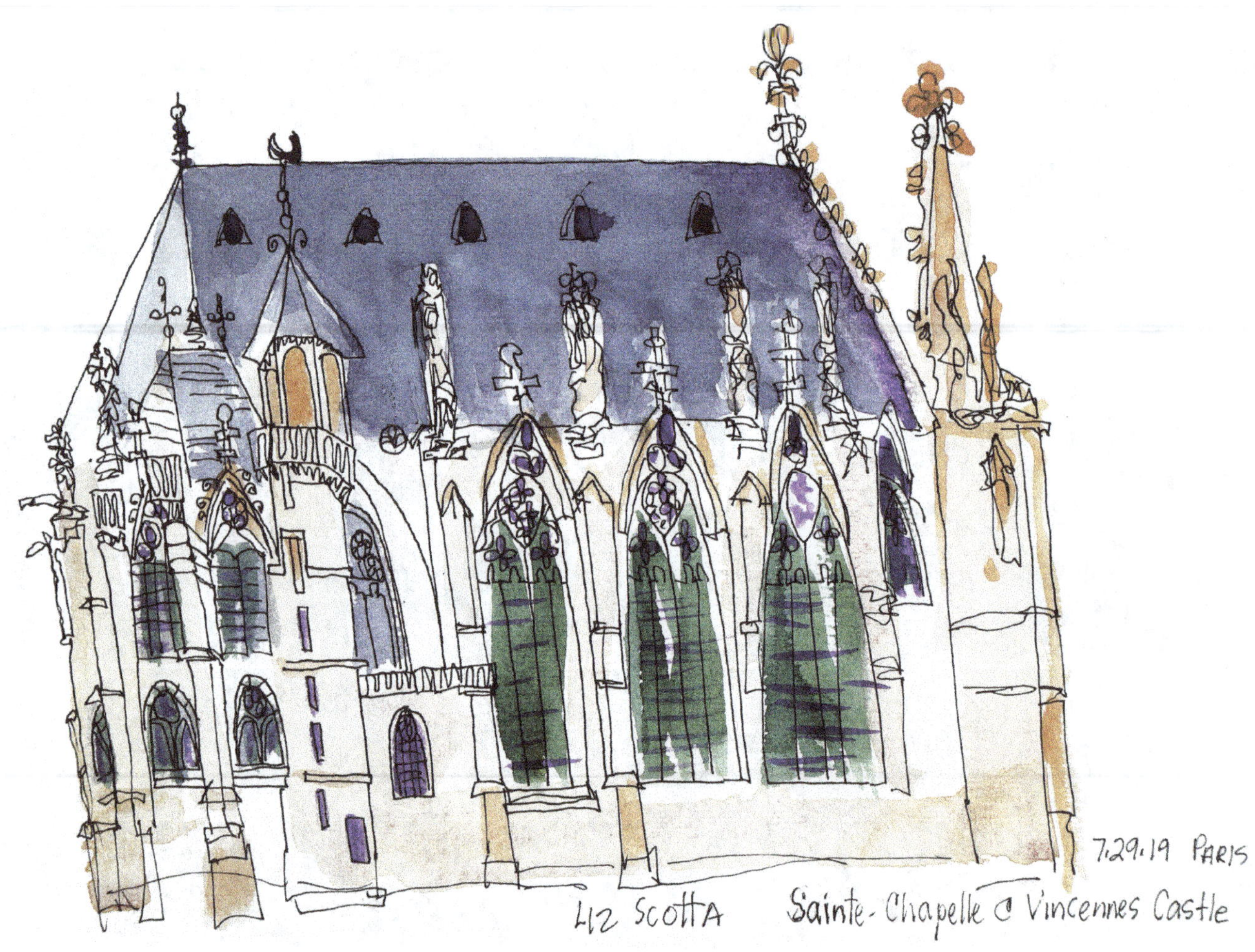

SAINTE-CHAPELLE AT VINCENNES CHÂTEAU
PARIS

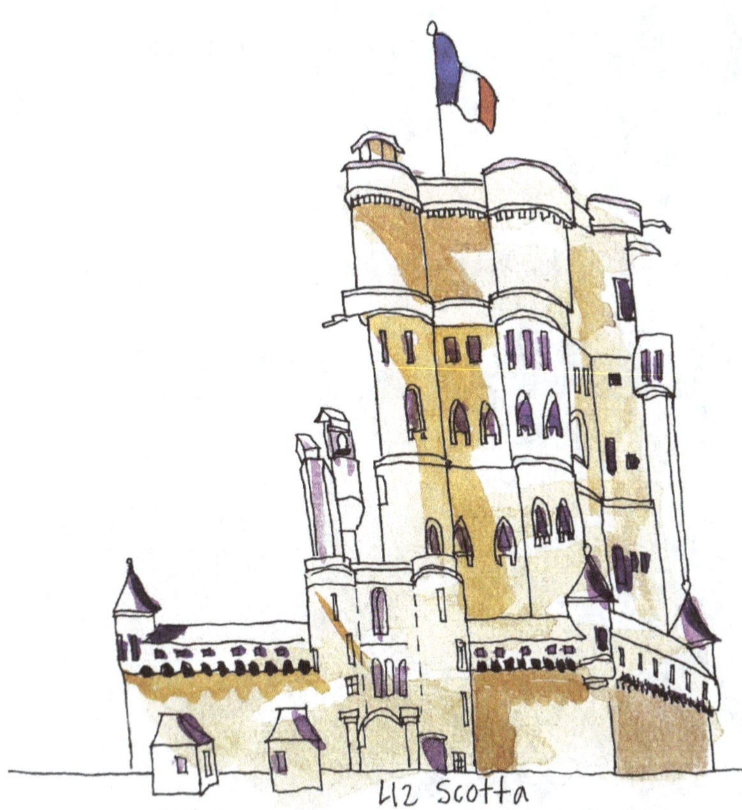

VINCENNES CHÂTEAU
PARIS

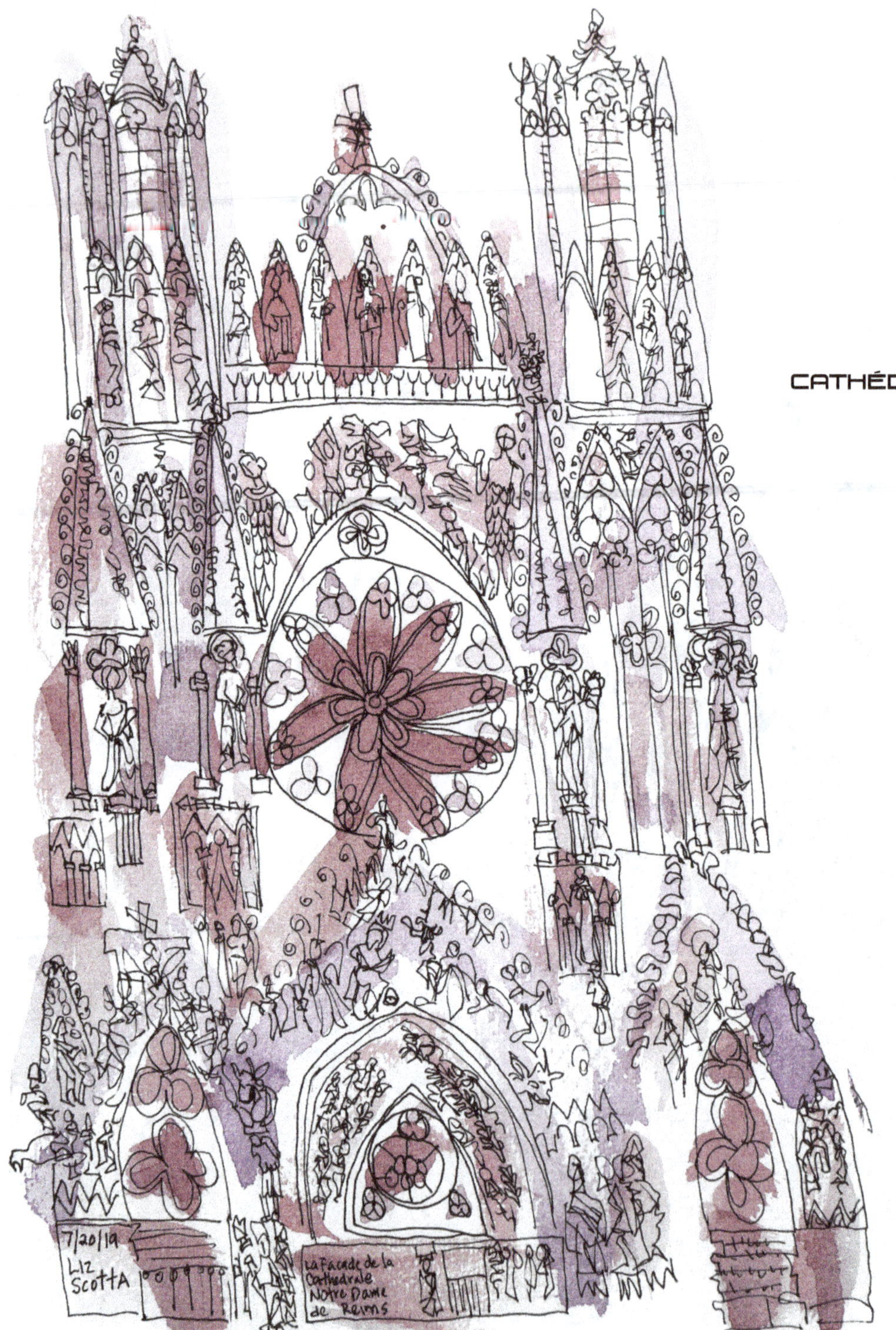

CATHÉDRALE DE REIMS
REIMS

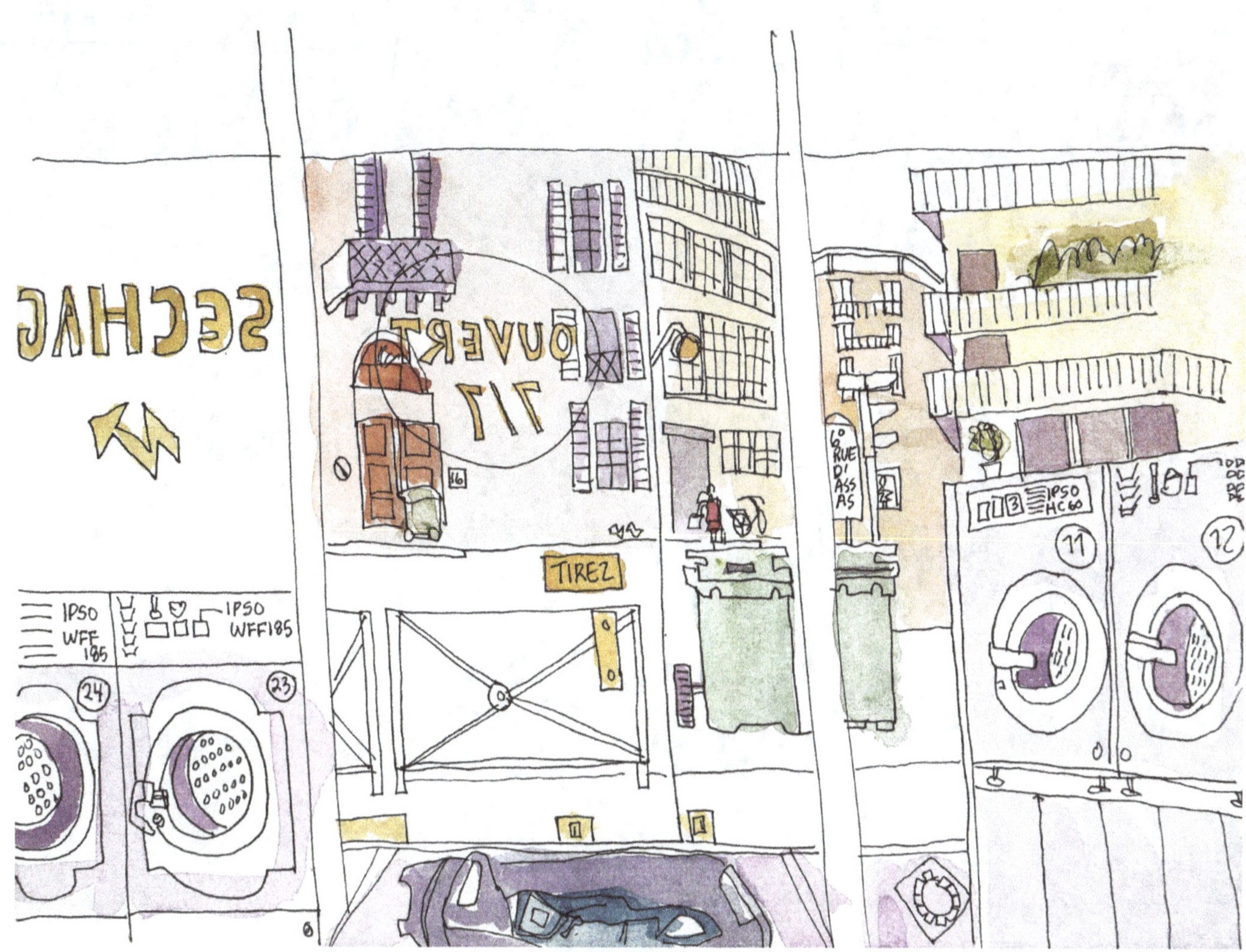

LAUNDROMAT
PARIS

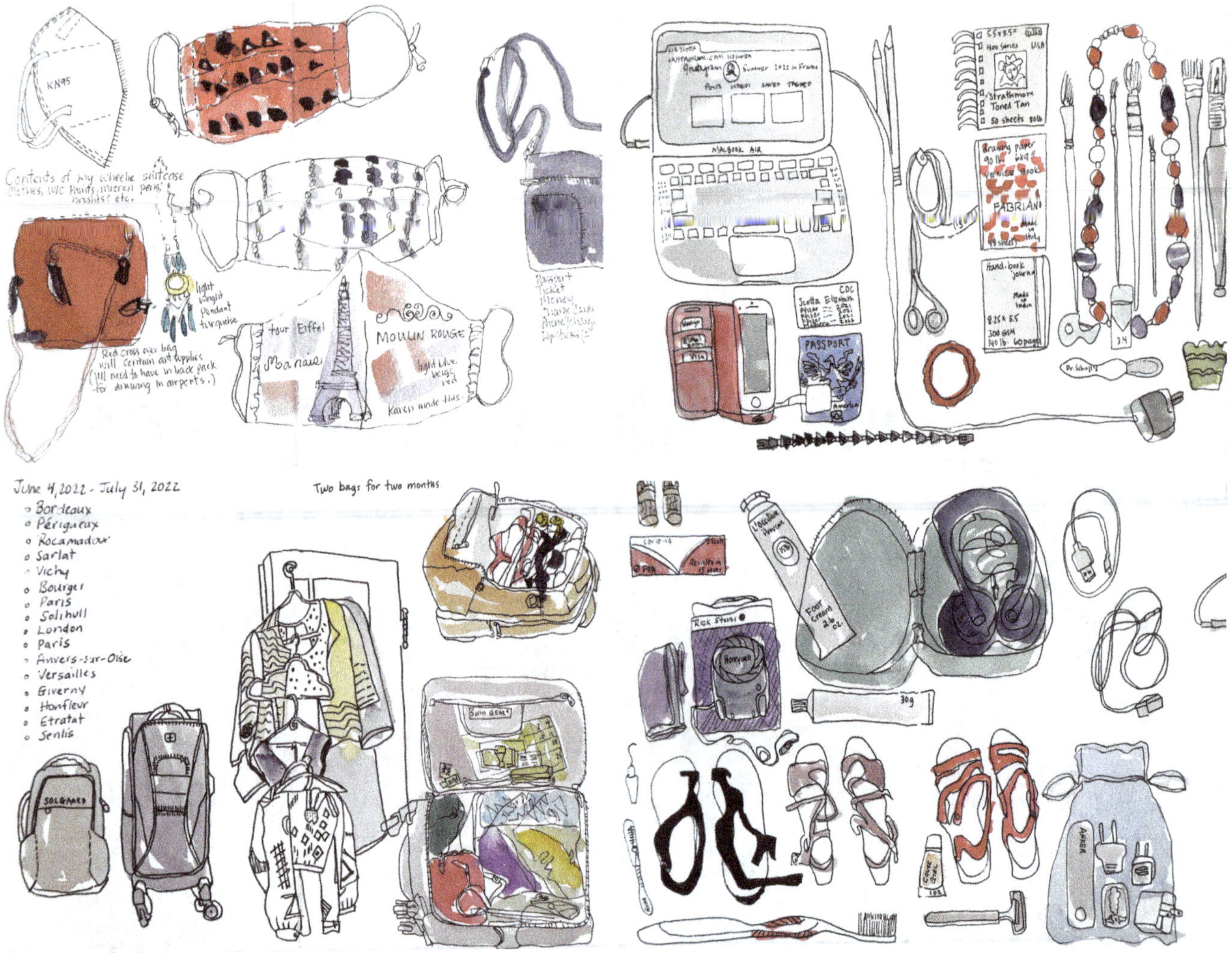

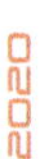

KN95
Contents of my wheelie suitcase
clothes, WC paints, murern paris, brushes etc.
light weight pendant turquoise
Red cross ear bag with certain art supplies (will need to have in back pack for drawing in airports.)
Tour Eiffel
Ma nave
MOULIN ROUGE
light olive, beige, red
Karen made this.
MACBOOK AIR
Passport Ticket Money Mastercard PhoneJersey lipstick?
Summer 2022 in France
Paris Senlis Anvers Tauned
5.5 x 8.5 100 Series USA
Strathmore Toned Tan 50 sheets 80lb
FABRIANO
Hand-book journal
Made in India
8.25 x 5.5 300 GSM 140 lb 60 pages
Juella Elizabeth
CDC
PASSPORT
VISA
Amelia
Dr. Scholl's
June 4, 2022 - July 31, 2022
o Bordeaux
o Périgueux
o Rocamadour
o Sarlat
o Vichy
o Bourges
o Paris
o Solihull
o London
o Paris
o Anvers-sur-Oise
o Versailles
o Giverny
o Honfleur
o Etratat
o Senlis
Two bags for two months
SOLGAARD
L'OCCITANE
Foot Cream 2.6 oz
30 g
Rick Steves
Honeyman
COLGATE
APPLE
LUGGAGE

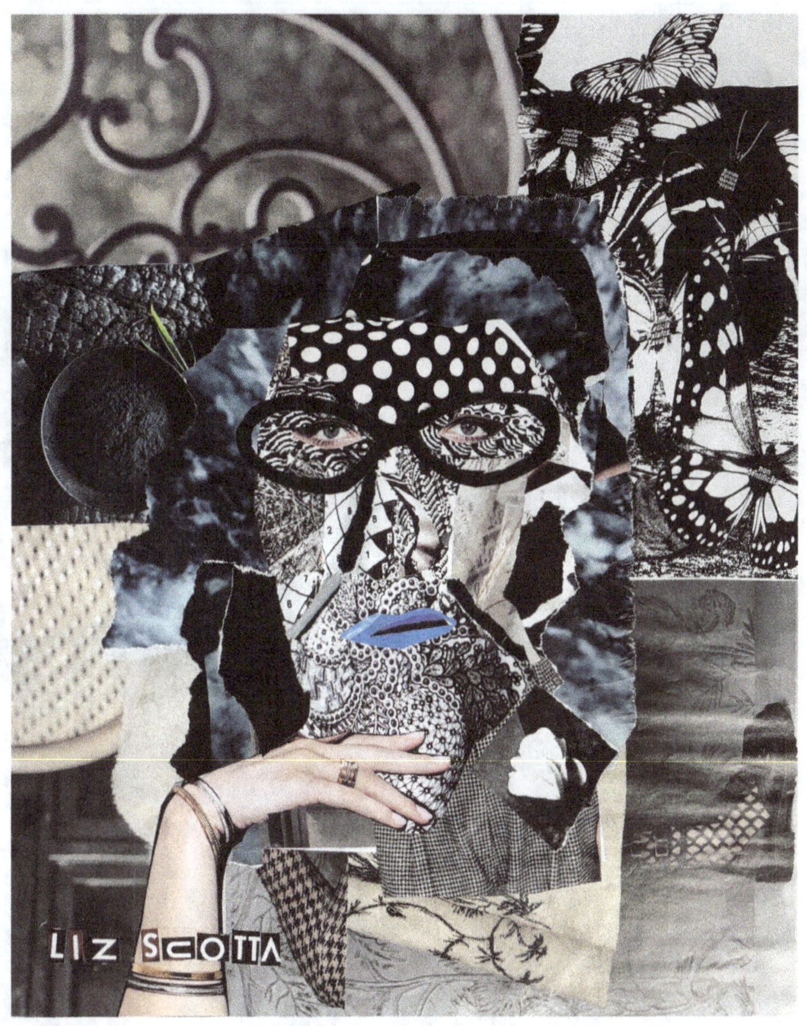

SELF-PORTRAIT

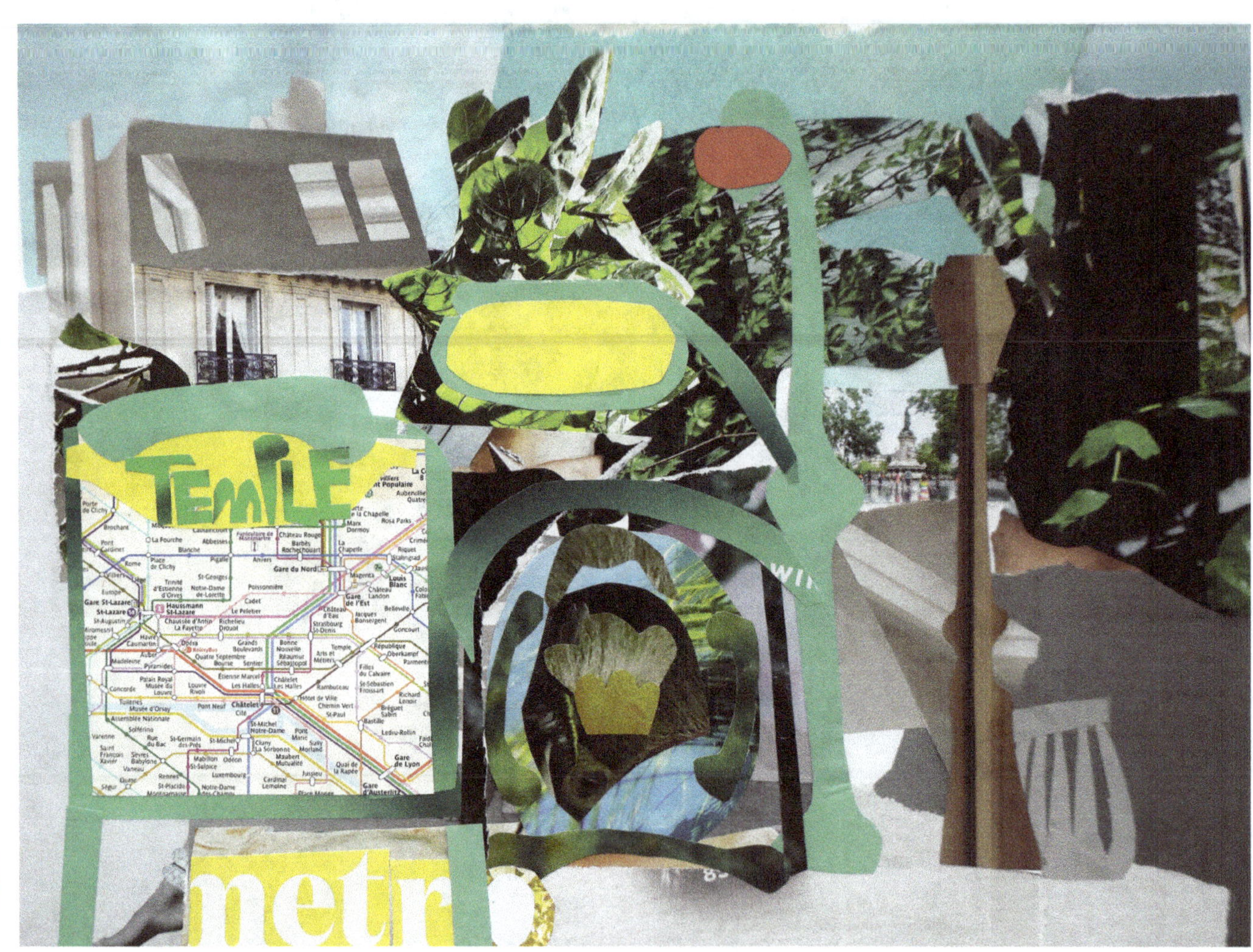
TEMPLE
metro
METRO TEMPLE
PARIS

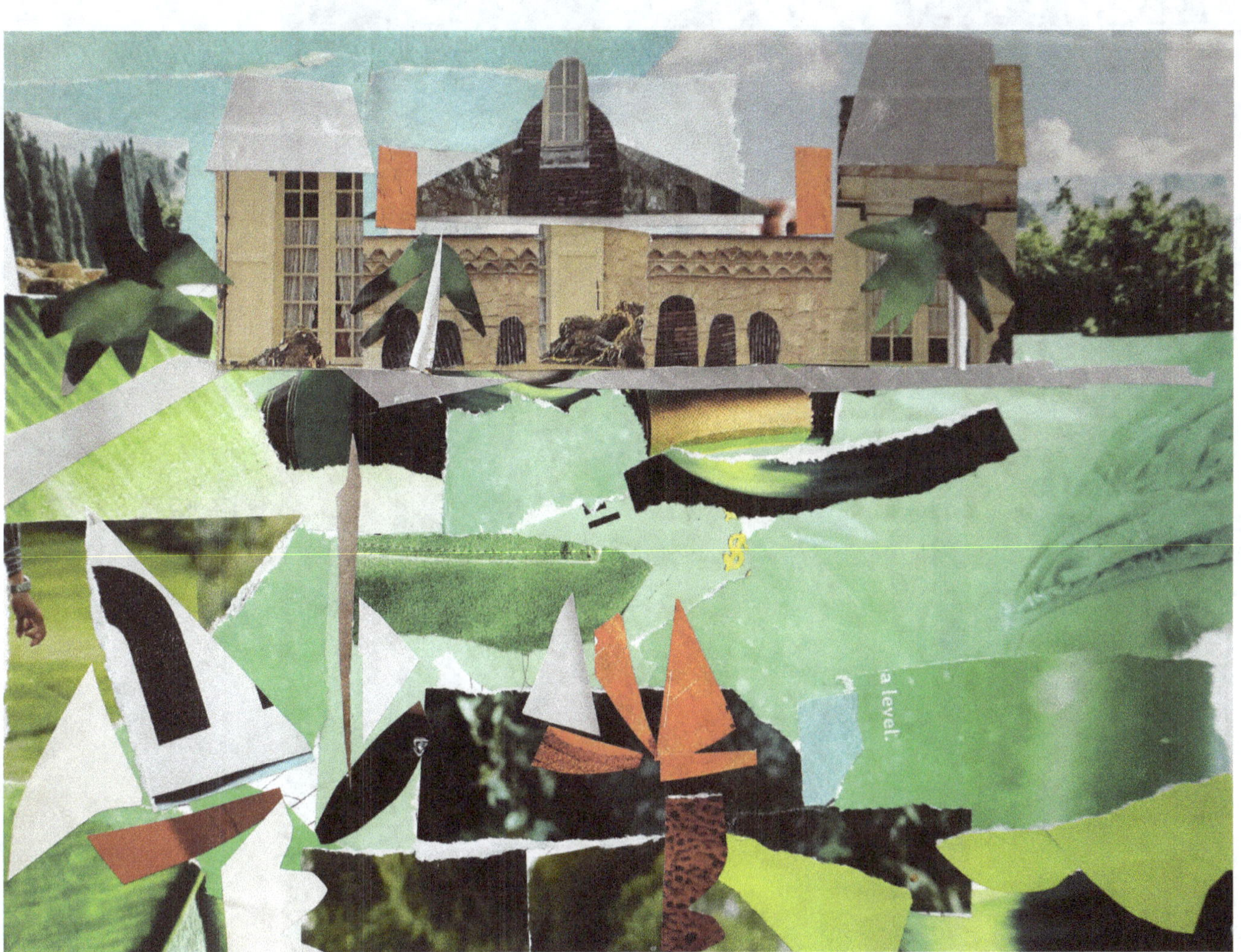

LUXEMBOURG GARDEN
PARIS

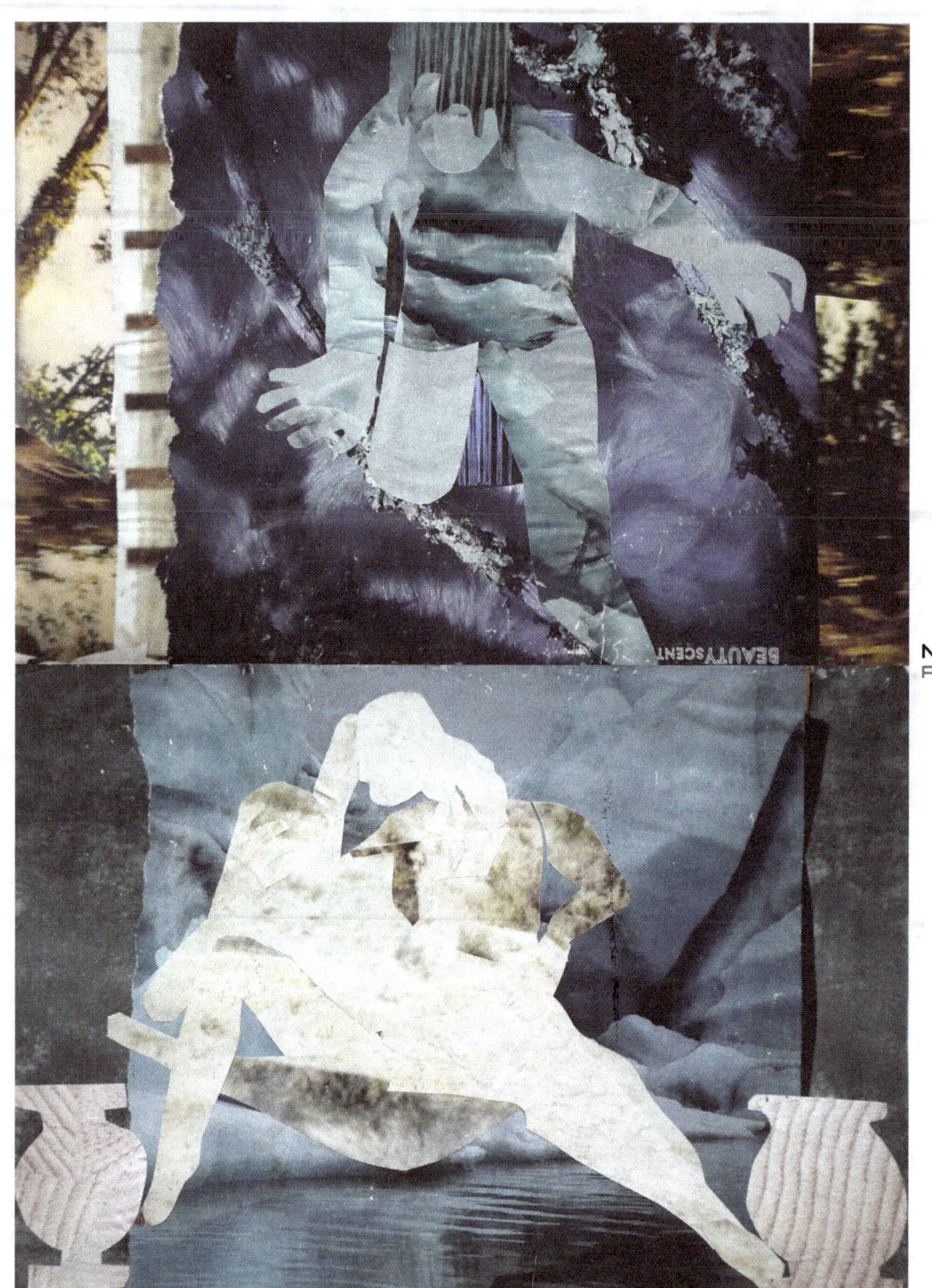

MEDICI FOUNTAIN
PARIS

2020

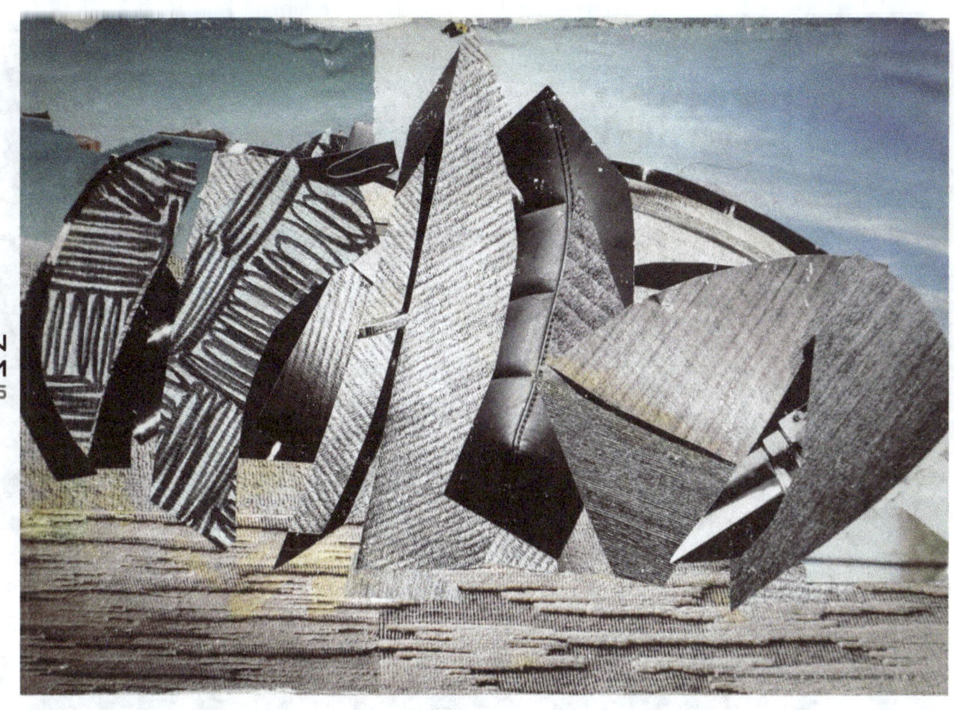

LOUIS VUITTON
FOUNDATION MUSEUM
PARIS

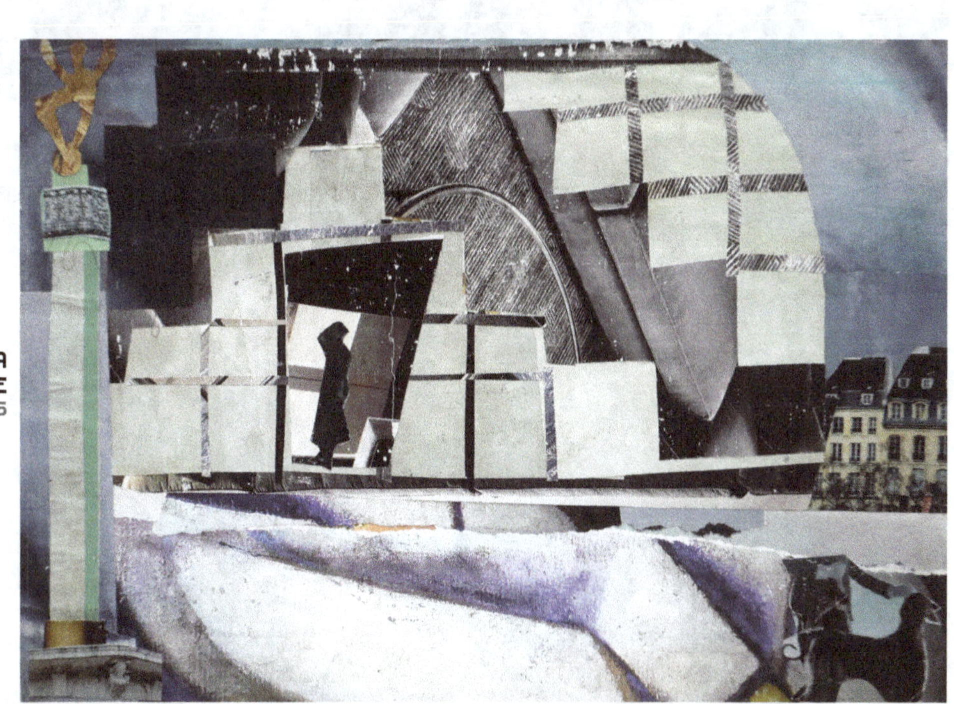

BASTILLE OPERA
HOUSE
PARIS

2020

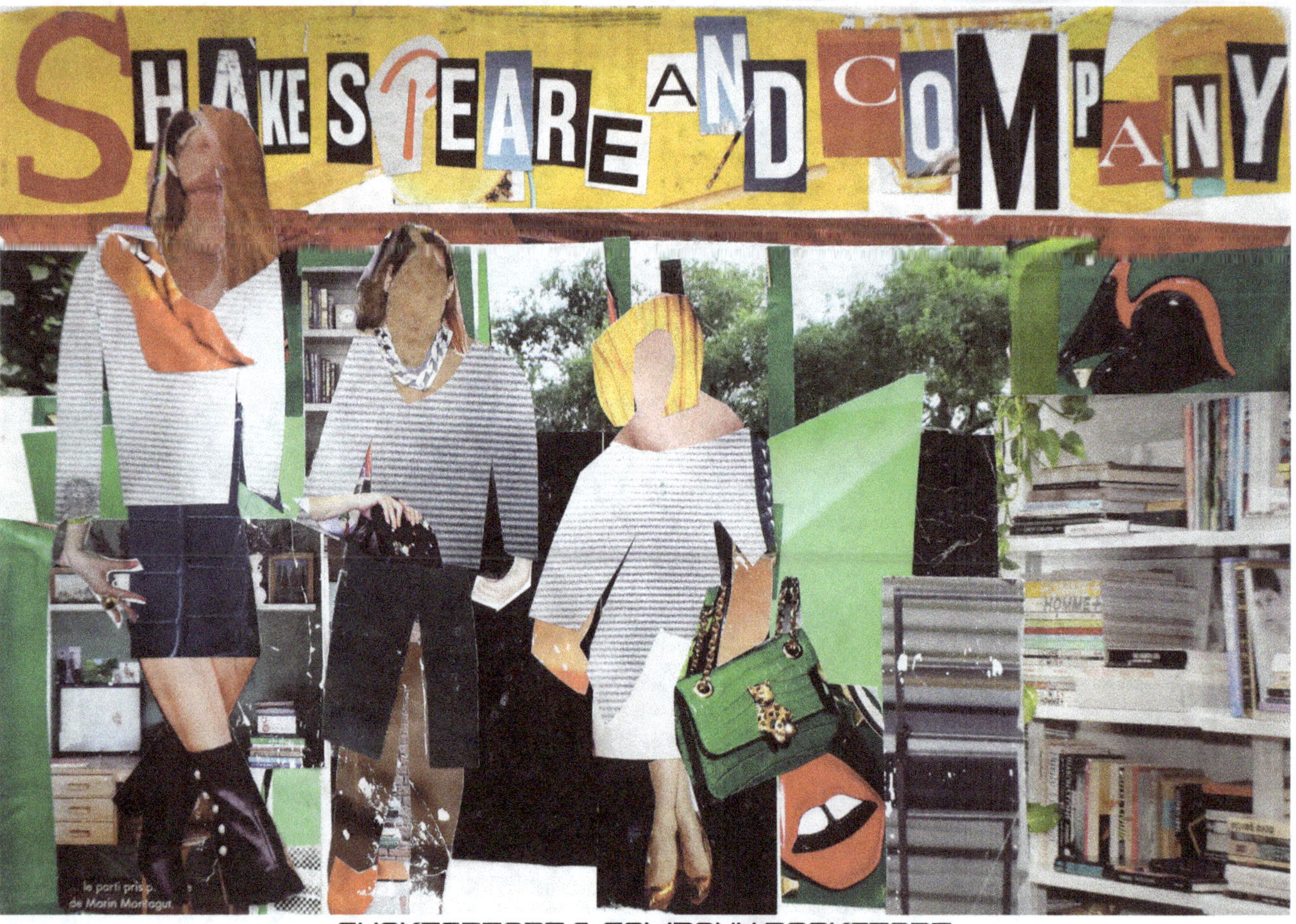

SHAKESPEARE & COMPANY BOOKSTORE
PARIS

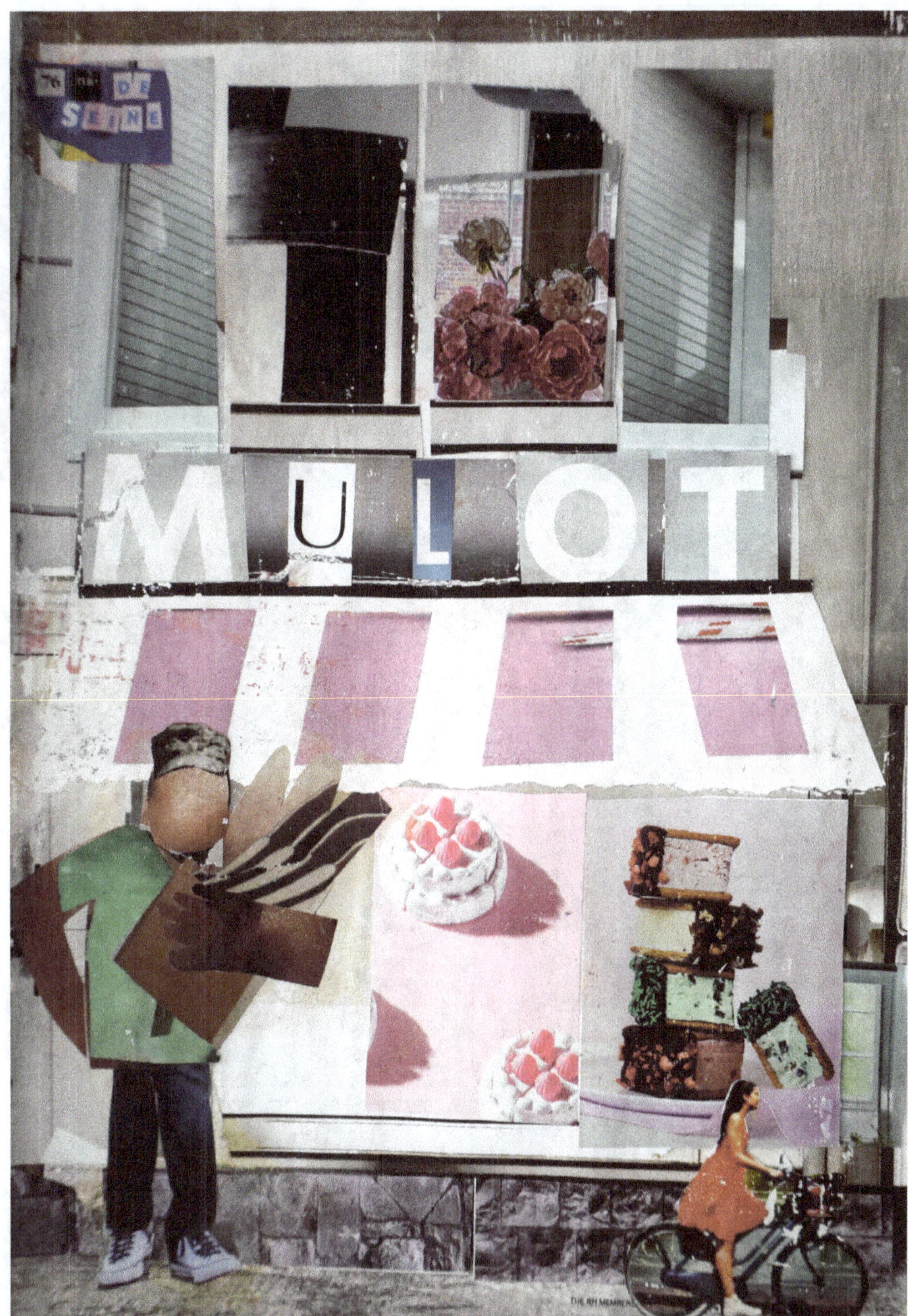

MULOT
PASTRY SHOP
PARIS

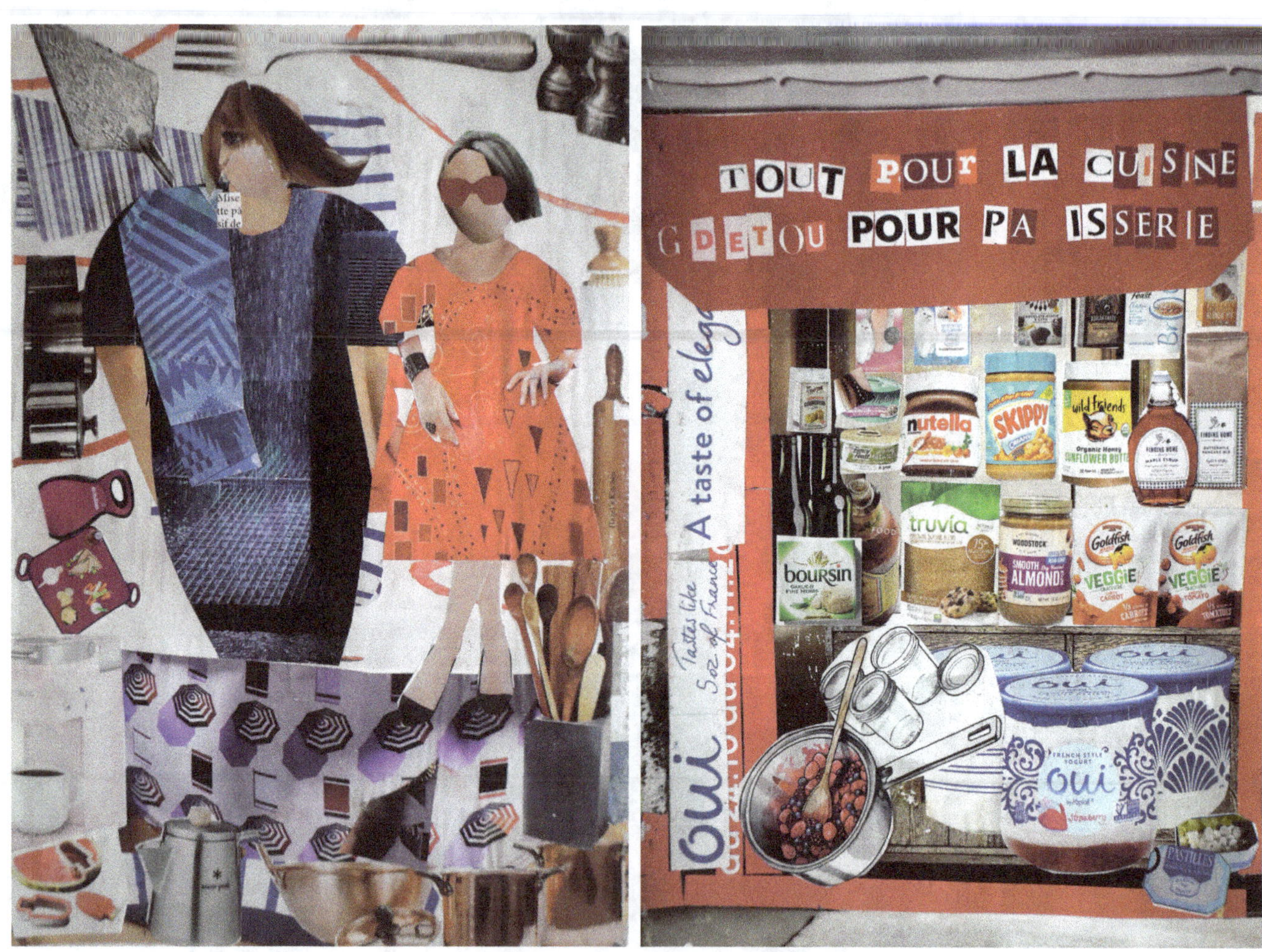

G. DETOU FOOD STORE
PARIS

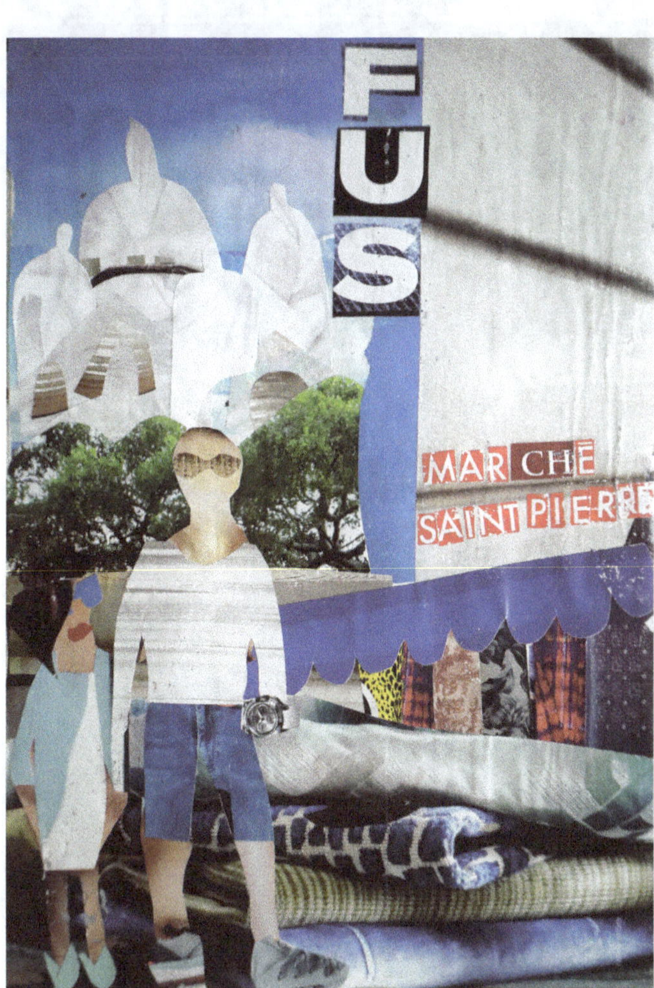

MARCHÉ SAINT-PIERRE FABRIC STORE
PARIS

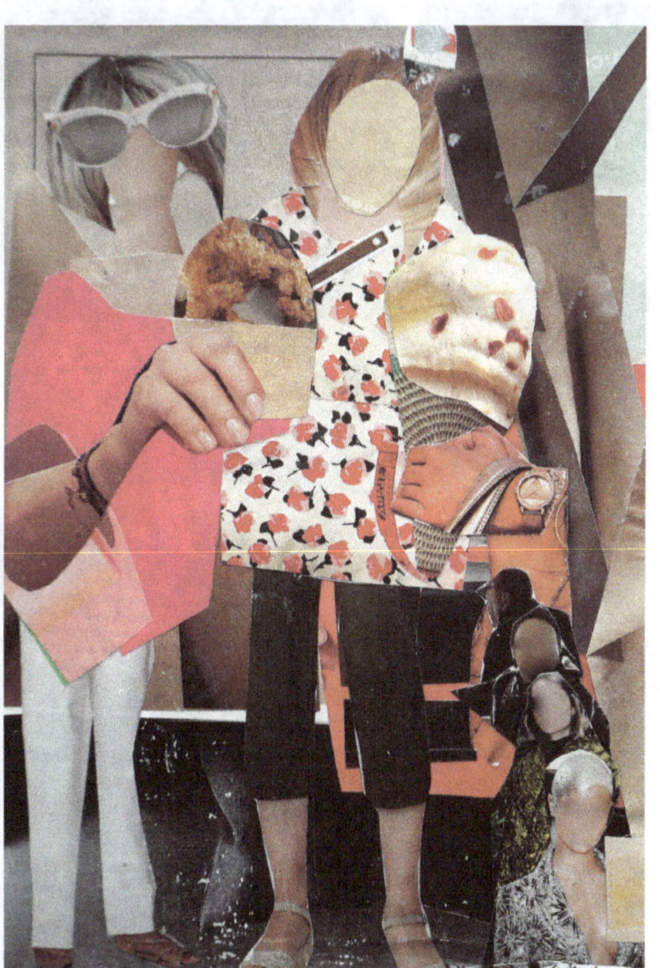

EATING AN AMORINO'S ICE CREAM CONE
PARIS

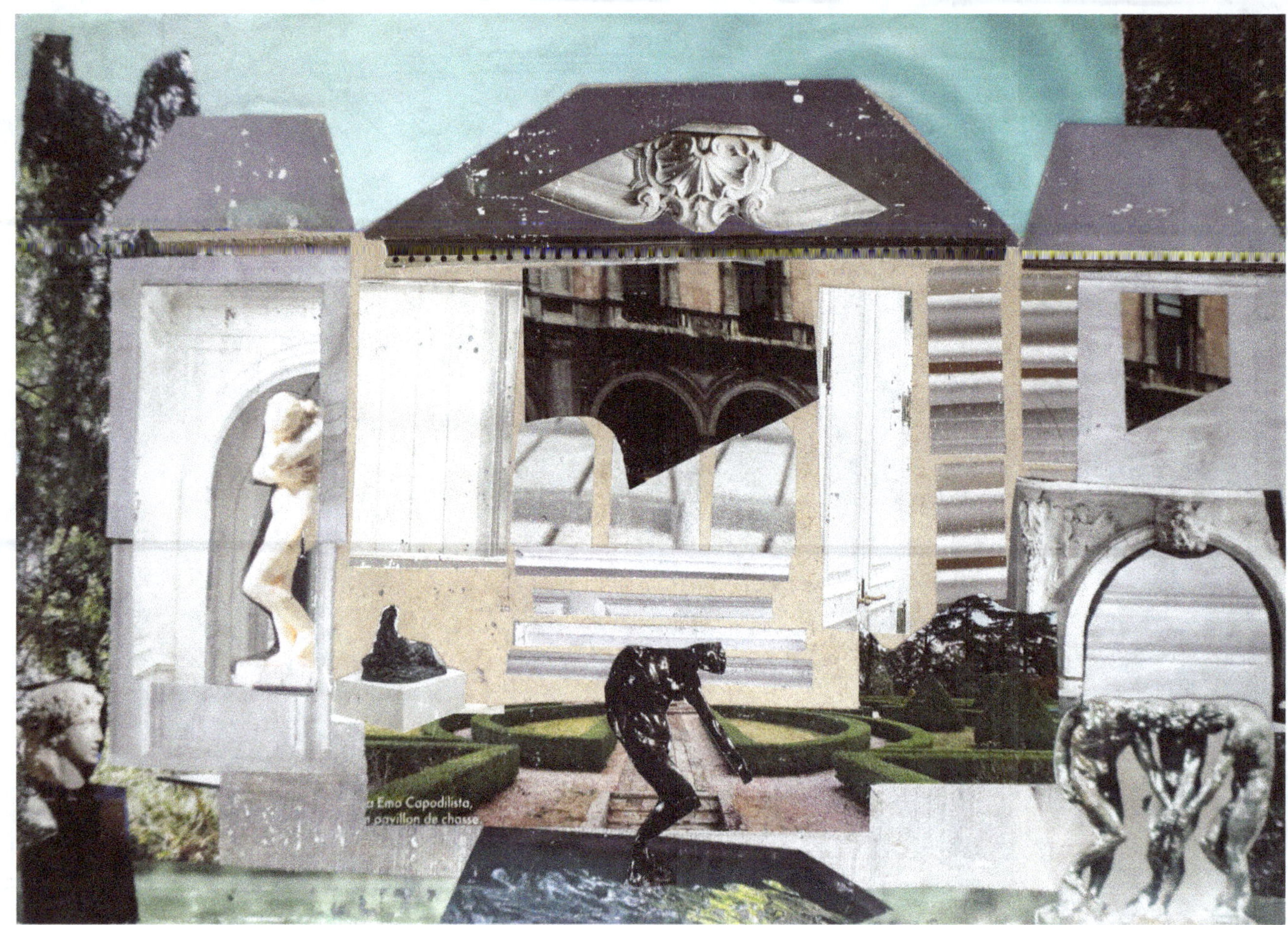

MUSÉE RODIN
PARIS

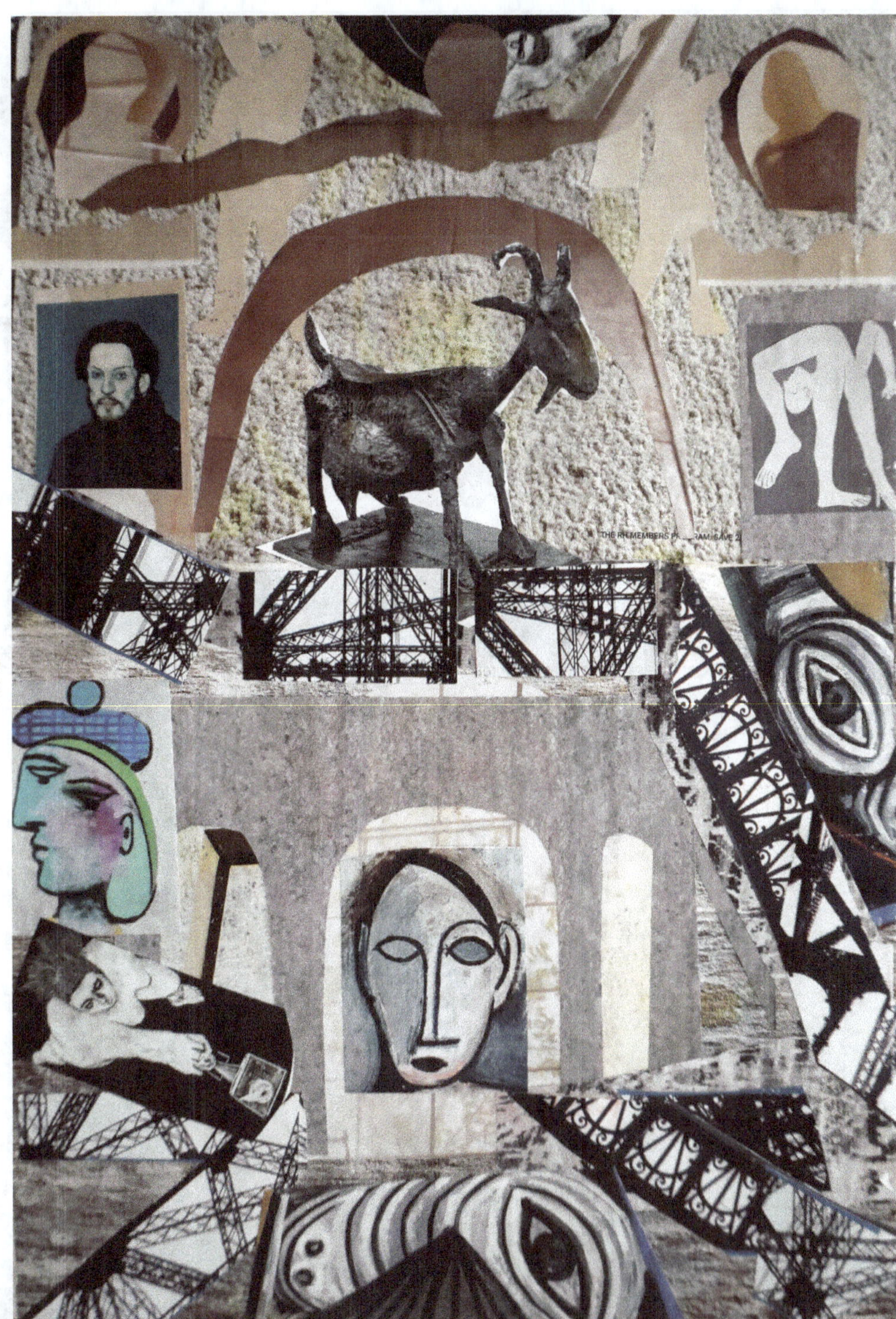

MUSÉE PICASSO
PARIS

2020

FONTAINE
SAINT-MICHEL
PARIS

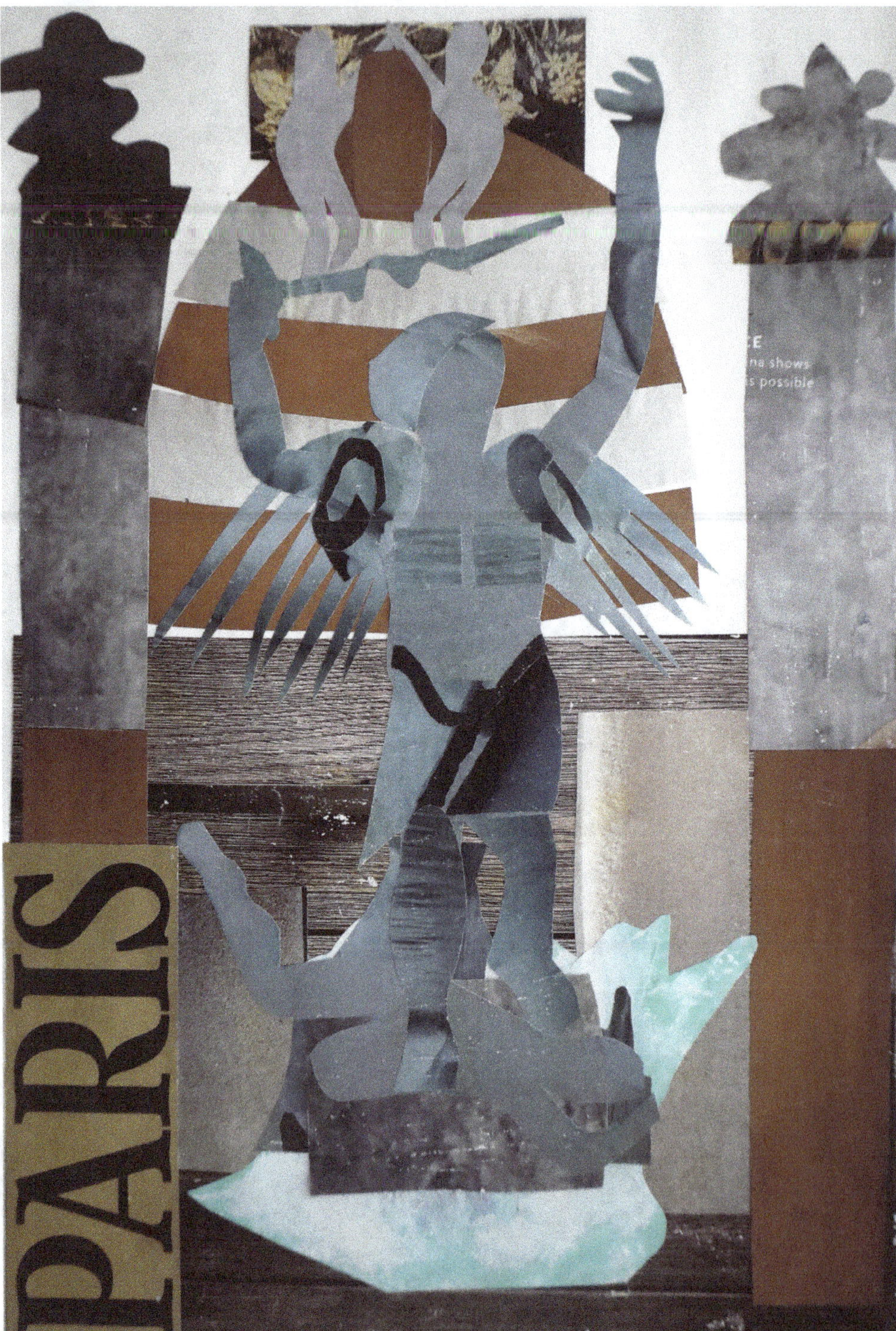

MOULIN ROUGE
PARIS

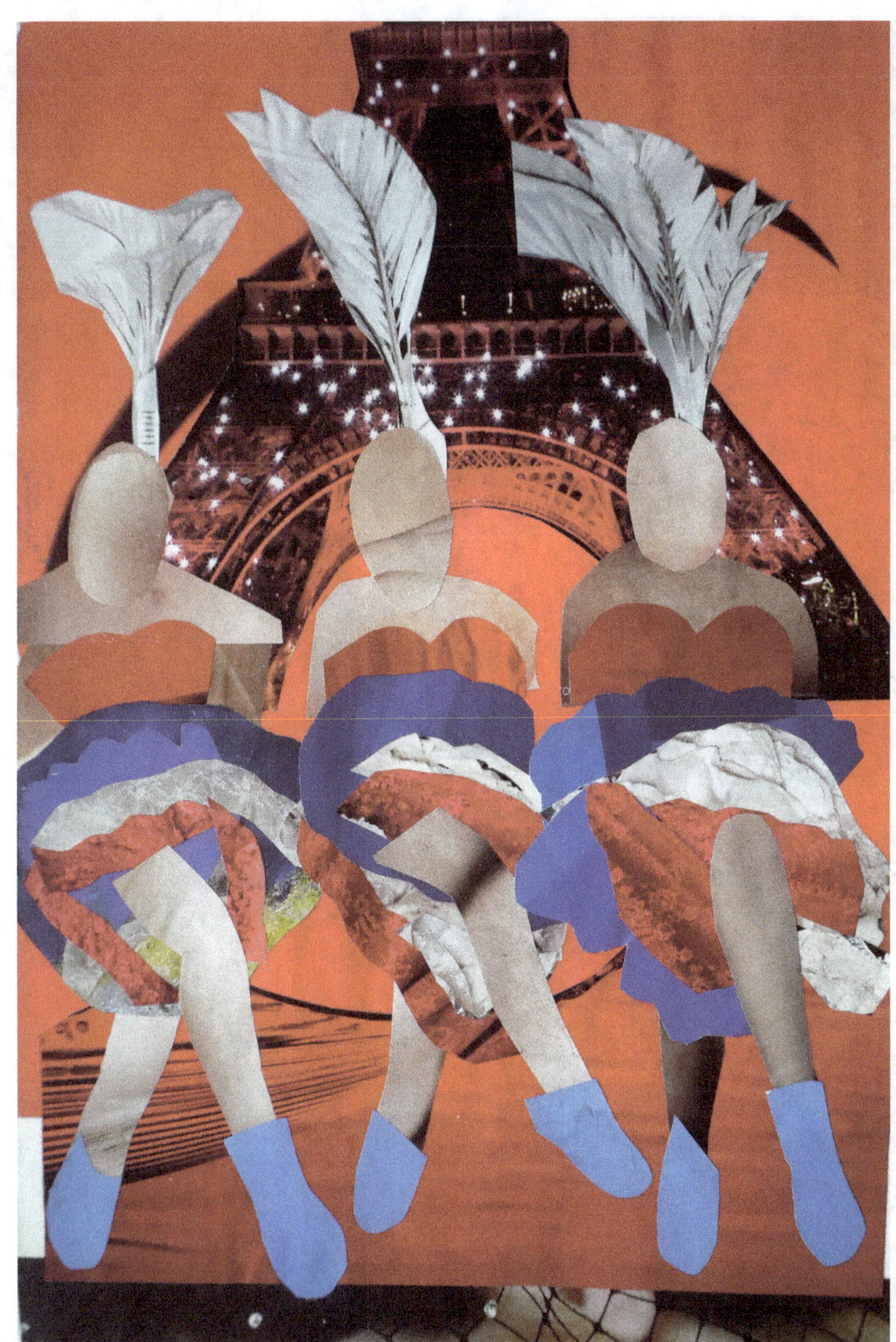

2020

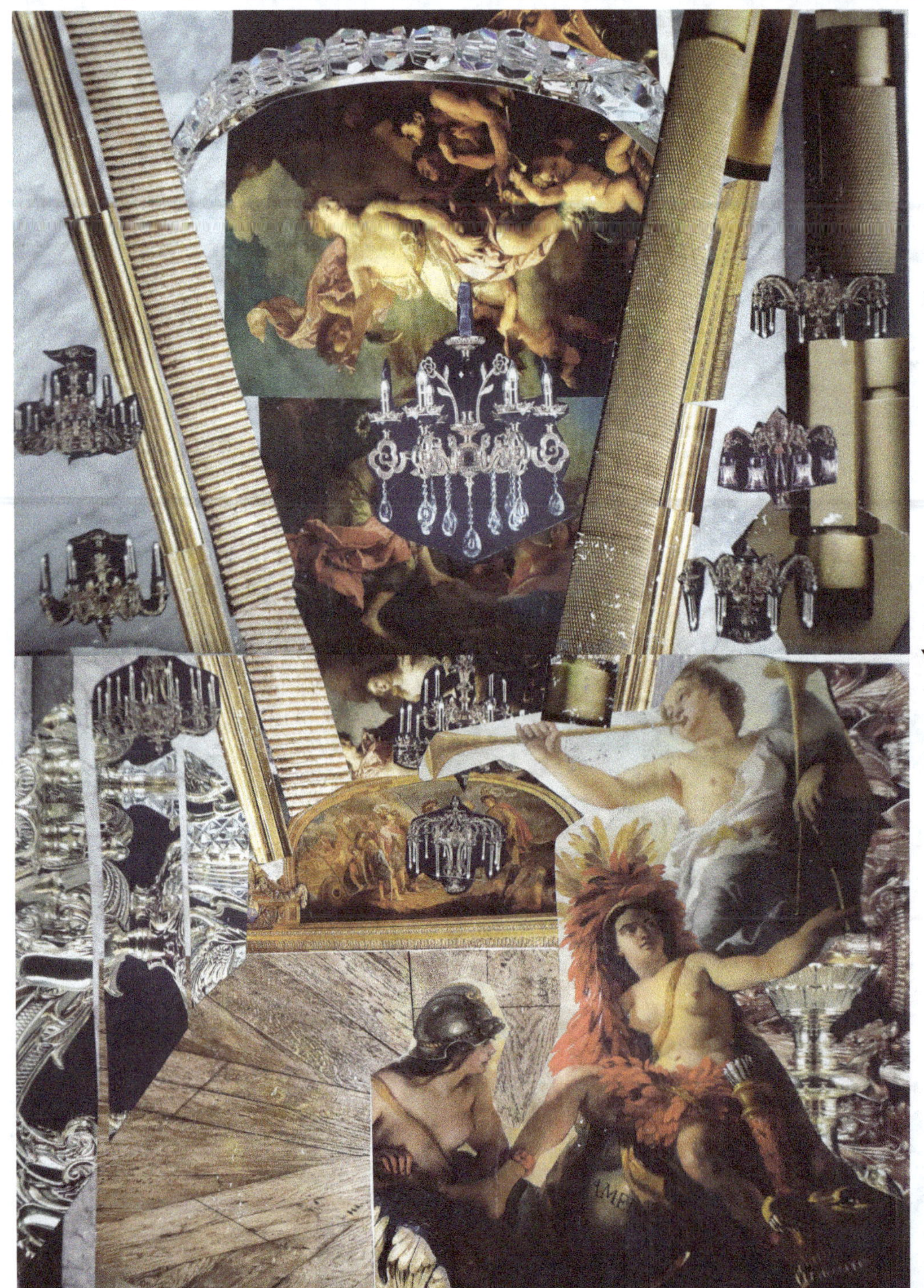

VERSAILLES

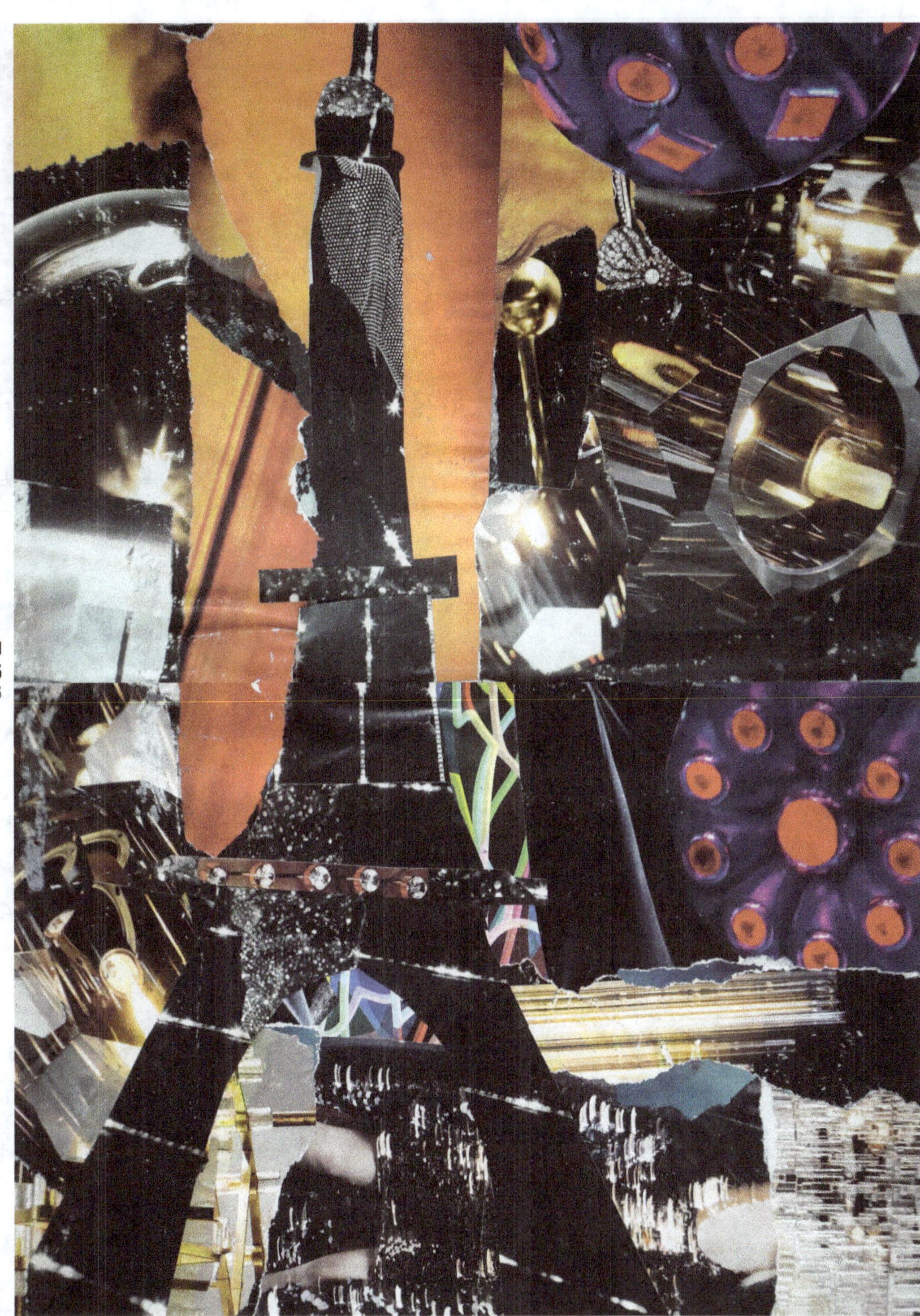

BASTILLE DAY
FIREWORKS
PARIS

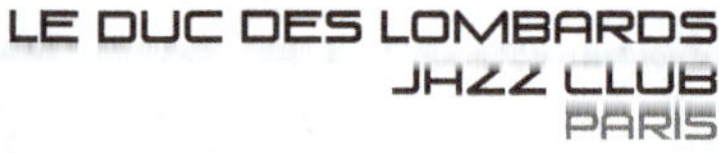
LE DUC DES LOMBARDS
JHZZ CLUB
PARIS

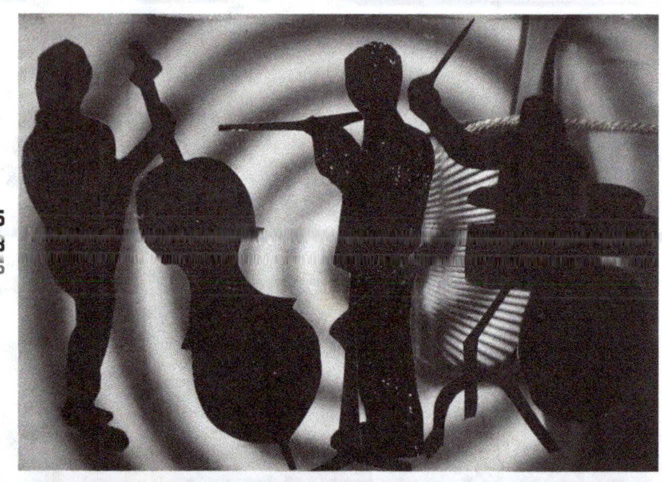

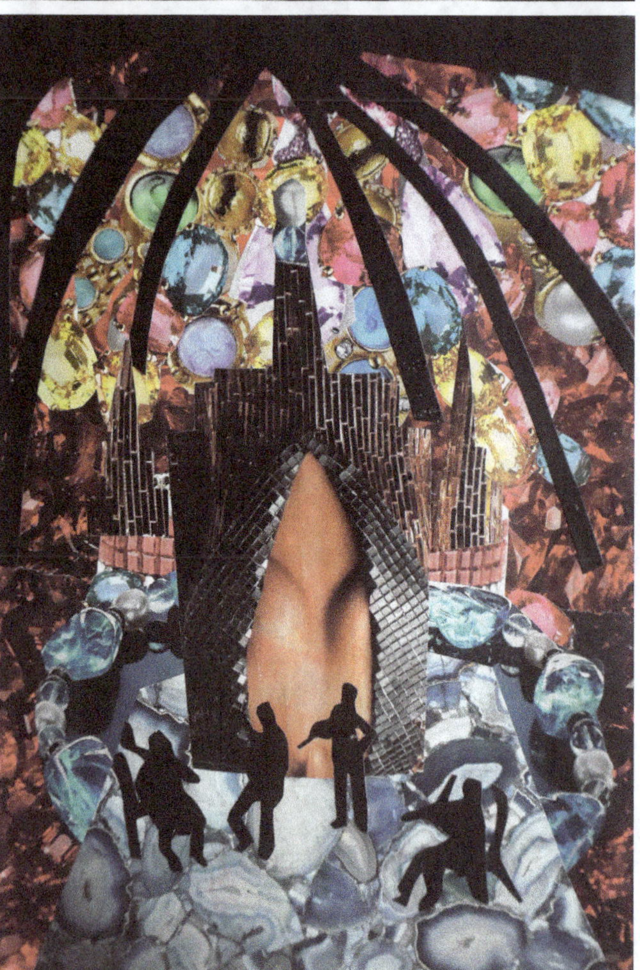
SAINTE-CHAPELLE CONCERT
PARIS

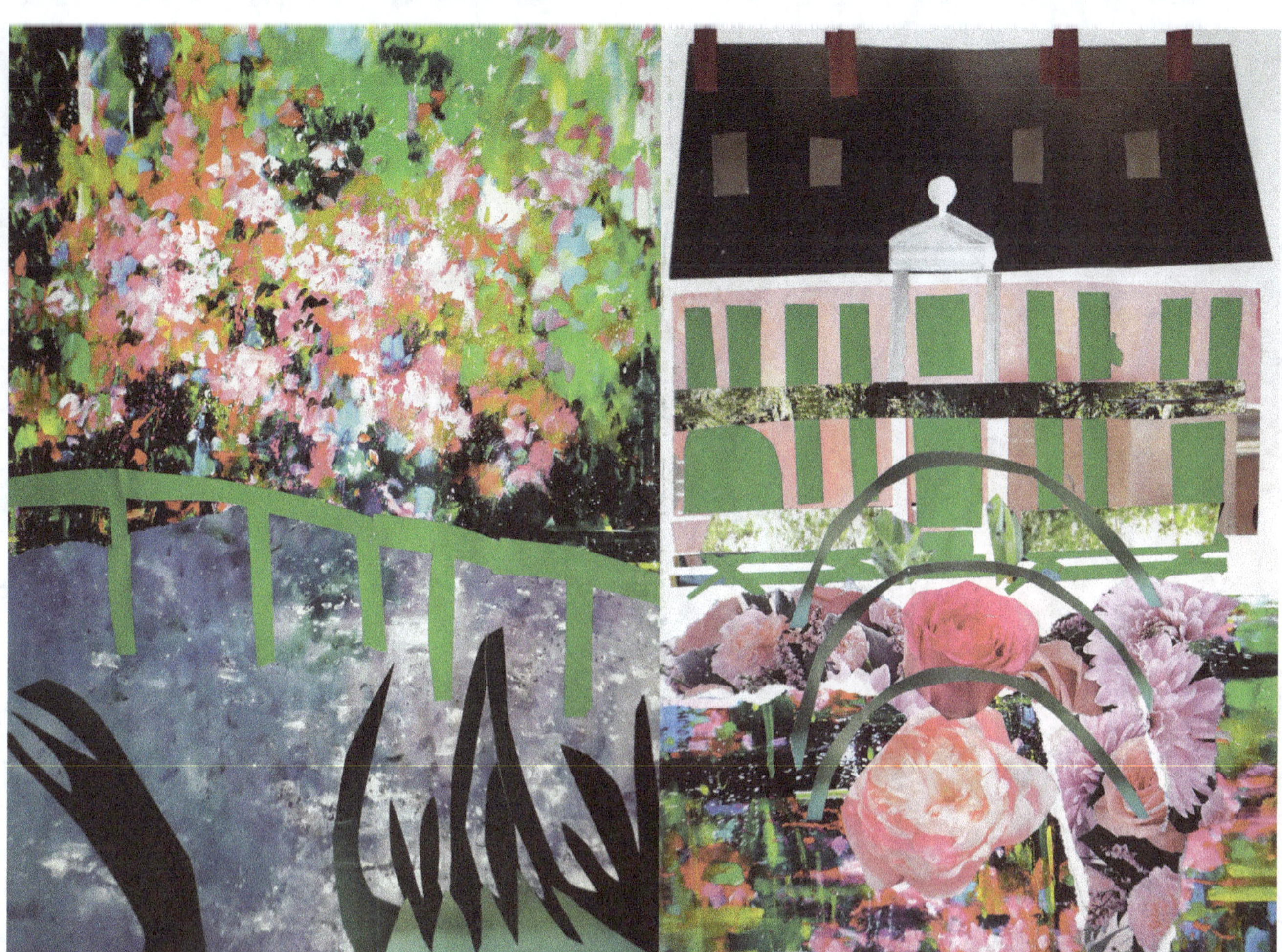

GIVERNY

2020

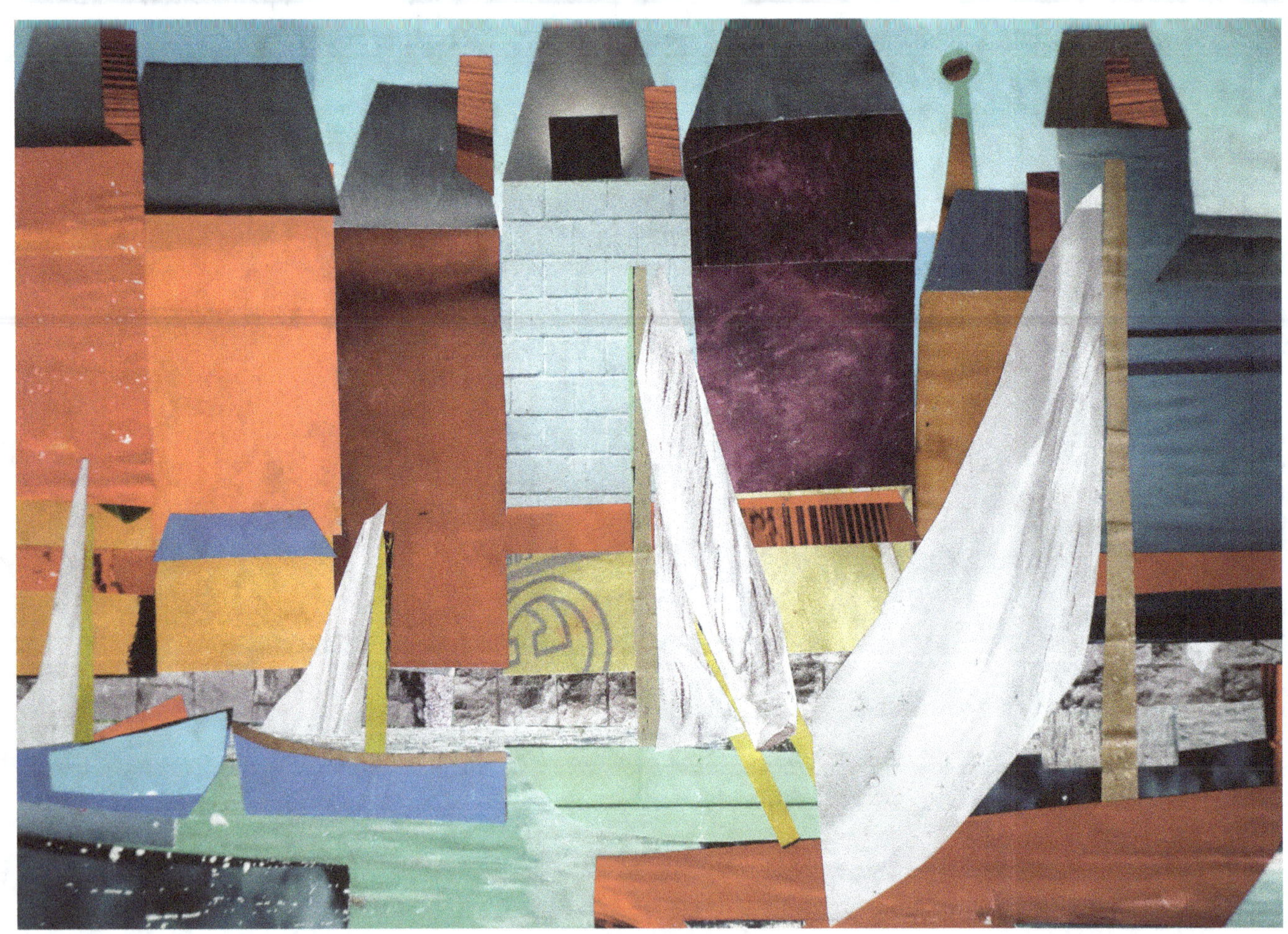

HONFLEUR

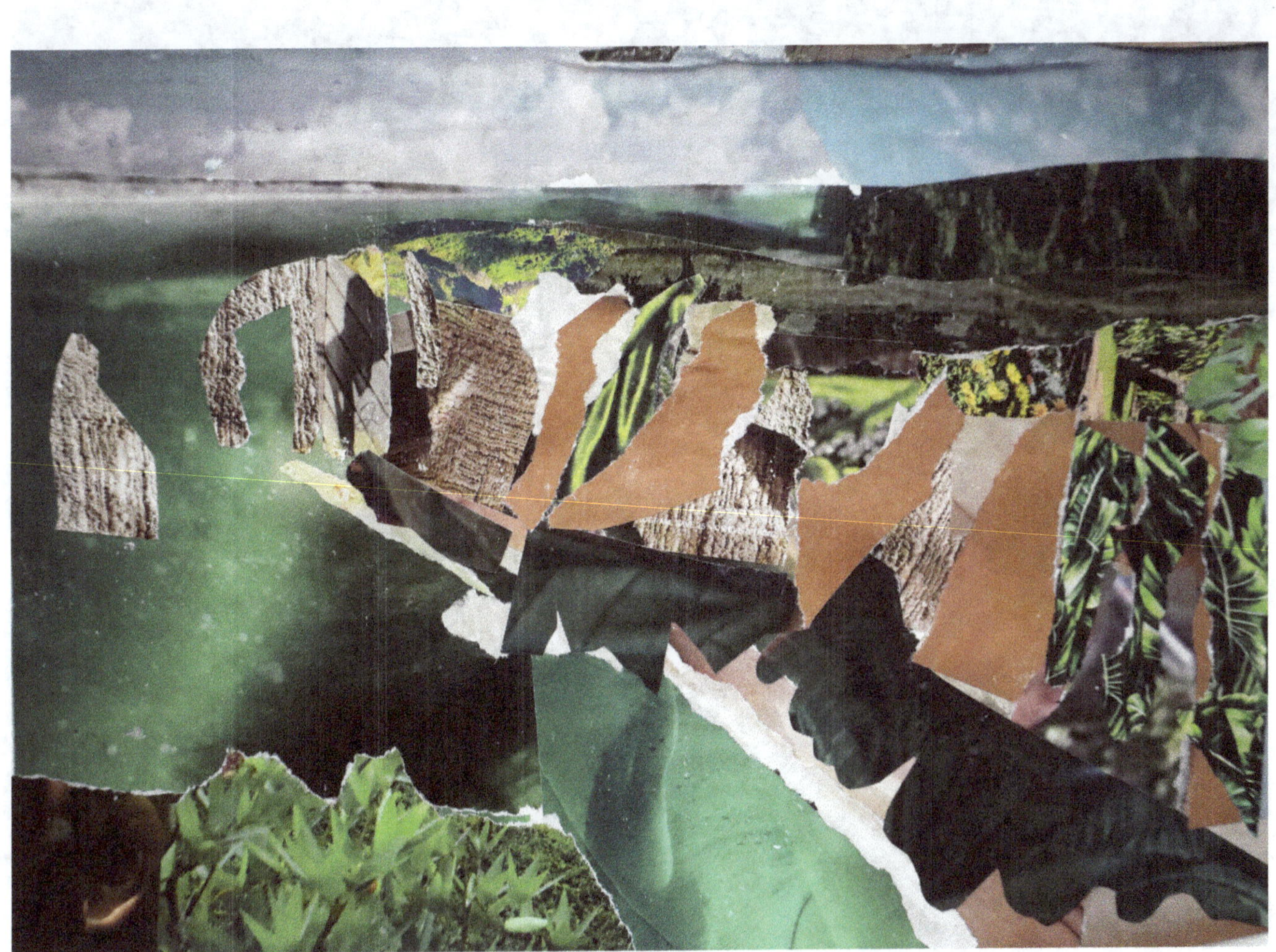

ÉTRETAT

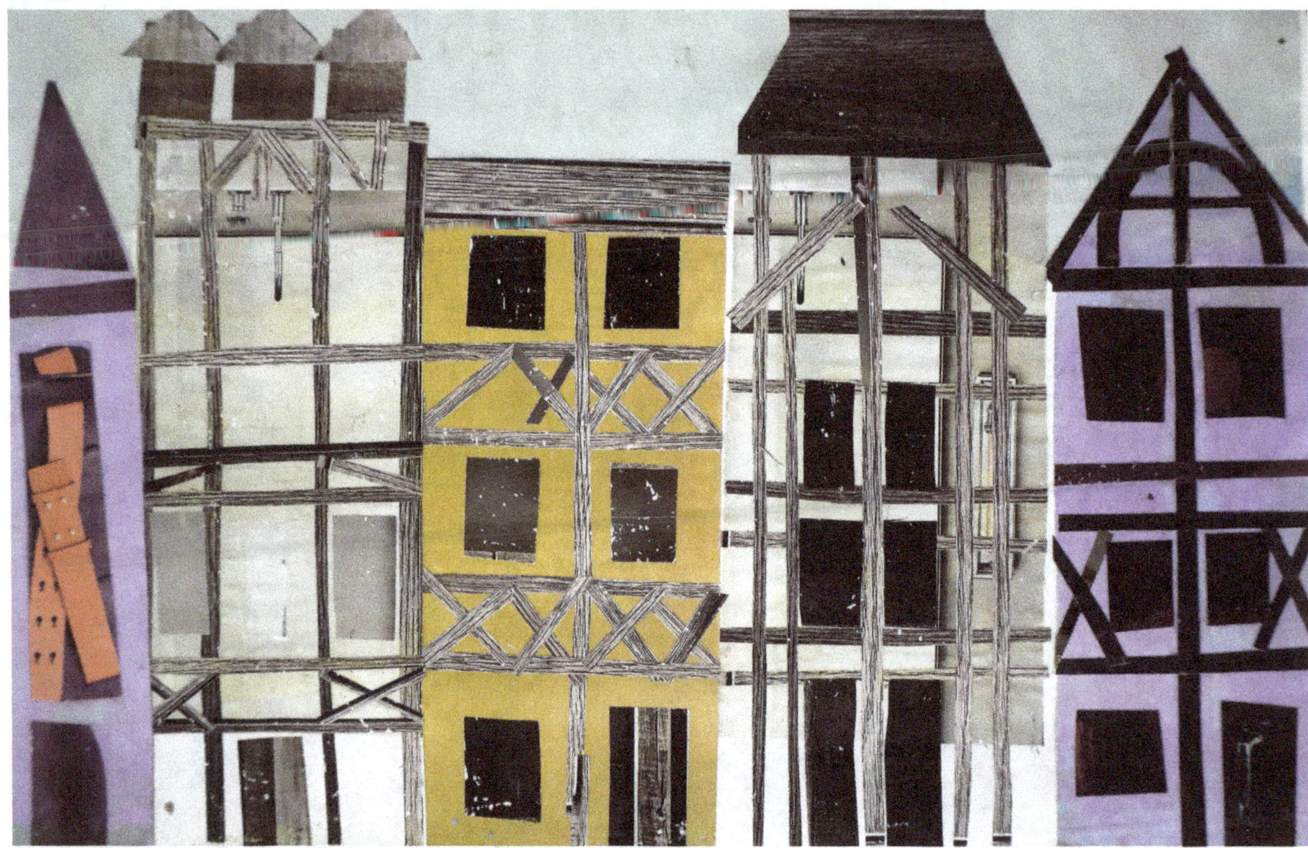

ROUEN

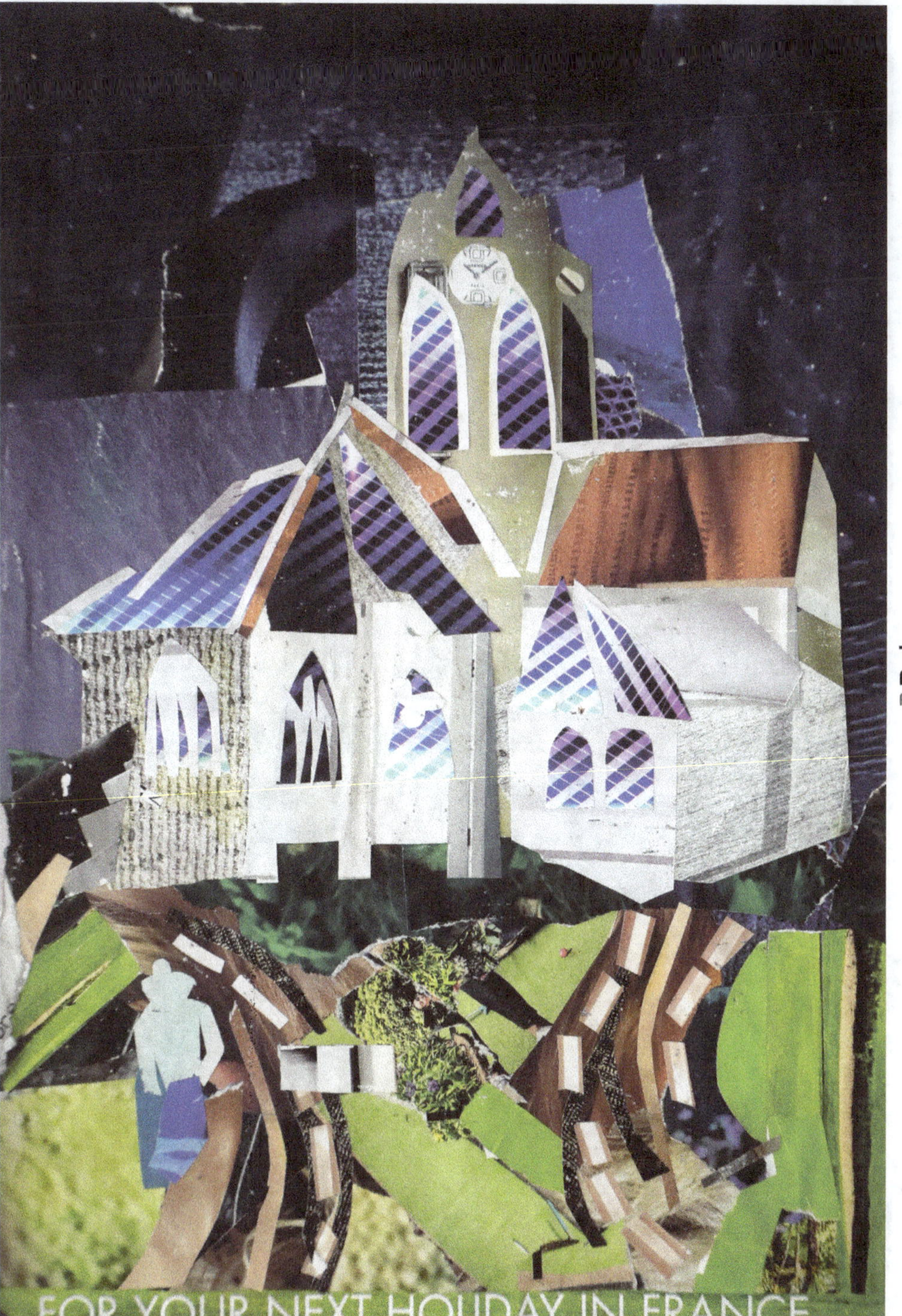

THE CHURCH
AT AUVERS
AUVERS-SUR-OISE

2020

2020

GOOD BYE TOAST

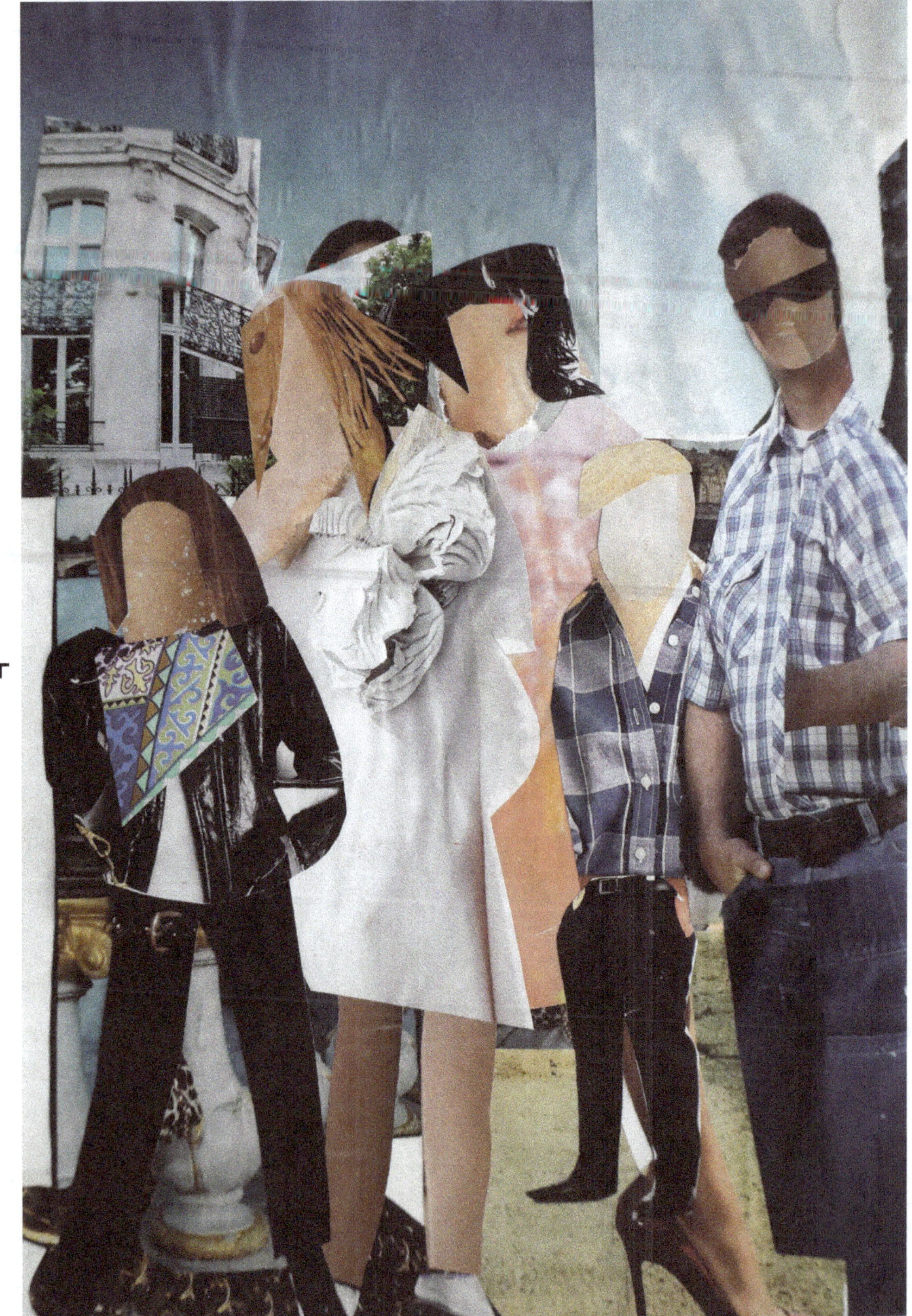

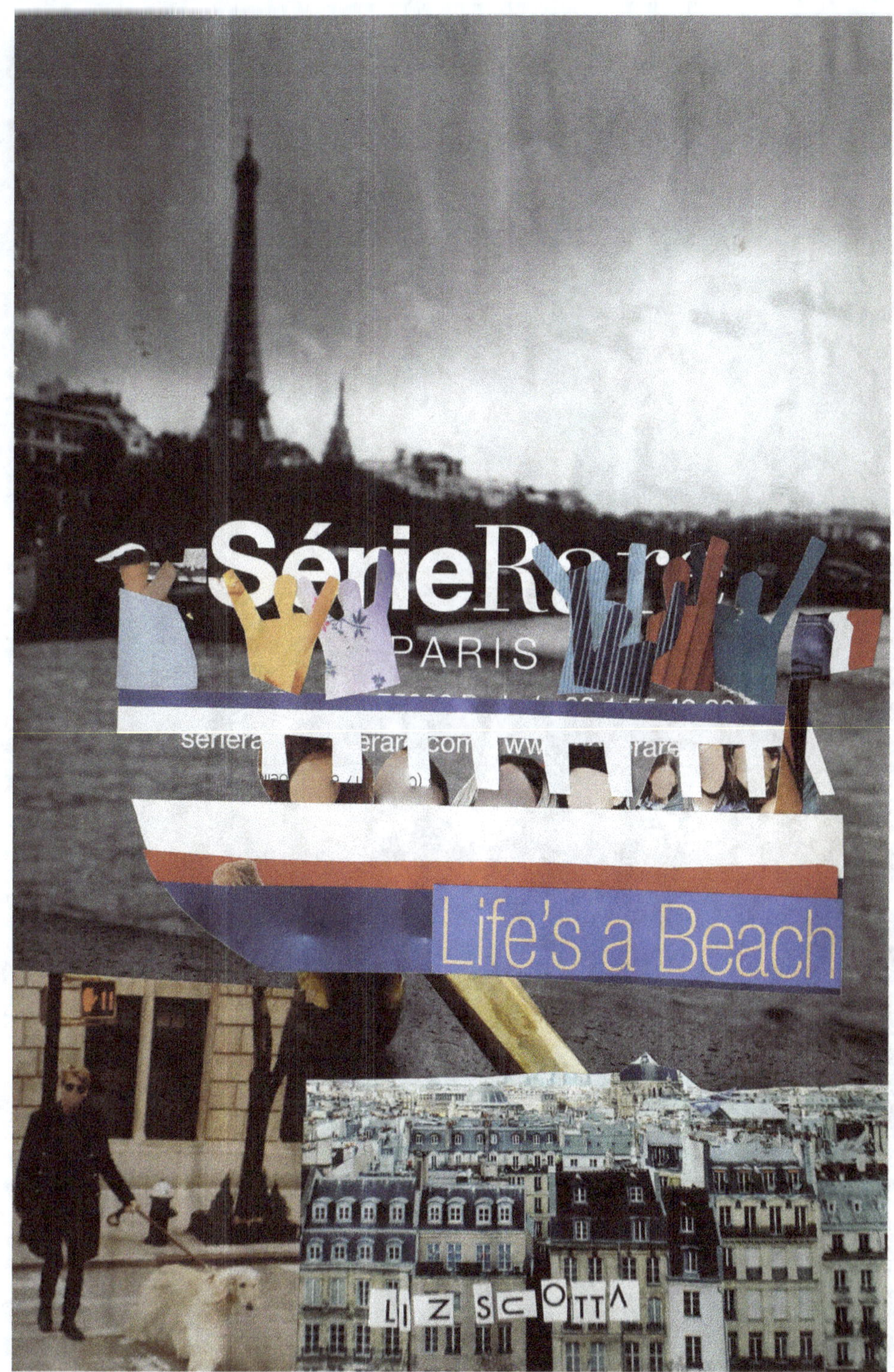

GOOD BYE BOAT RIDE
ON SEINE

2020

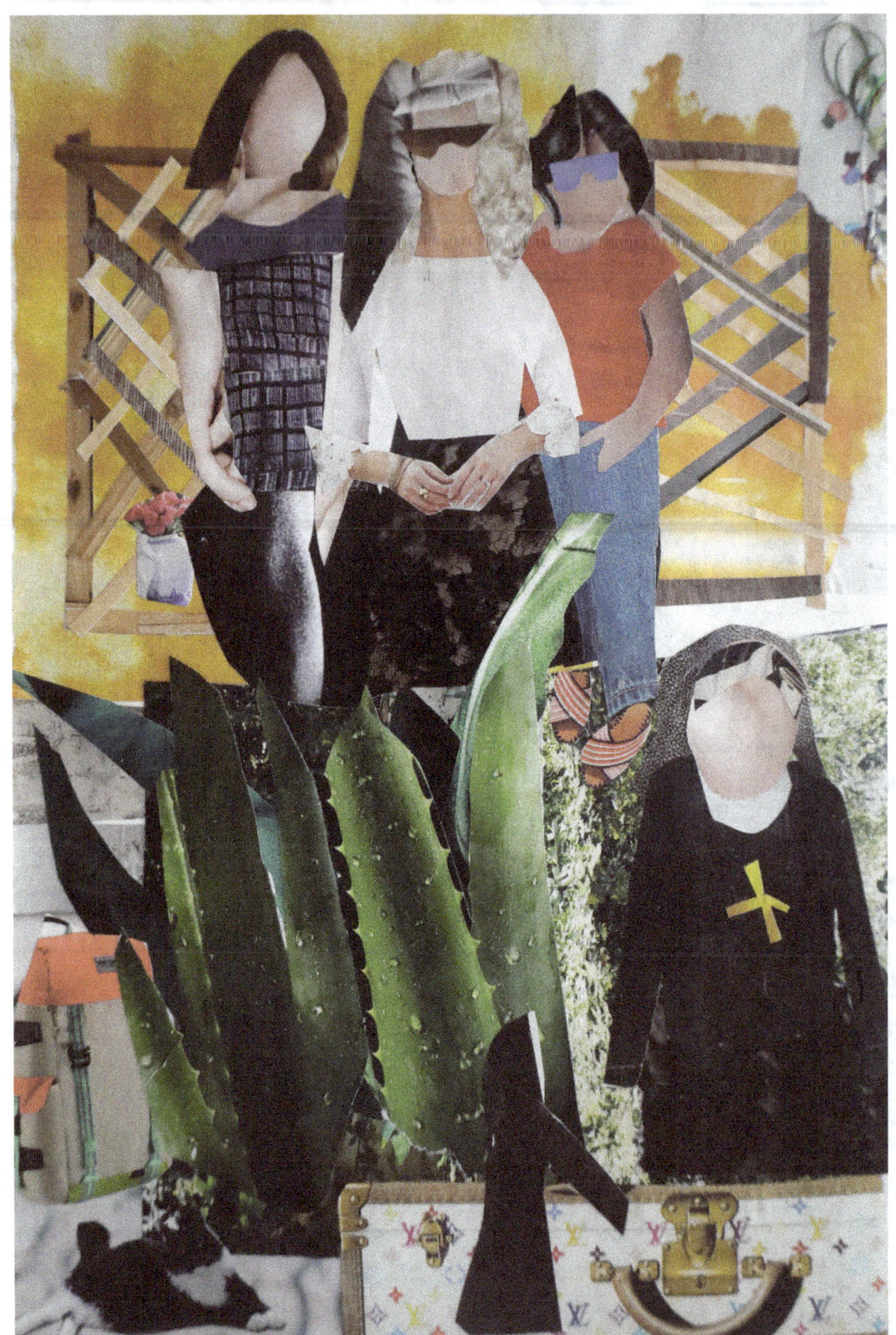

TOASTING THE END
OF MY
VIRTUAL VACATION

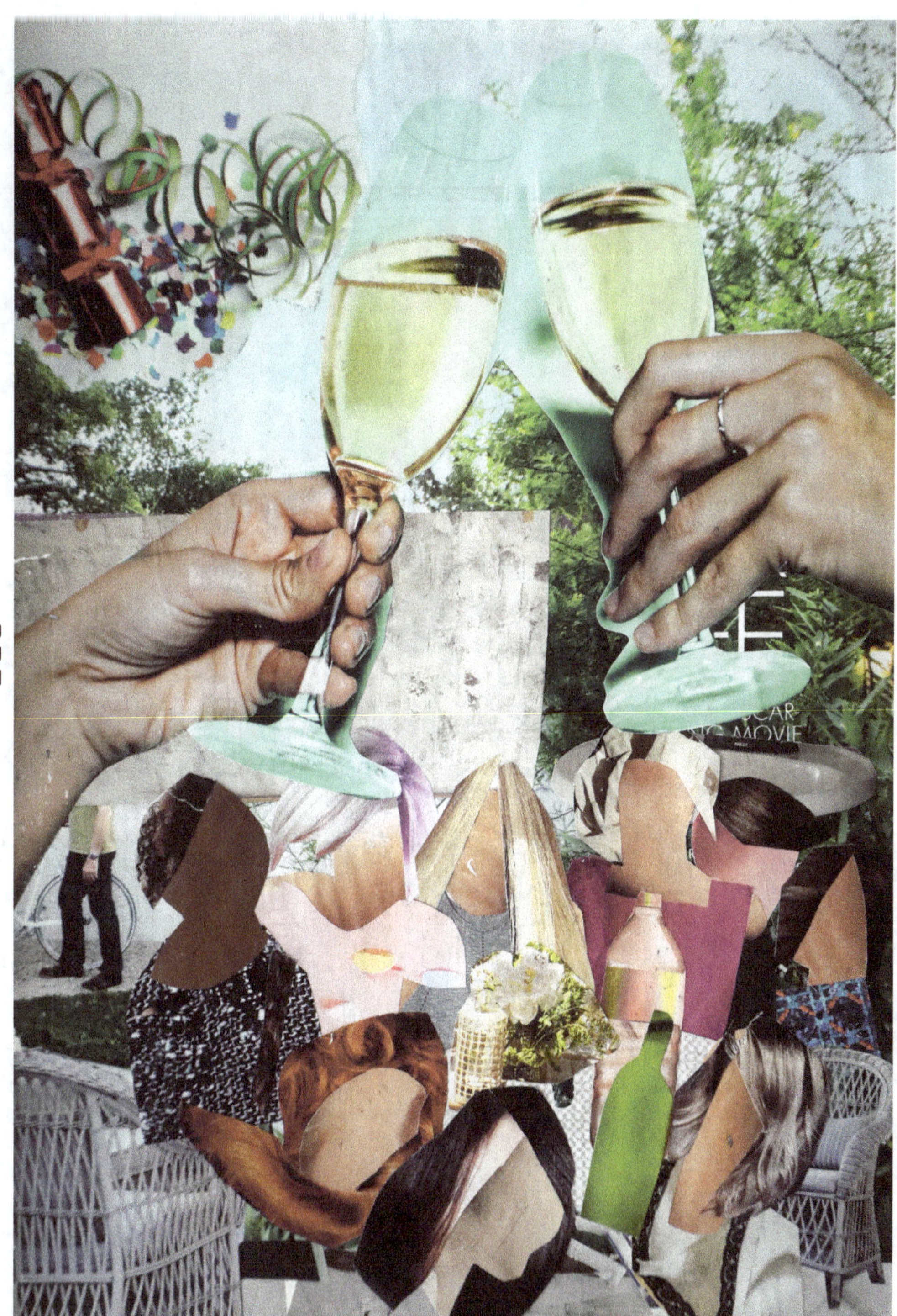

TOASTING THE END
OF MY
VIRTUAL VACATION

2020

2021

CAISSE DE EPARGNE AND CHAPELLE SAINTE-MARIE
NEVERS

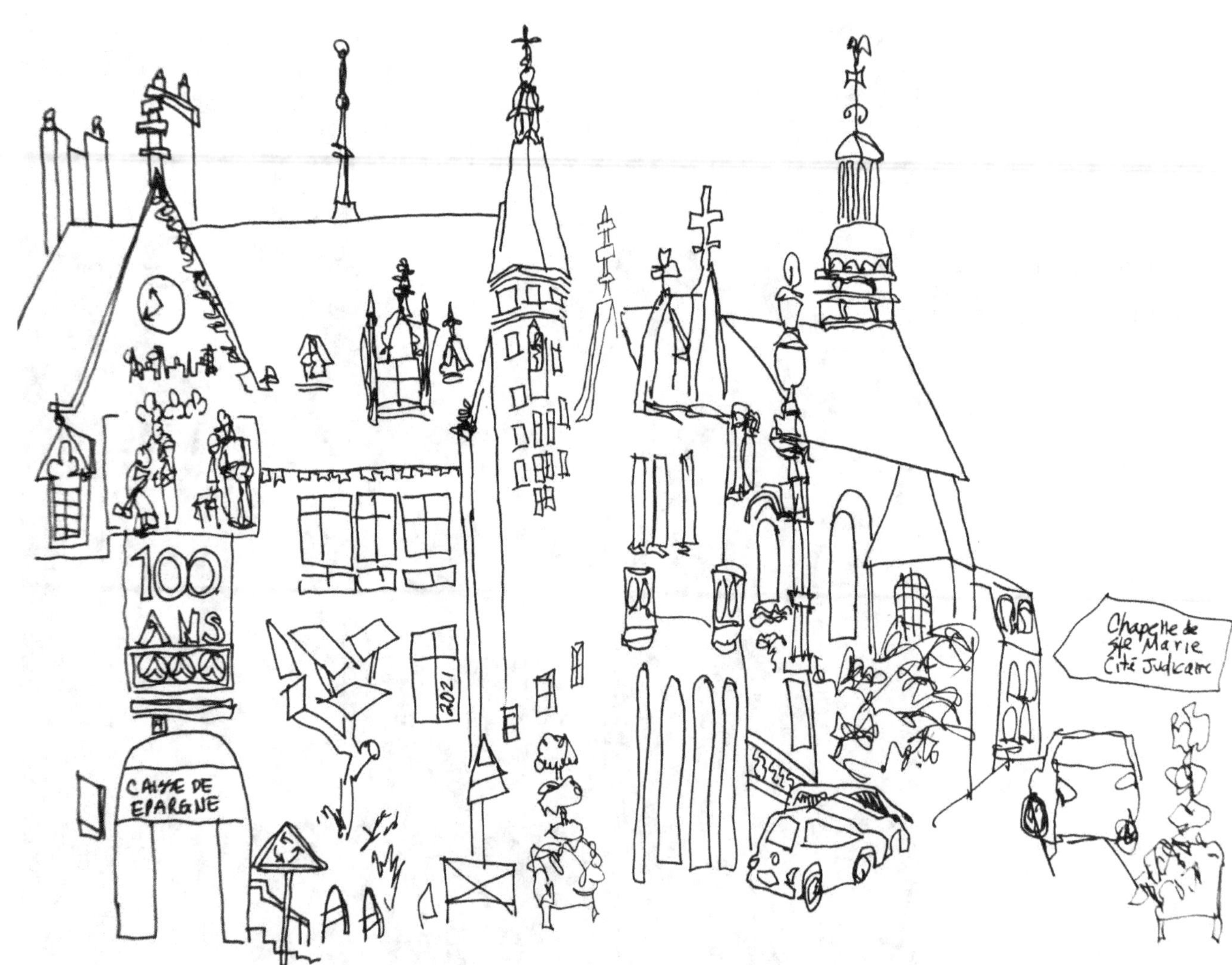

BAR HÔTEL DE NEVERS
NEVERS

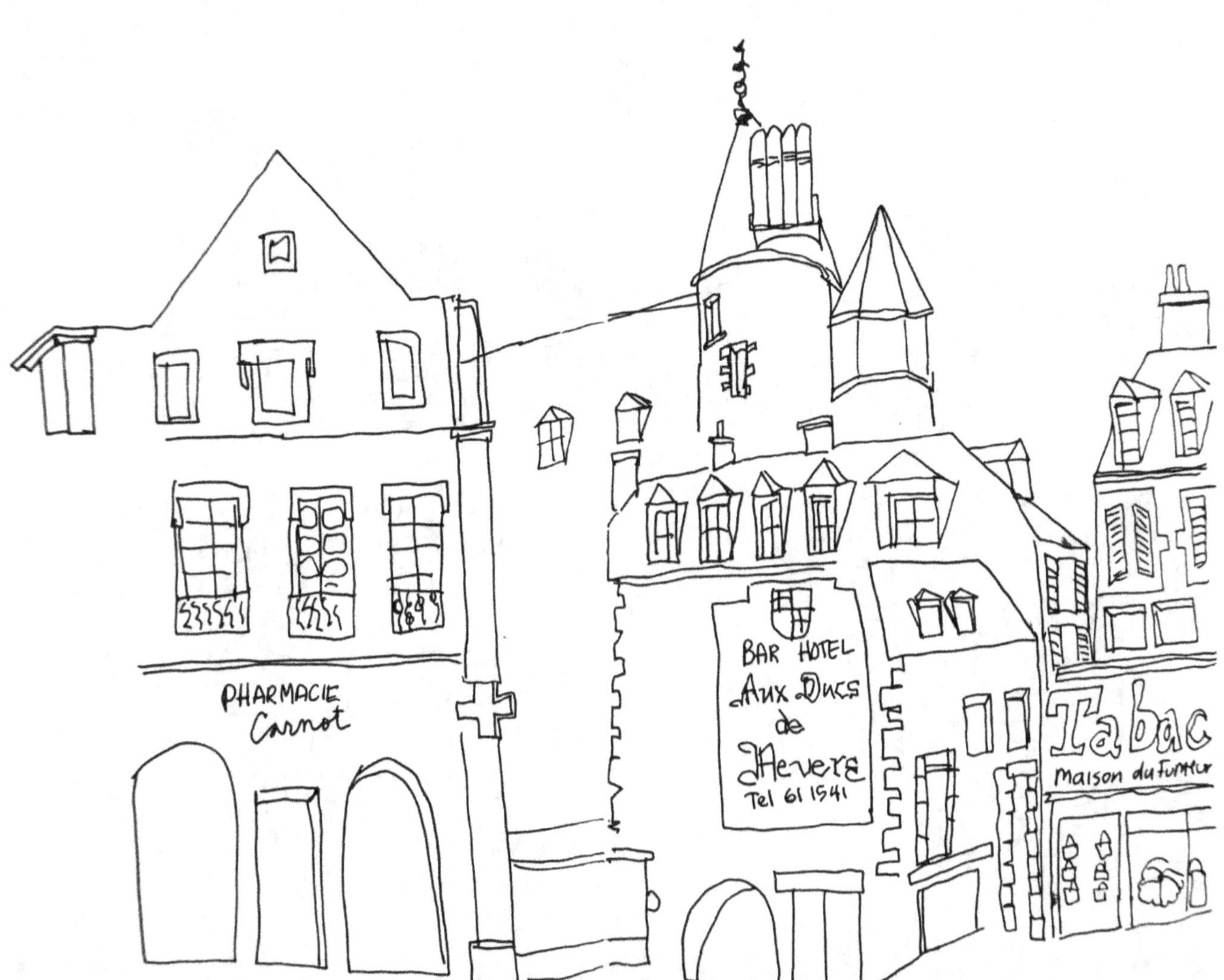

2021

HOTEL D'ANGLETERRE
BOURGES

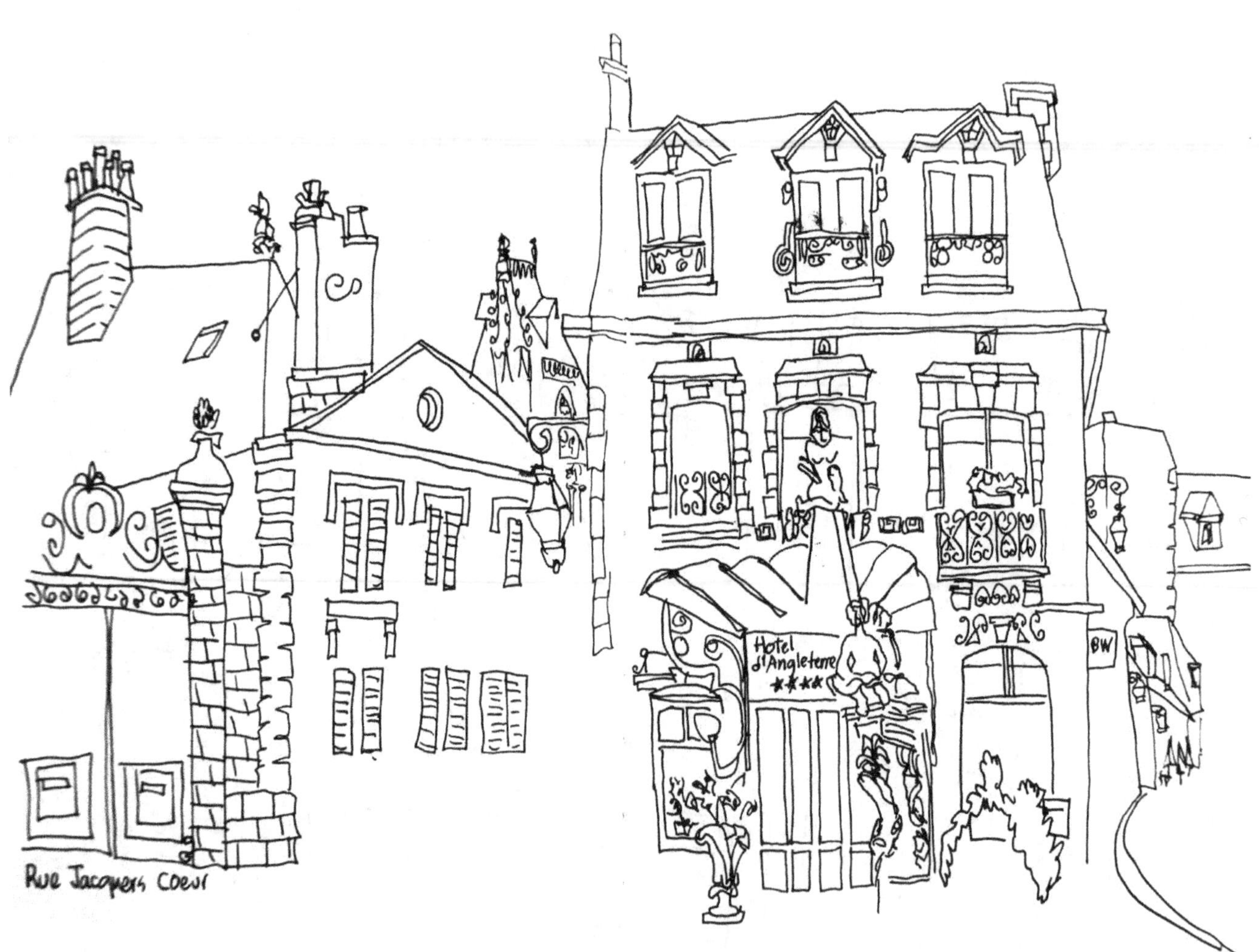

BOURGES

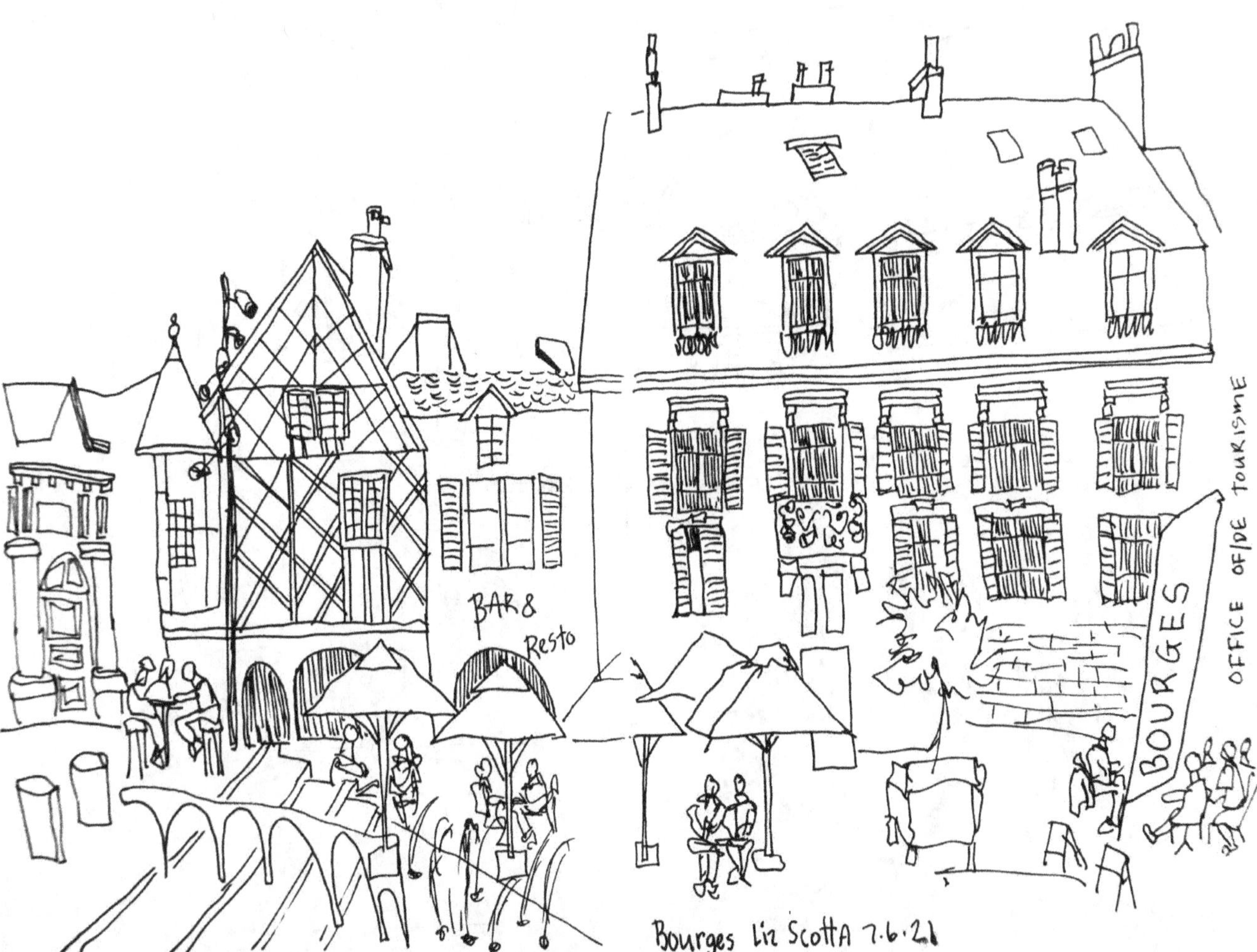

Bourges Liz Scotta 7.6.21

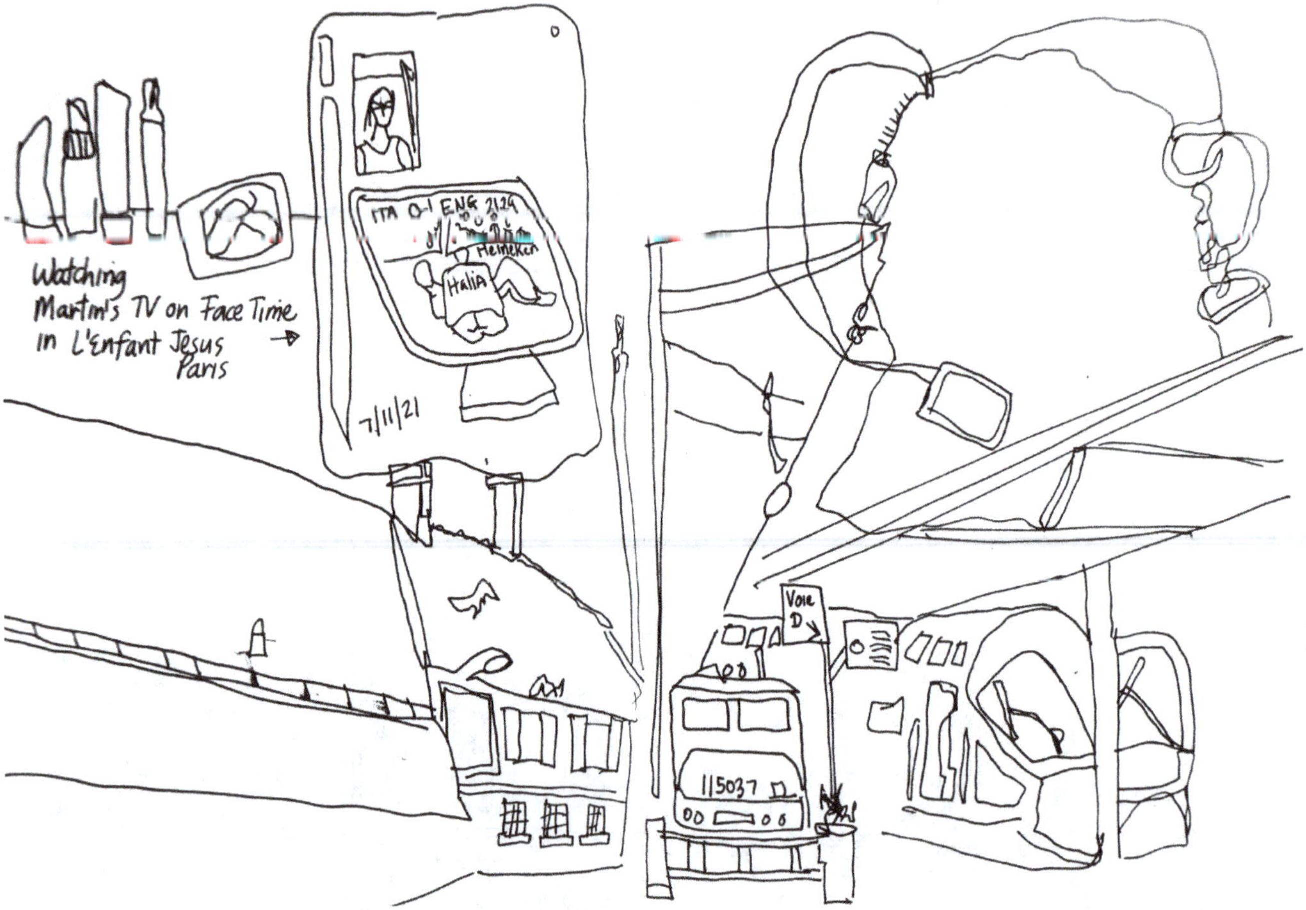

Watching
Martin's TV on Face Time
in L'Enfant Jesus
Paris →

7/11/21

TRAINS AND GAMES

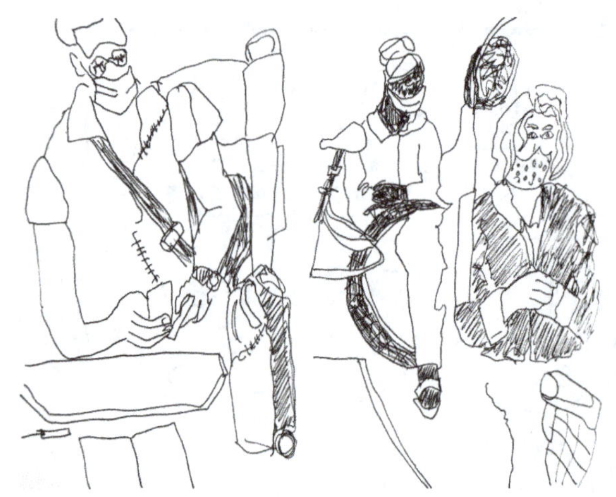

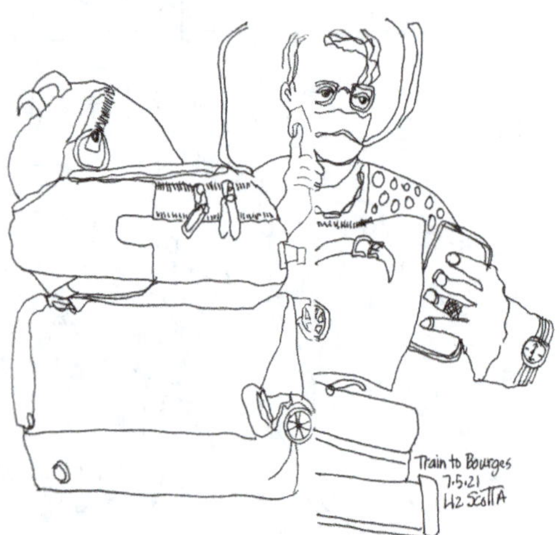

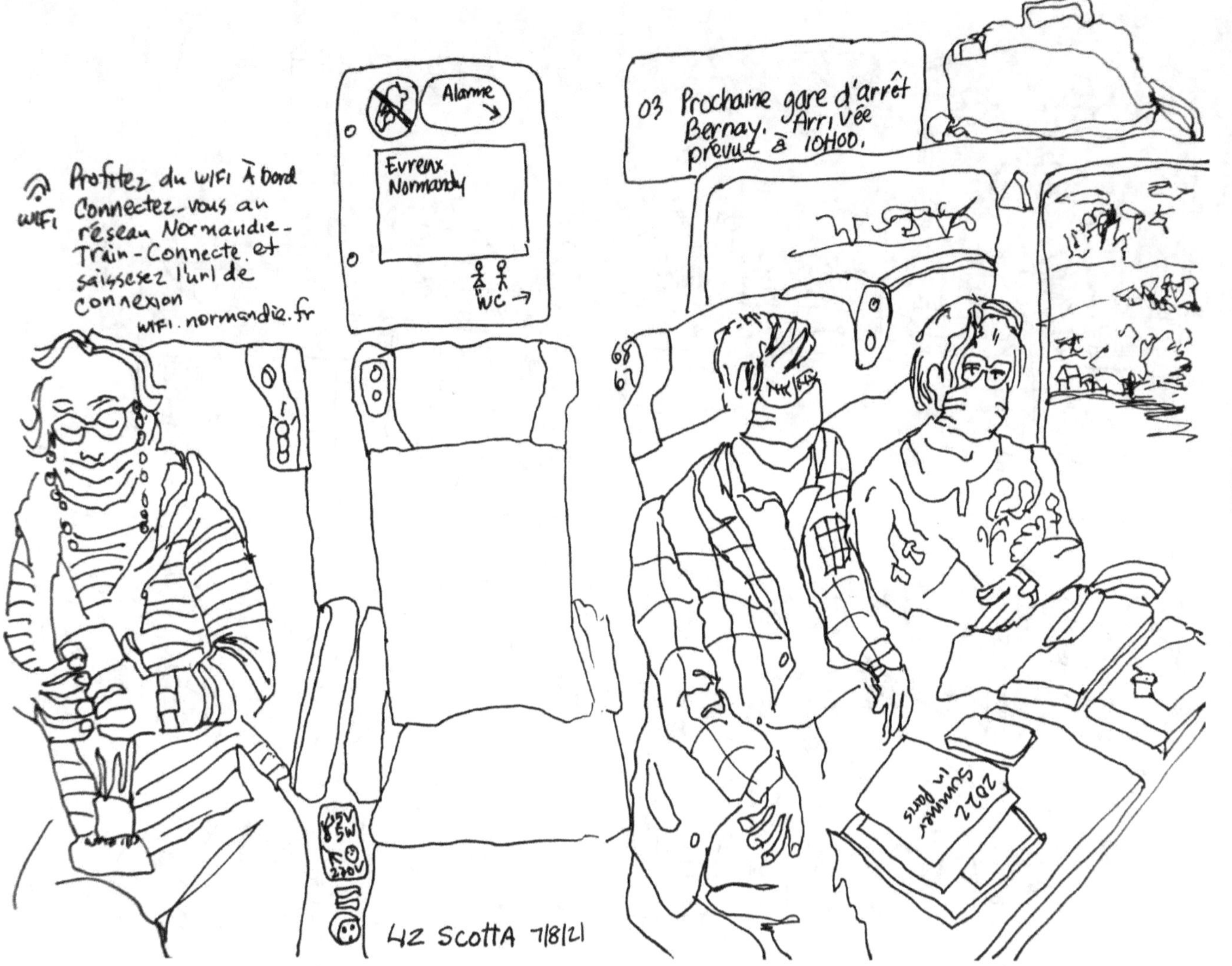

TRAIN TO NORMANDY

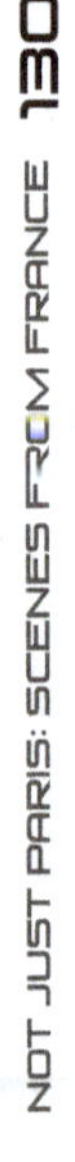

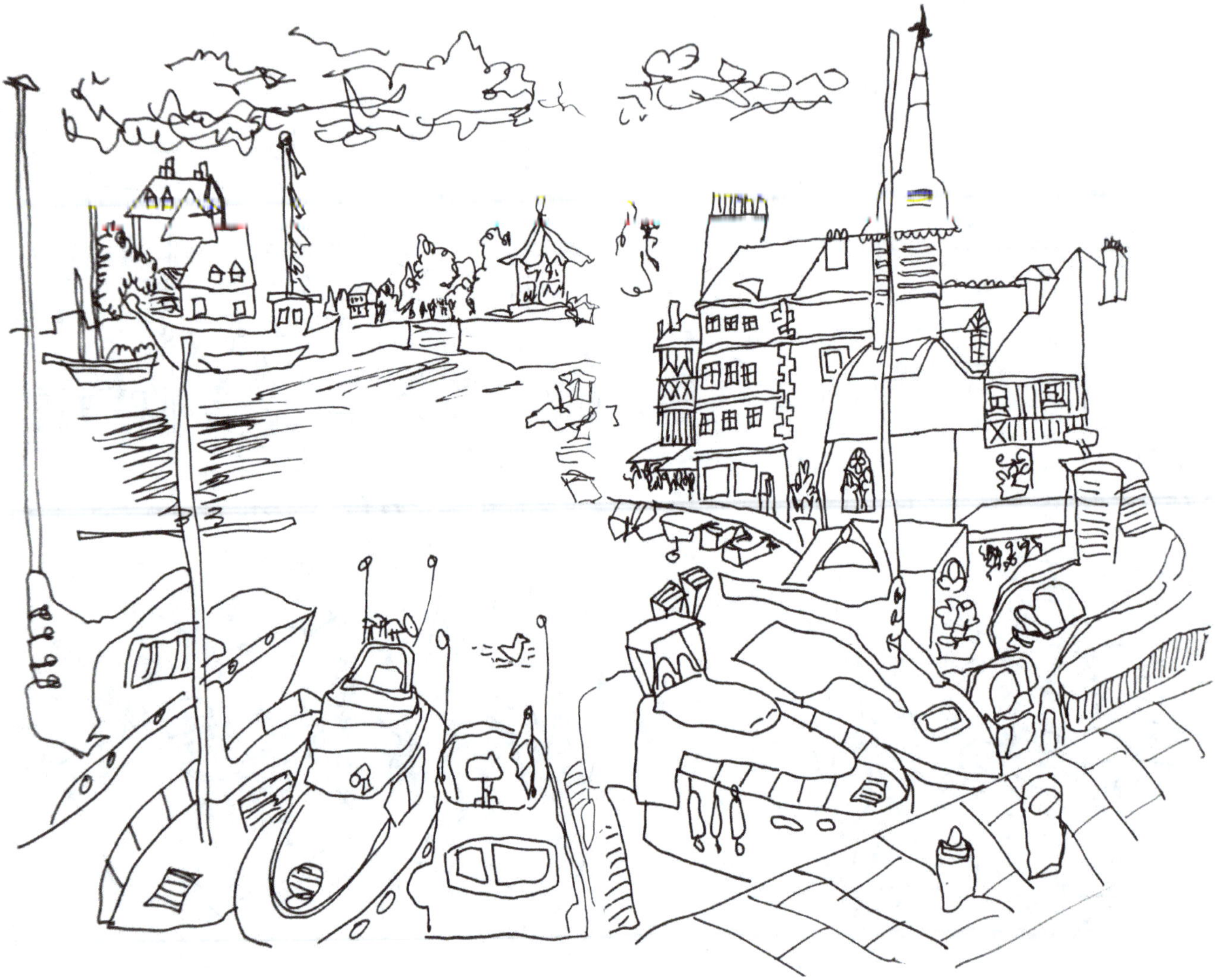

HONFLEUR HARBOR

PROMENADE EN
MAR
Decouverte du
Pont de
Normandie
le
bistro
du port
Honfleur
LIZ
SCOTTA

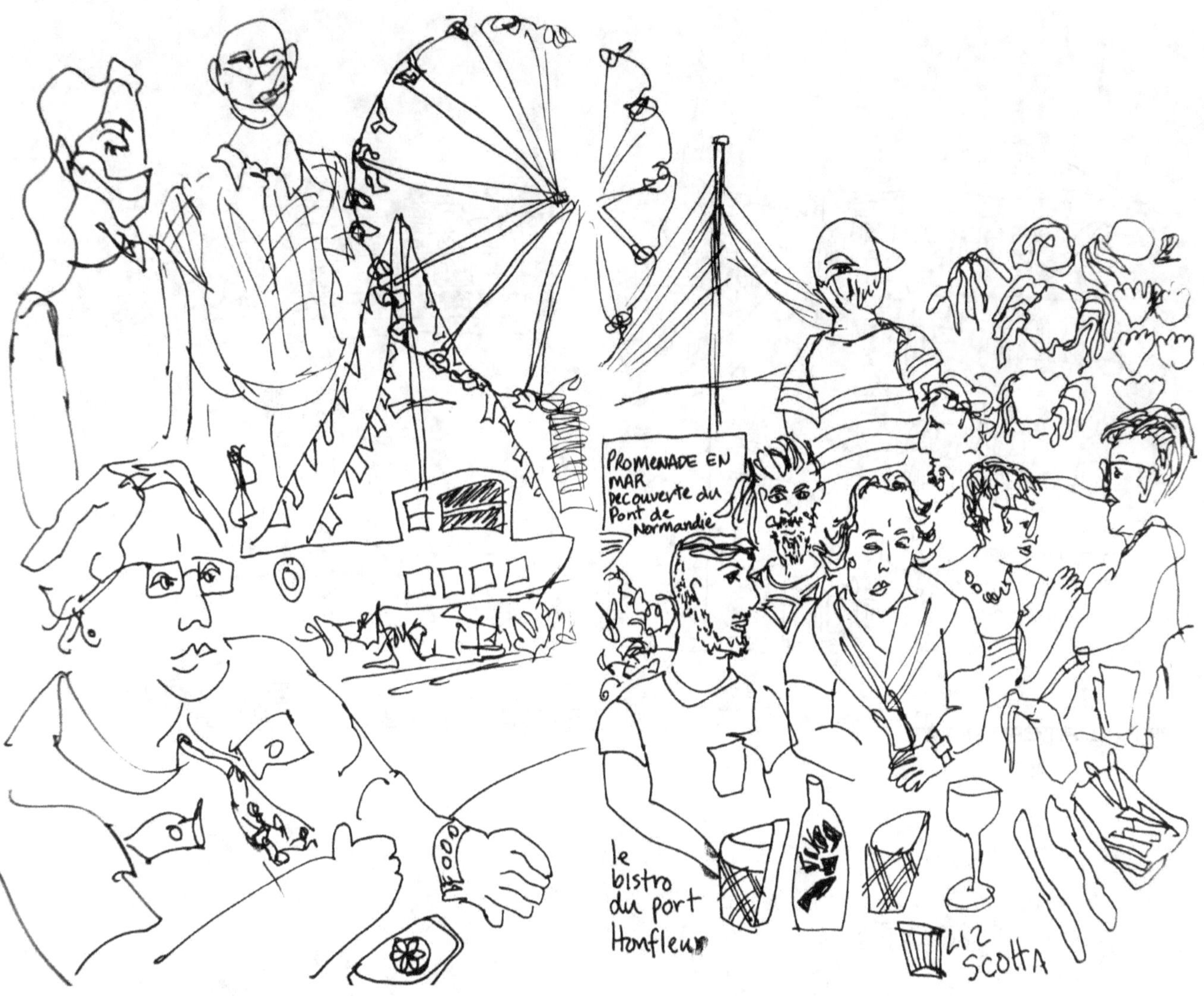

HONFLEUR

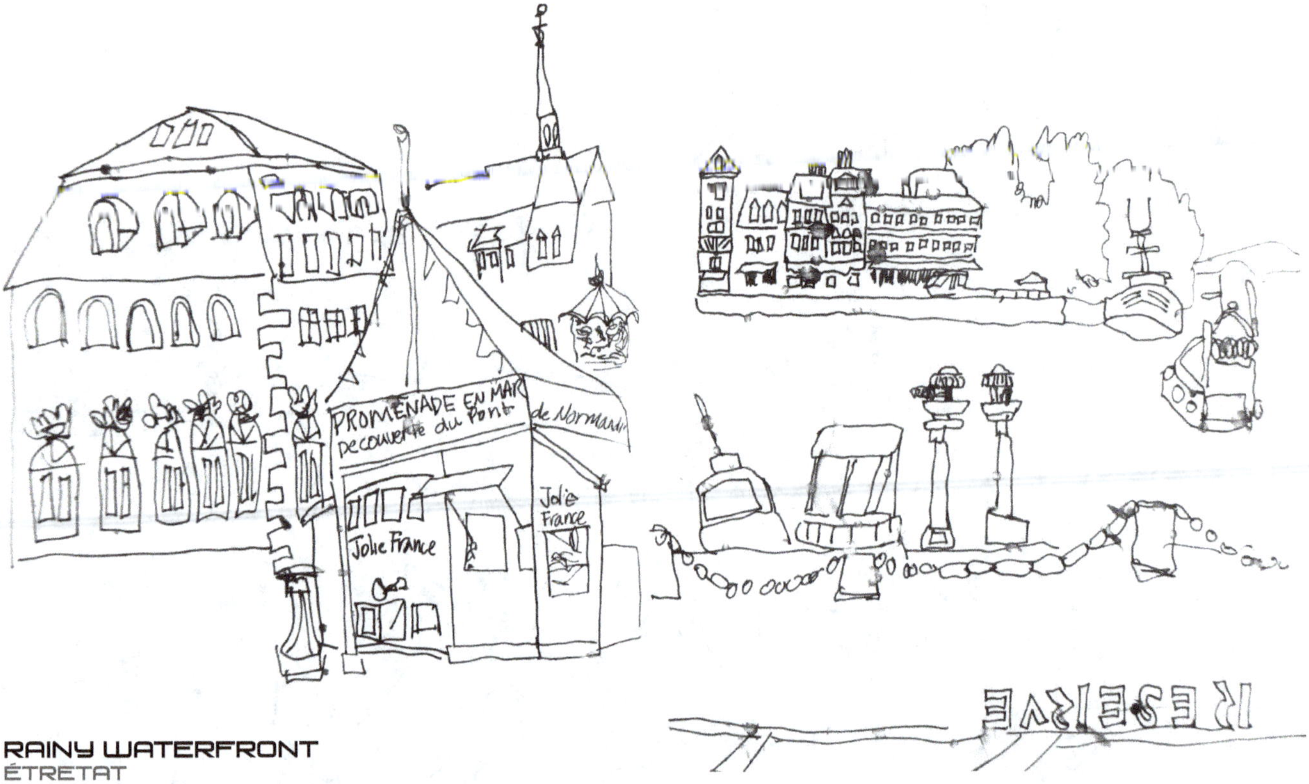

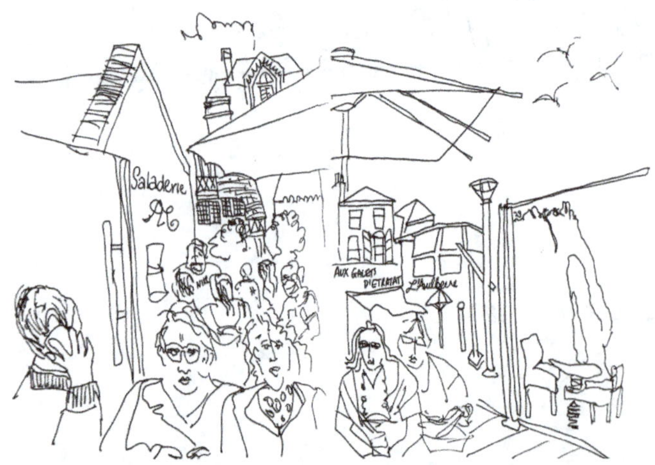

RAINY WATERFRONT
ÉTRETAT

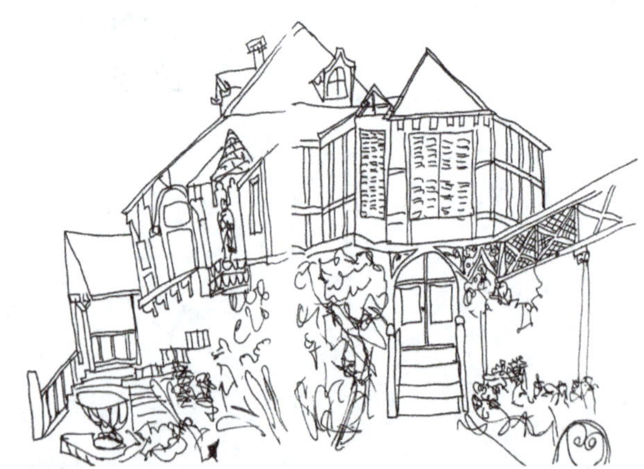

SEAFOOD RESTAURANT
ÉTRETAT

MAISON LEBLANC (ARSÈNE LUPIN HOUSE)
ÉTRETAT

FRIENDS

BULLETIN BOARD

2021

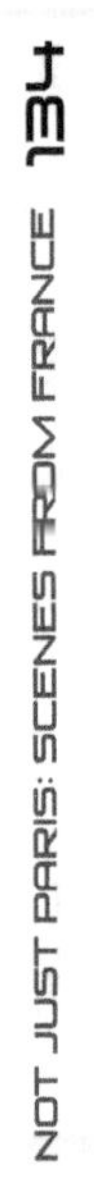

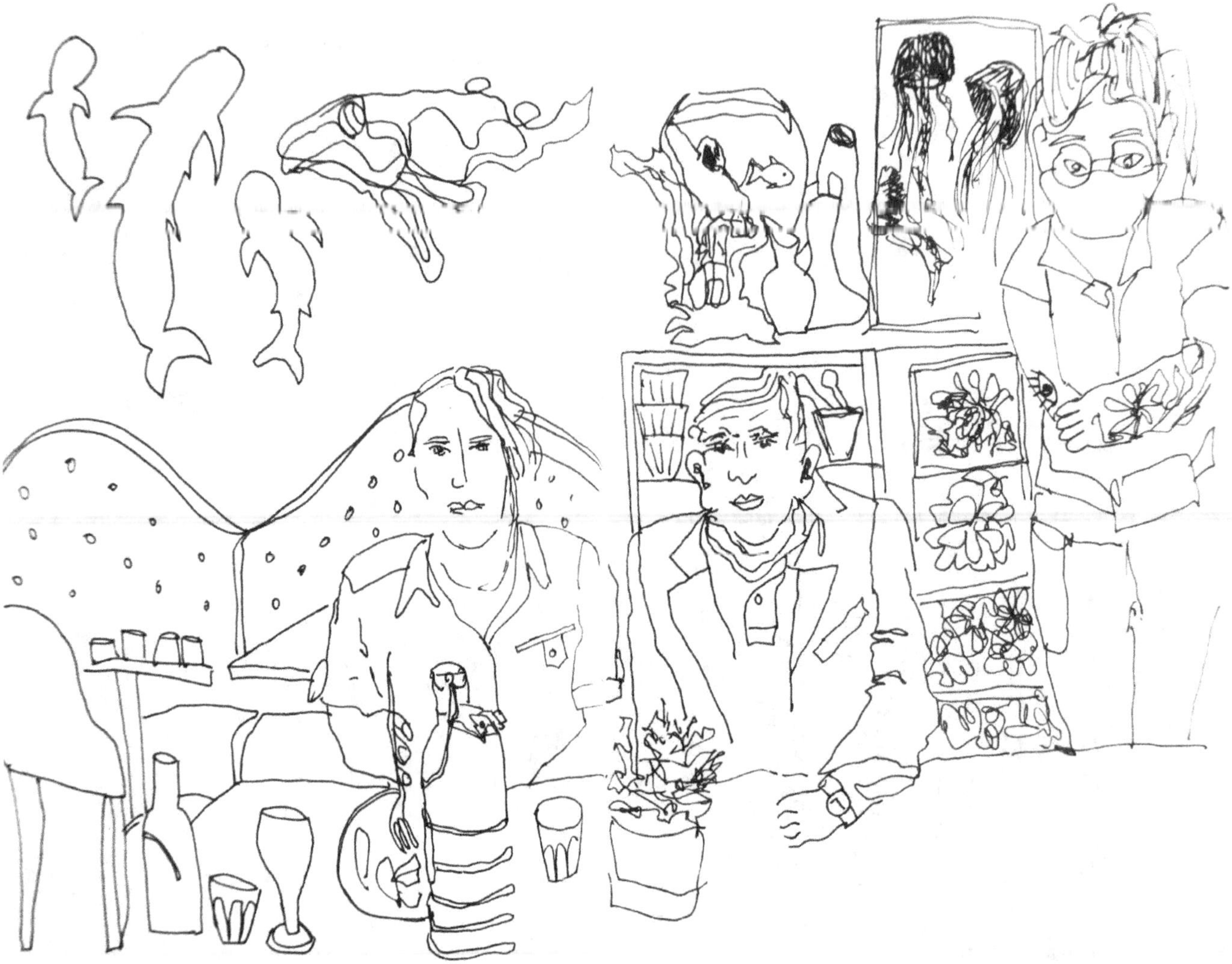

SEAFOOD RESTAURANT
BAYEUX

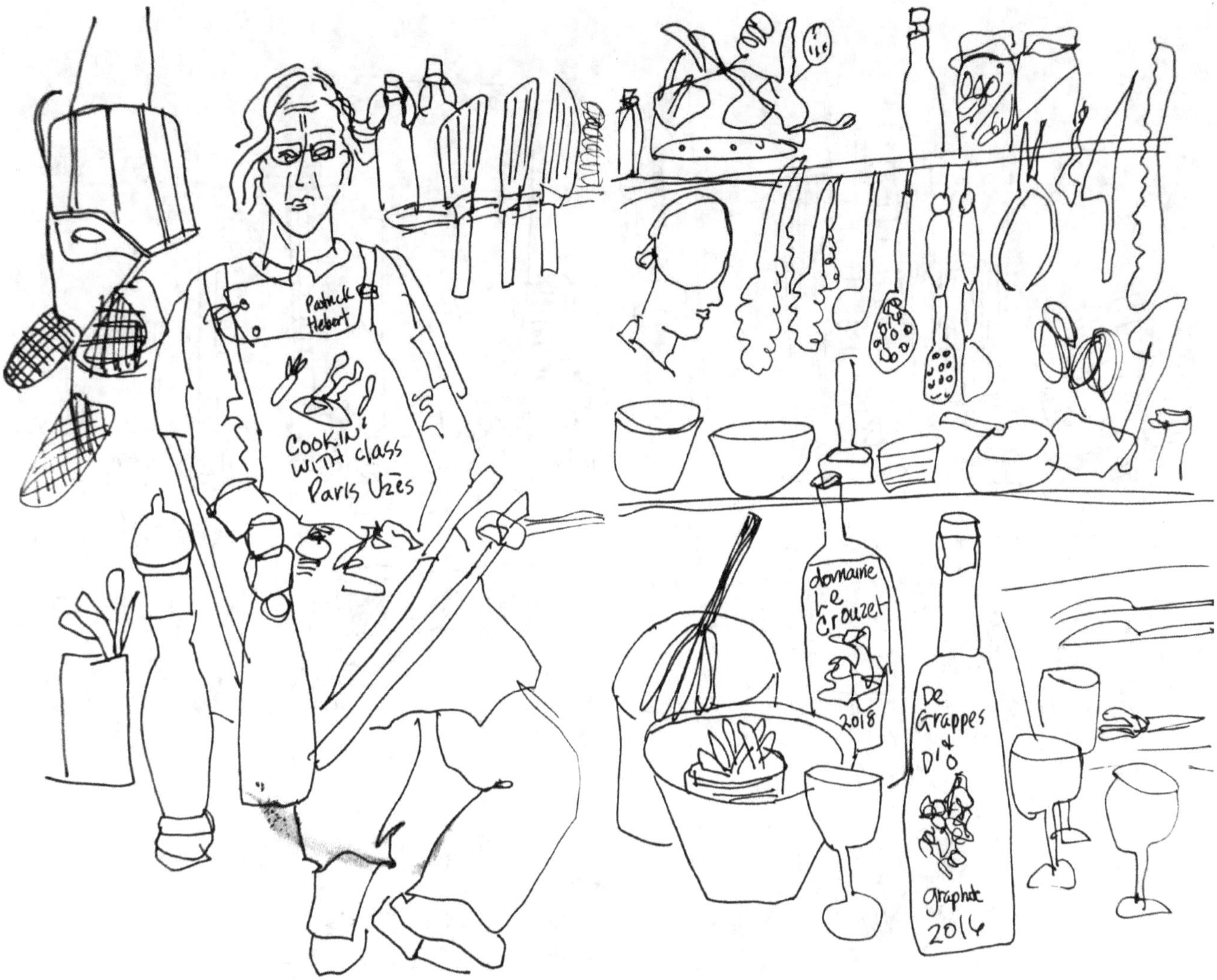

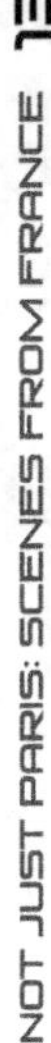

COOKING WITH CLASS SCHOOL
PARIS

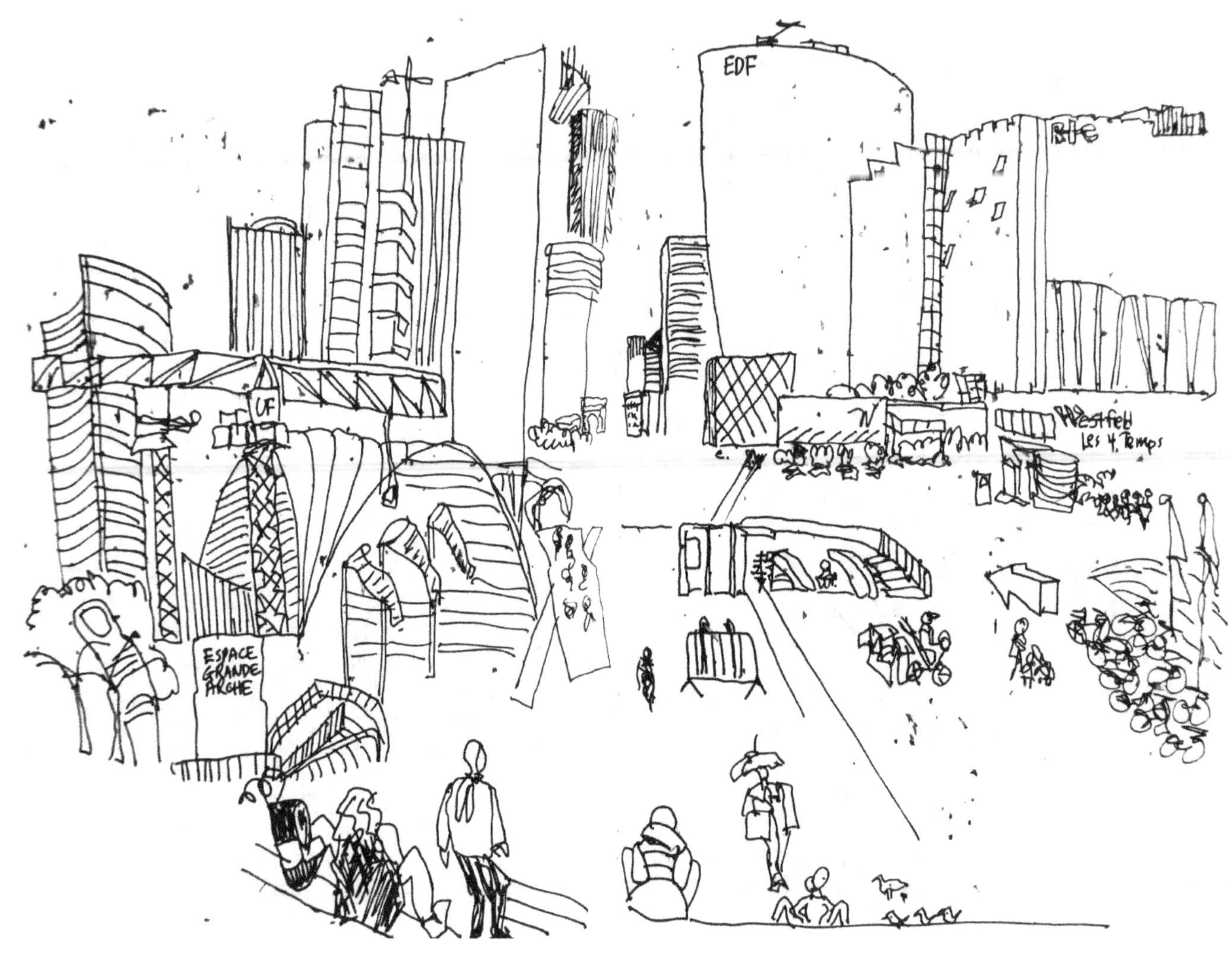

VIEW FROM LA DÉFENSE
PARIS

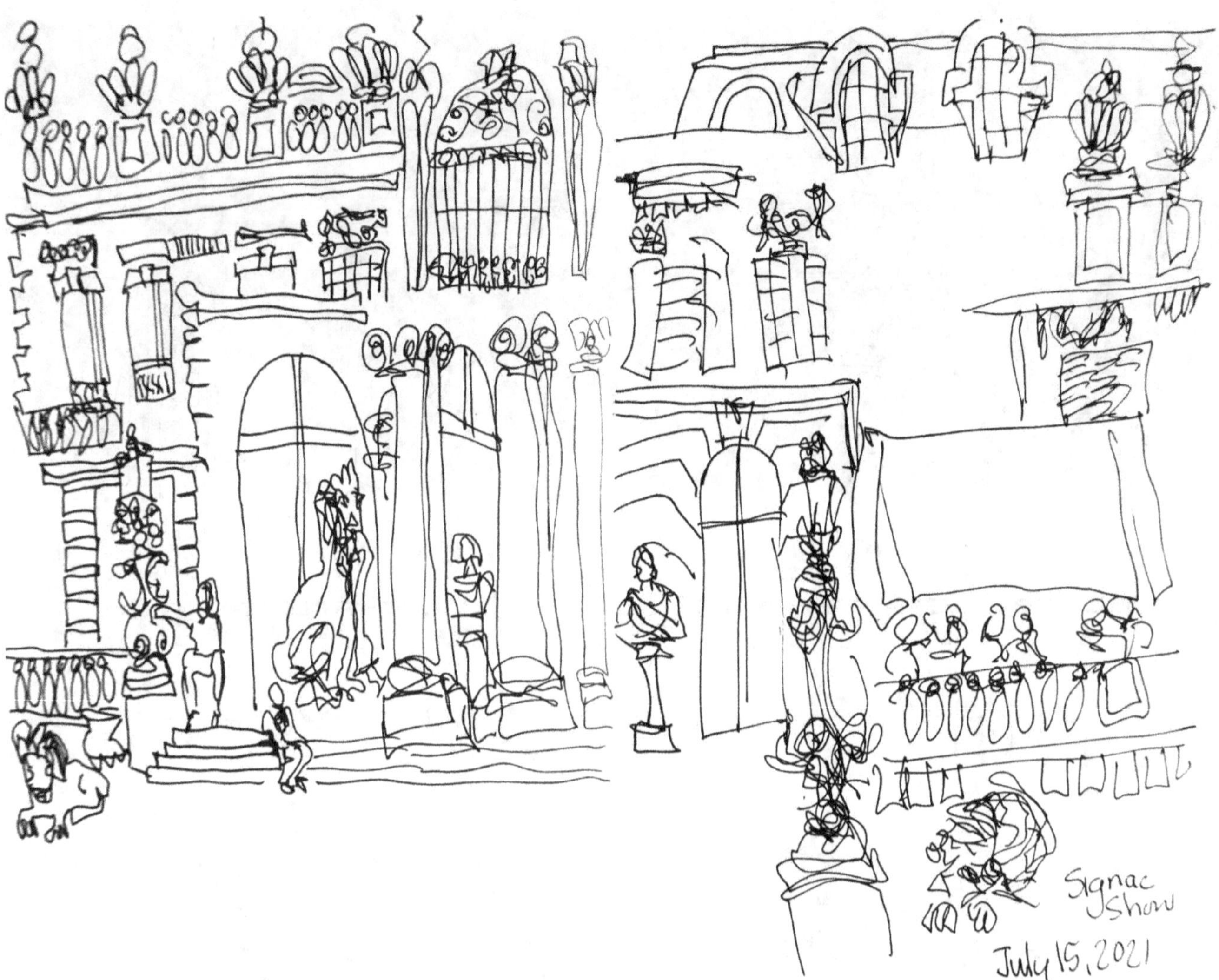

MUSÉE JACQUEMART-ANDRÉ
PARIS

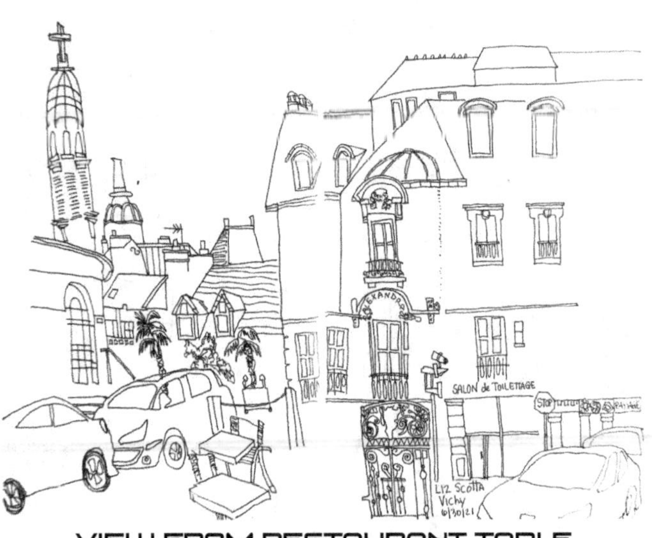

VIEW FROM RESTAURANT TABLE
VICHY

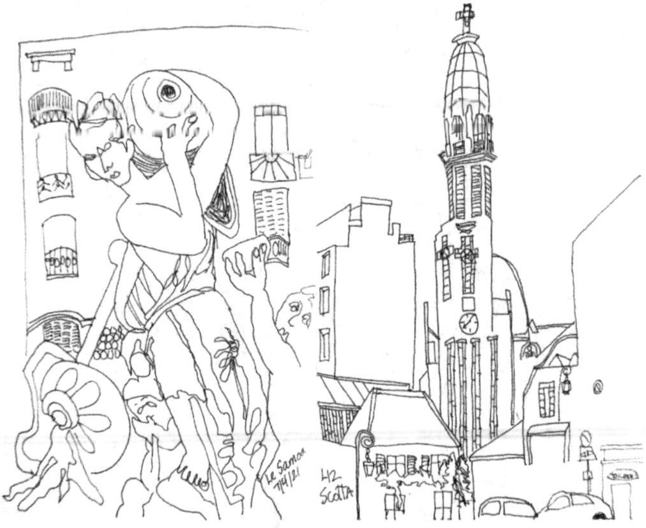

LUNCH AT LE SAMOA
VICHY

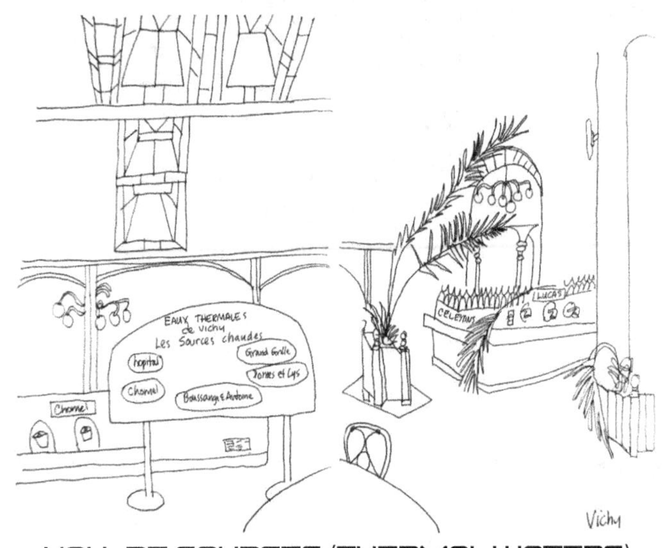

HALL DE SOURCES (THERMAL WATERS)
VICHY

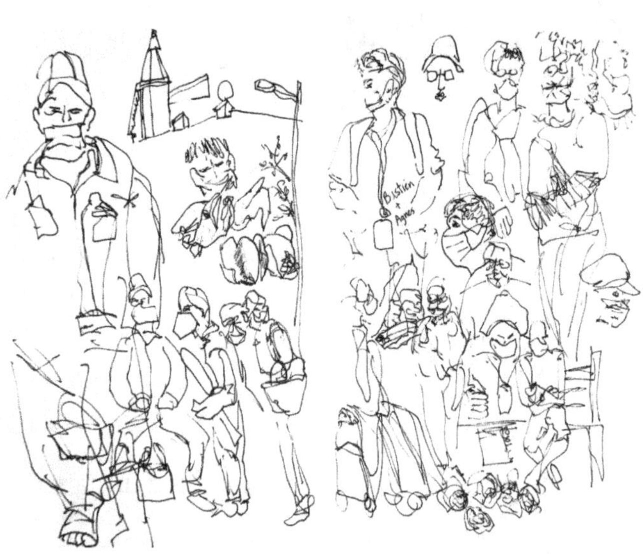

MASKED CUSTOMERS AT MARKET
VICHY

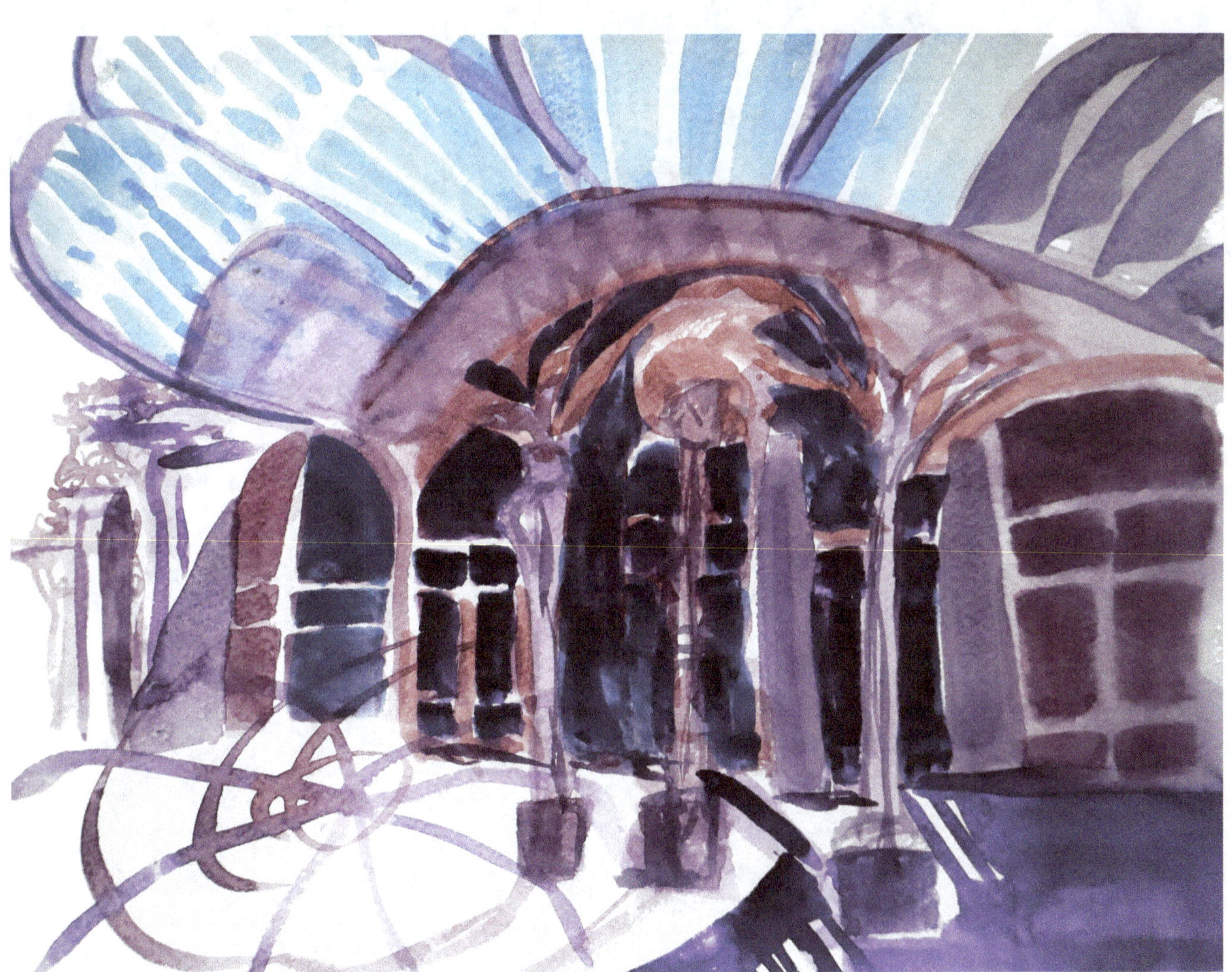

CASINO
VICHY

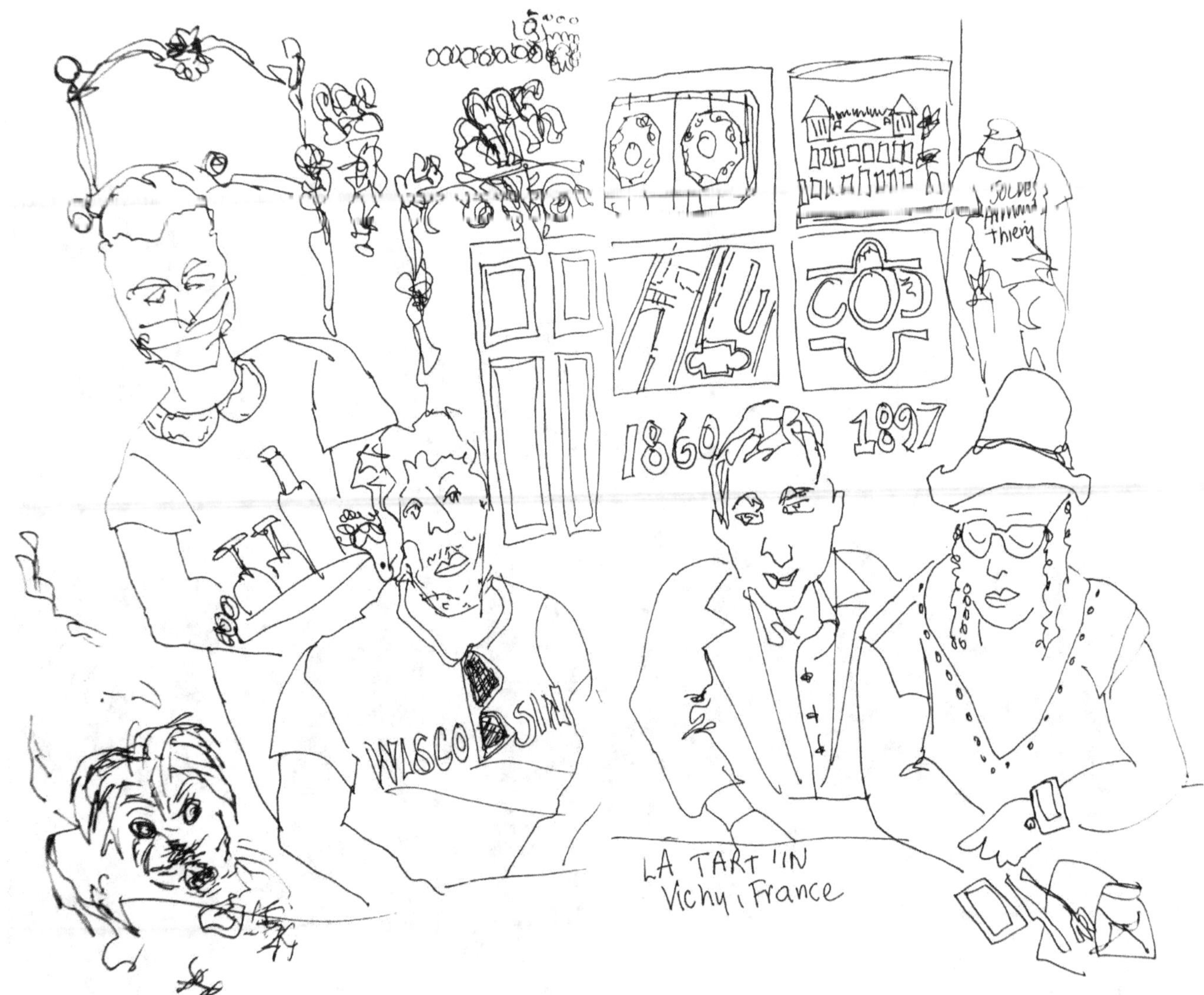

LA TARTIN RESTAURANT VICHY
VICHY

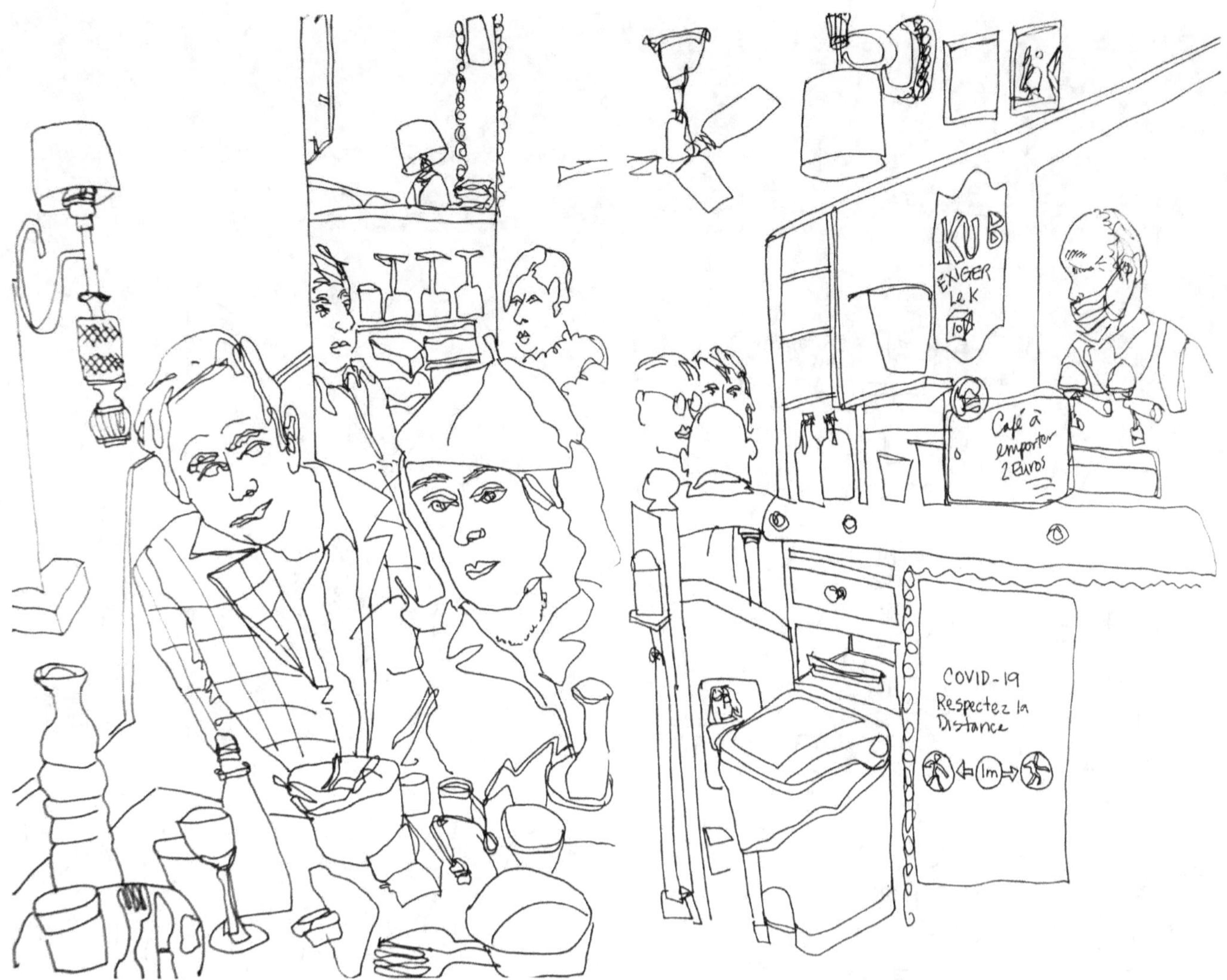

"COVID" DINNER
PARIS

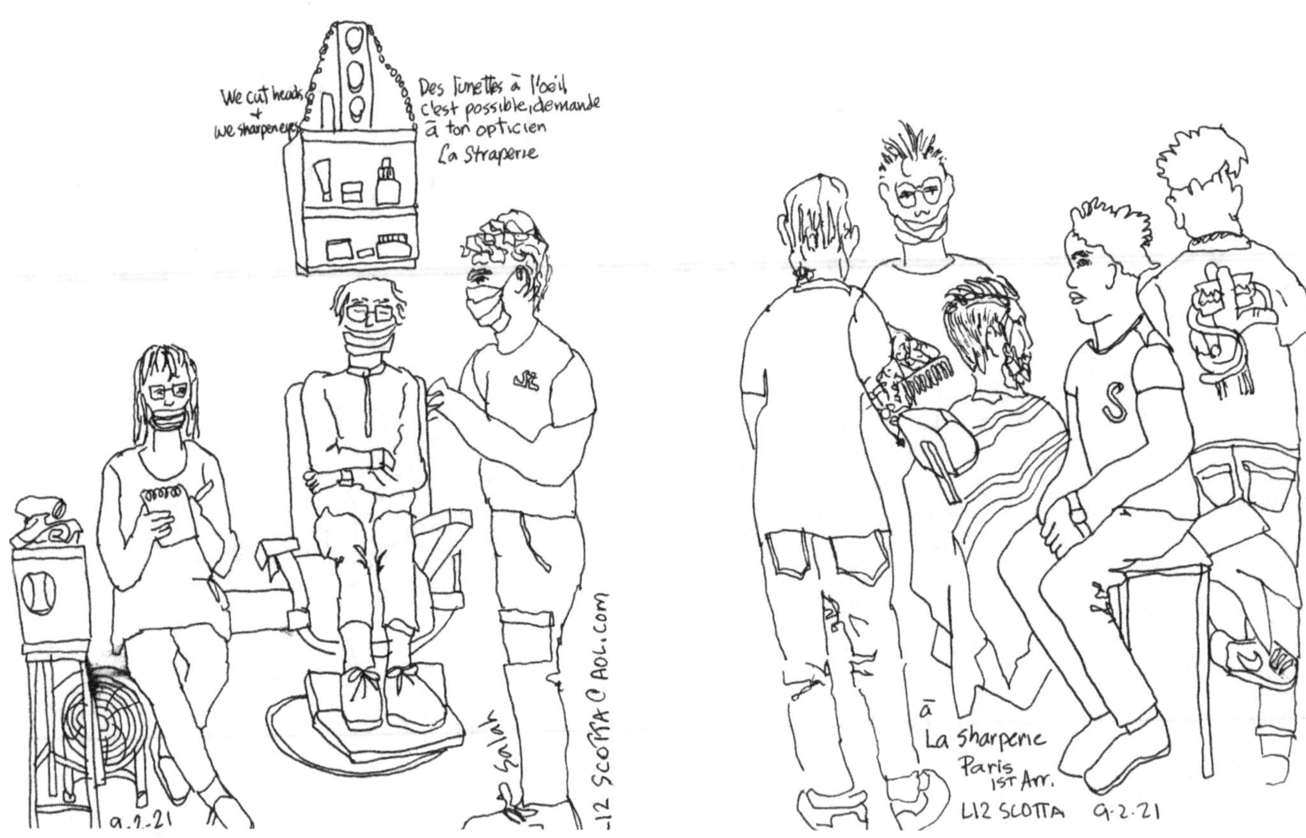

LA STRAPERIE BARBER SHOP
PARIS

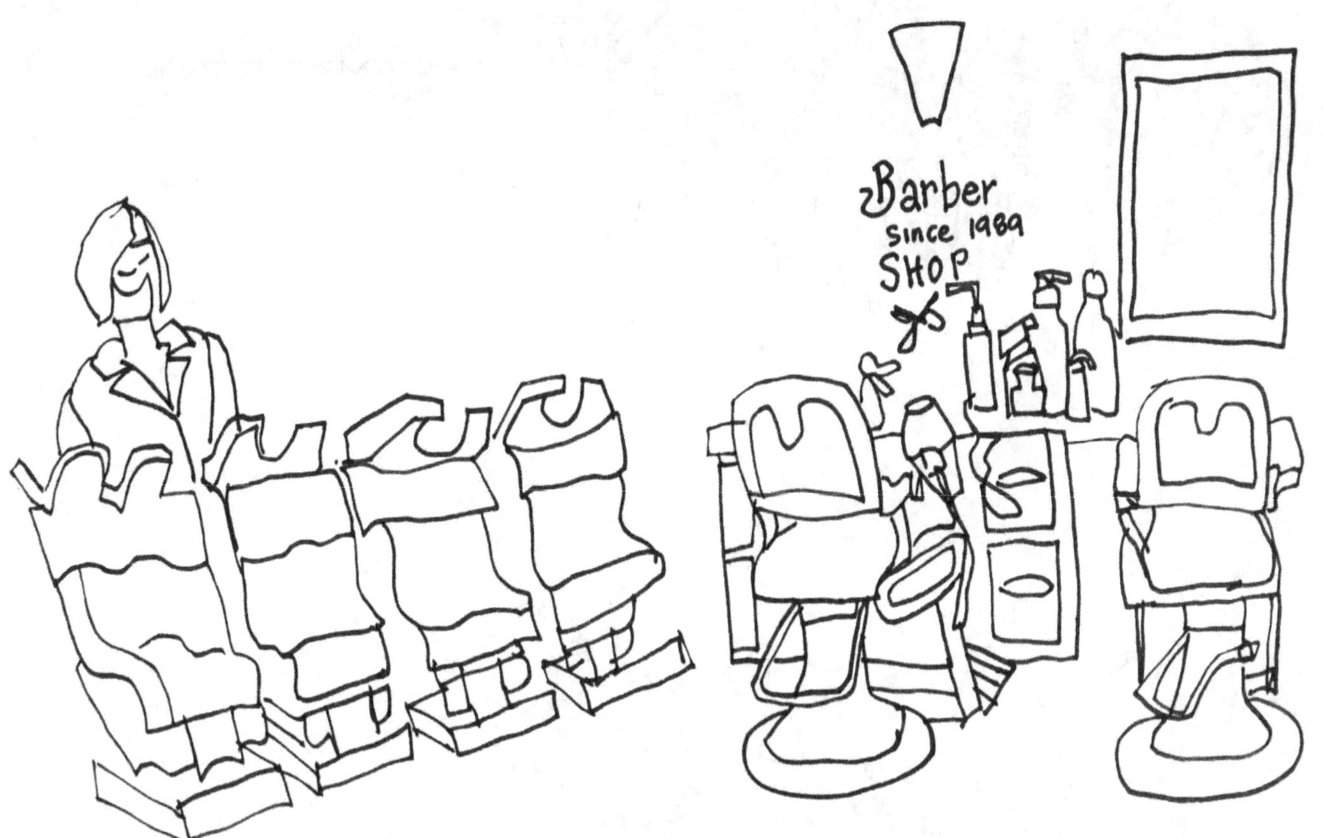

HAIR SALON
PARIS

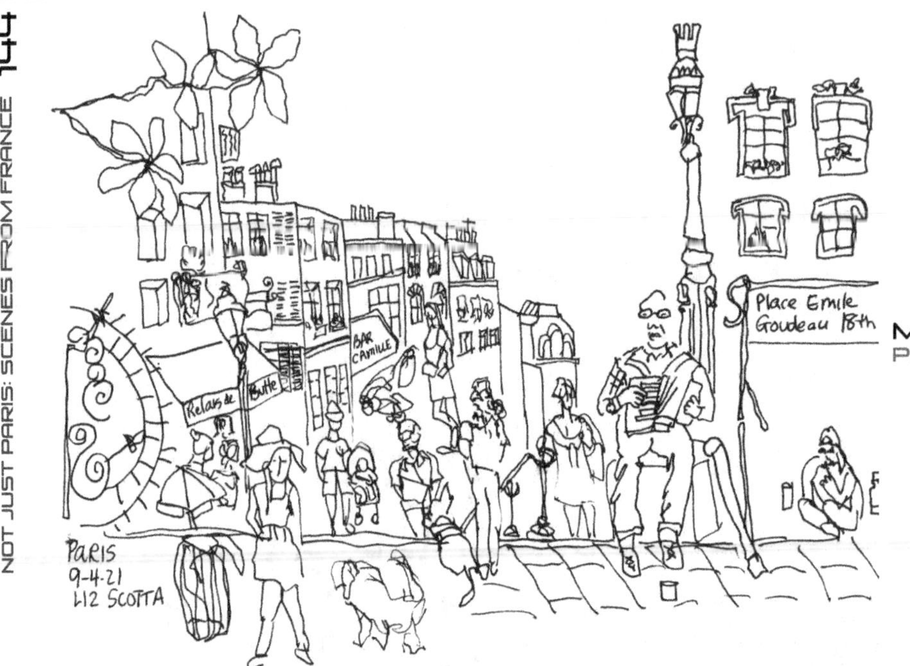

MONTMARTRE PARK
PARIS

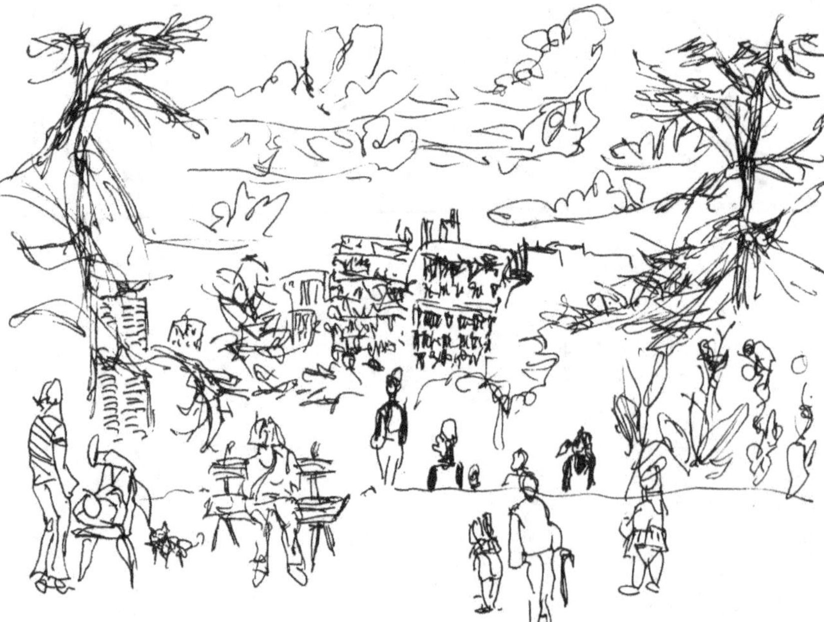

PARC BUTTE CHAUMONT
PARIS

PARC BUTTE CHAUMONT
PARIS

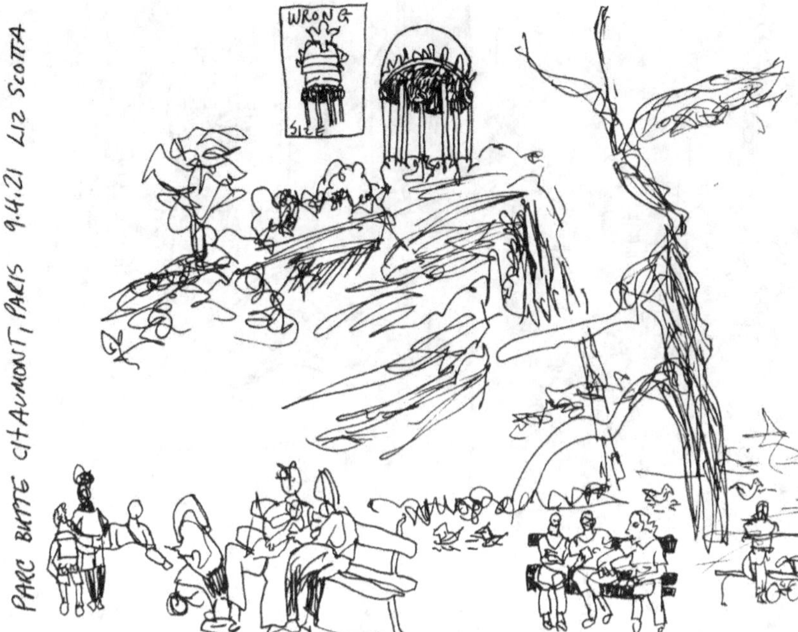

HOP ON-HOP OFF BUS
PARIS

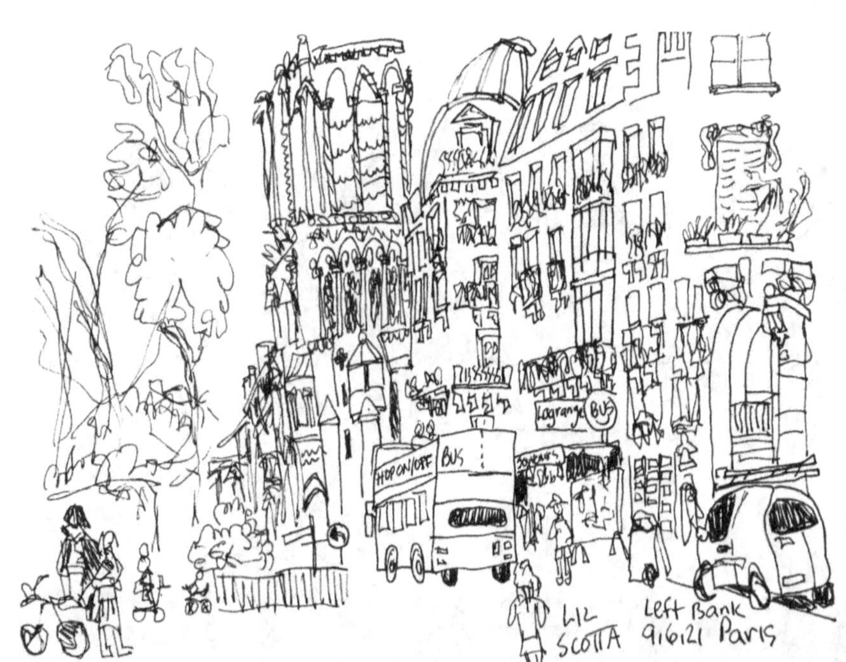

2021

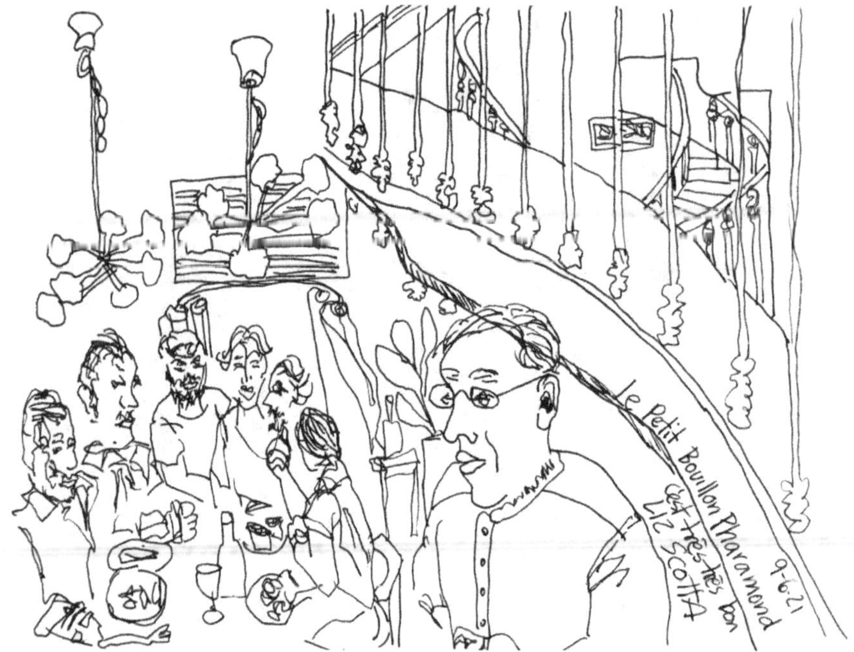

LE PETITE BOUILLON PHARAMOND
PARIS

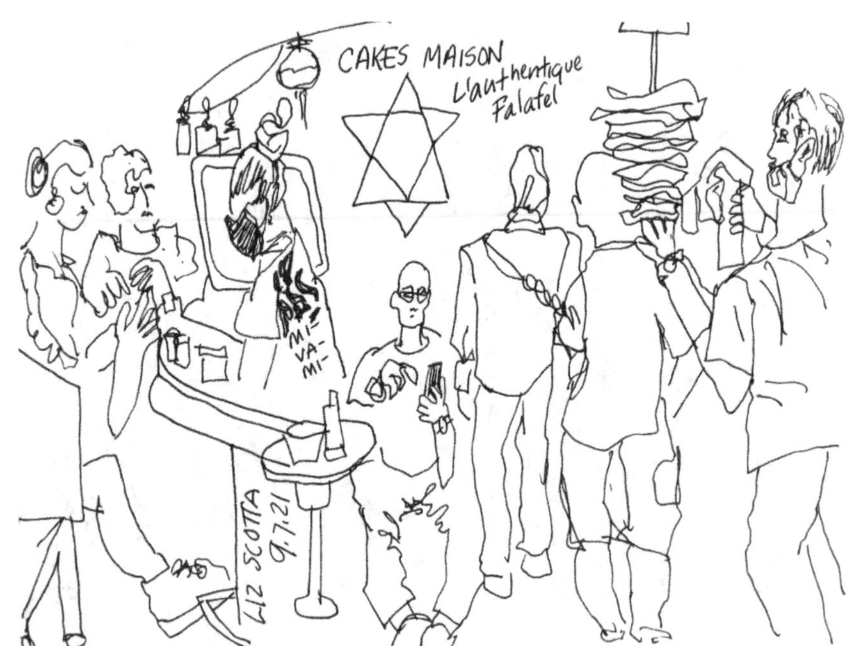

AUTHENTIQUE FALAFEL RESTAURANT
PARIS

COOKING WITH CLASS SCHOOL
PARIS

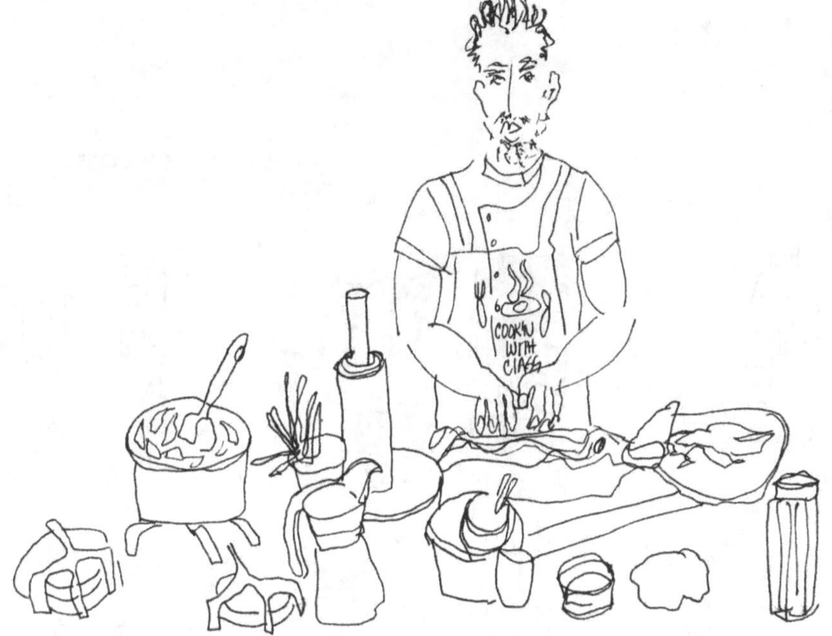

MUSÉE CARNAVALET
PARIS

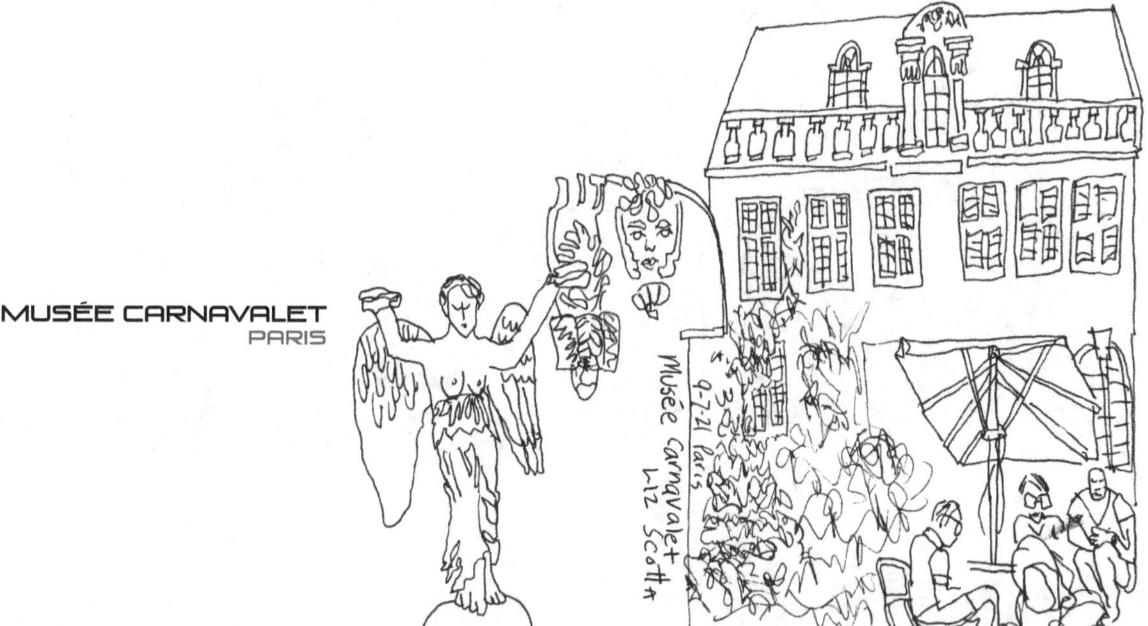

2021

L'EMPIRE HÔTEL
PARIS

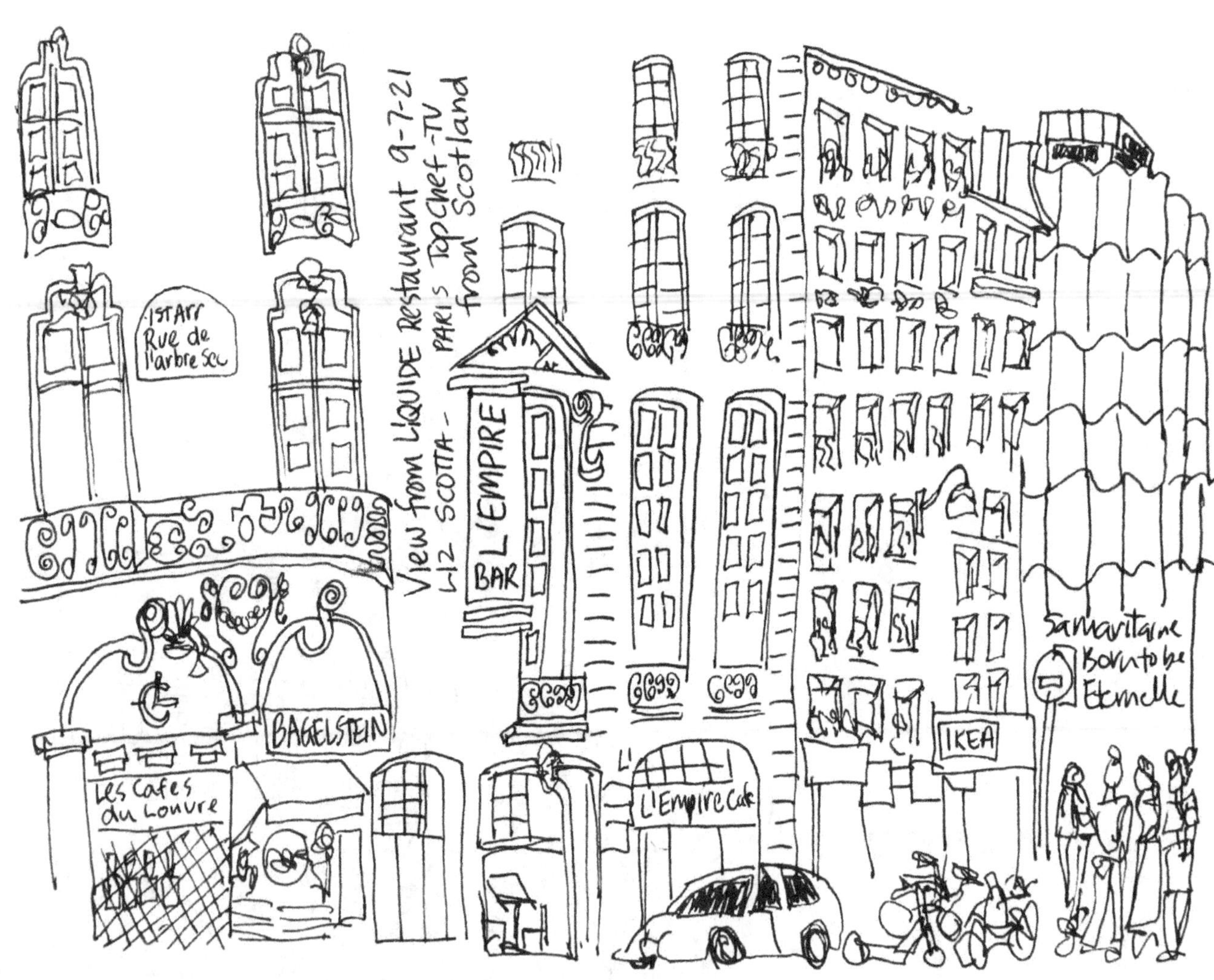

LA DÉFENSE
PARIS

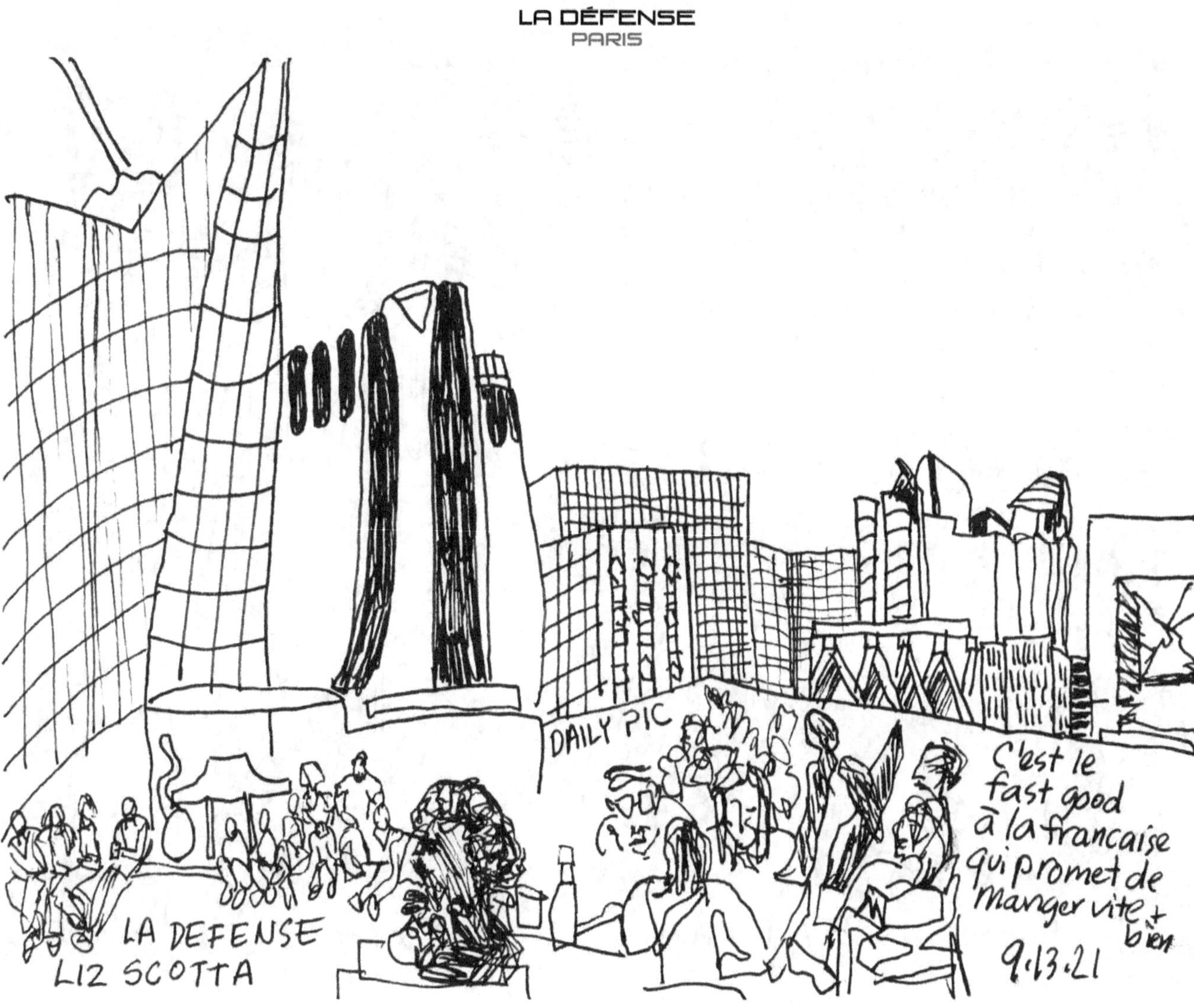

VIEW FROM LE SAINT-ANDRÉ MONTPARNASSE CAFE
PARIS

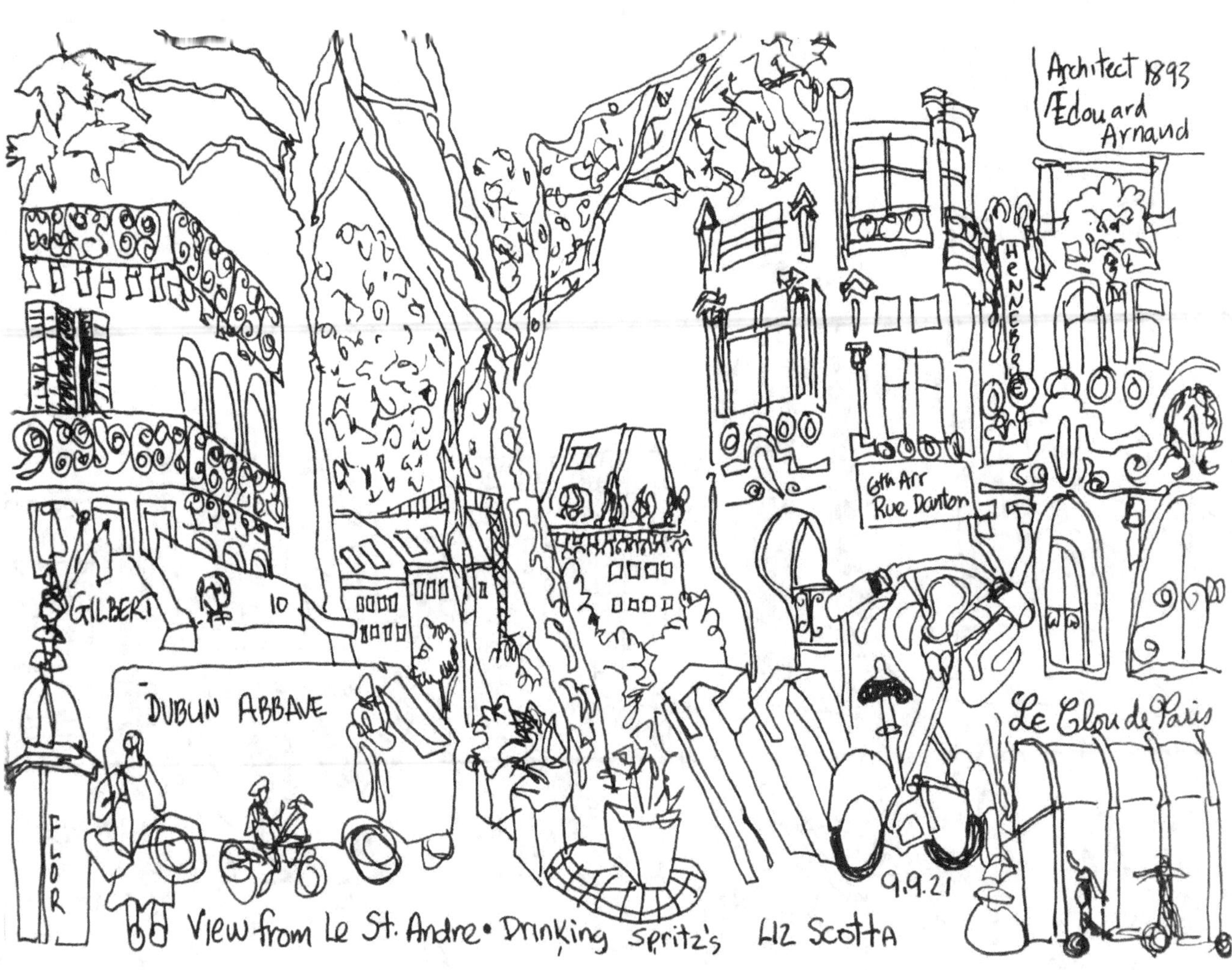

LA BOURSE DE COMMERCE
PARIS

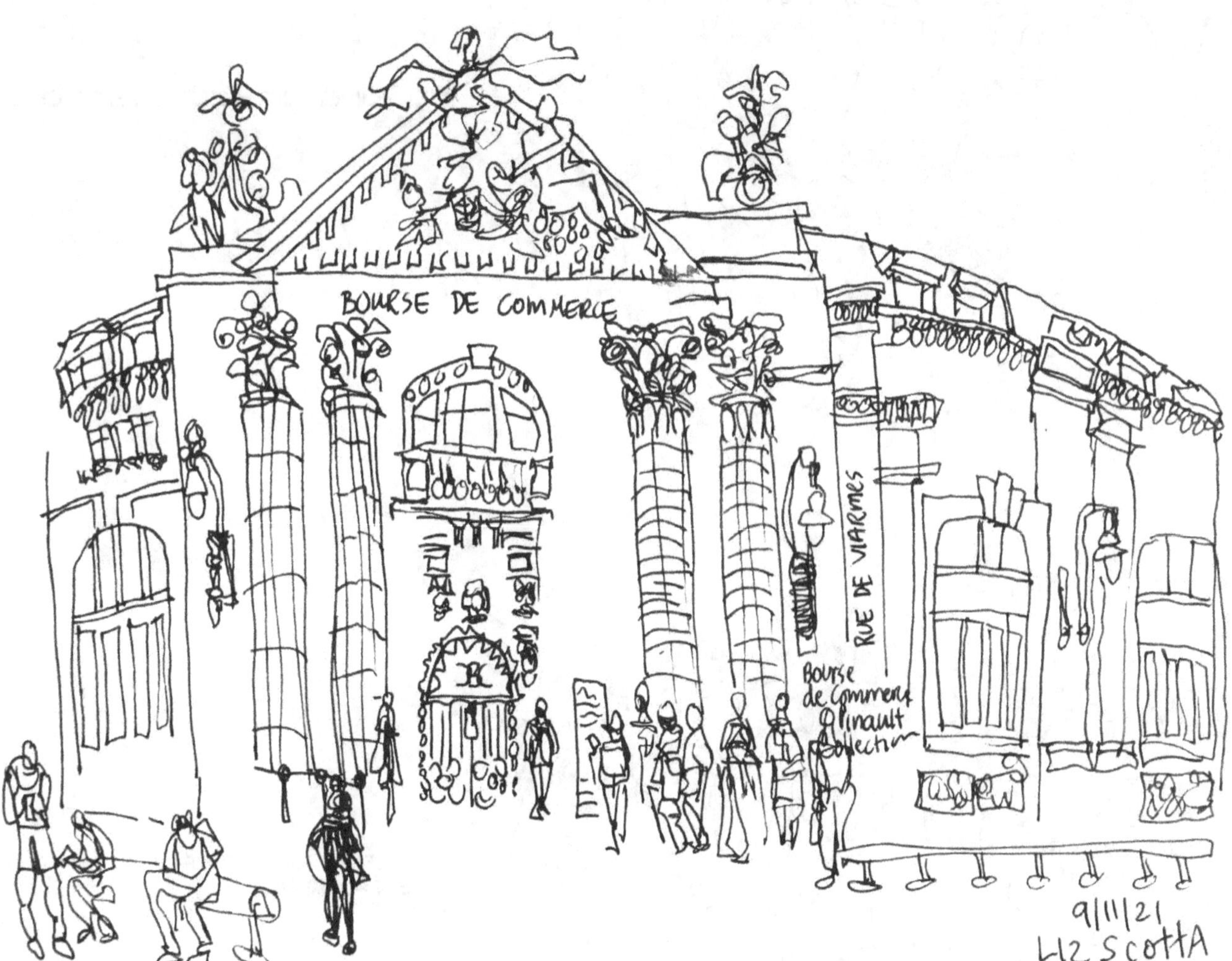

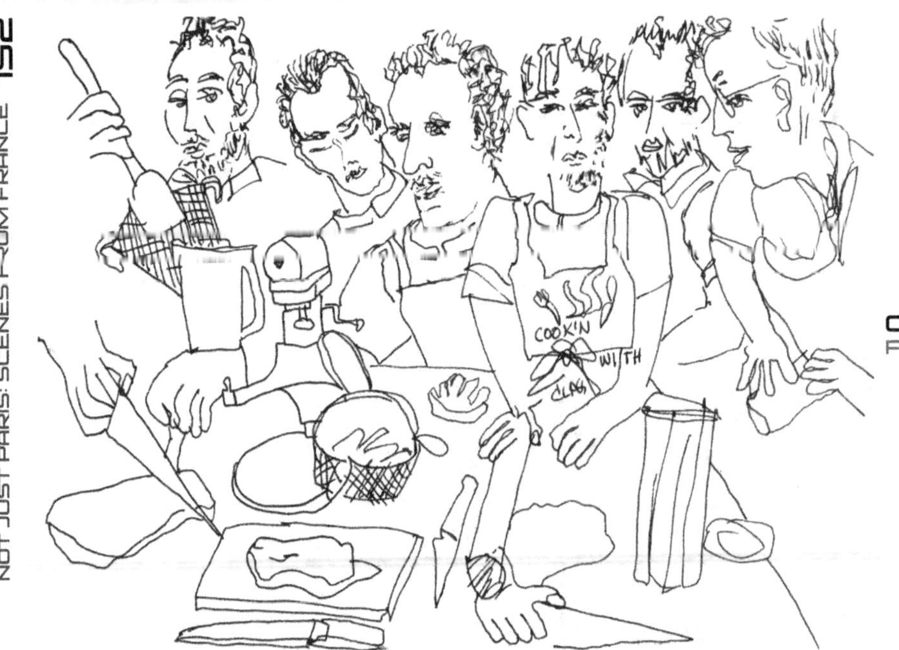

COOKING WITH CLASS SCHOOL
PARIS

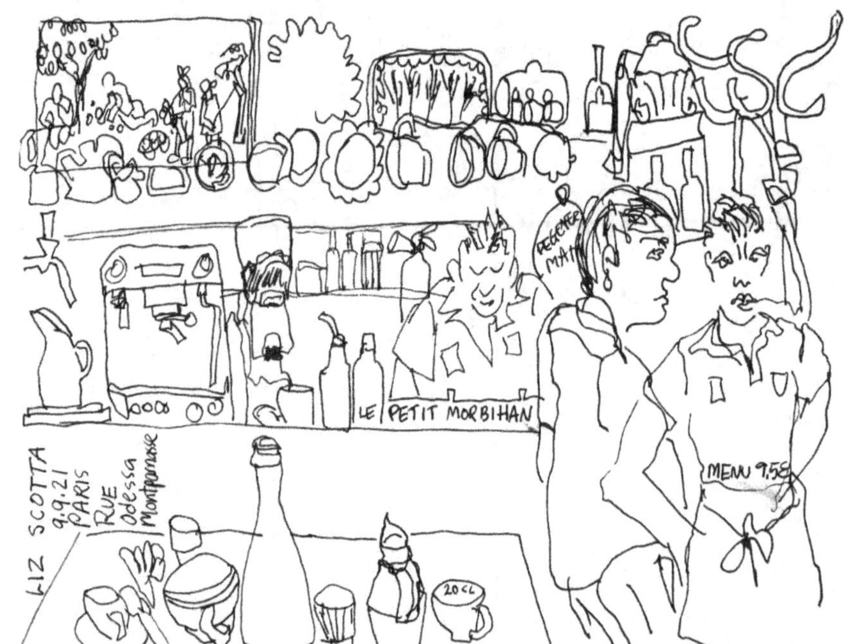

LE PETIT MORBIHAN
RESTAURANT
PARIS

ANTIQUE MARKET
PARIS

2021

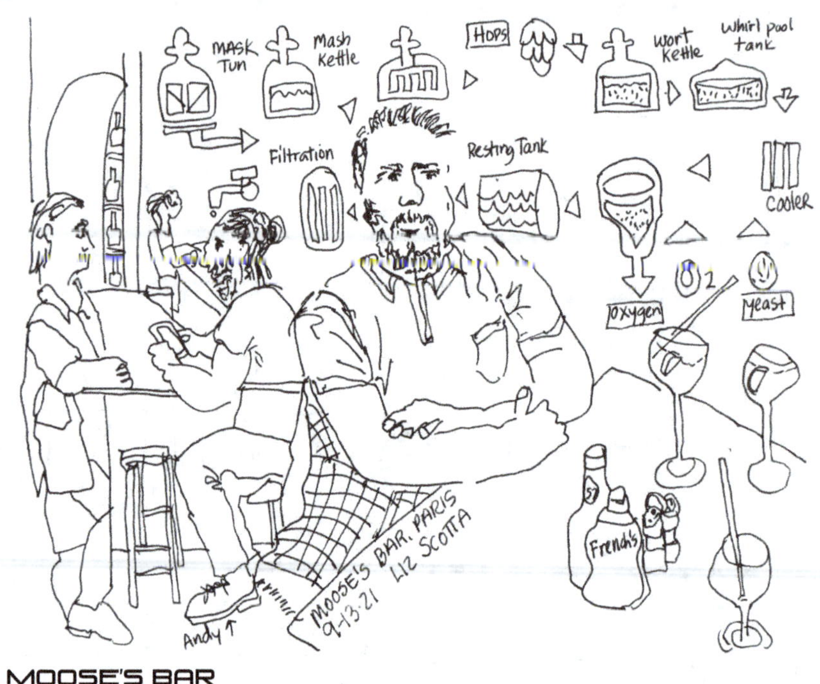

MOOSE'S BAR
PARIS

AU PIED DE COCHON RESTAURANT
PARIS

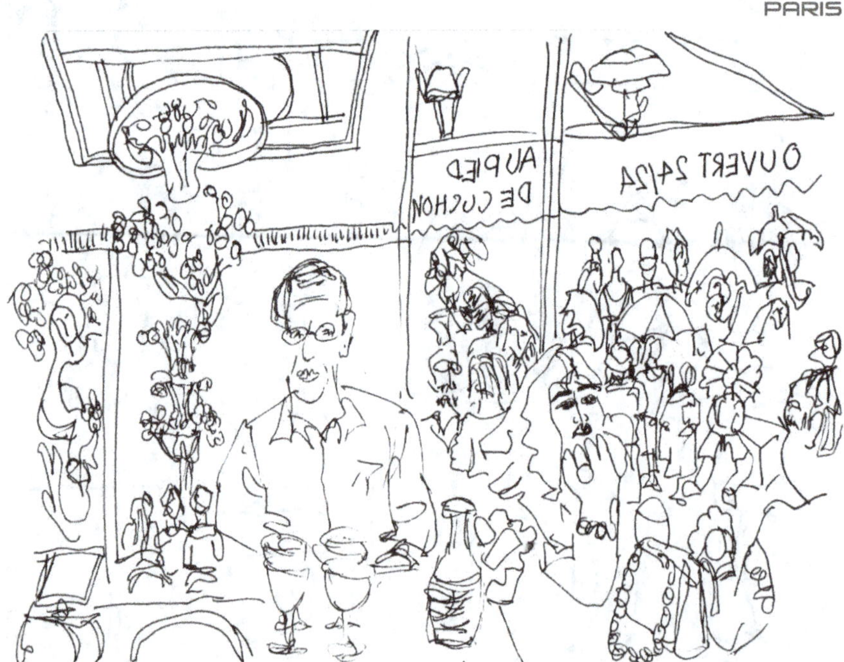

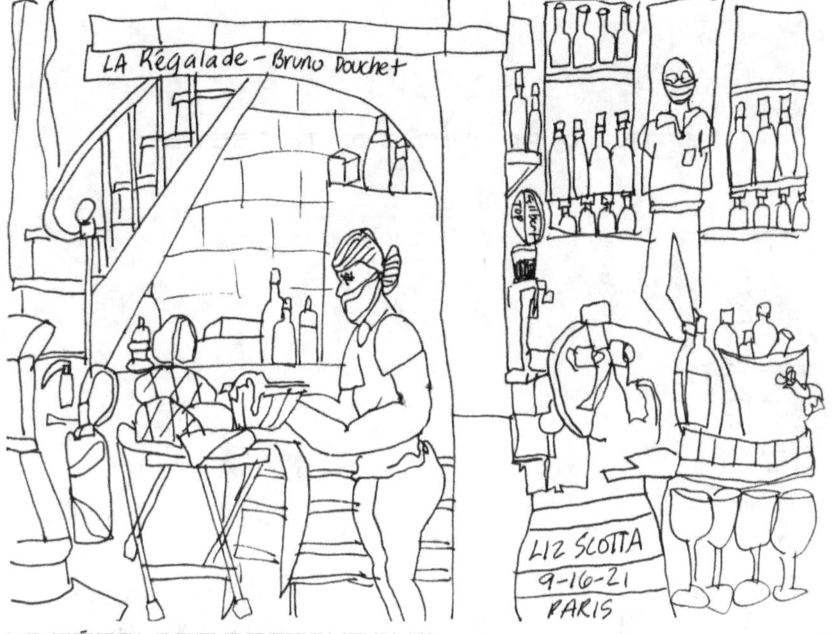

LA RÉGALADE RESTAURANT
PARIS

MUSÉE JACQUEMART ANDRÉ
PARIS

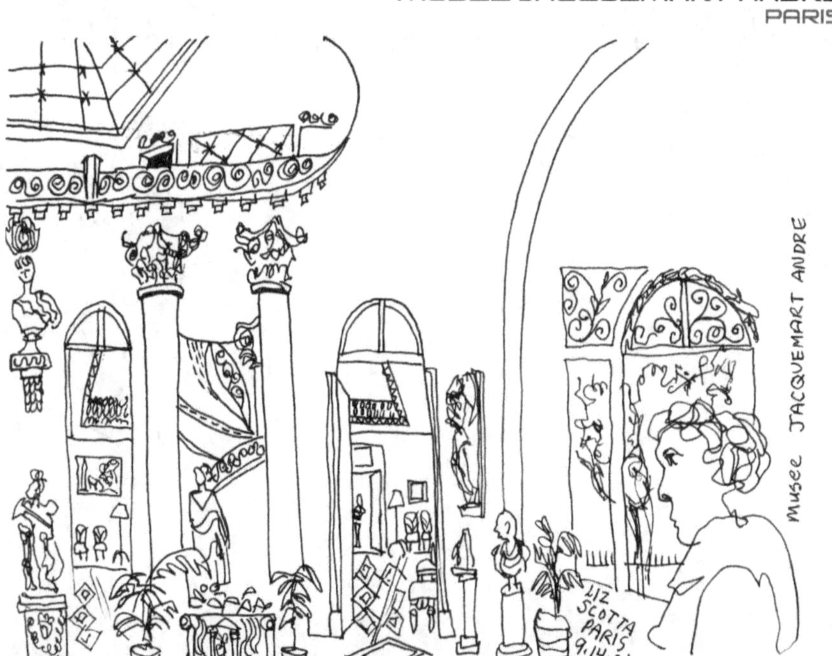

BATEAUX PARISIENS ON THE SEINE
PARIS

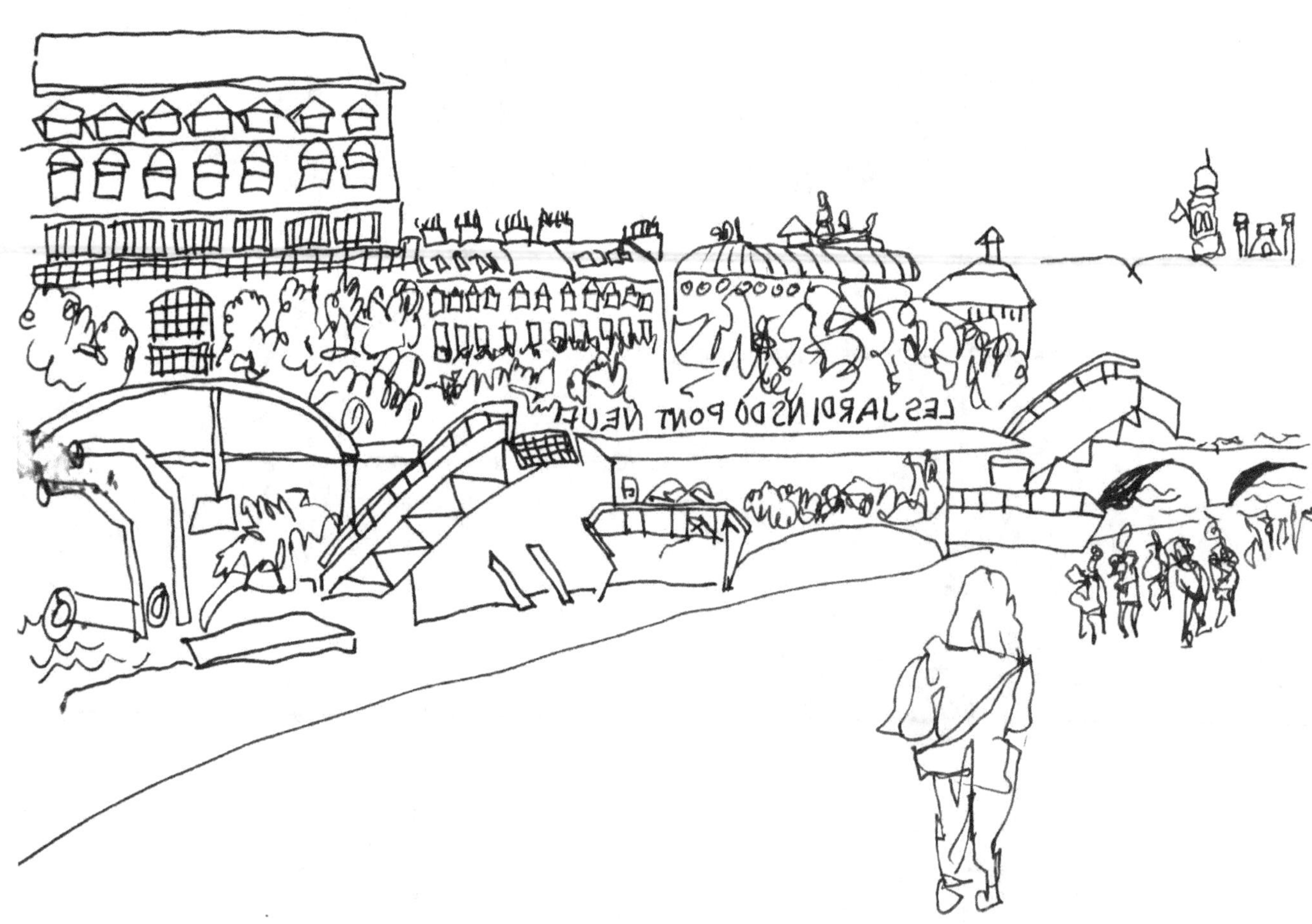

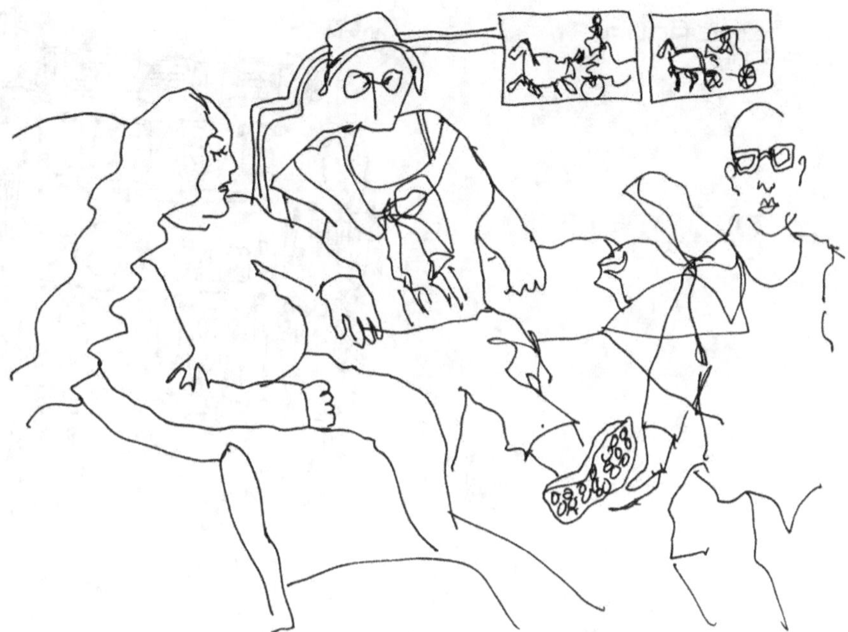

LIZ AND BARBARA
PARIS

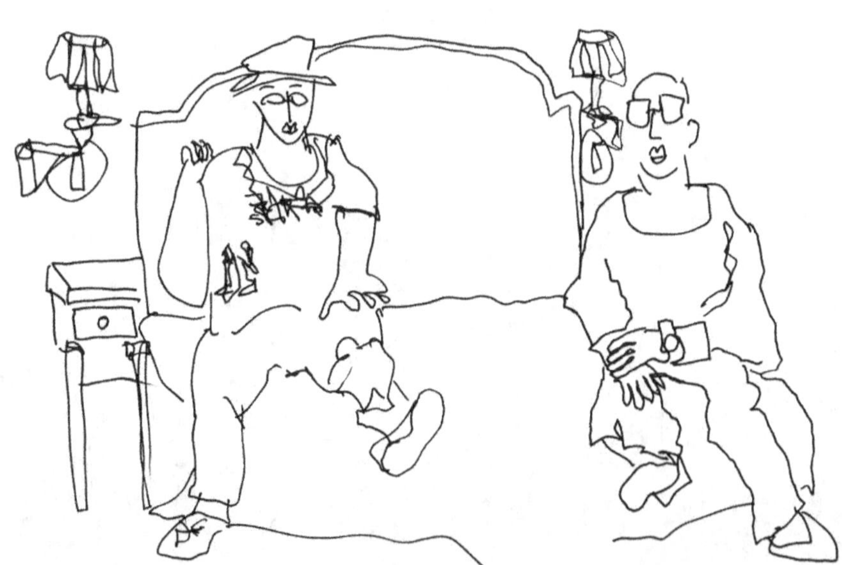

CINÉ AQUA
PARIS

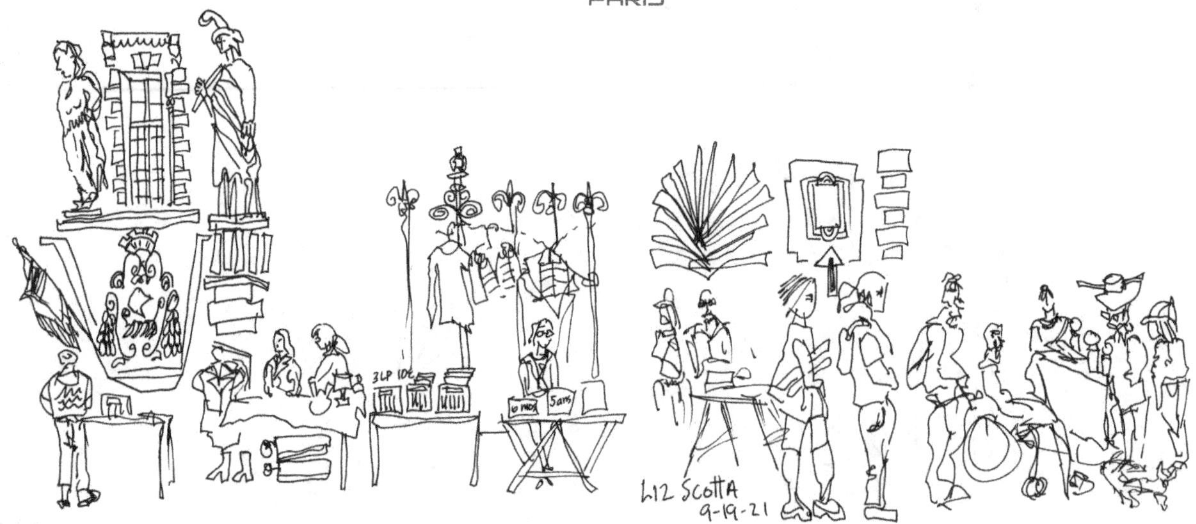

FLEA MARKET
PARIS

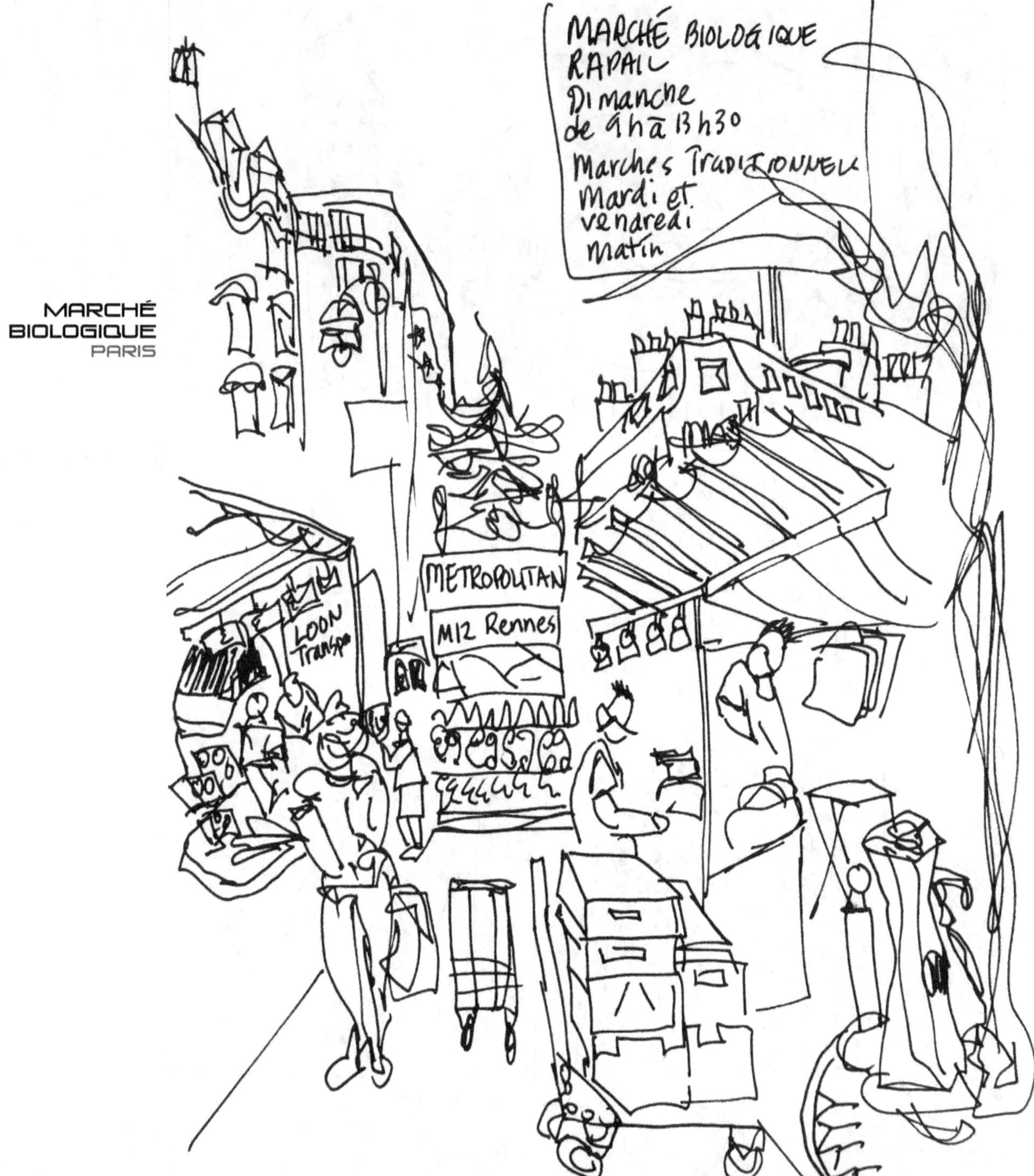

MARCHÉ
BIOLOGIQUE
PARIS

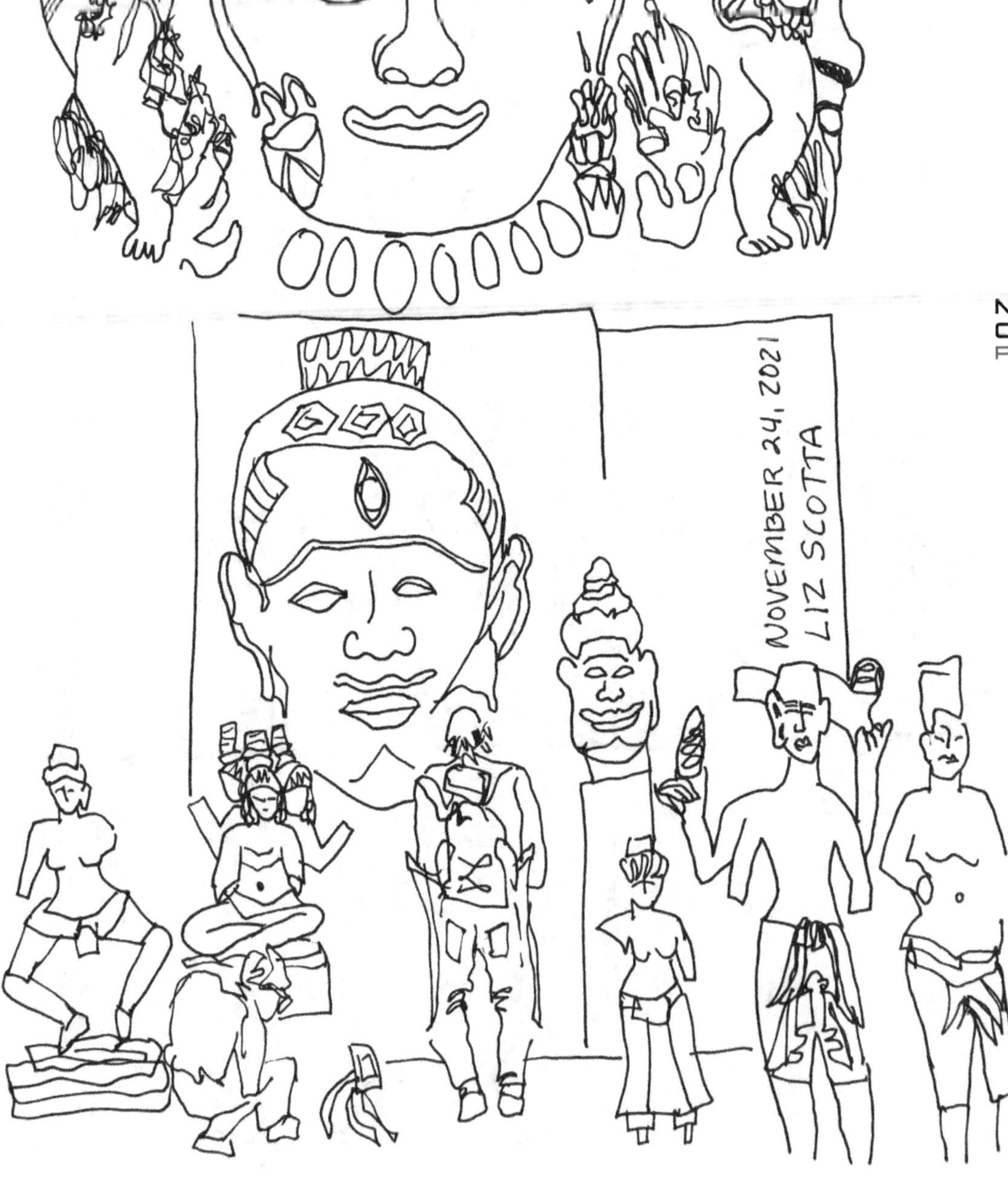
MUSÉE GUIMET
OF ASIAN ARTS
PARIS
NOVEMBER 24, 2021
LIZ SCOTTA

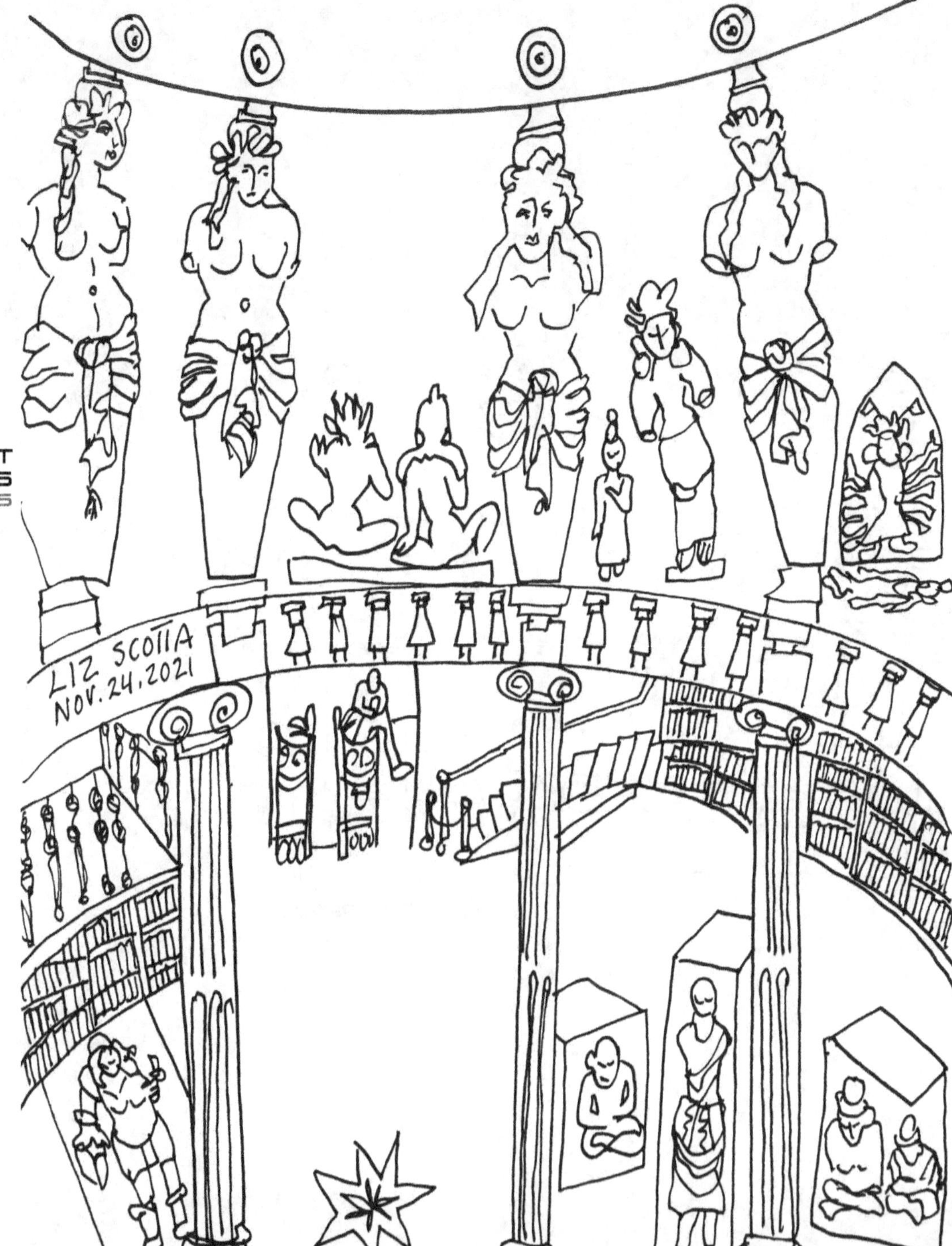
MUSÉE GUIMET
OF ASIAN ARTS
PARIS
LIZ SCOTTA
NOV. 24, 2021
2021

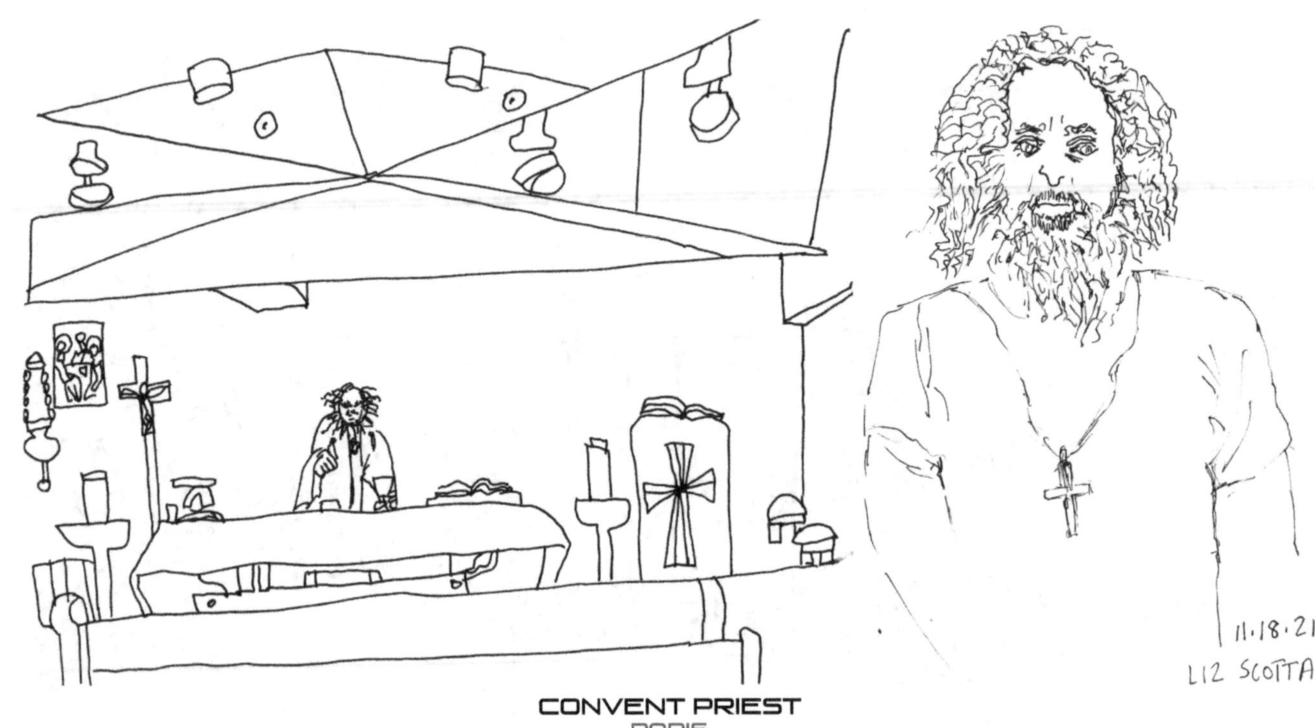

CONVENT PRIEST
PARIS

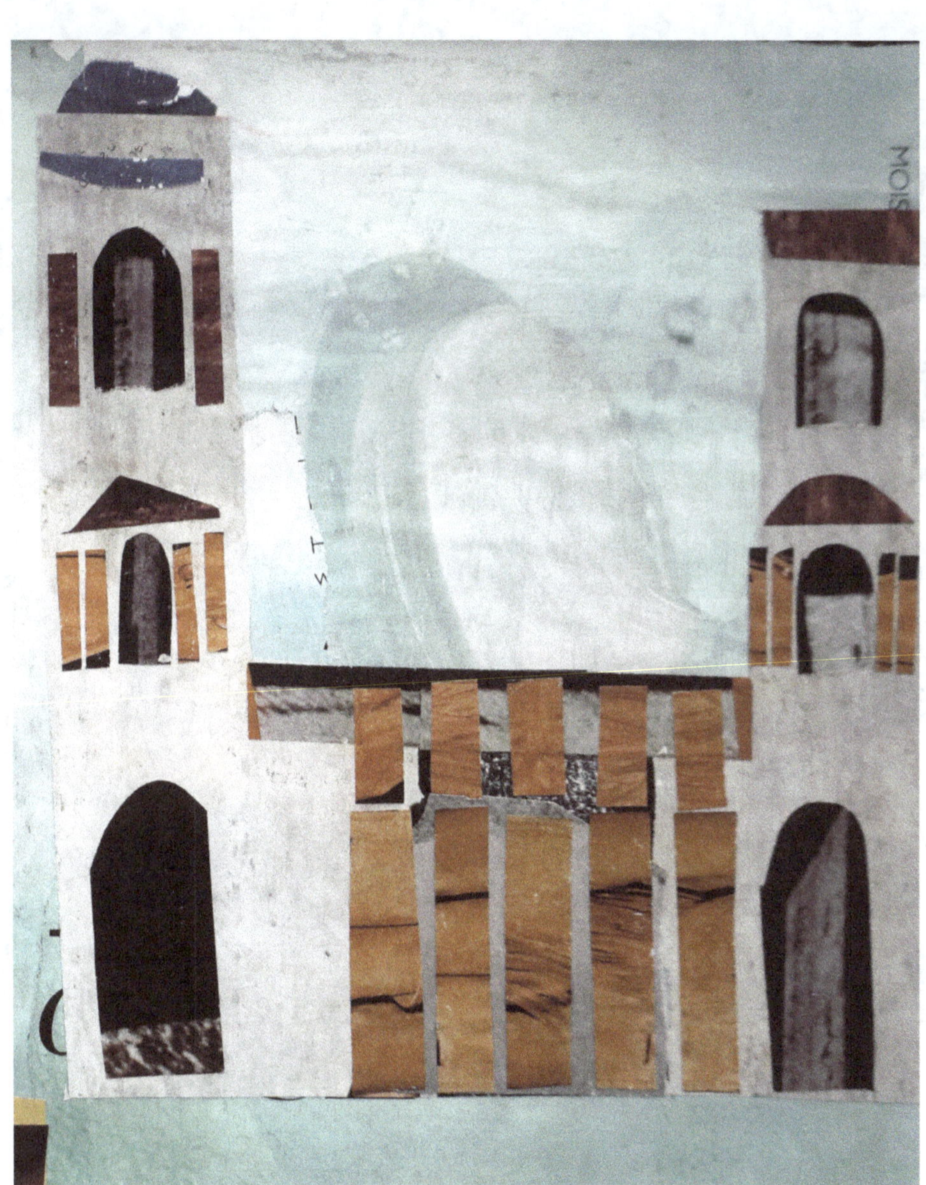

SAINT-SULPICE
PARIS

2021

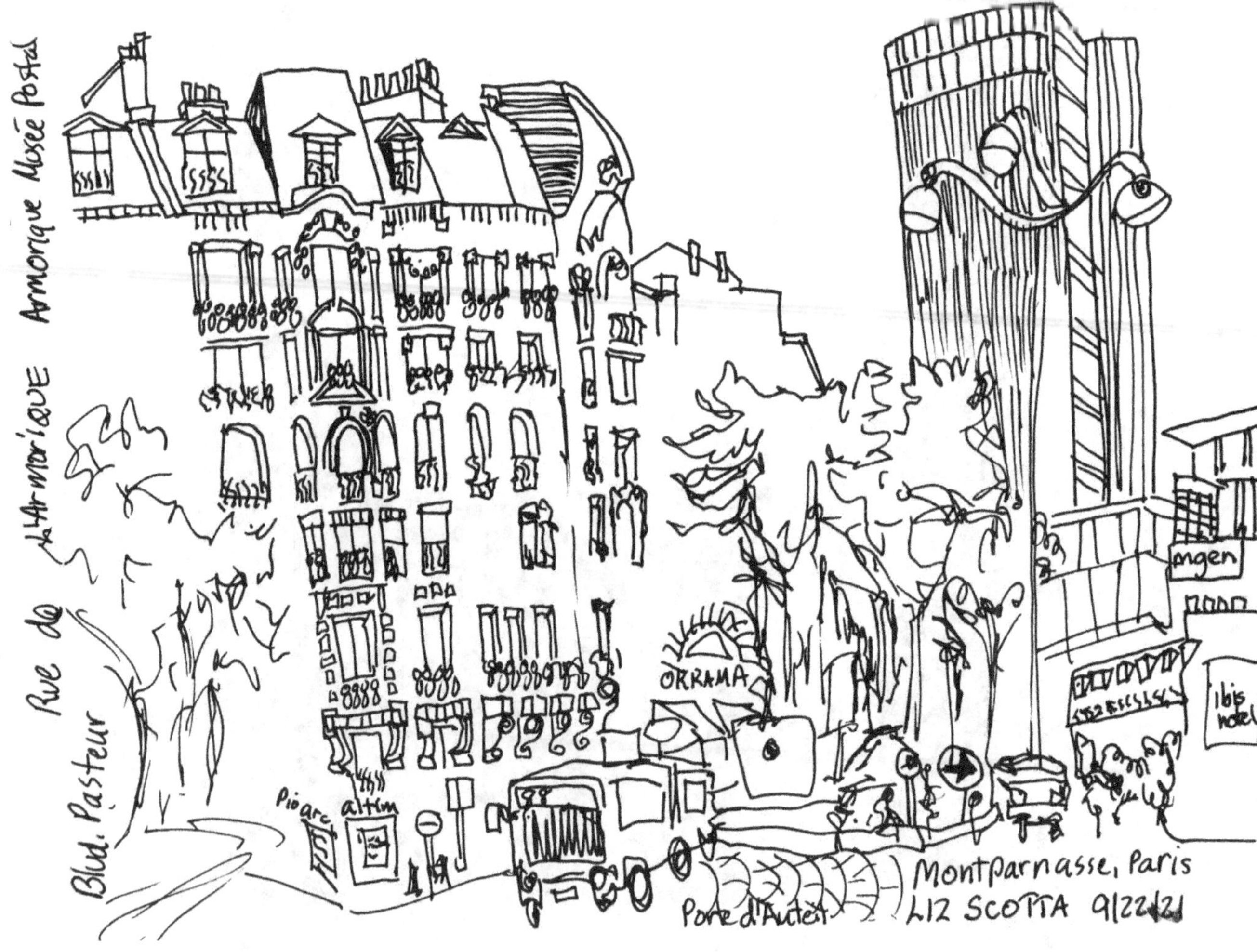
Rue de l'Armorique Armorique Musée Postal
Blvd. Pasteur
ORRAMA
ngen
ibis hotel
Montparnasse, Paris
LIZ SCOTTA 9/22/21
Porte d'Auteil

VILLE DE NEUILLY
PARIS

2021

2021

CAISSE DE EPARGNE
NEVERS

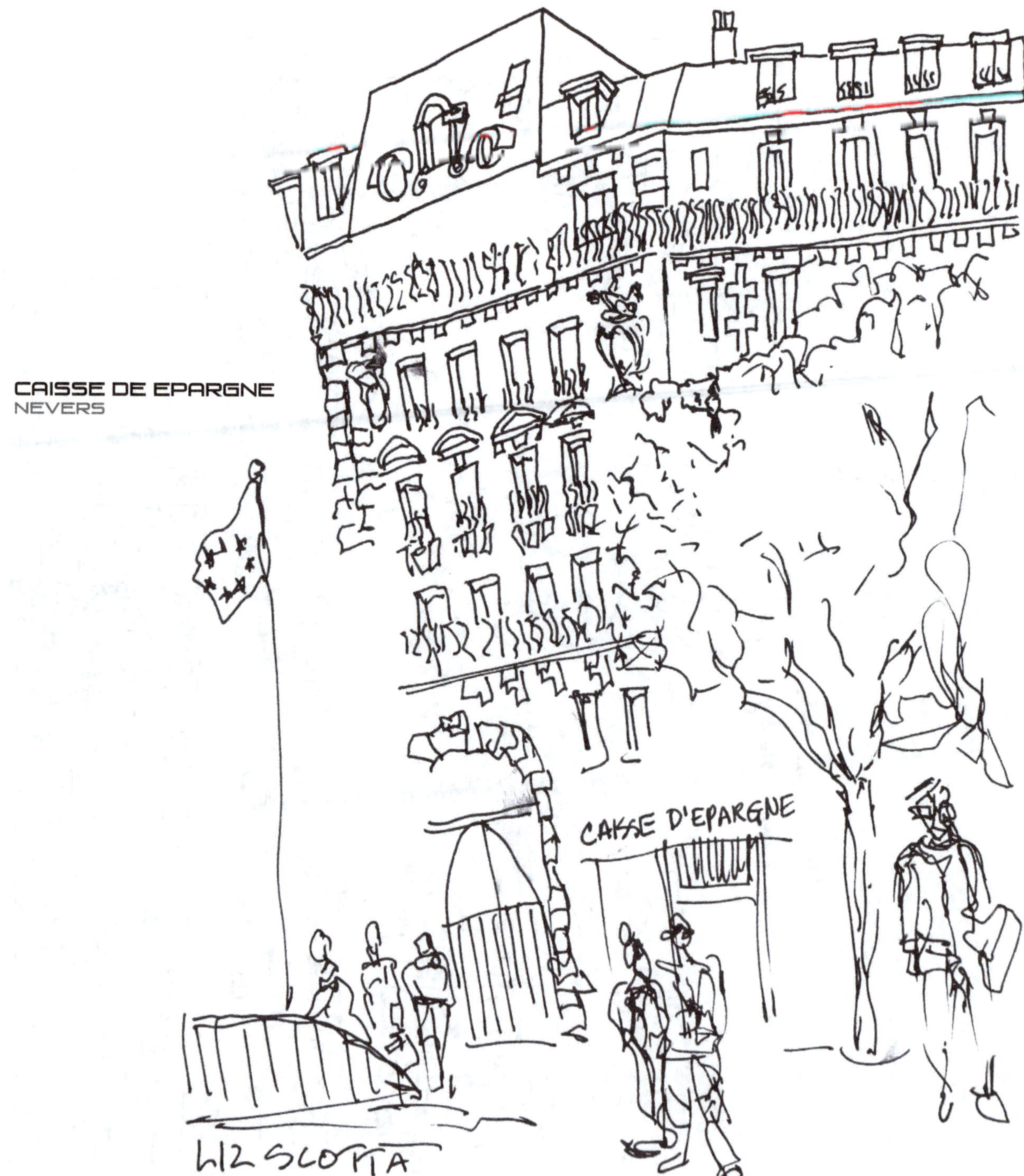

SAINT-SULPICE
PARIS

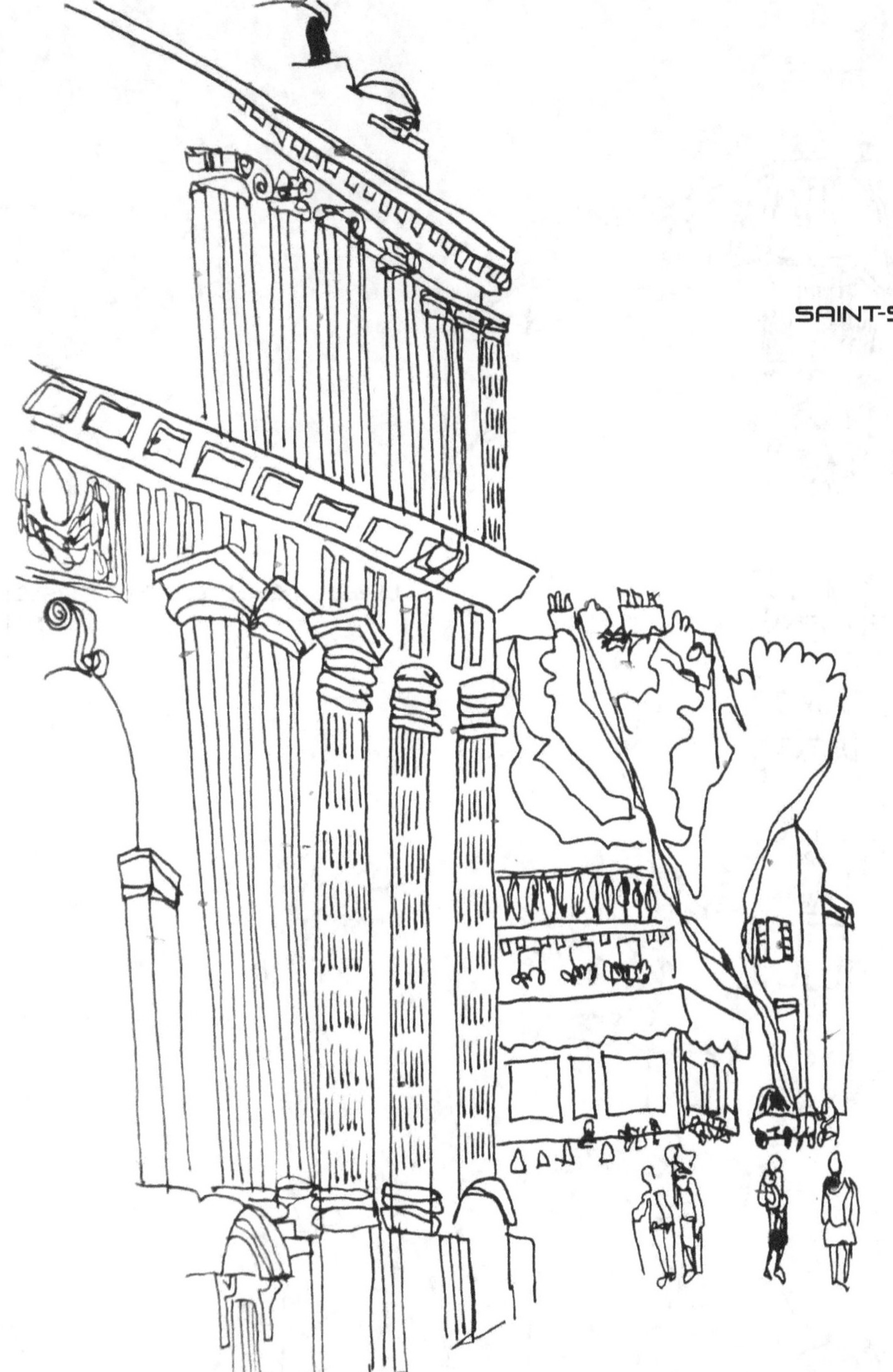

2021

2021

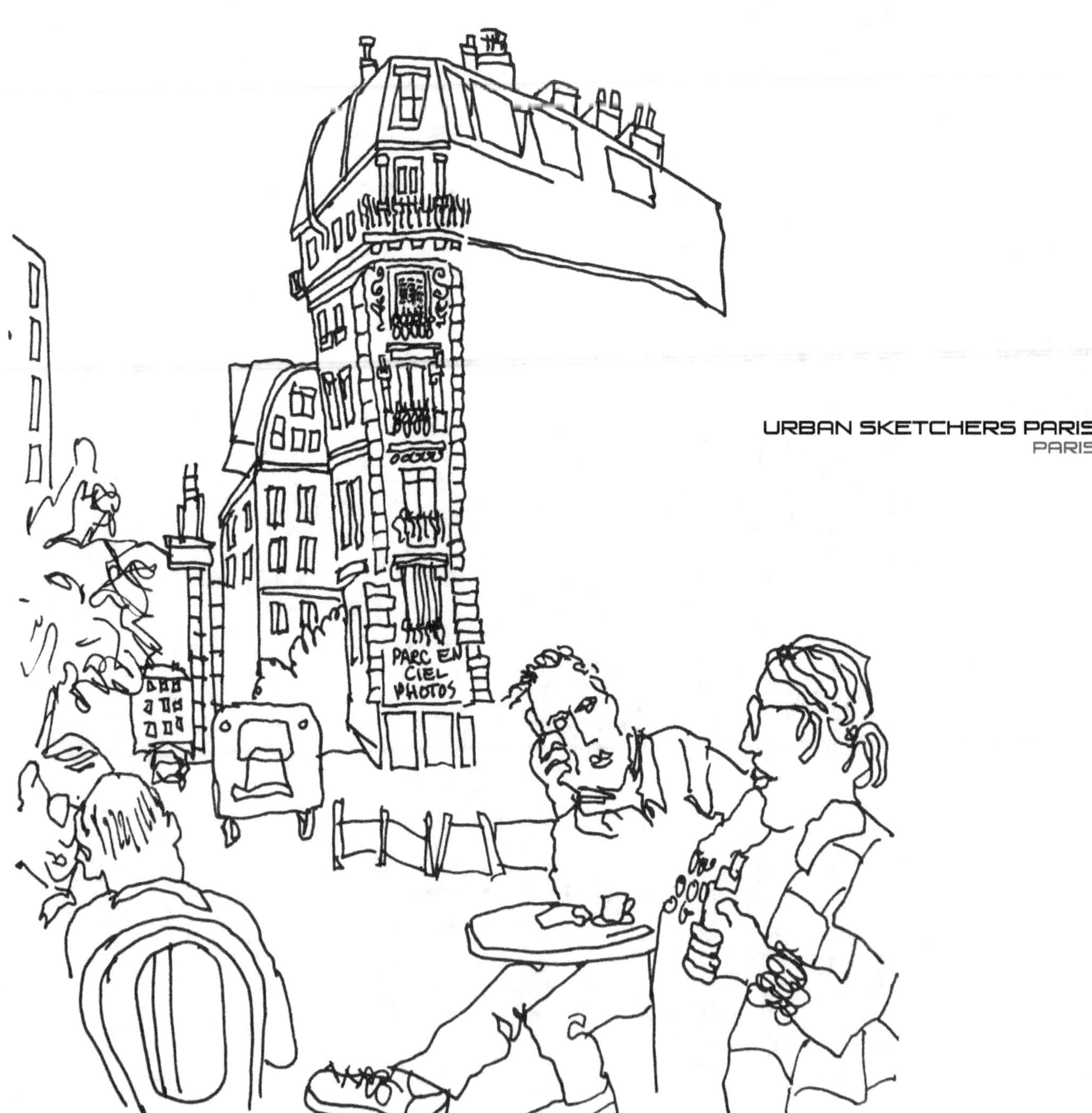

URBAN SKETCHERS PARIS
PARIS

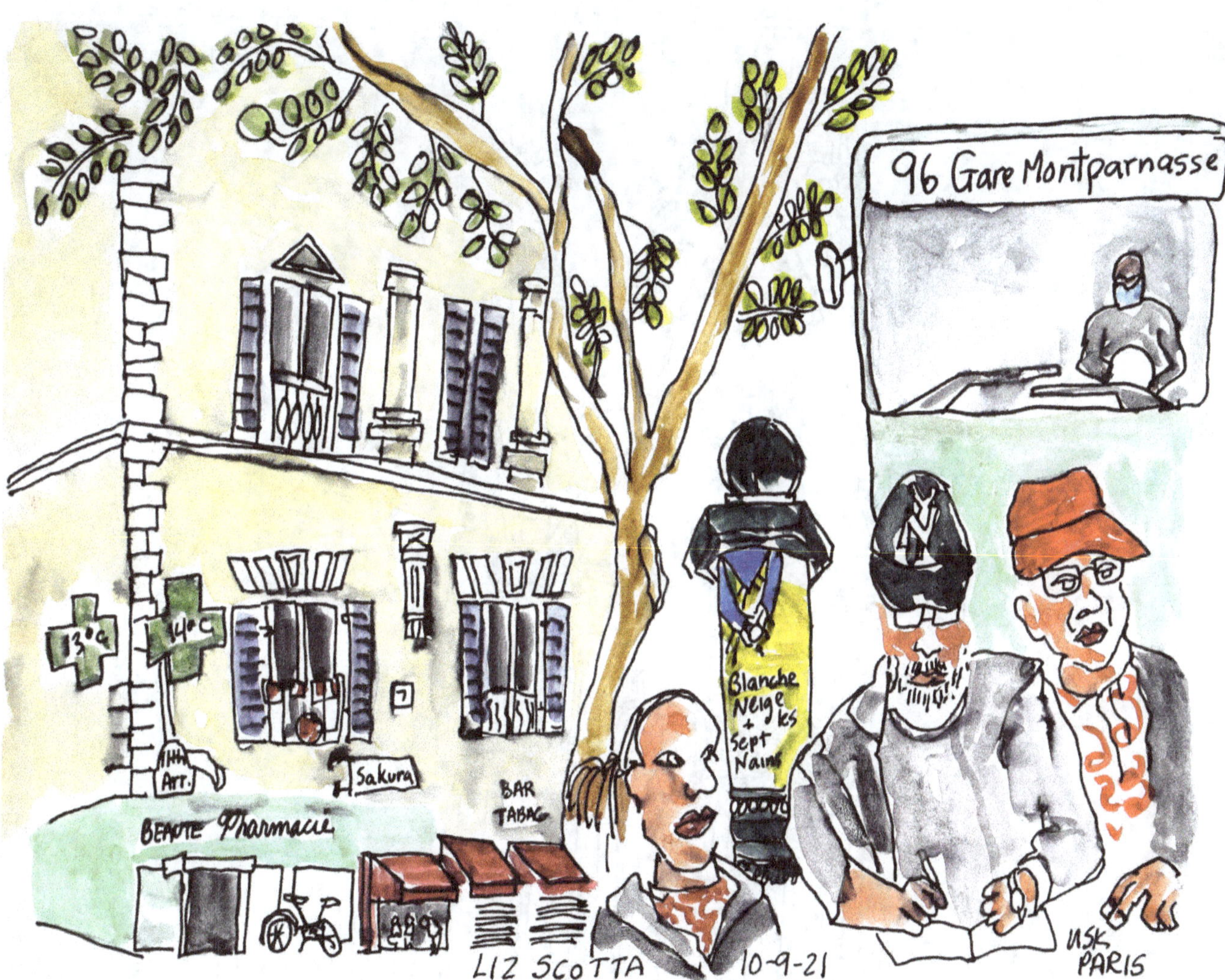

URBAN SKETCHERS PARIS
PARIS

2021

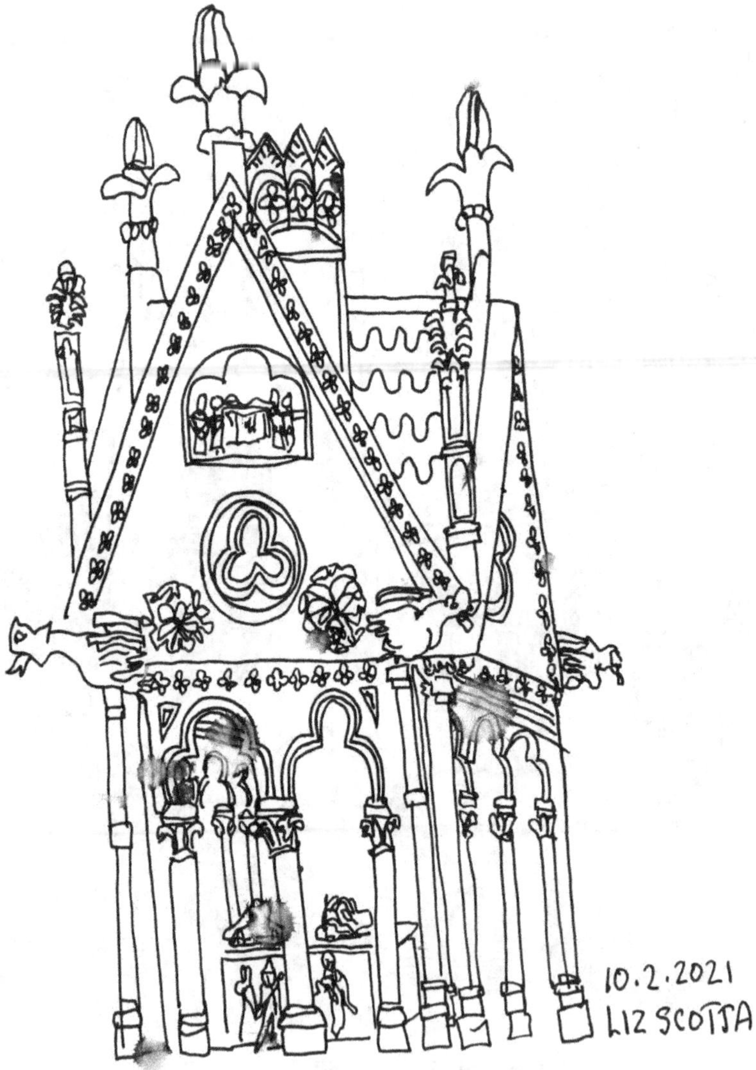

RAINY DAY AT CIMÈTIERE PÈRE LACHAISE
PARIS

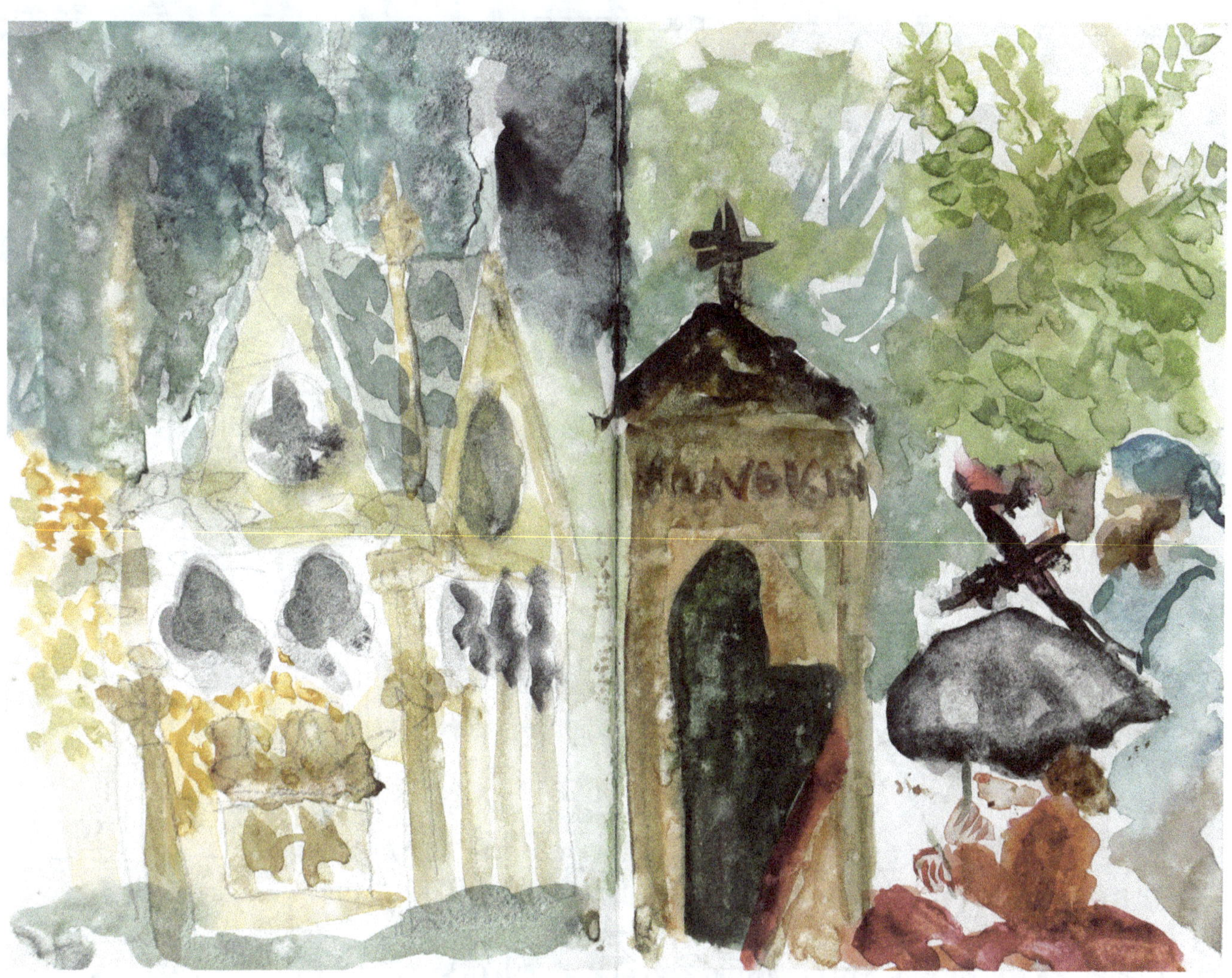

TOMB OF ABELARD AND HELOISE
PARIS

TROCADERO
PARIS

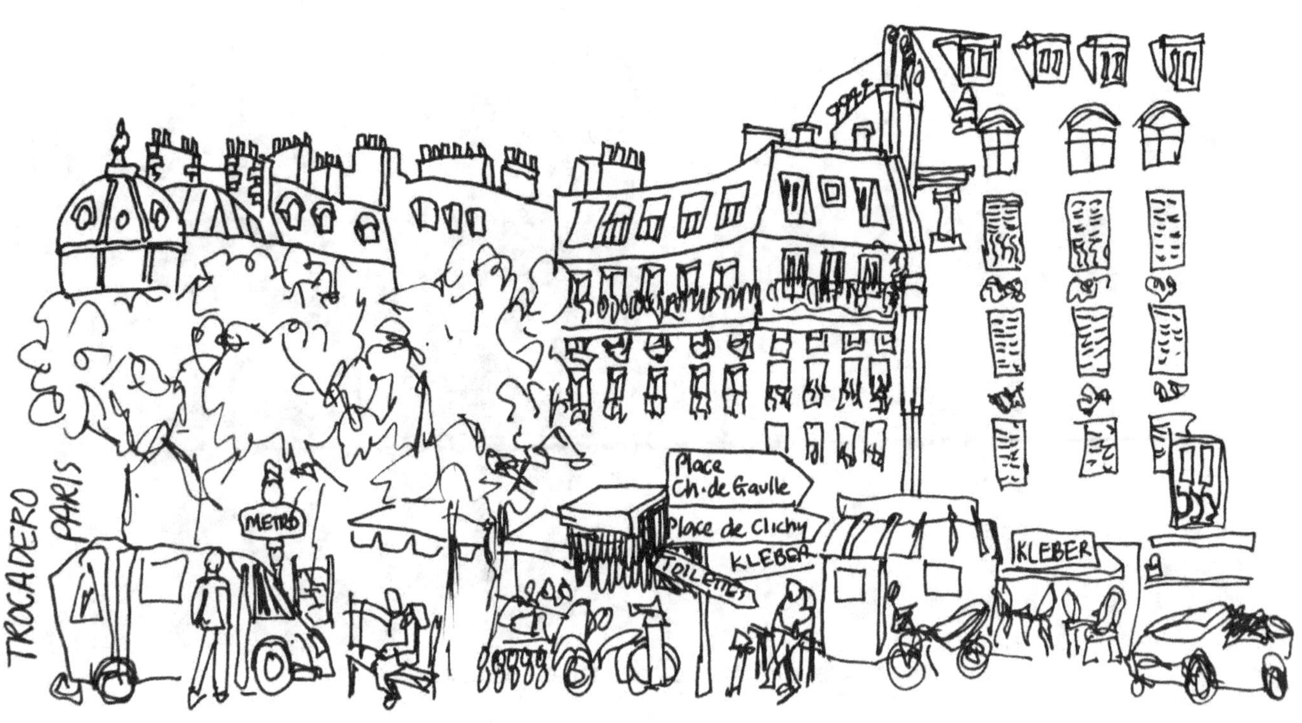

TROCADERO
PARIS

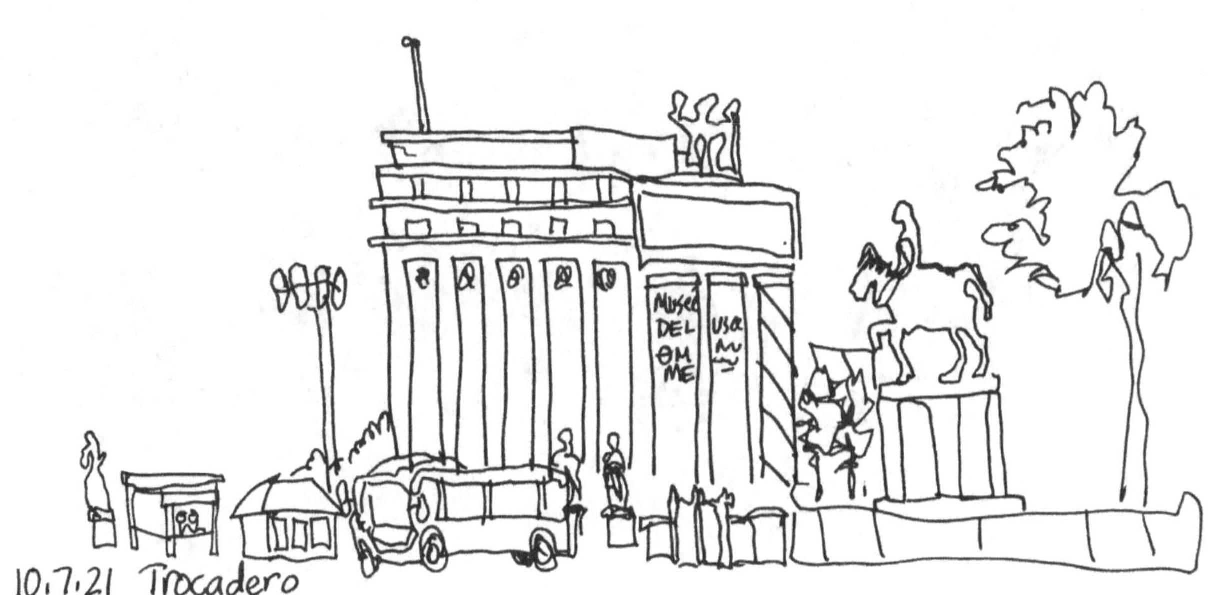

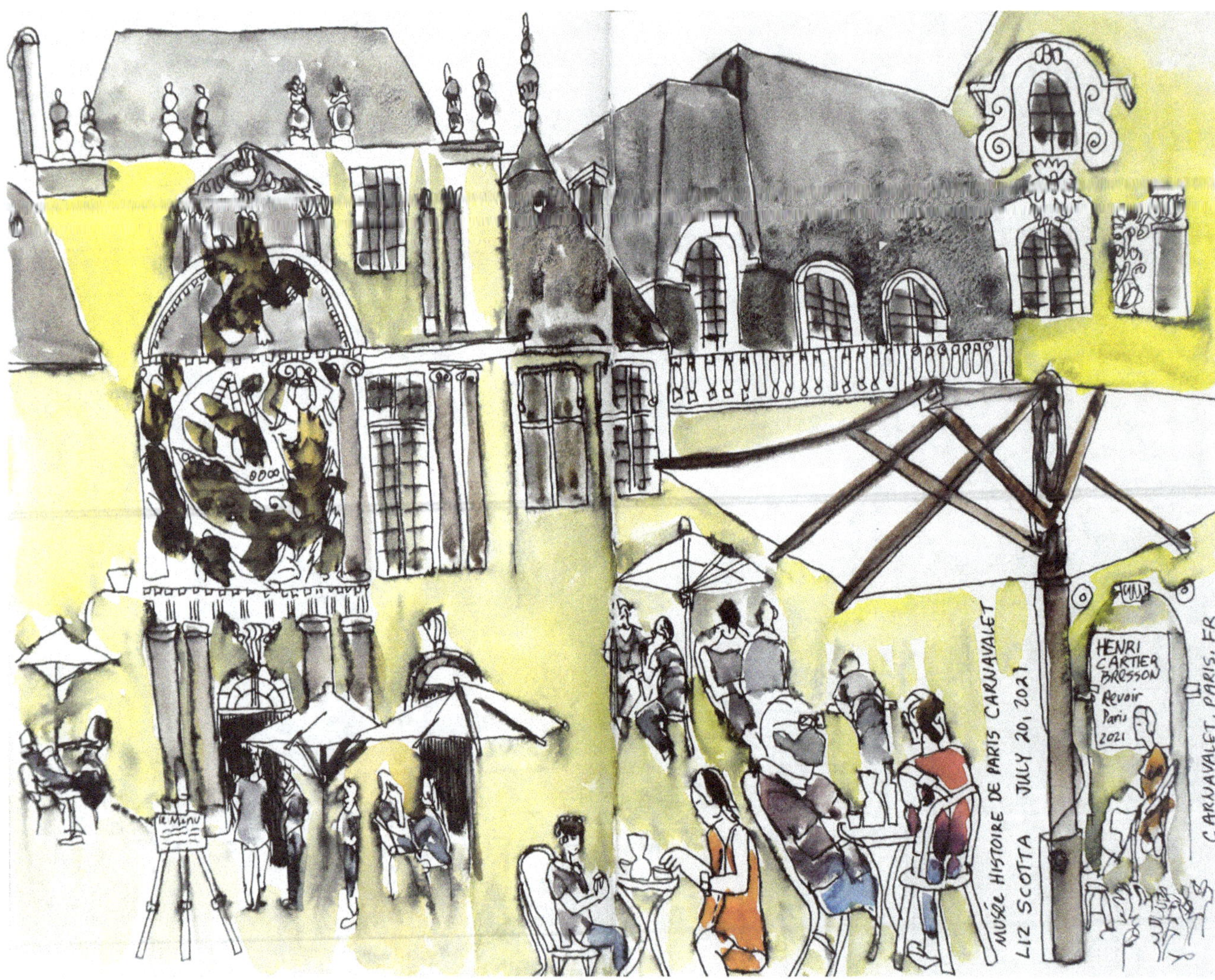

MUSÉE CARNAVALET
PARIS

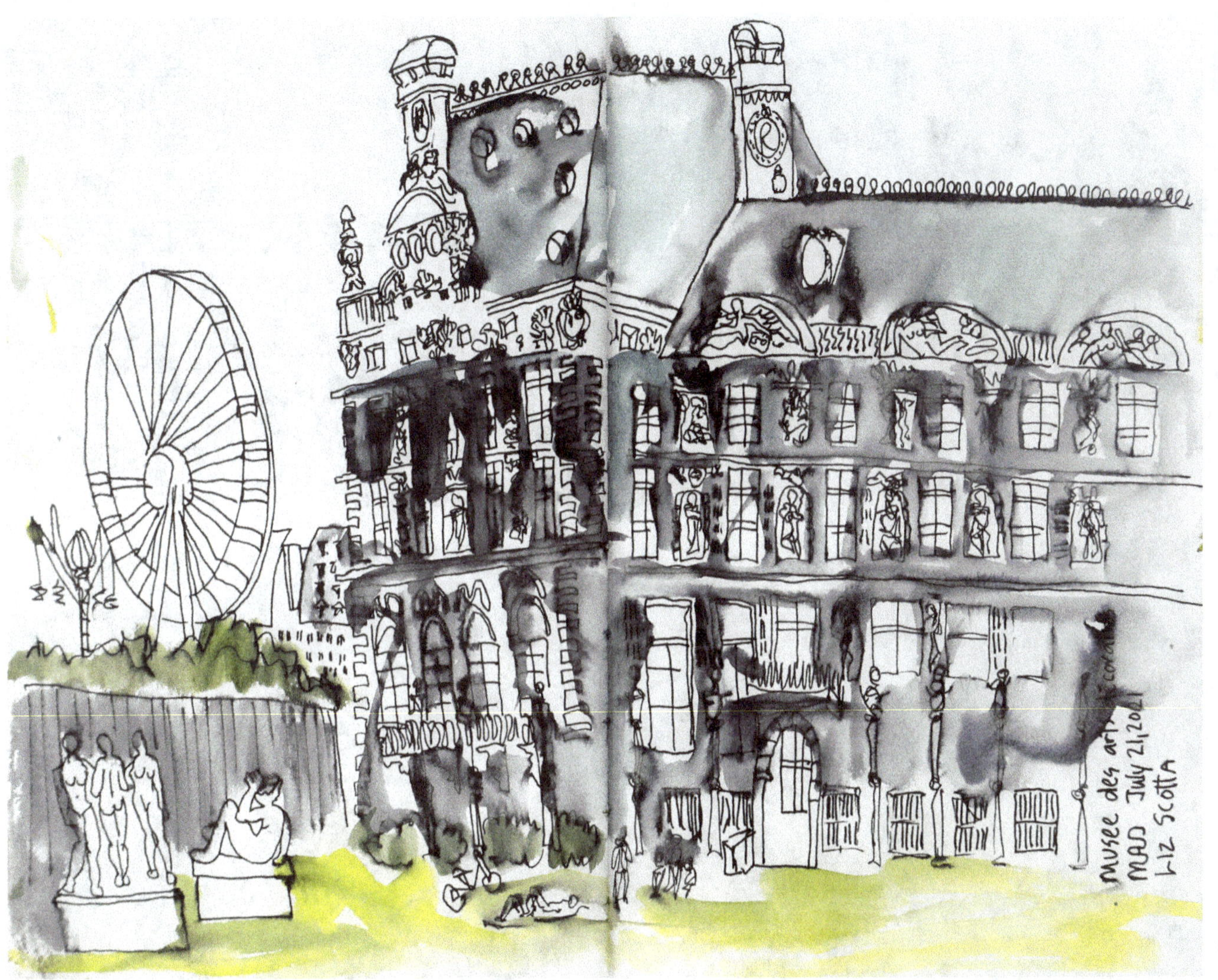

MUSÉE DES ARTS DÉCORATIFS
PARIS

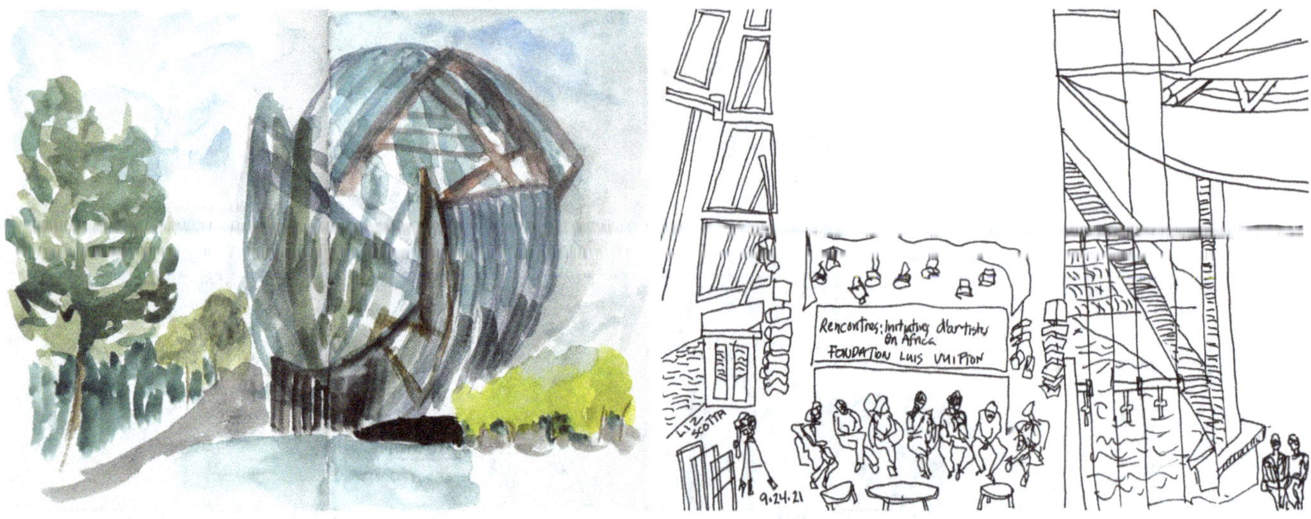

LOUIS VUITTON FOUNDATION MUSEUM
PARIS

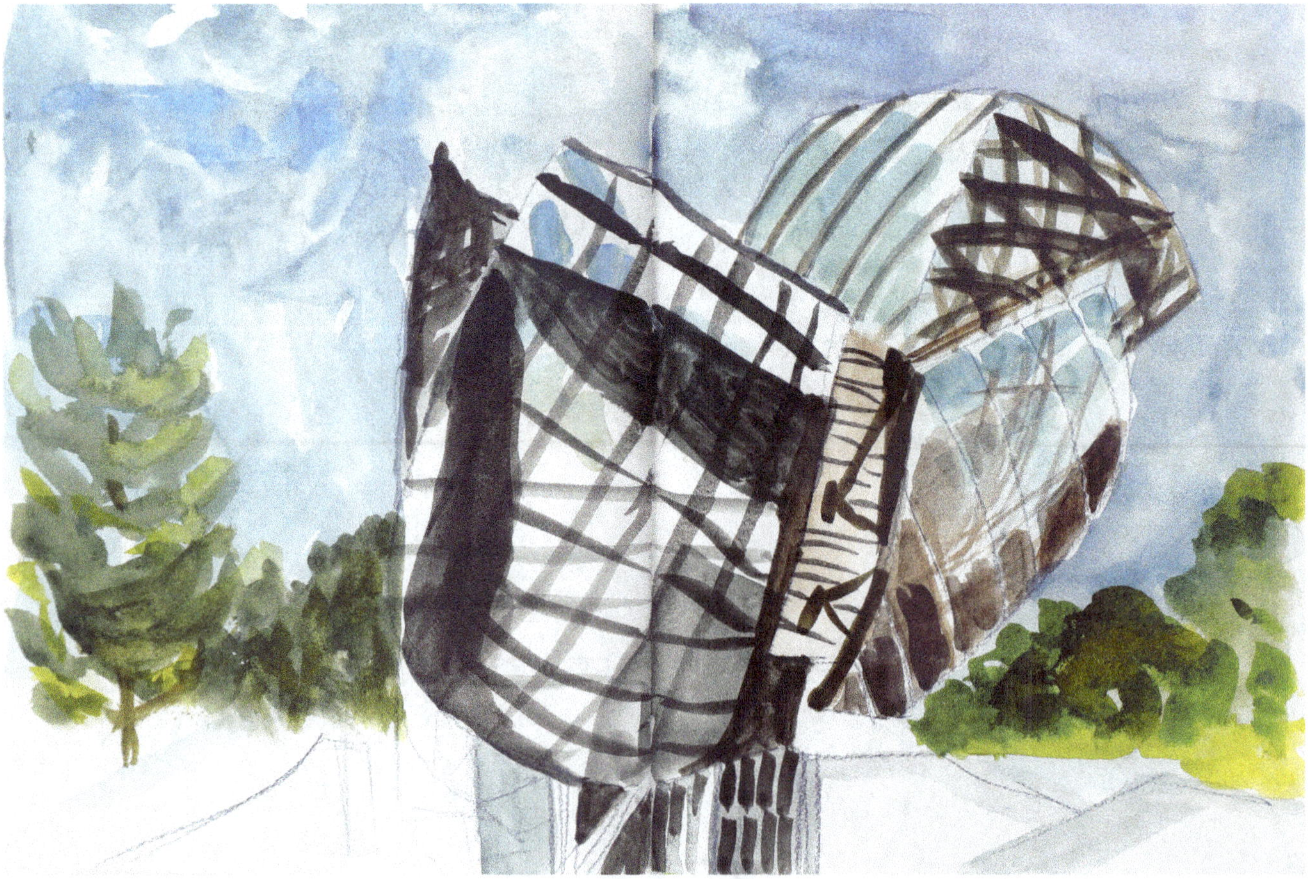

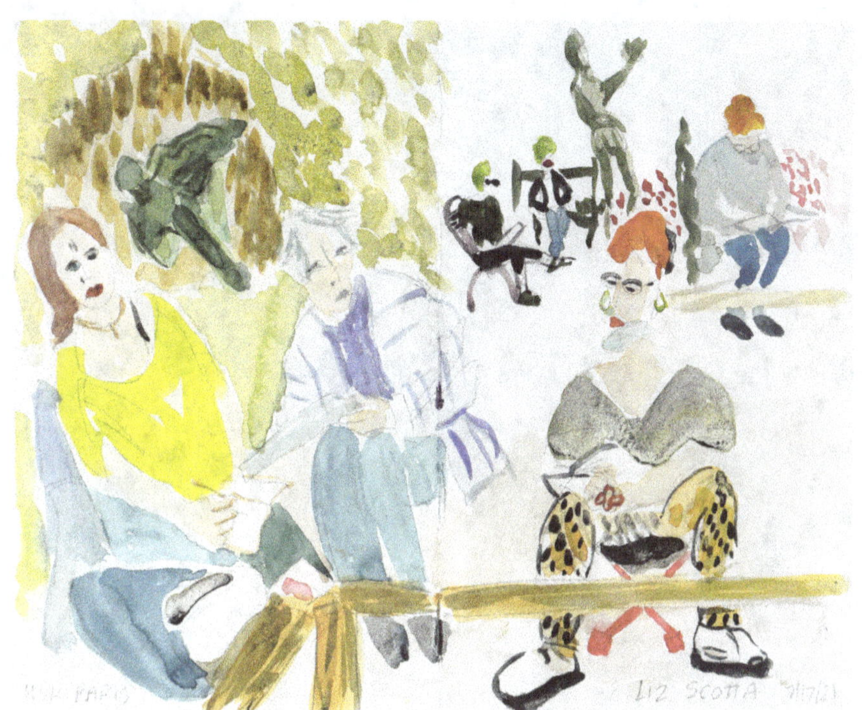

URBAN SKETCHERS PARIS
PARIS

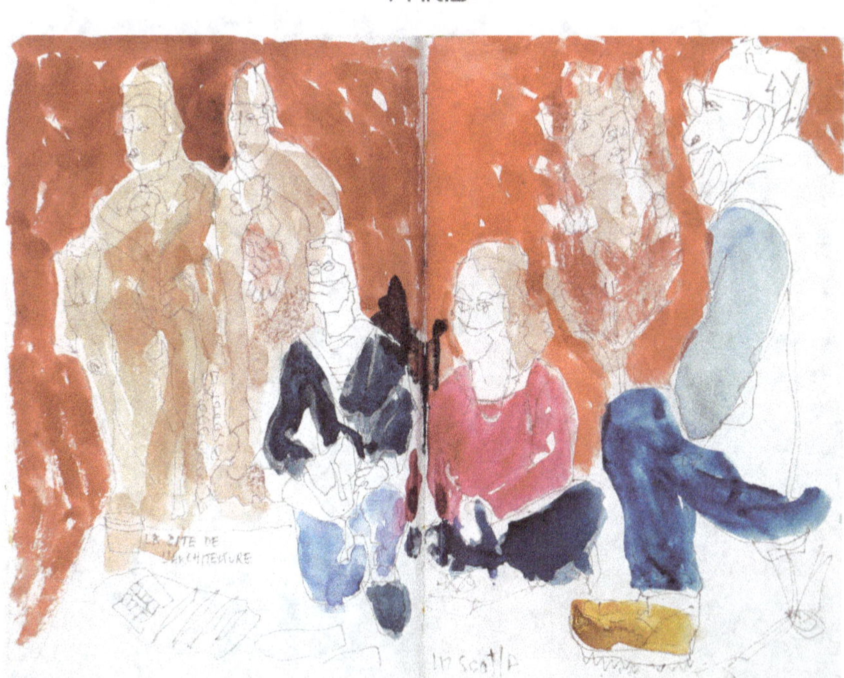

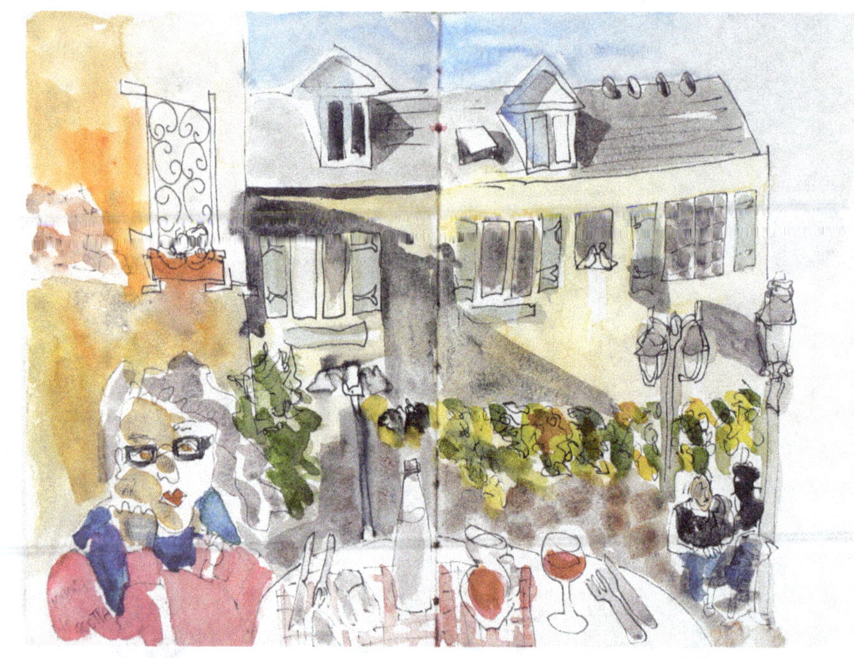

LUNCH AT MONTMARTRE
PARIS

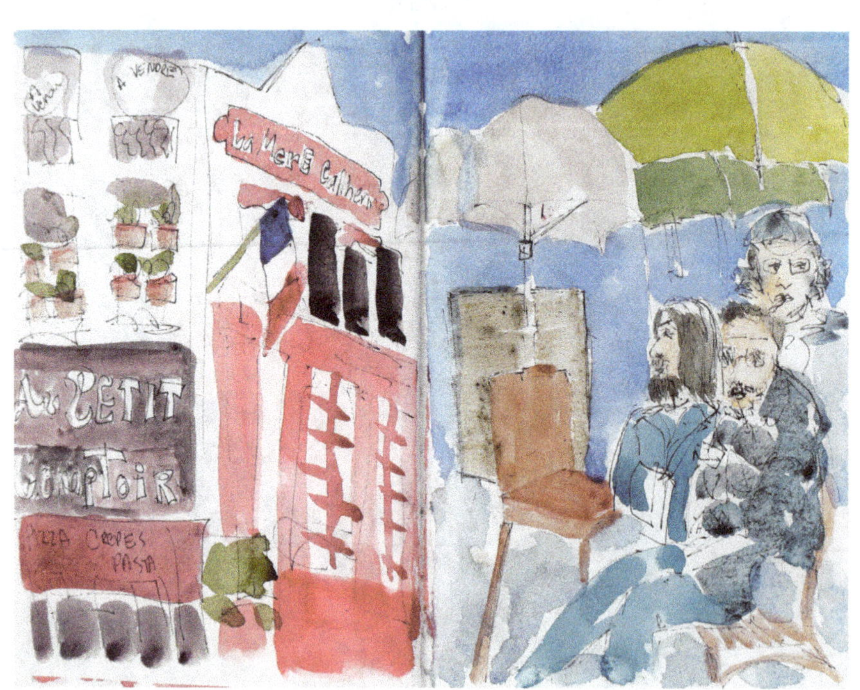

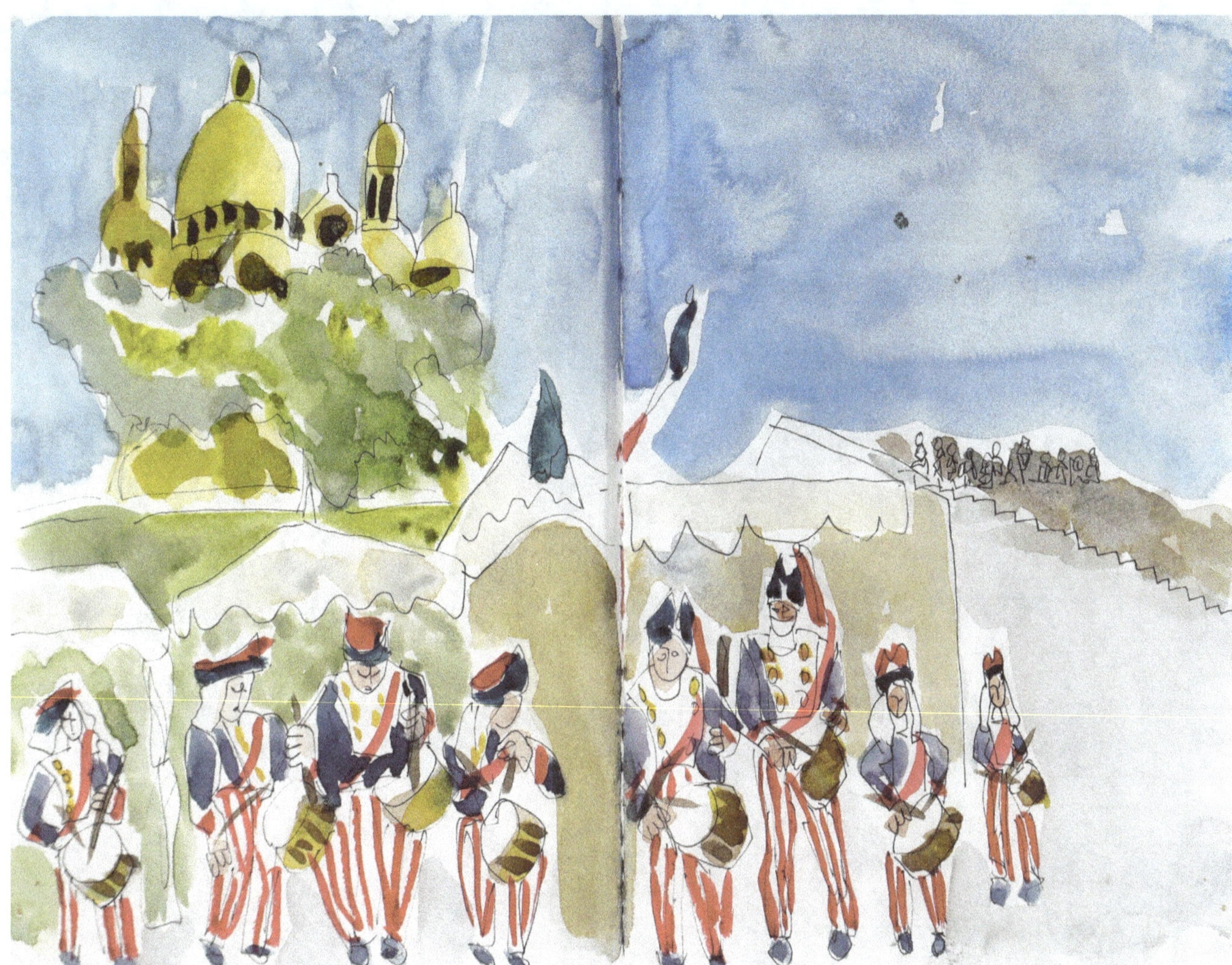

CELEBRATION AT MONTMARTRE
PARIS

BELLEVILLE
PARIS

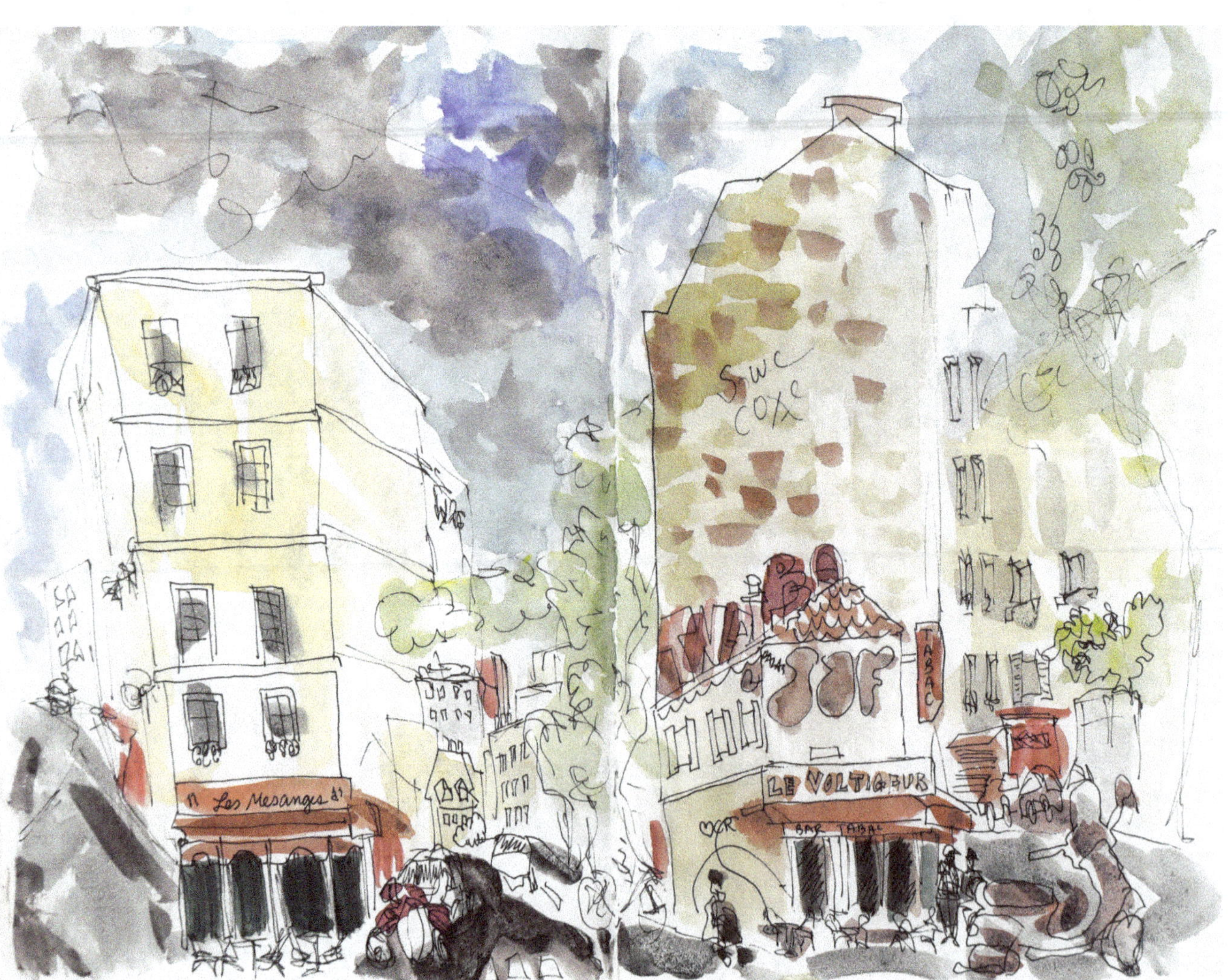

BELLEVILLE
PARIS

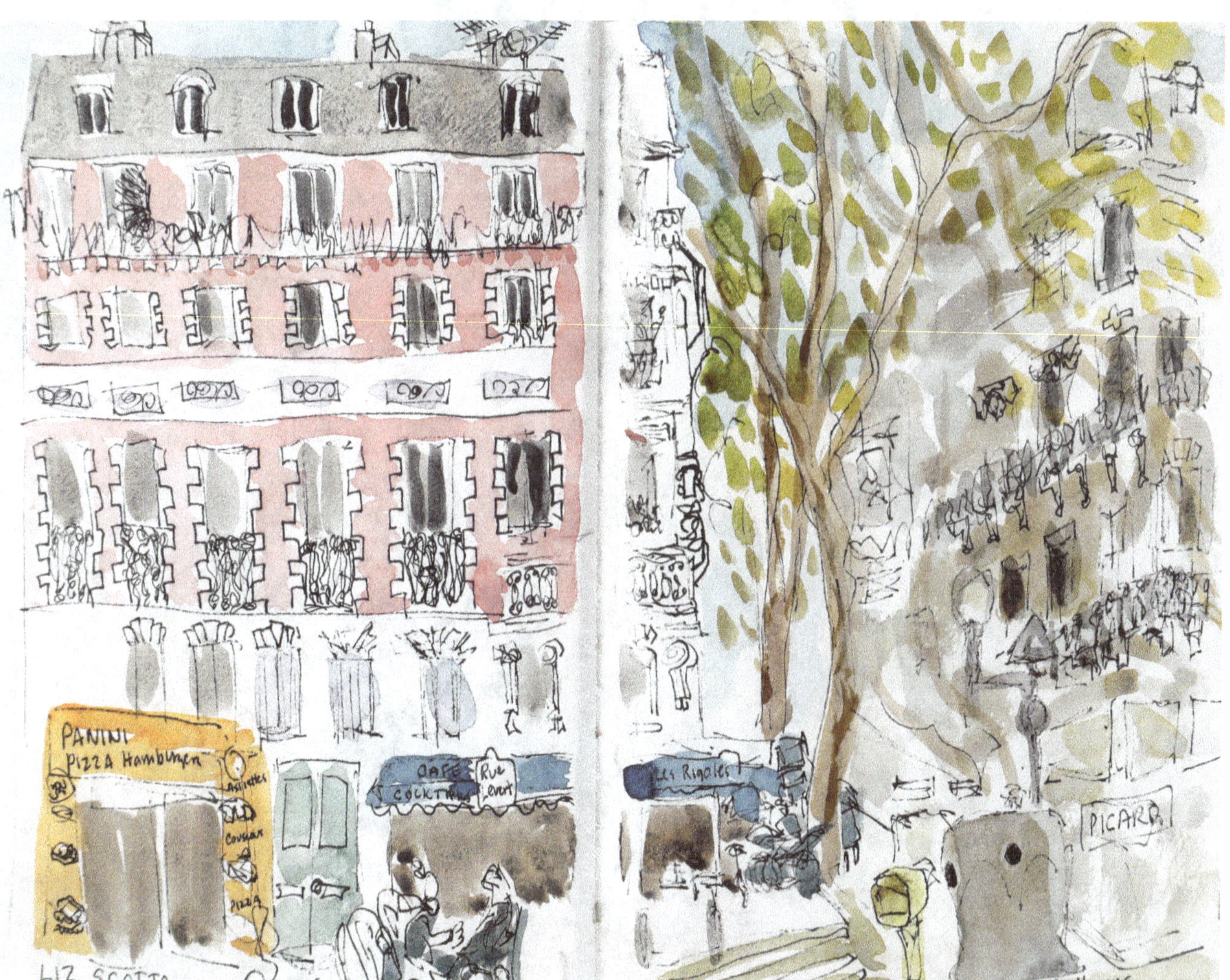

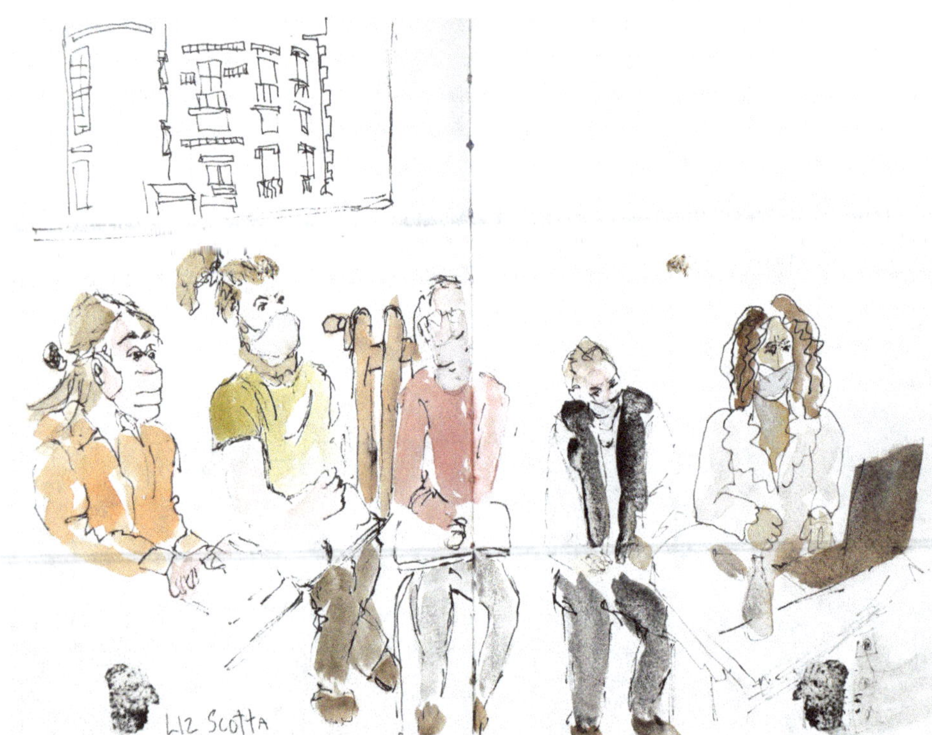
LIZ SCOTTA
ALLIANCE FRANÇAISE
PARIS

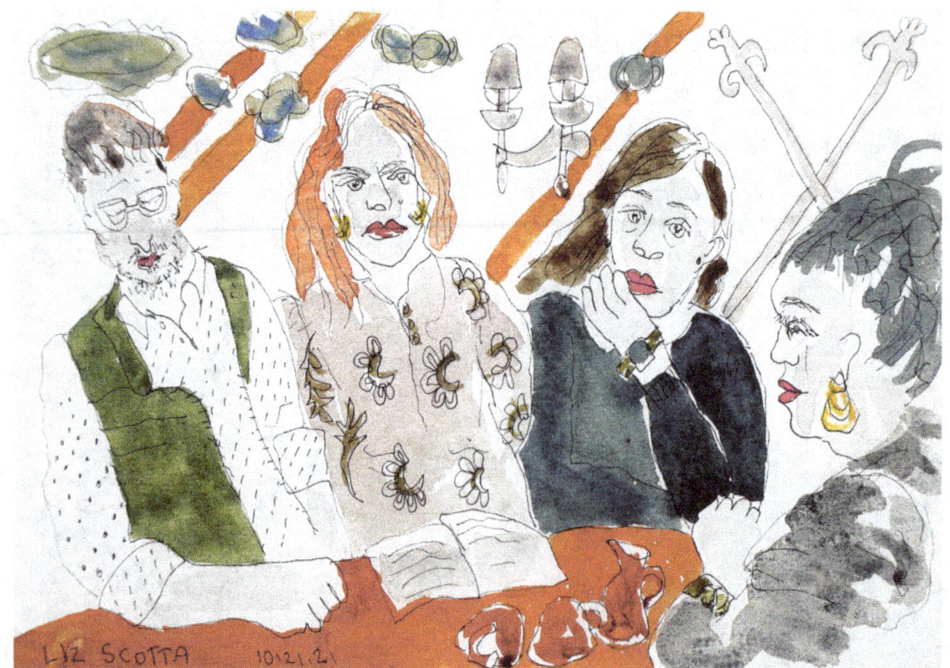
LIZ SCOTTA   10·21·21

ALLIANCE FRANÇAISE CLASSROOM
PARIS

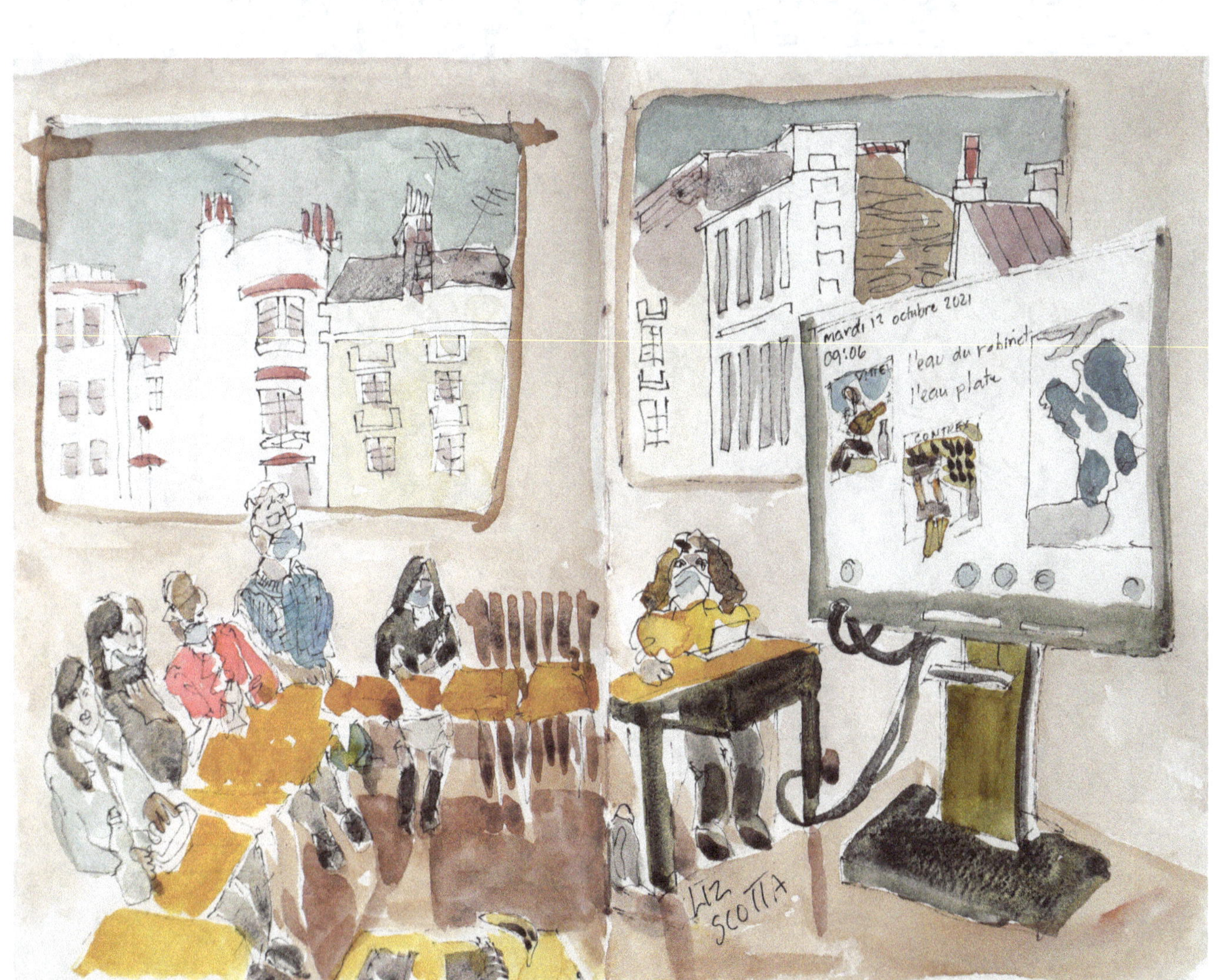

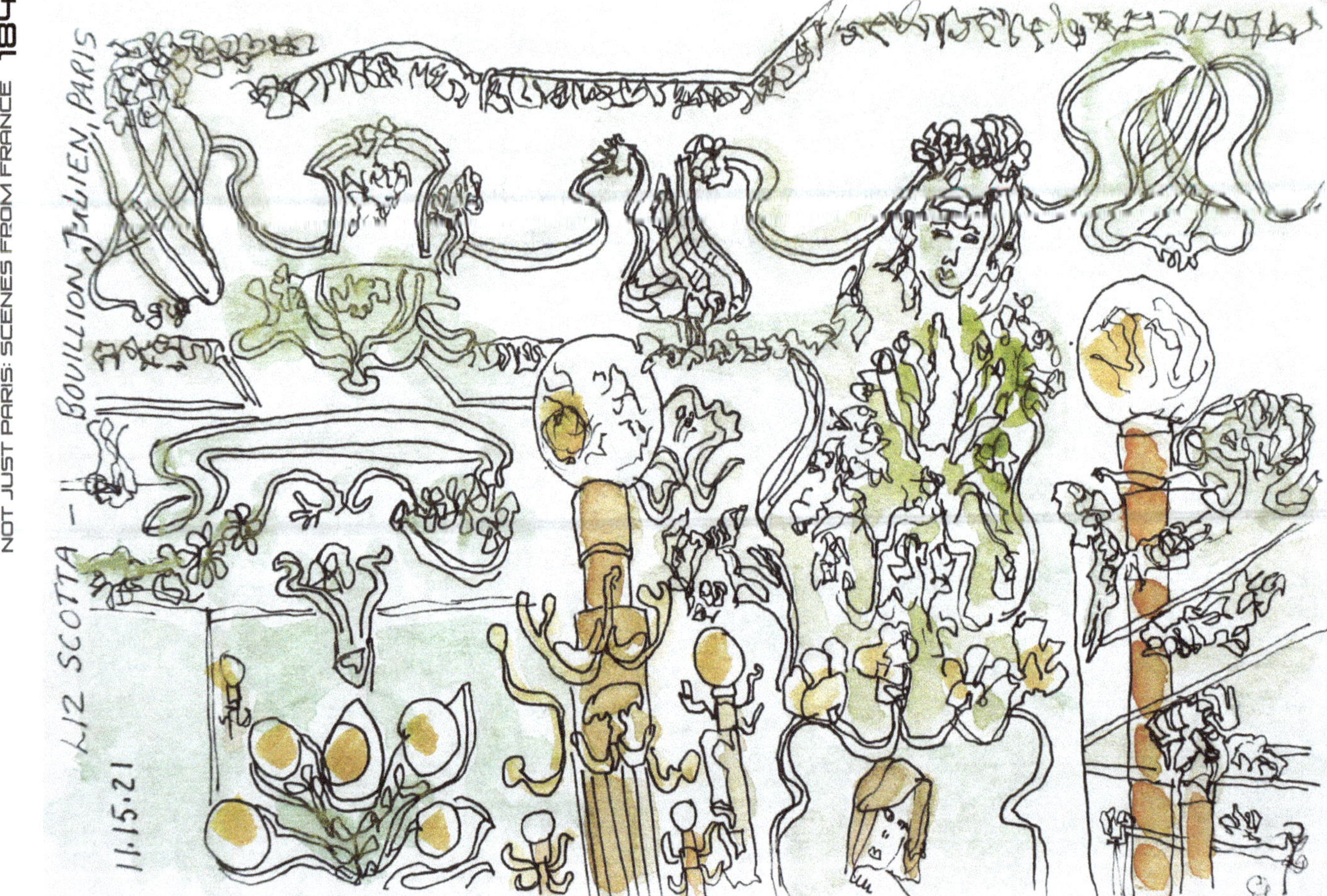

BOUILLON JULIEN RESTAURANT
PARIS

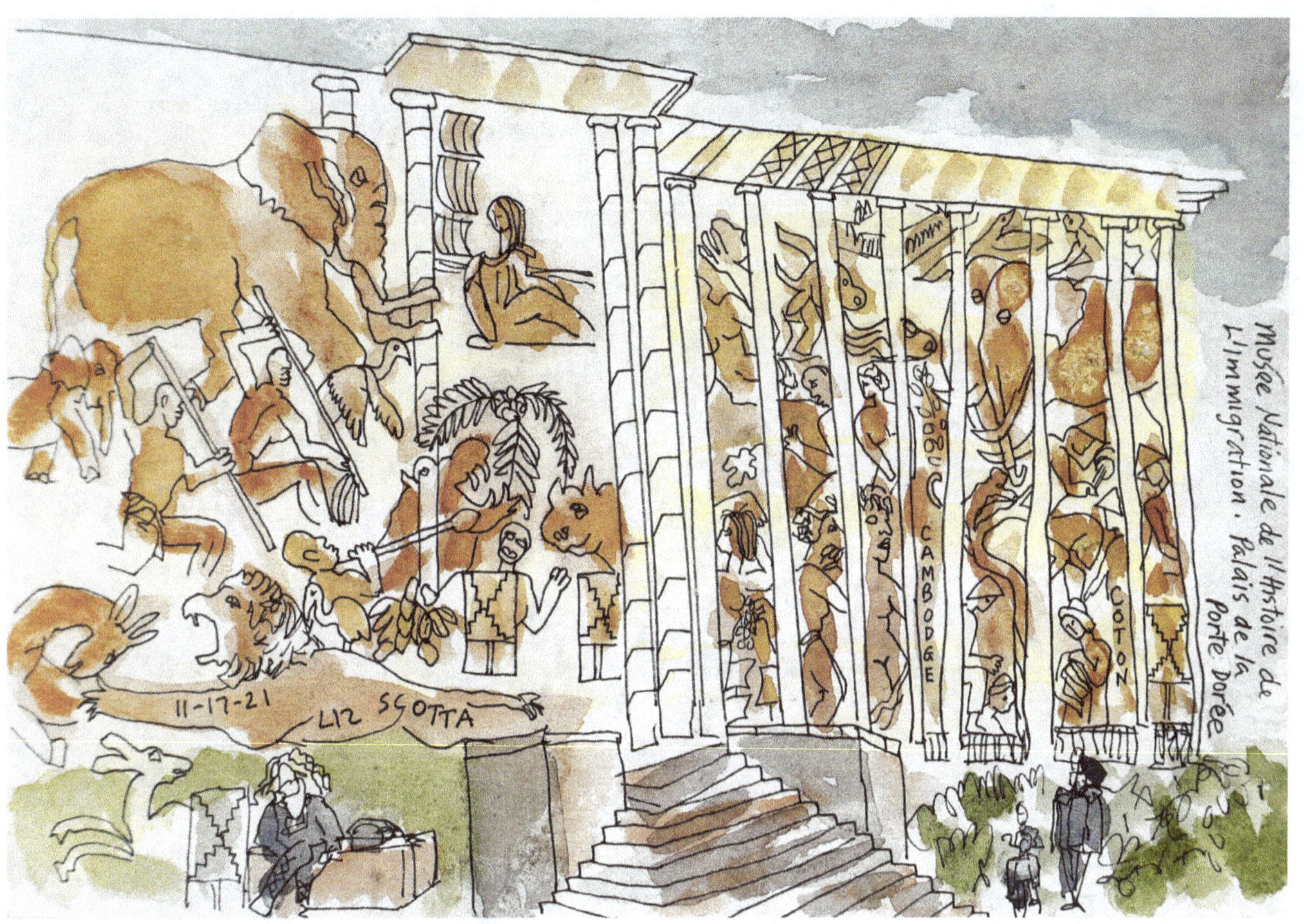

MUSÉE NATIONAL DE L'HISTOIRE DE L'IMMIGRATION
PARIS

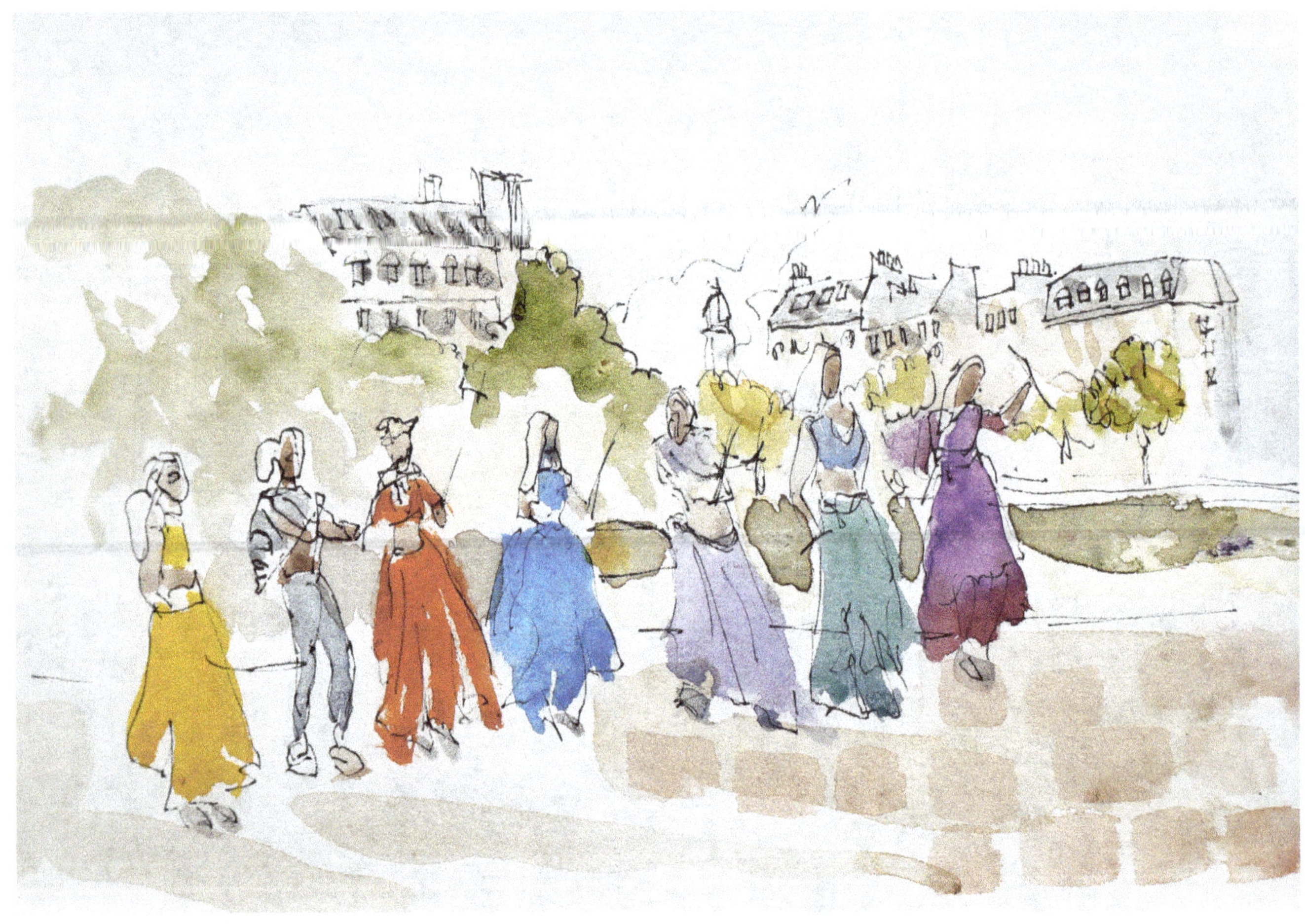

INDIAN DANCERS ALONG THE SEINE
PARIS

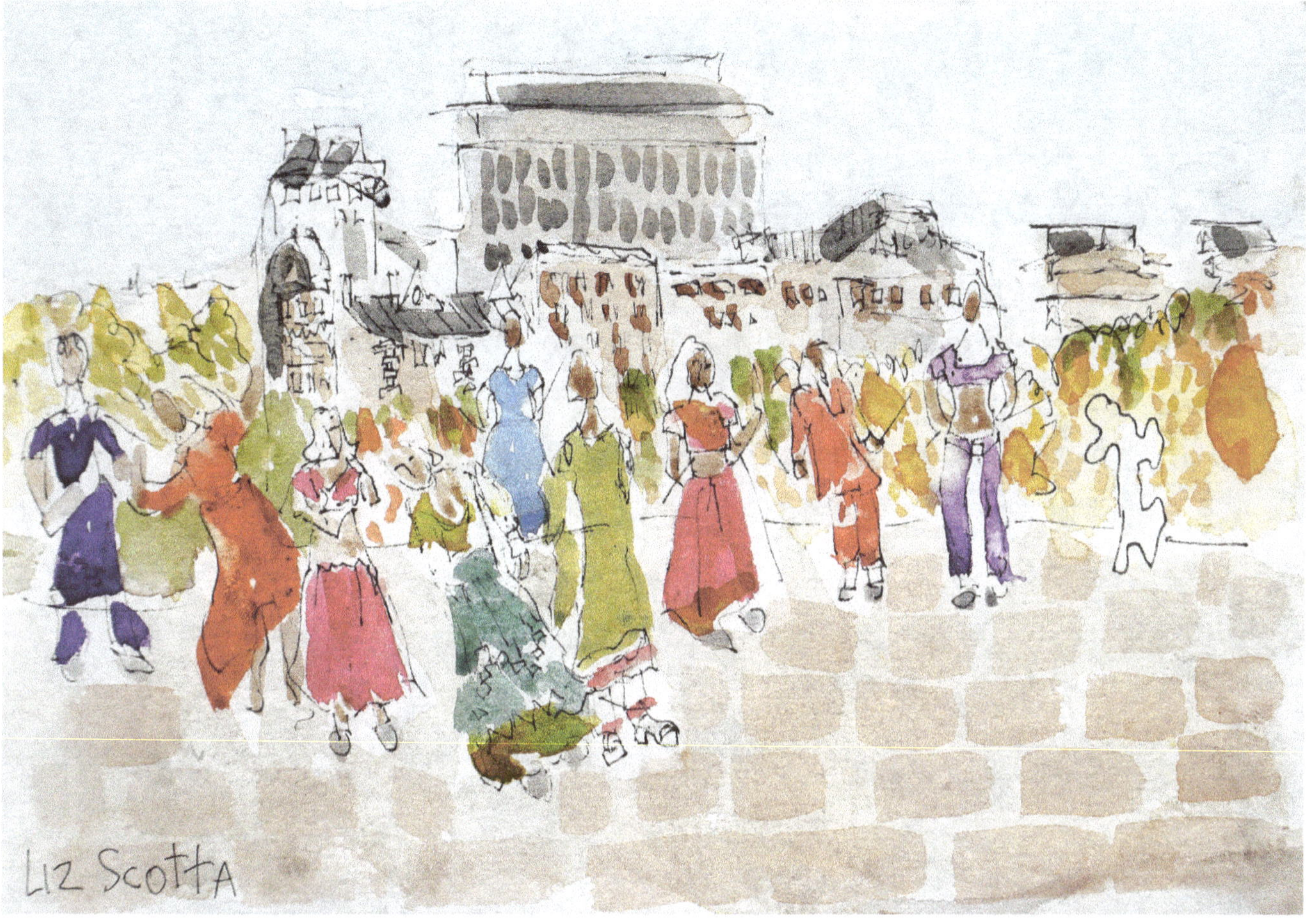

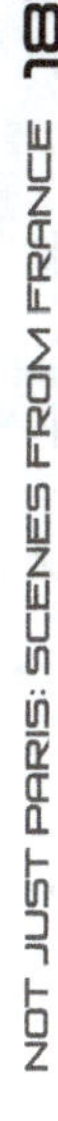

INDIAN DANCERS ALONG THE SEINE
PARIS

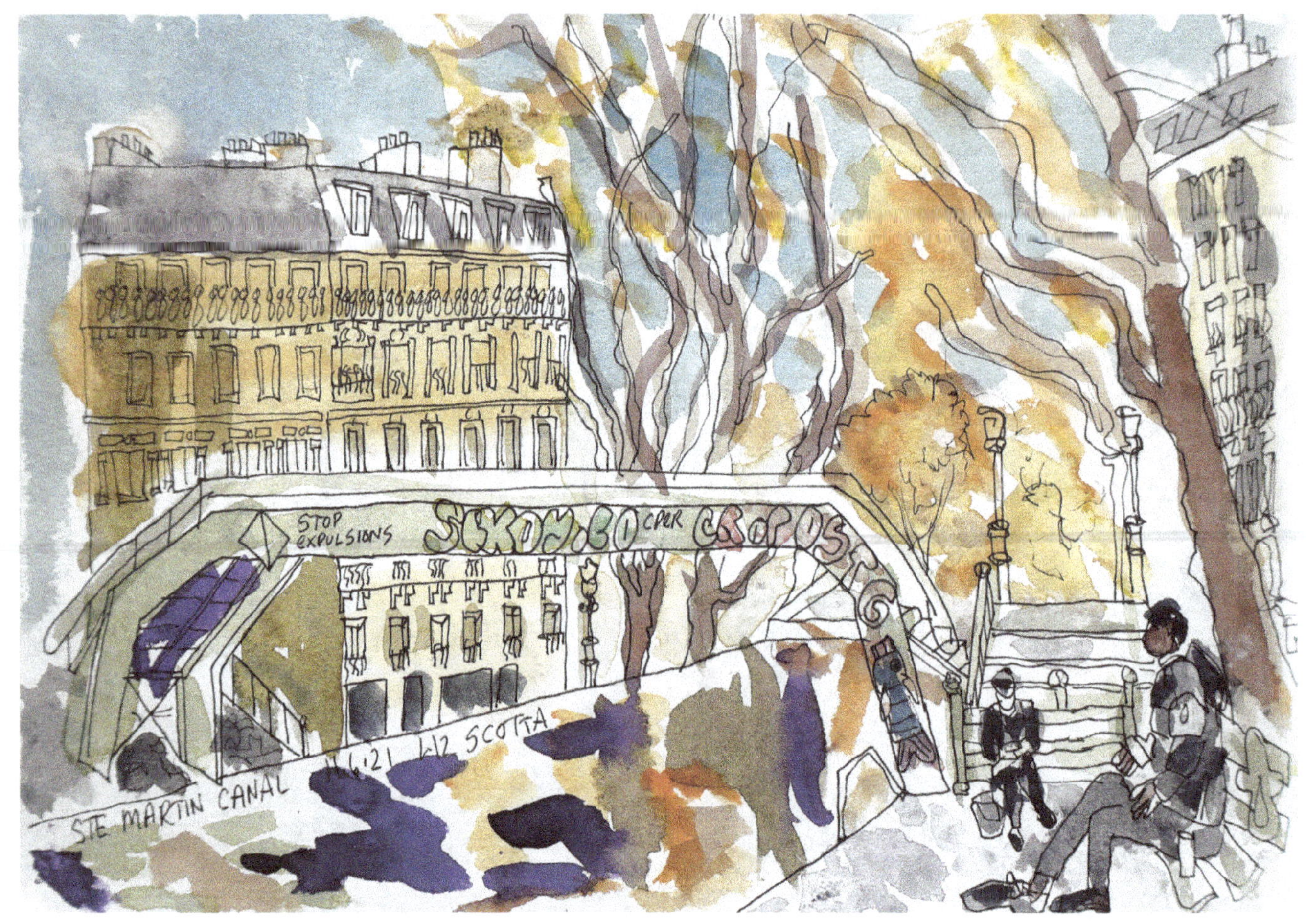

CANAL SAINT-MARTIN
PARIS

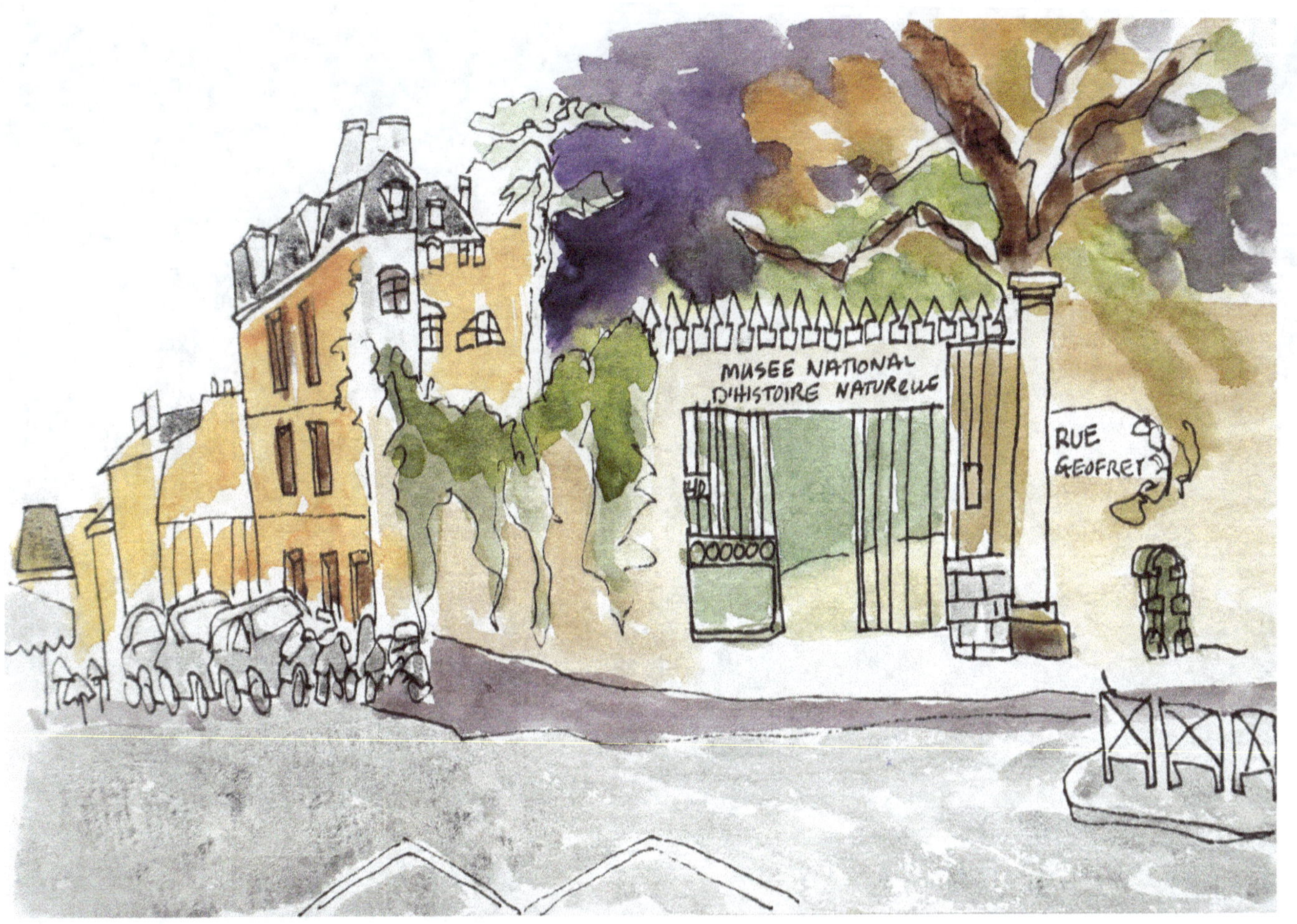

MUSÉE NATIONAL D'HISTOIRE NATURELLE
PARIS

2021

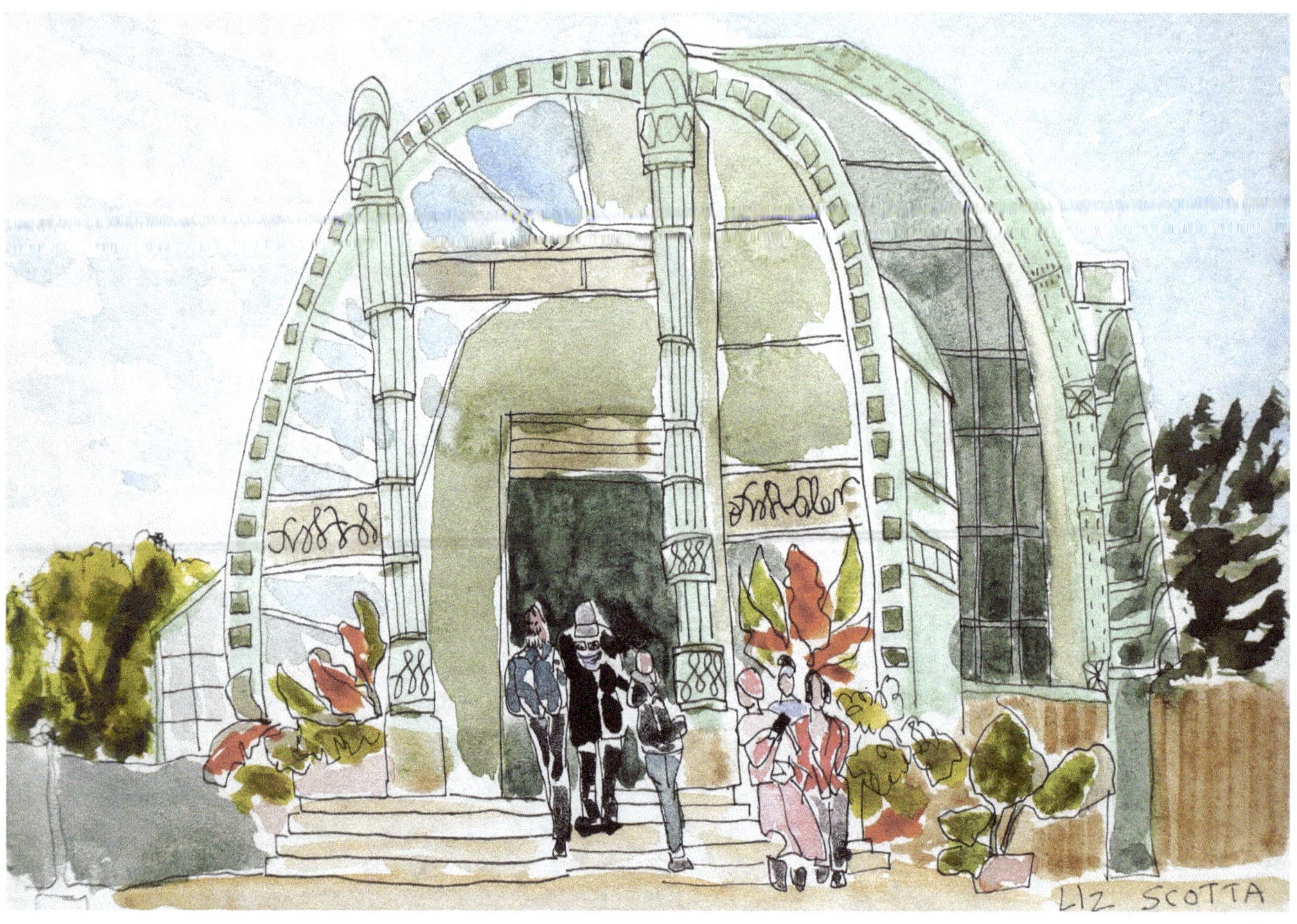

JARDIN DES PLANTES
PARIS

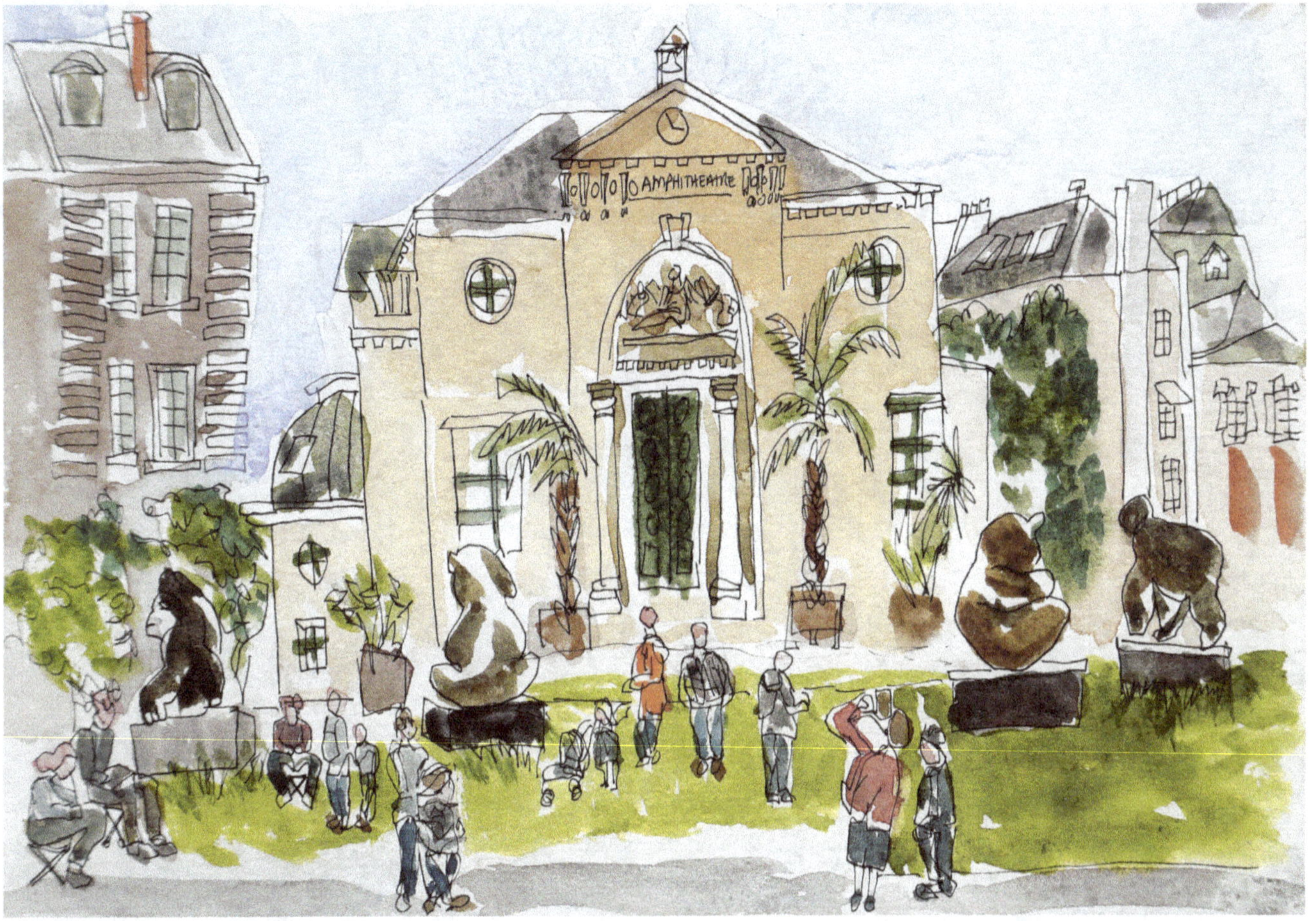

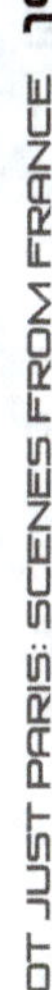

GRAND AMPHITHÉÂTRE, JARDIN DES PLANTES
PARIS

2021

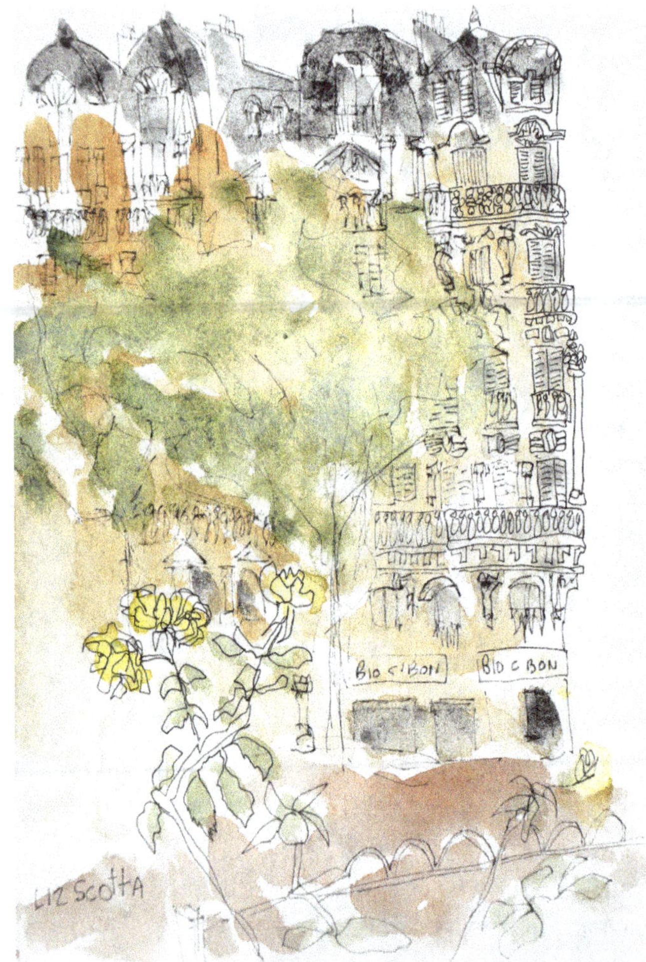

SQUARE COURTELINE
PARIS

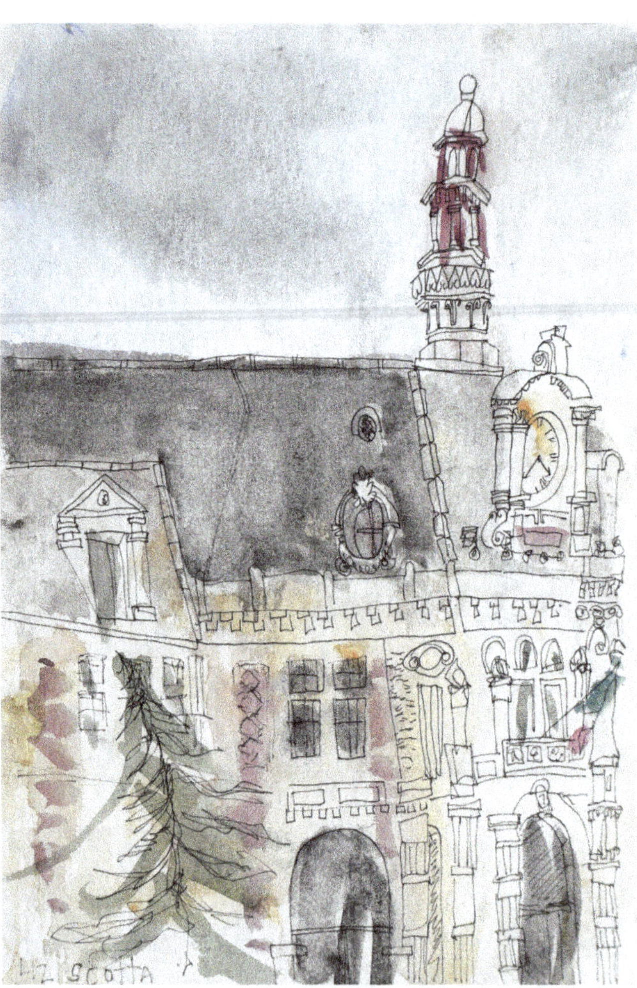

SQUARE EUGÈNE THOMAS
PARIS

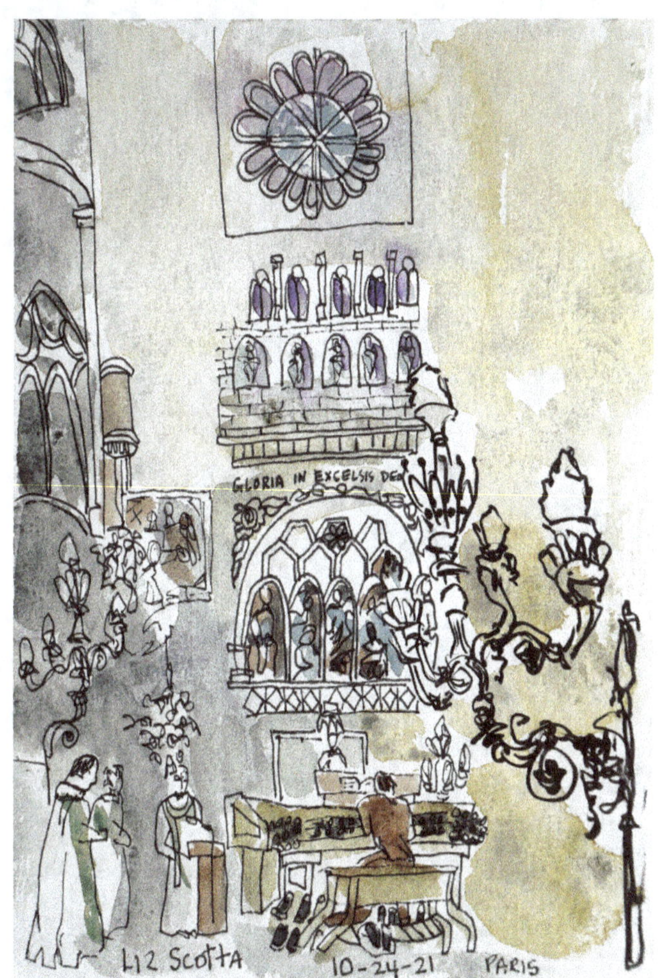

SAINT-EUSTACHE CHURCH
PARIS

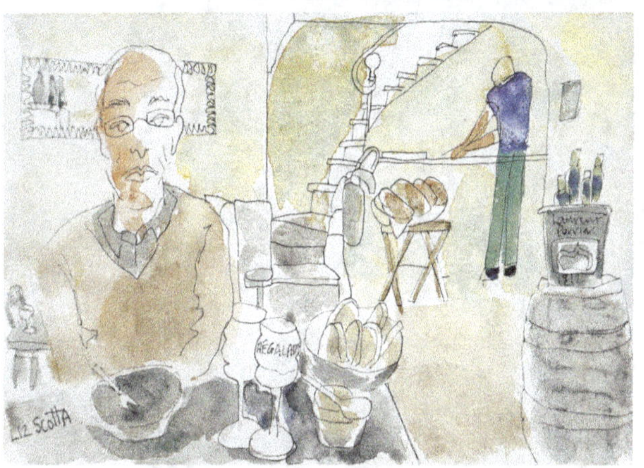

LA RÉGALADE RESTAURANT
PARIS

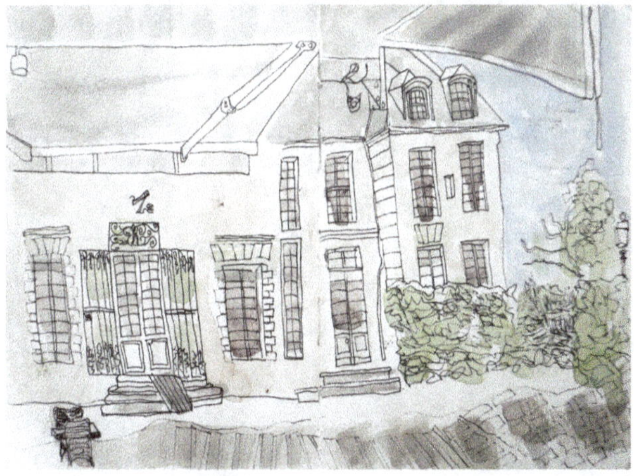

CHÂTEAU D'AUVERS
AUVERS-SUR-OISE

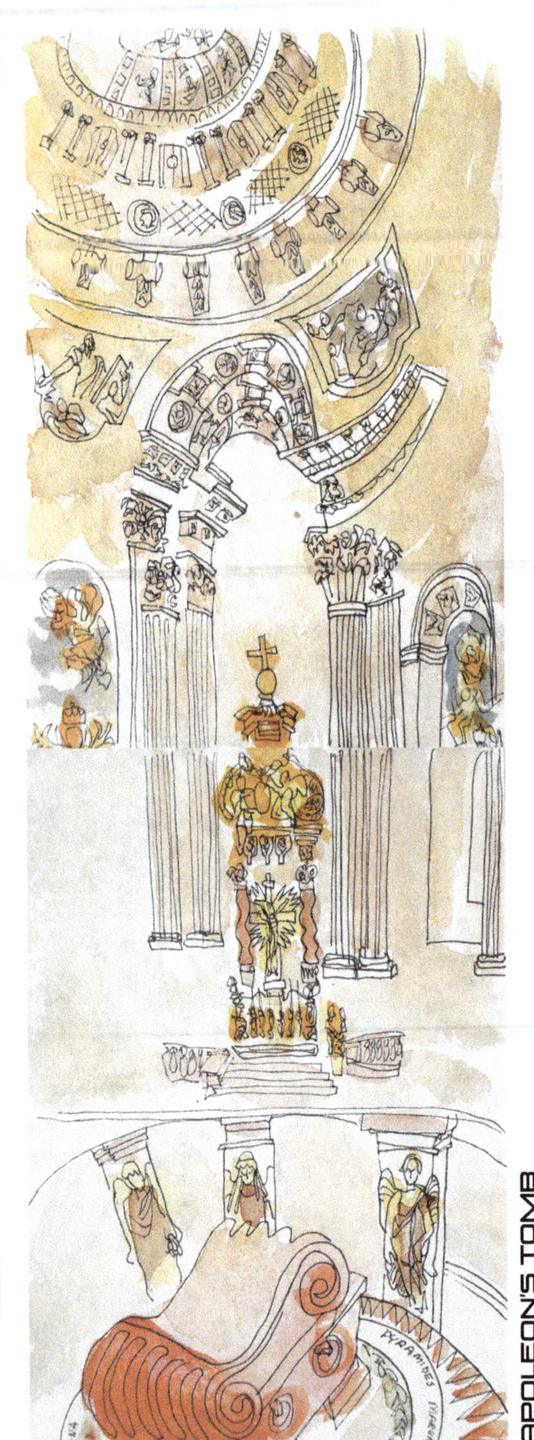

NAPOLEON'S TOMB
PARIS

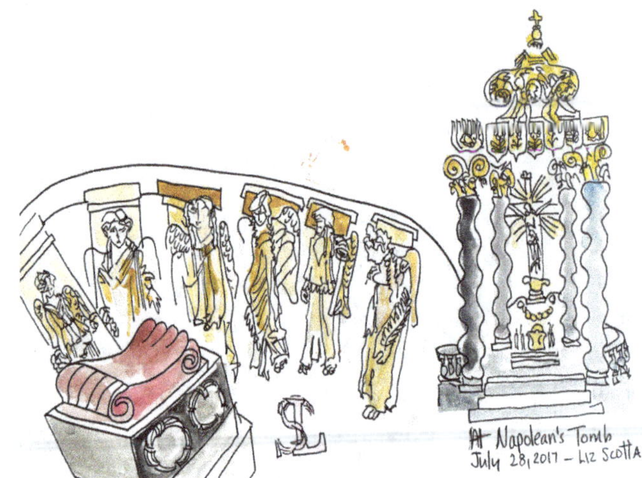

NAPOLEON'S TOMB
PARIS

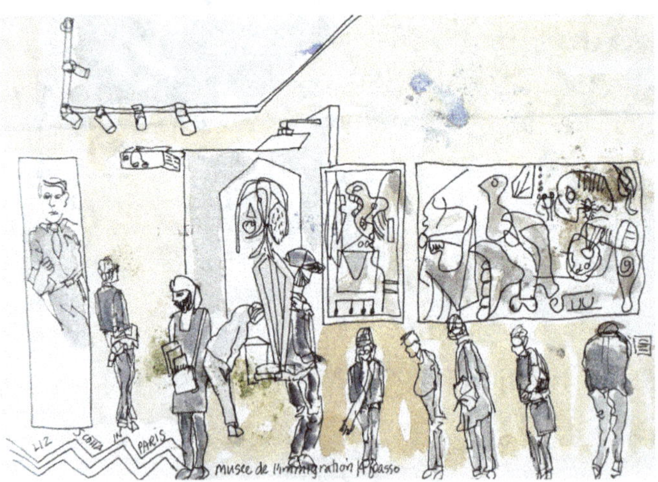

**MUSÉE NATIONAL DE L'HISTOIRE
DE L'IMMIGRATION**
PARIS

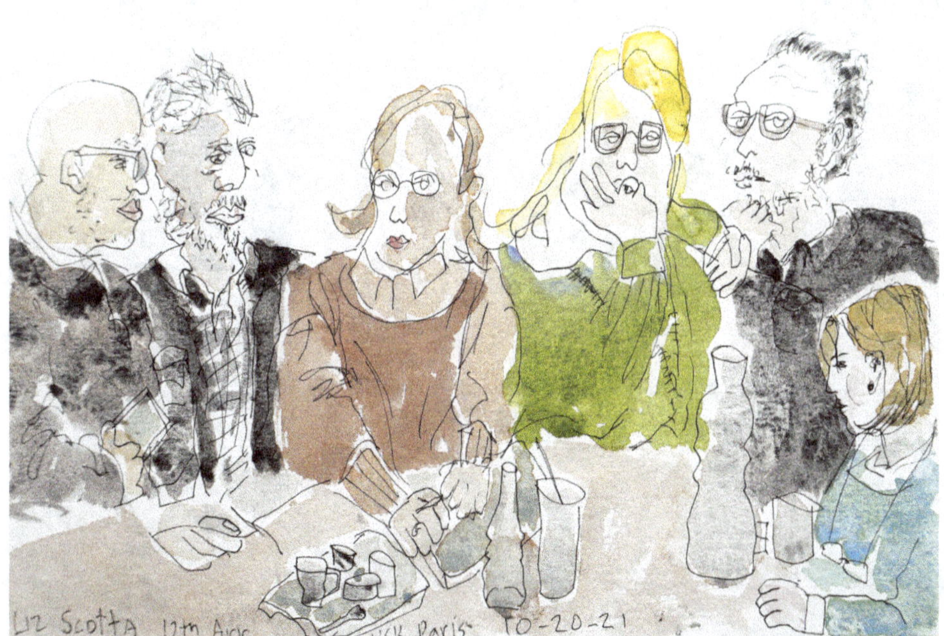

URBAN SKETCHERS PARIS
PARIS

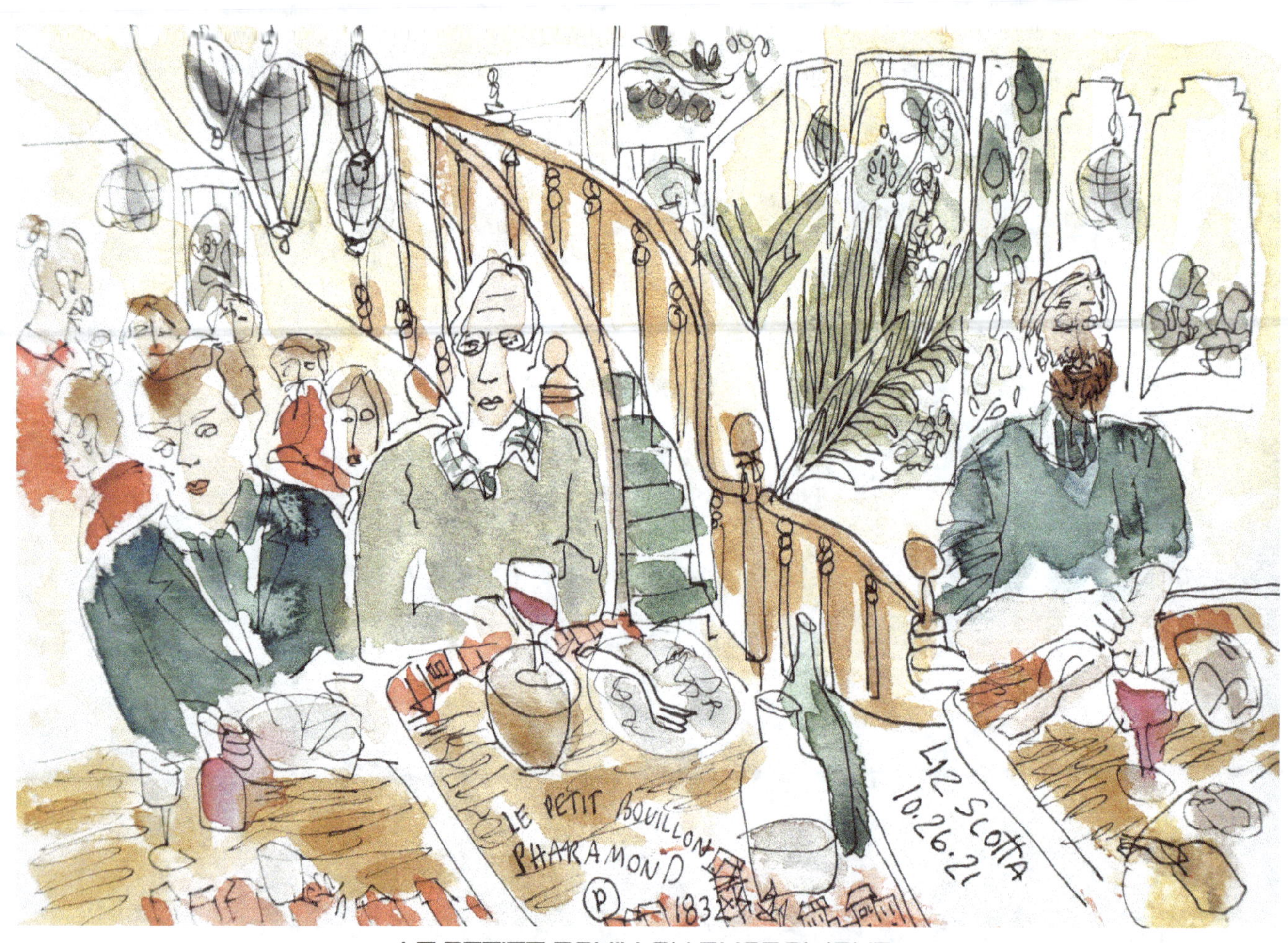

LE PETITE BOUILLON PHARAMOND
PARIS

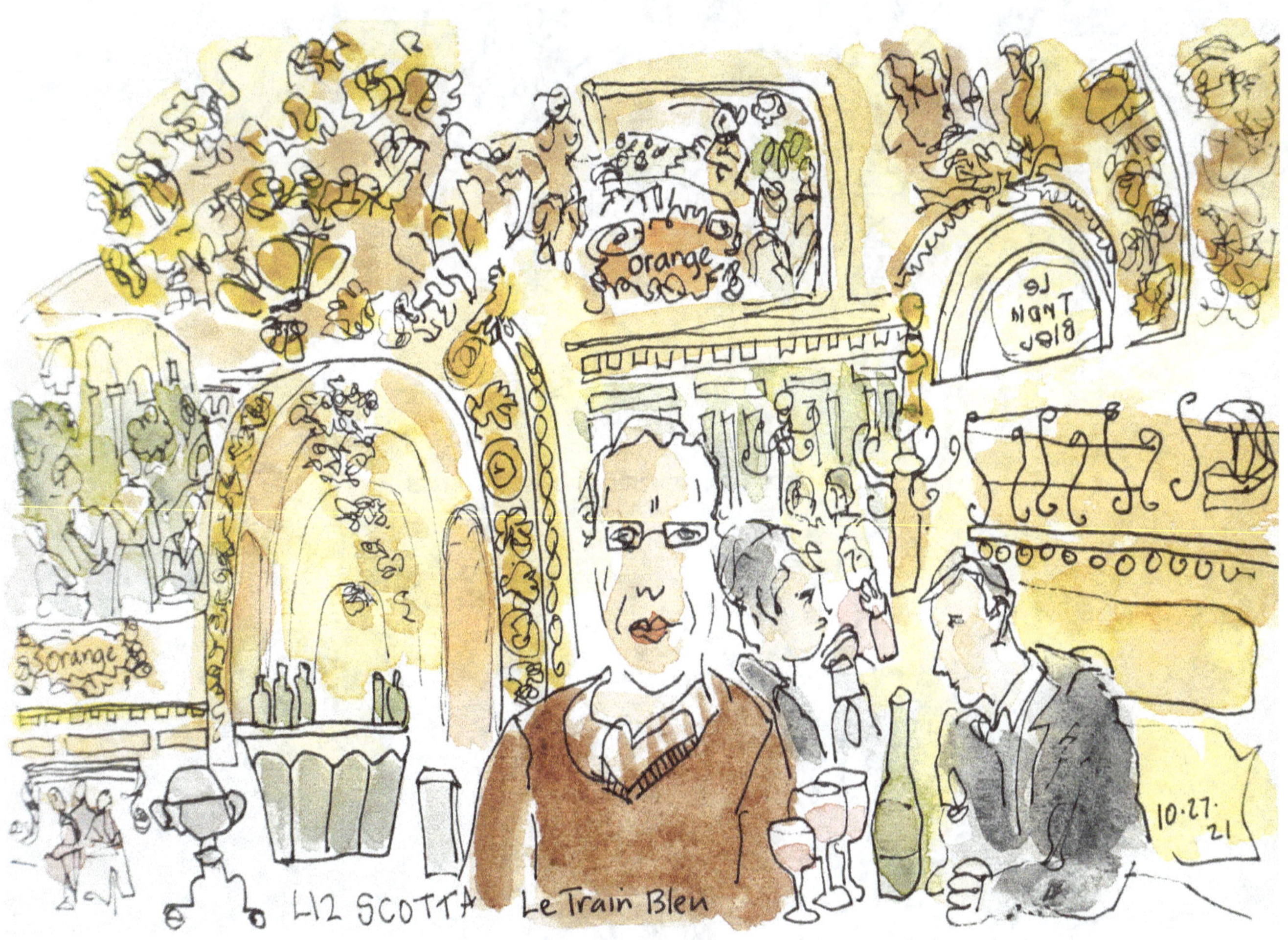

LE TRAIN BLEU
PARIS

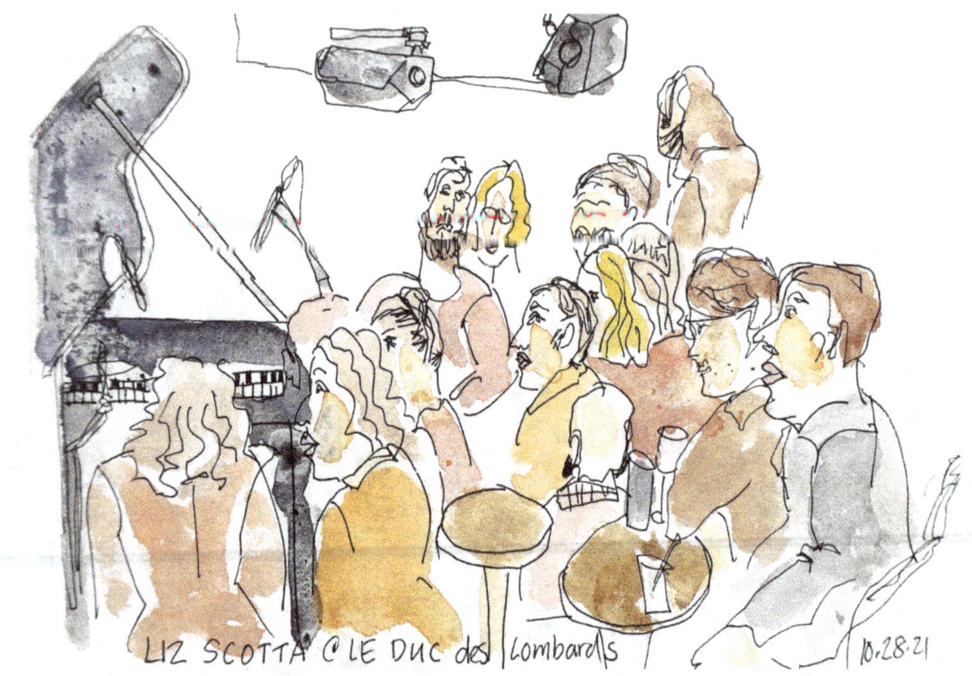

LE DUC DES LOMBARDS JAZZ CLUB
PARIS

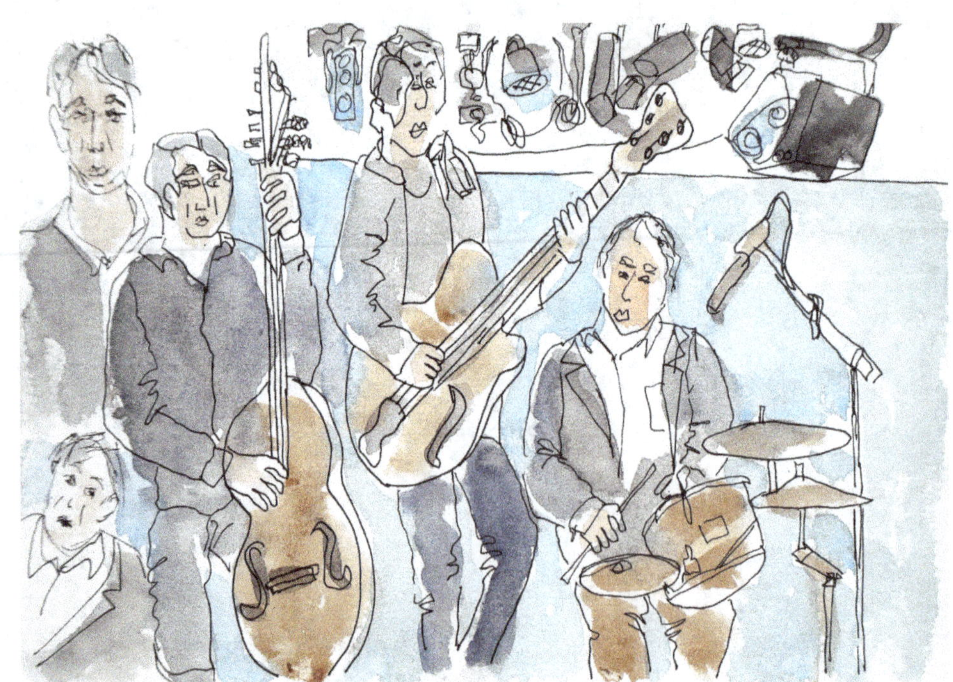

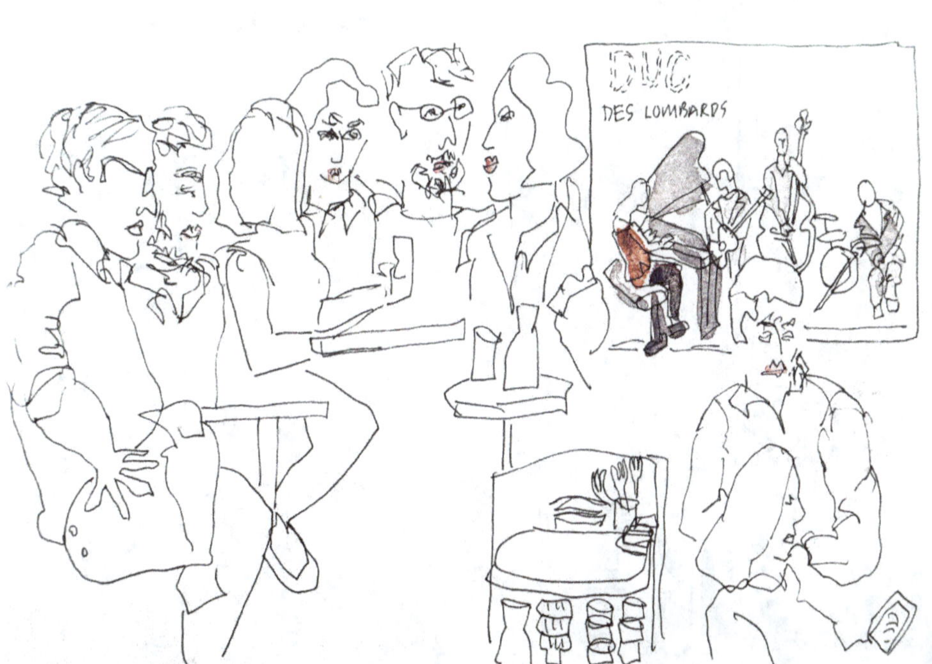

LE DUC DES LOMBARDS JAZZ CLUB
PARIS

BASTILLE SQUARE
PARIS

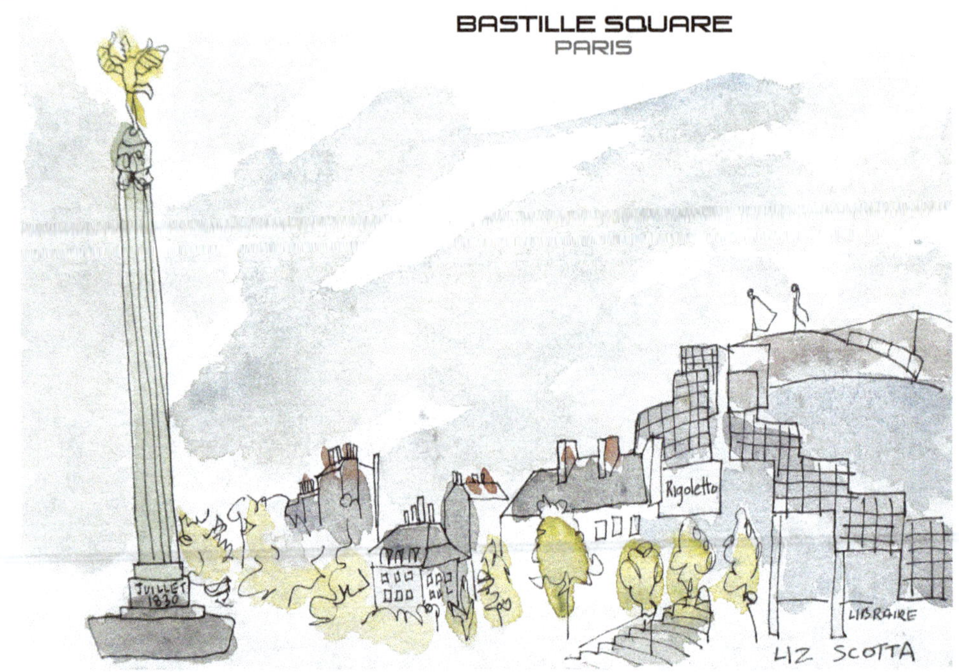

CAFÉ BASTILLE
PARIS

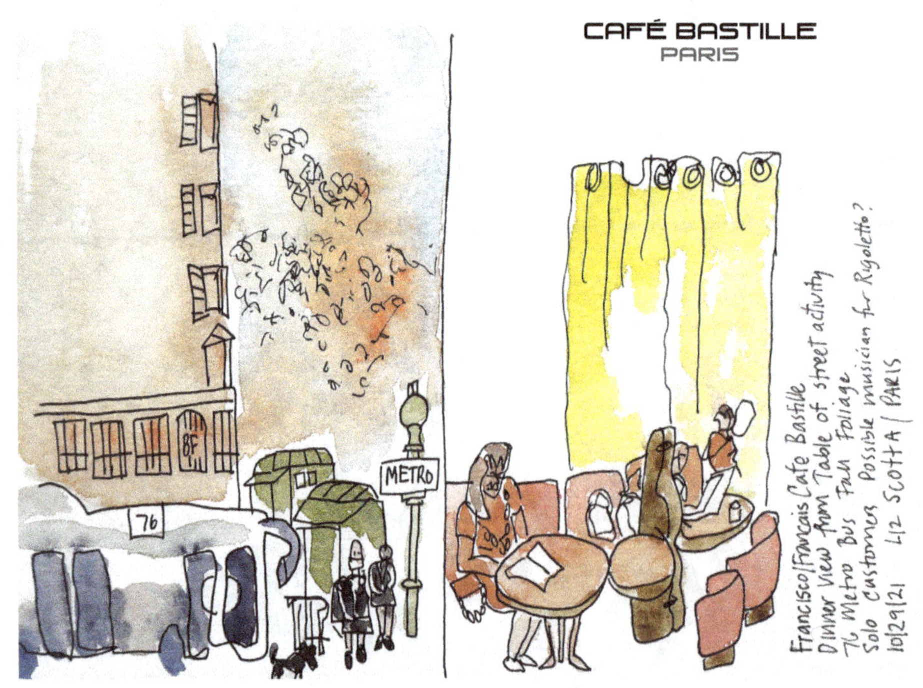

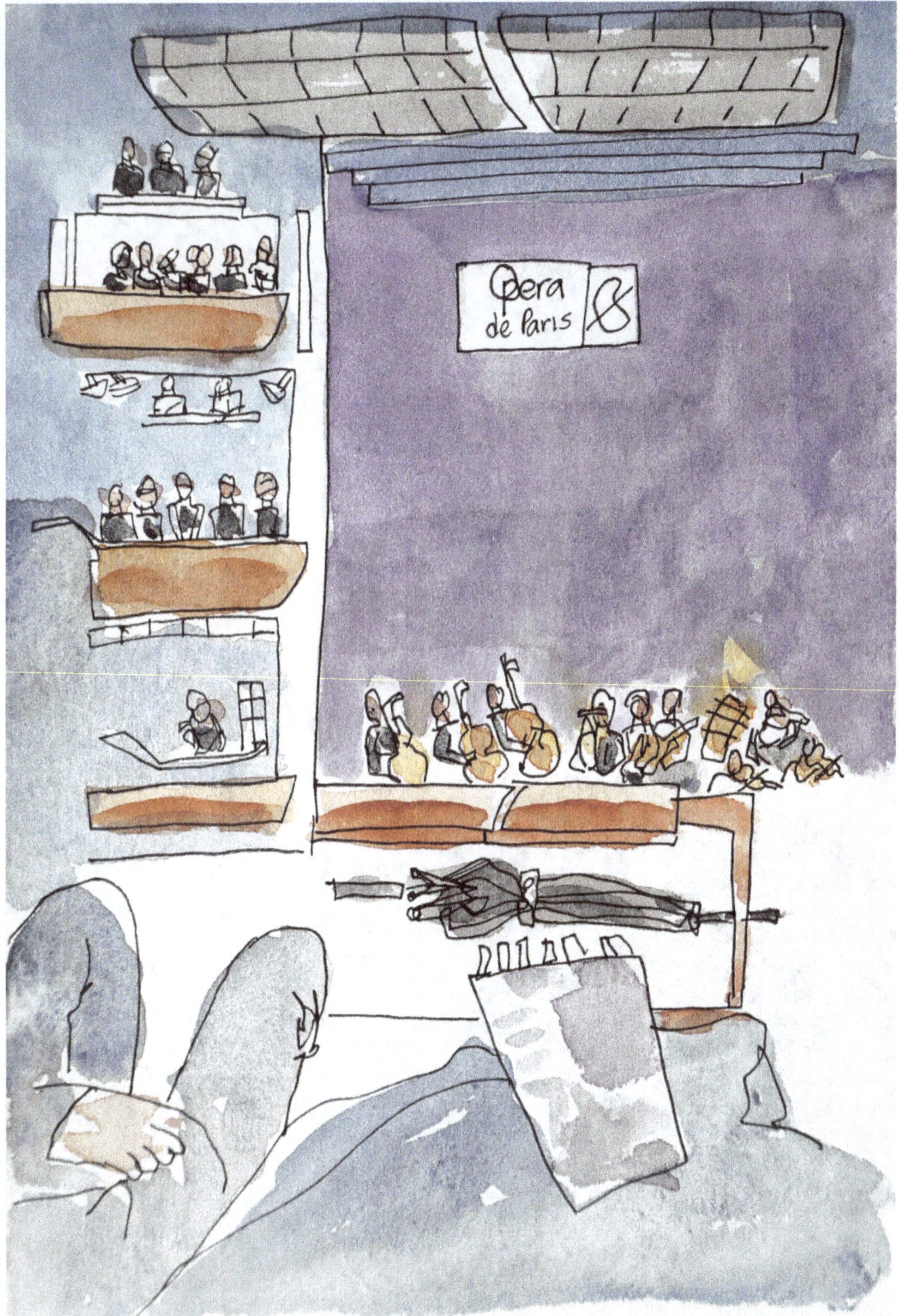

BASTILLE
OPERA HOUSE
PARIS

2021

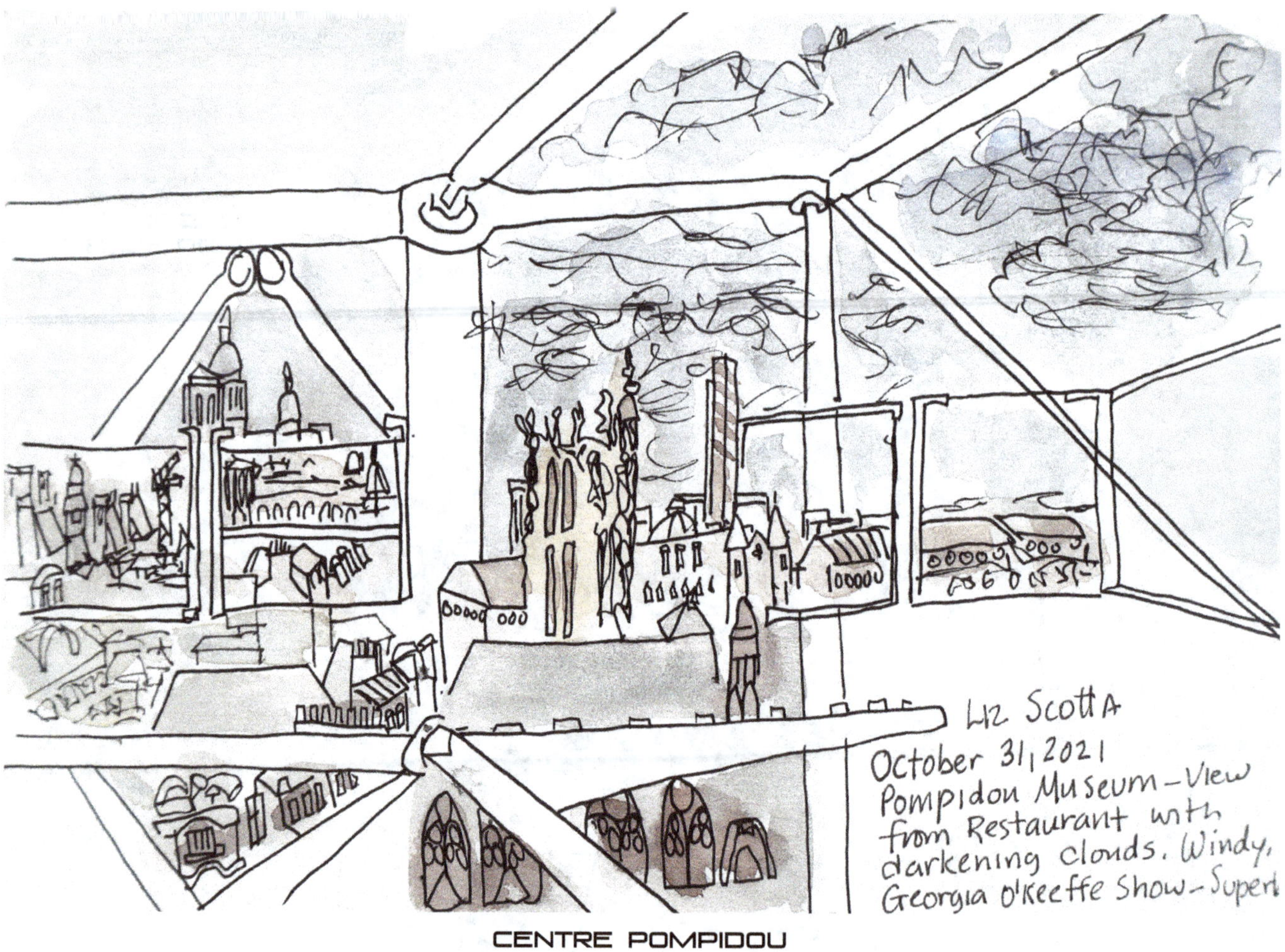

CENTRE POMPIDOU
PARIS

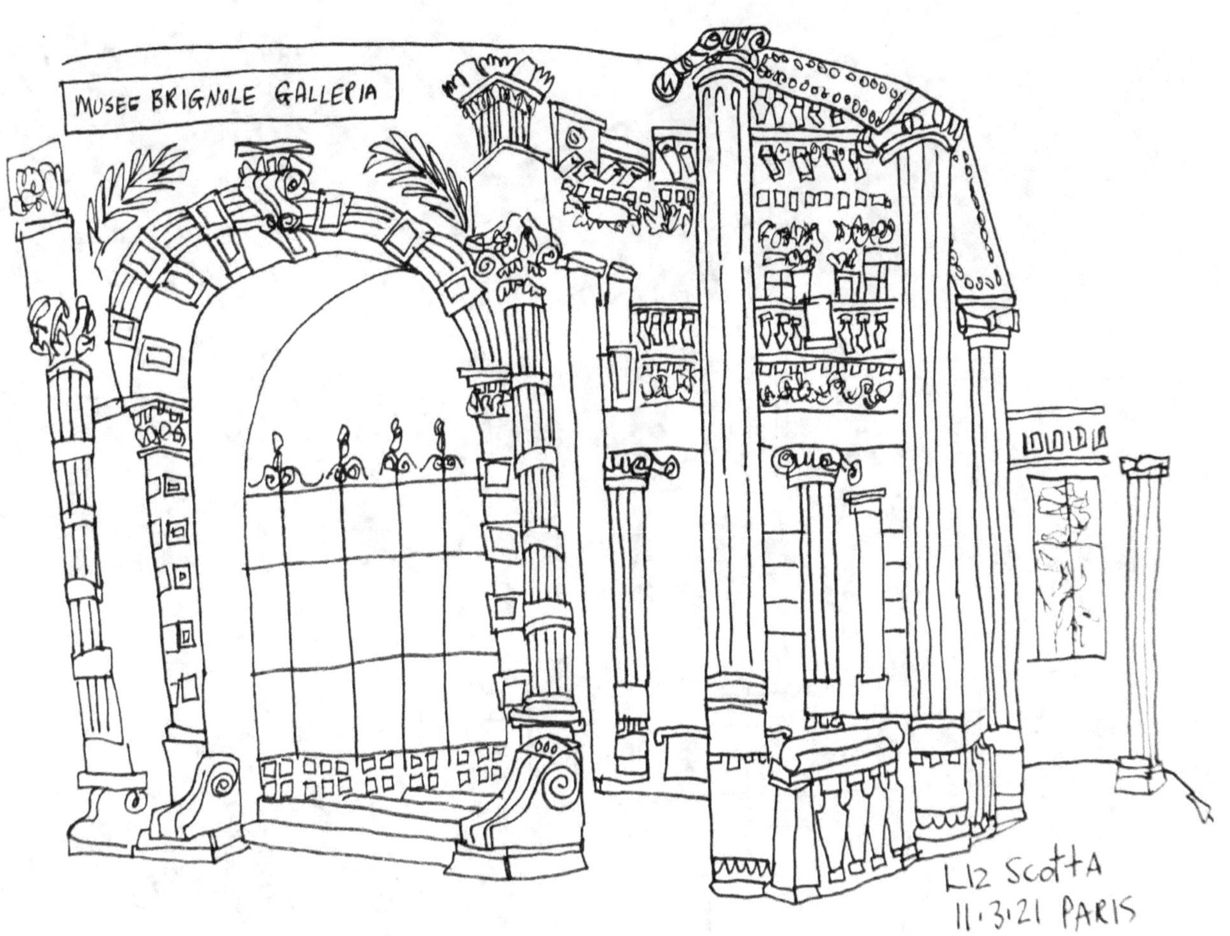

MUSÉE BRIGNOLE GALLERIA—FASHION MUSEUM
PARIS

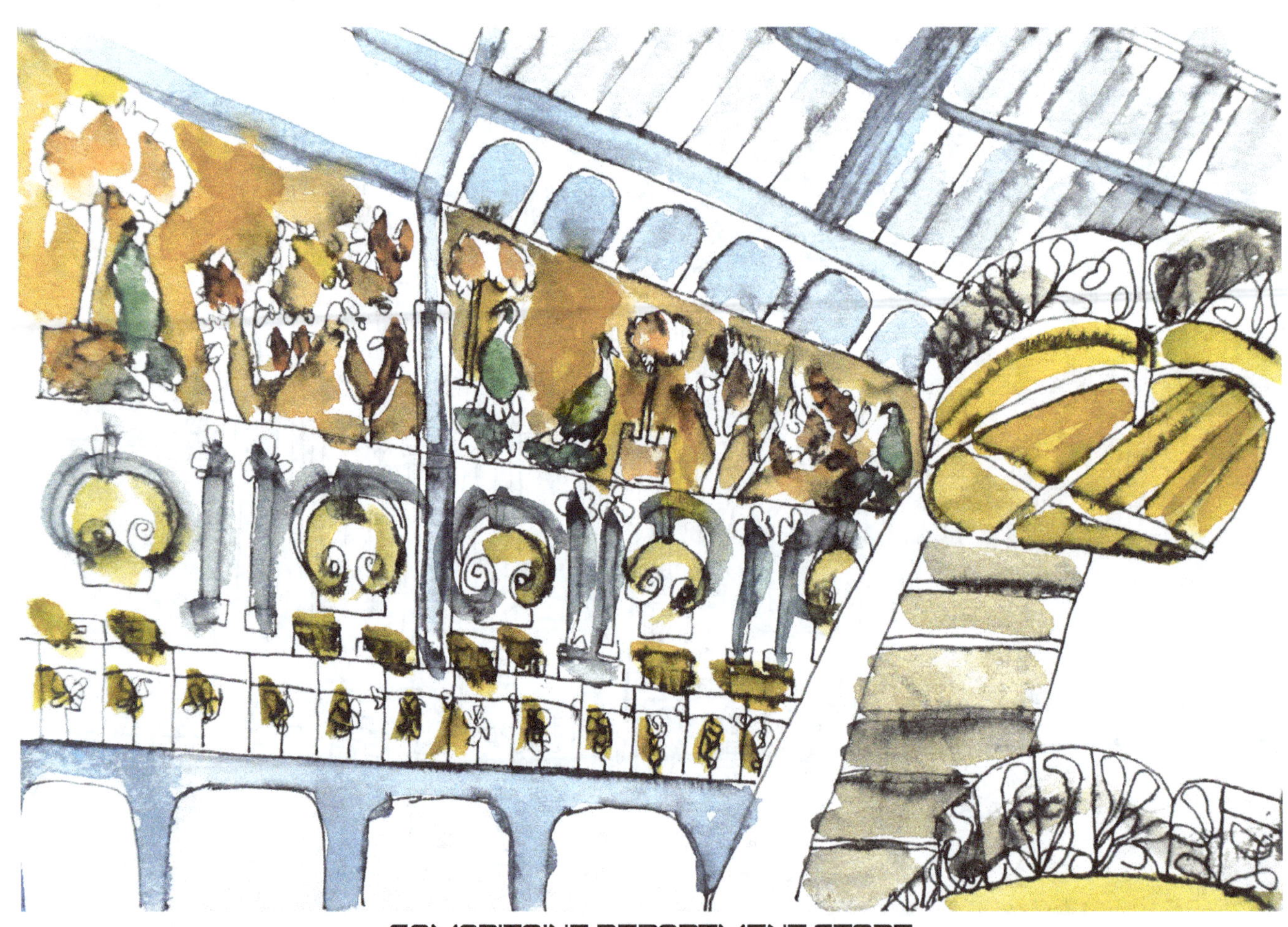

SAMARITAINE DEPARTMENT STORE
PARIS

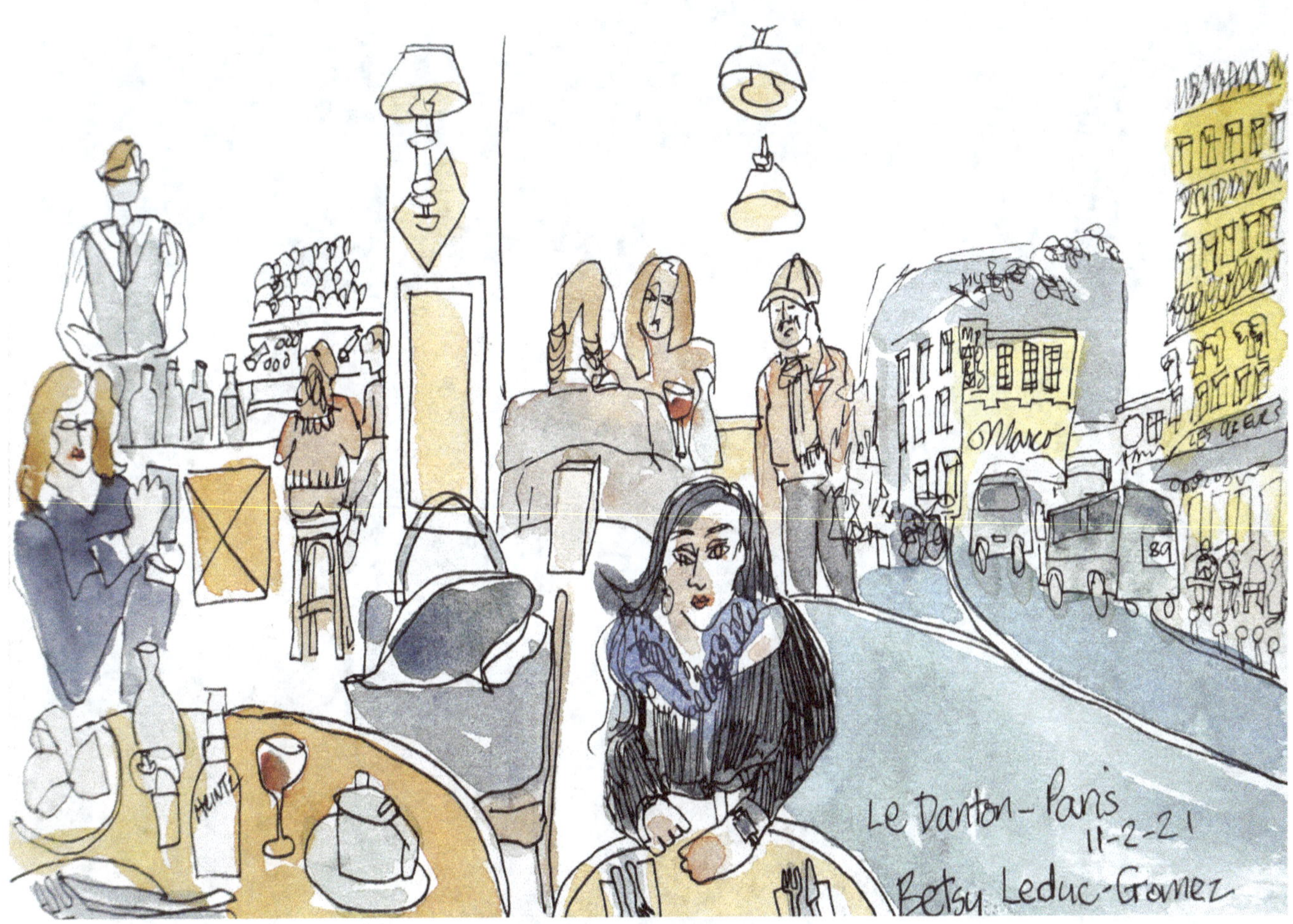

DANTON'S RESTAURANT
PARIS

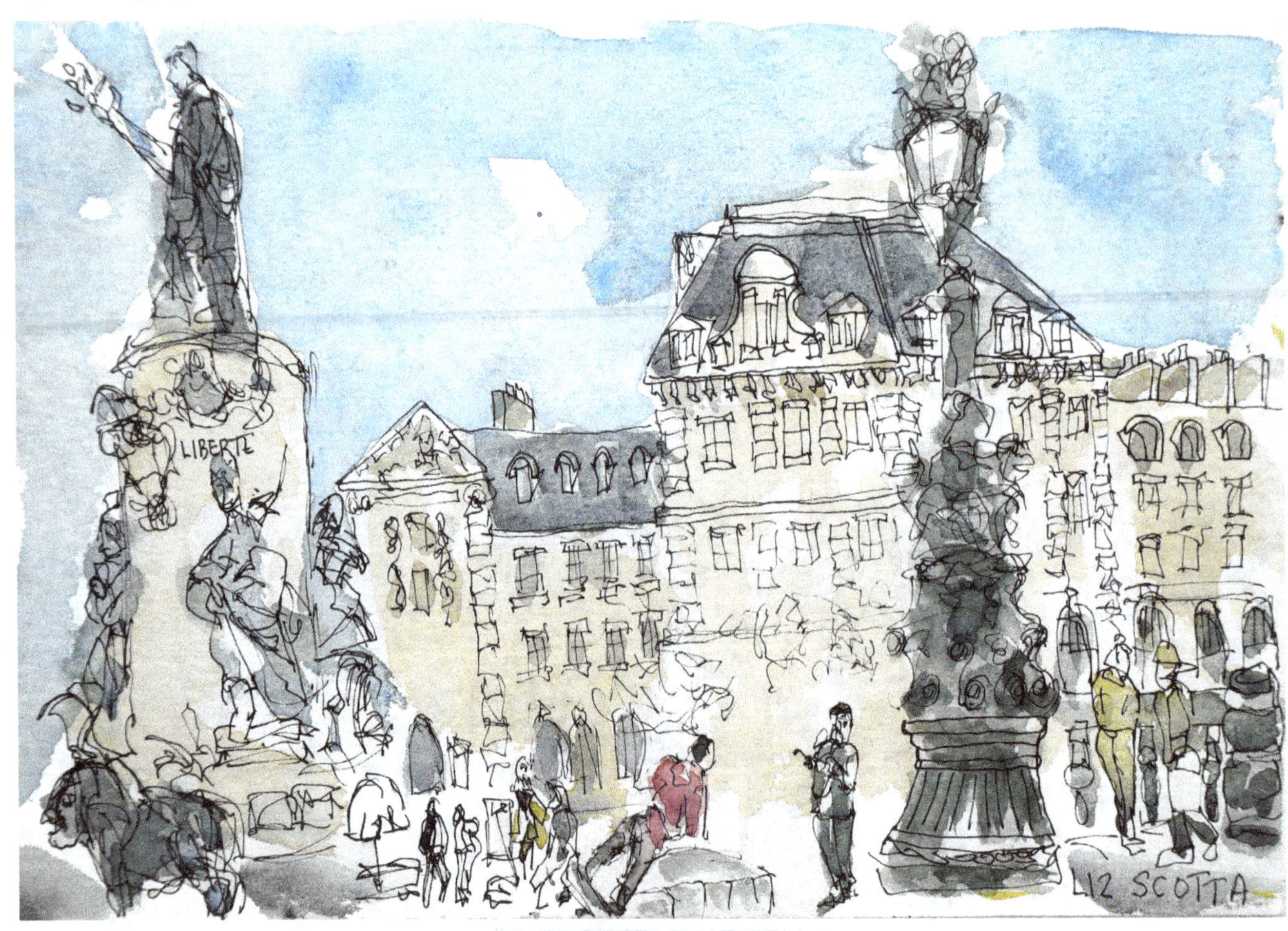

PLACE DE LA NATION
PARIS

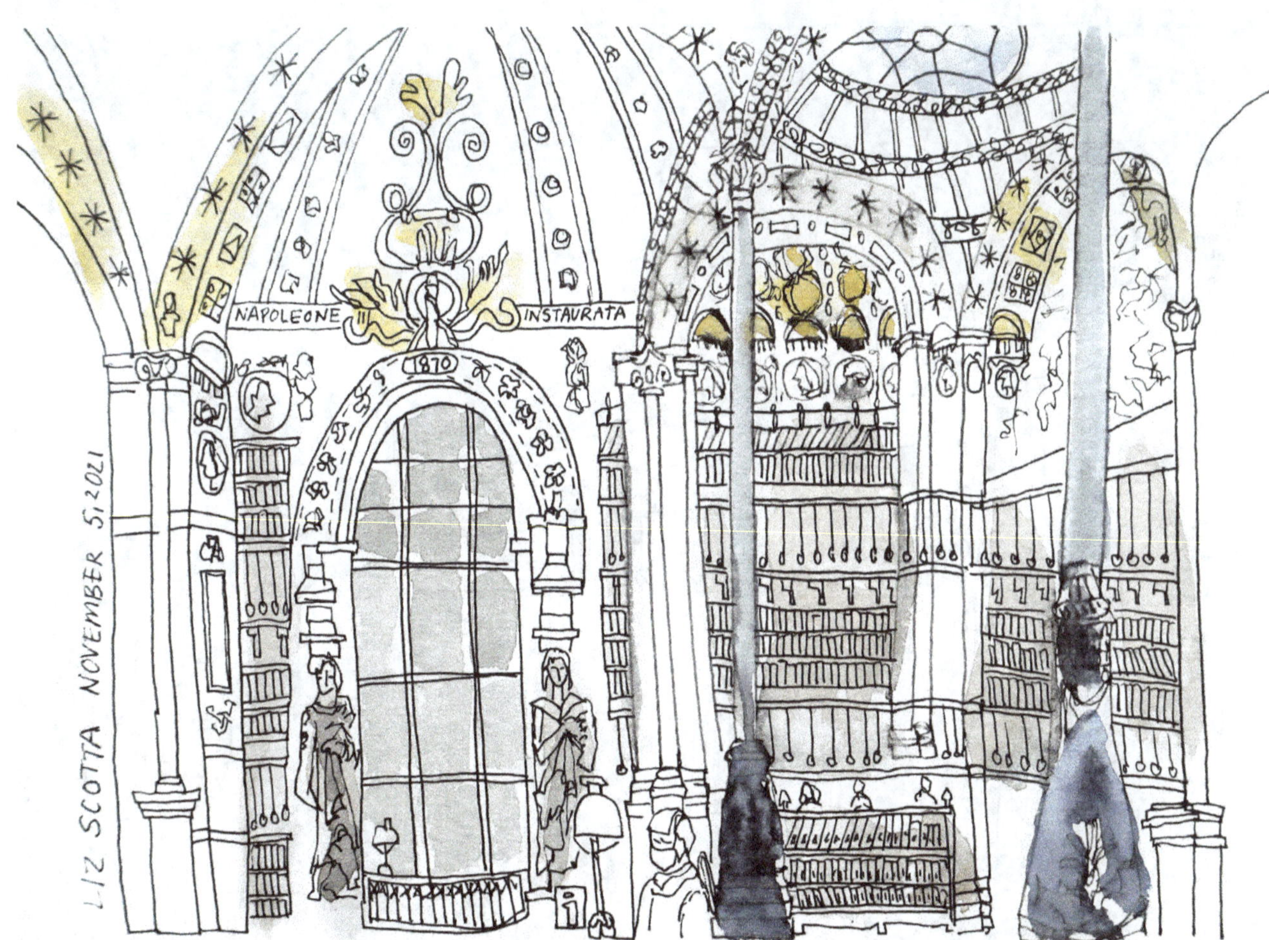

BIBLIOTHÈQUE NATIONALE RICHELIEU-LOUVOIS
PARIS

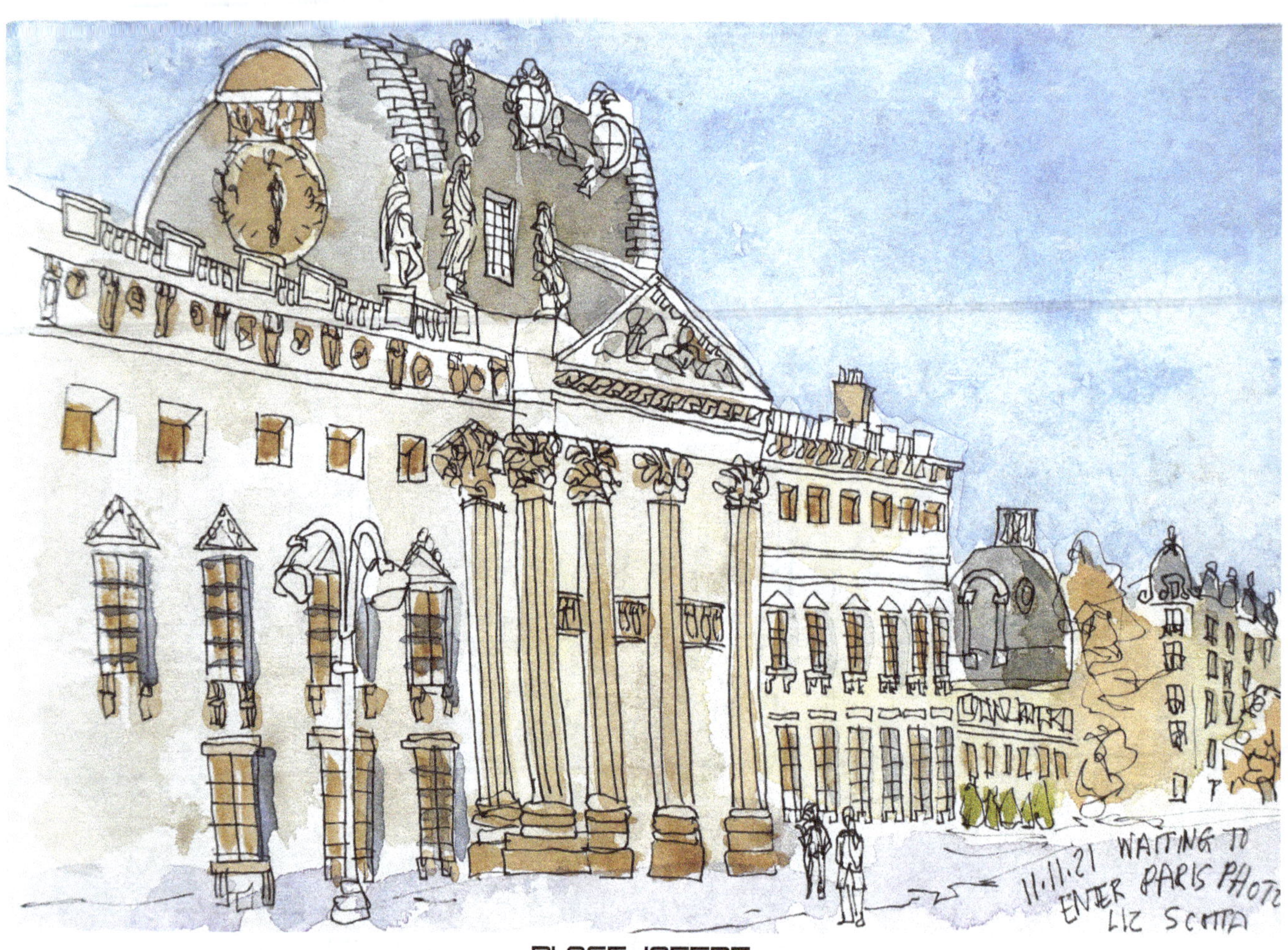

PLACE JOFFRE
PARIS

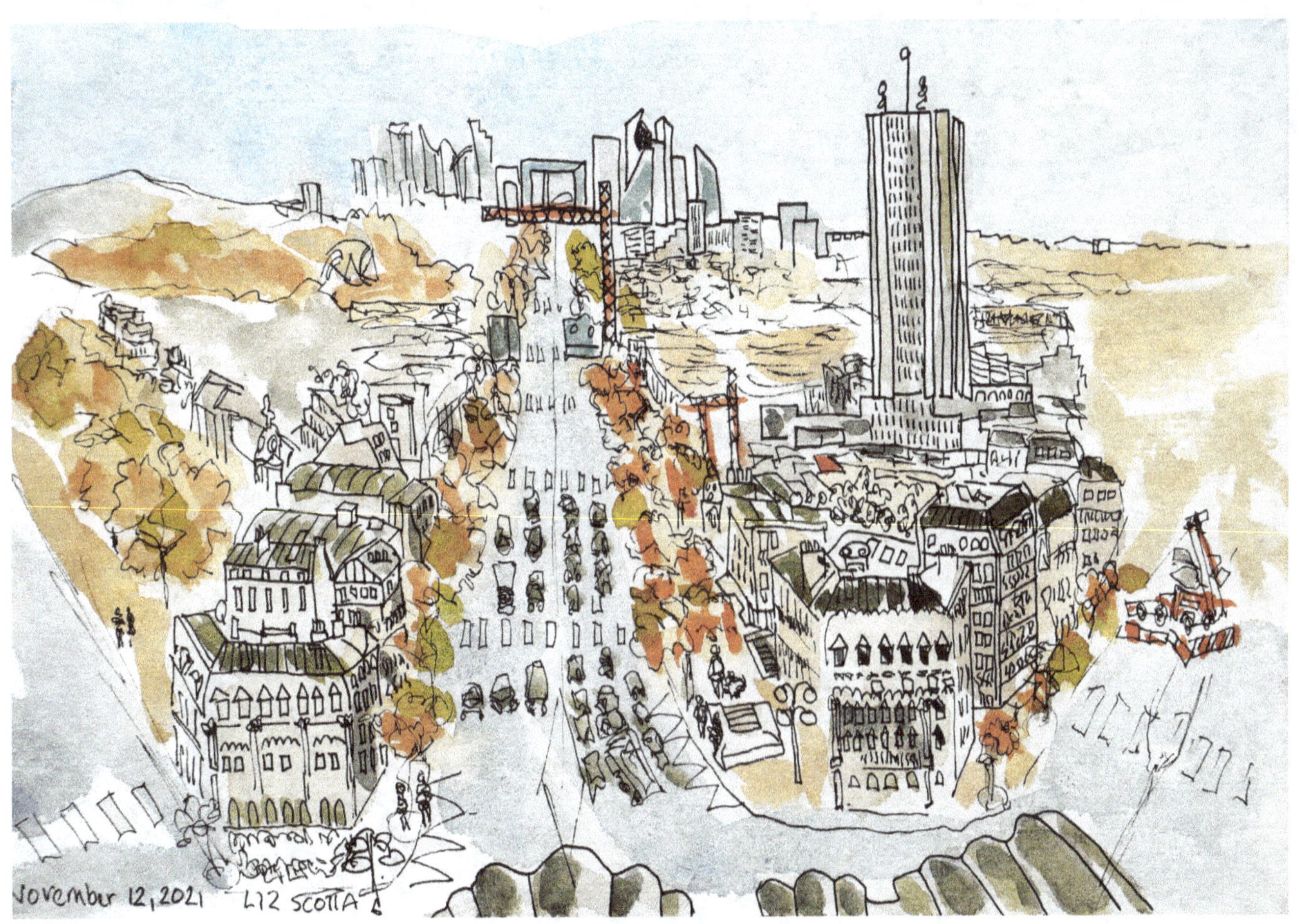

VIEW FROM ROOF OF ARC DE TRIOMPHE
PARIS

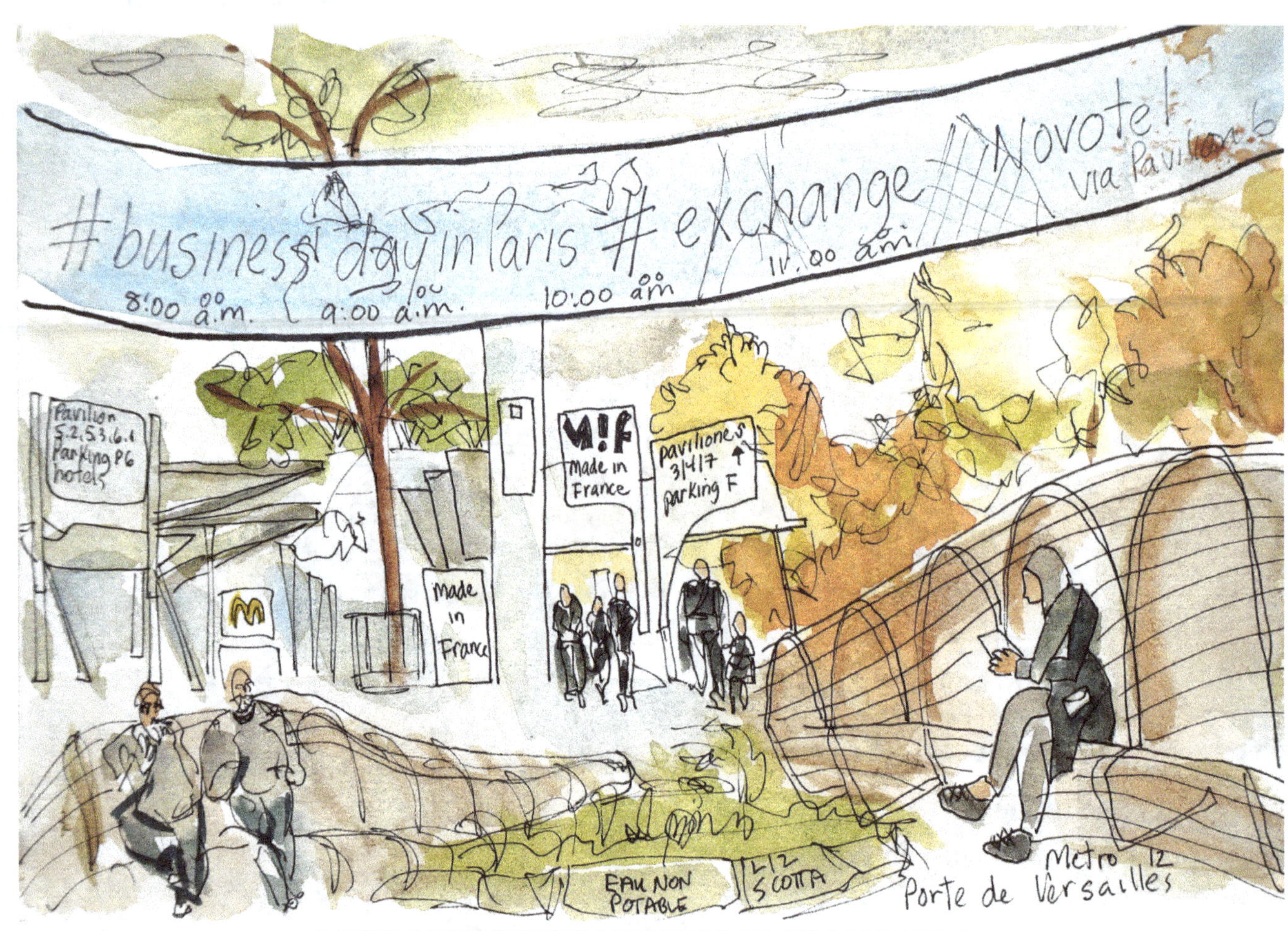

PORTE DE VERSAILLES CONVENTION CENTER
PARIS

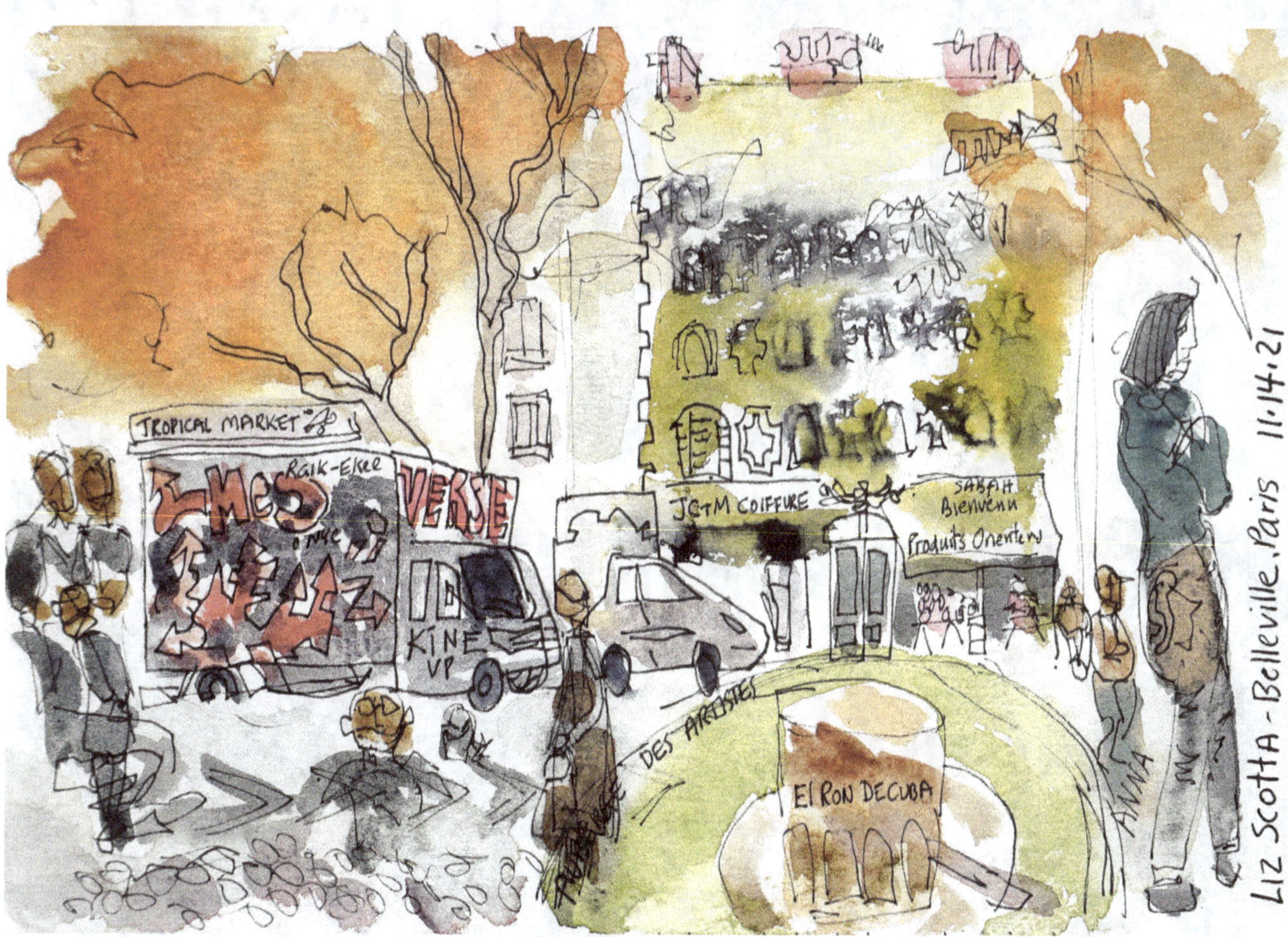

BELLEVILLE
PARIS

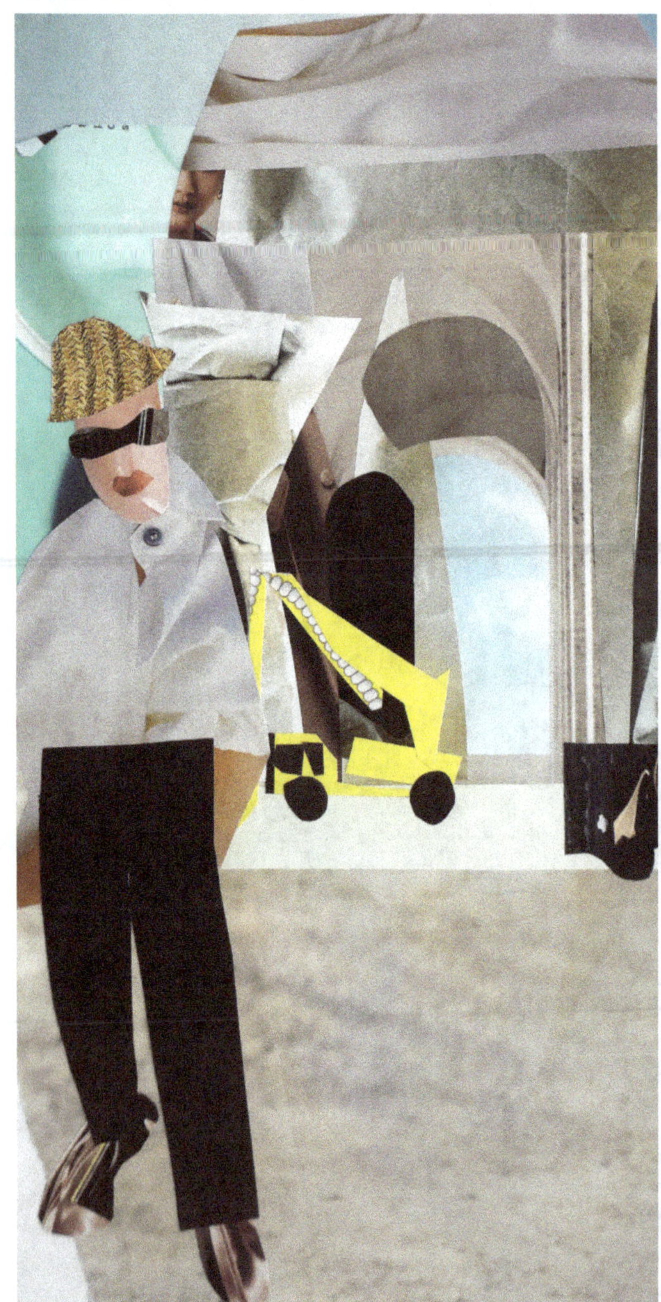

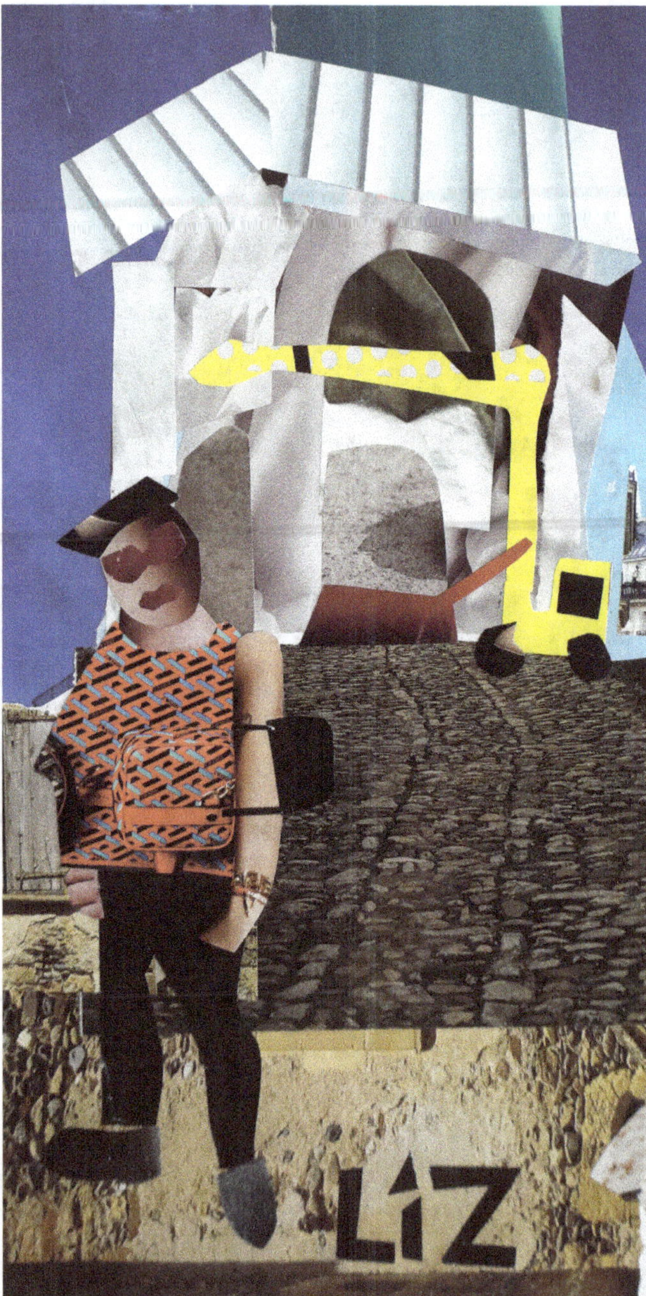

MARTIN AND LIZ
PARIS

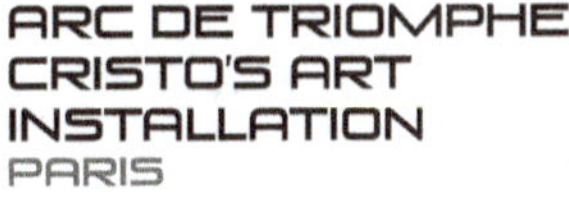

ARC DE TRIOMPHE
CRISTO'S ART
INSTALLATION
PARIS

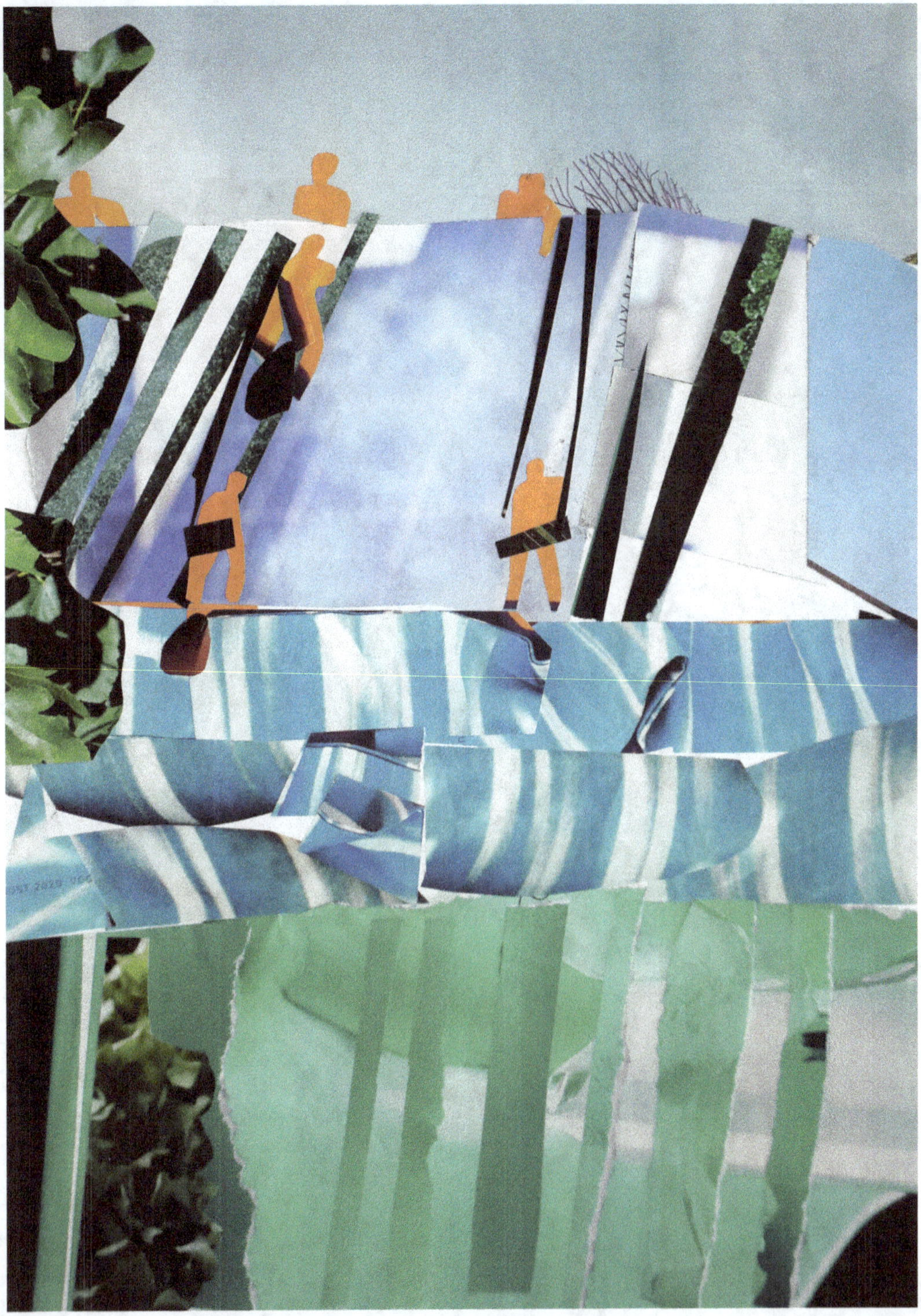

2021

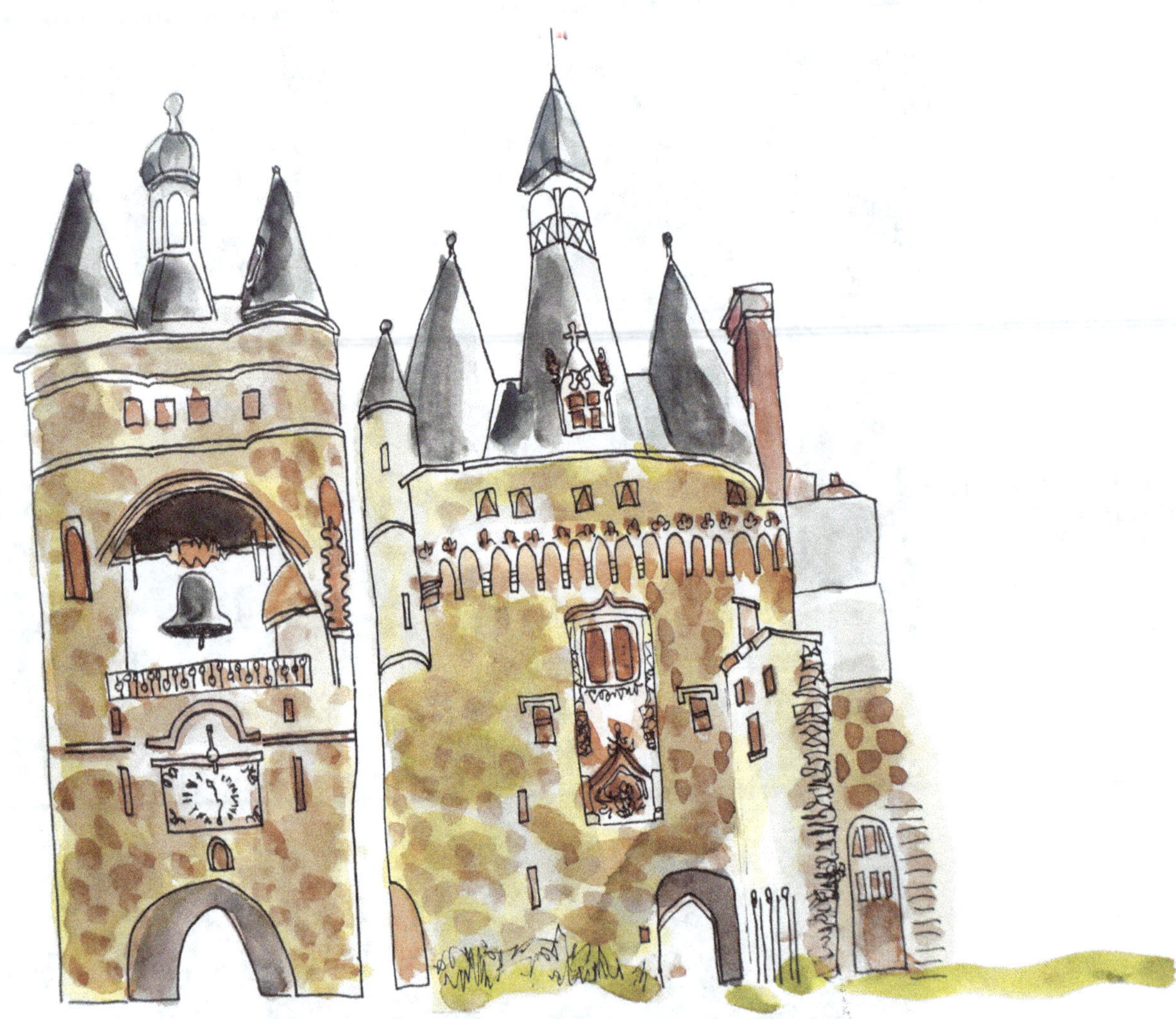

GROSSE CLOCHE AND PORTE CAILHAU
BORDEAUX

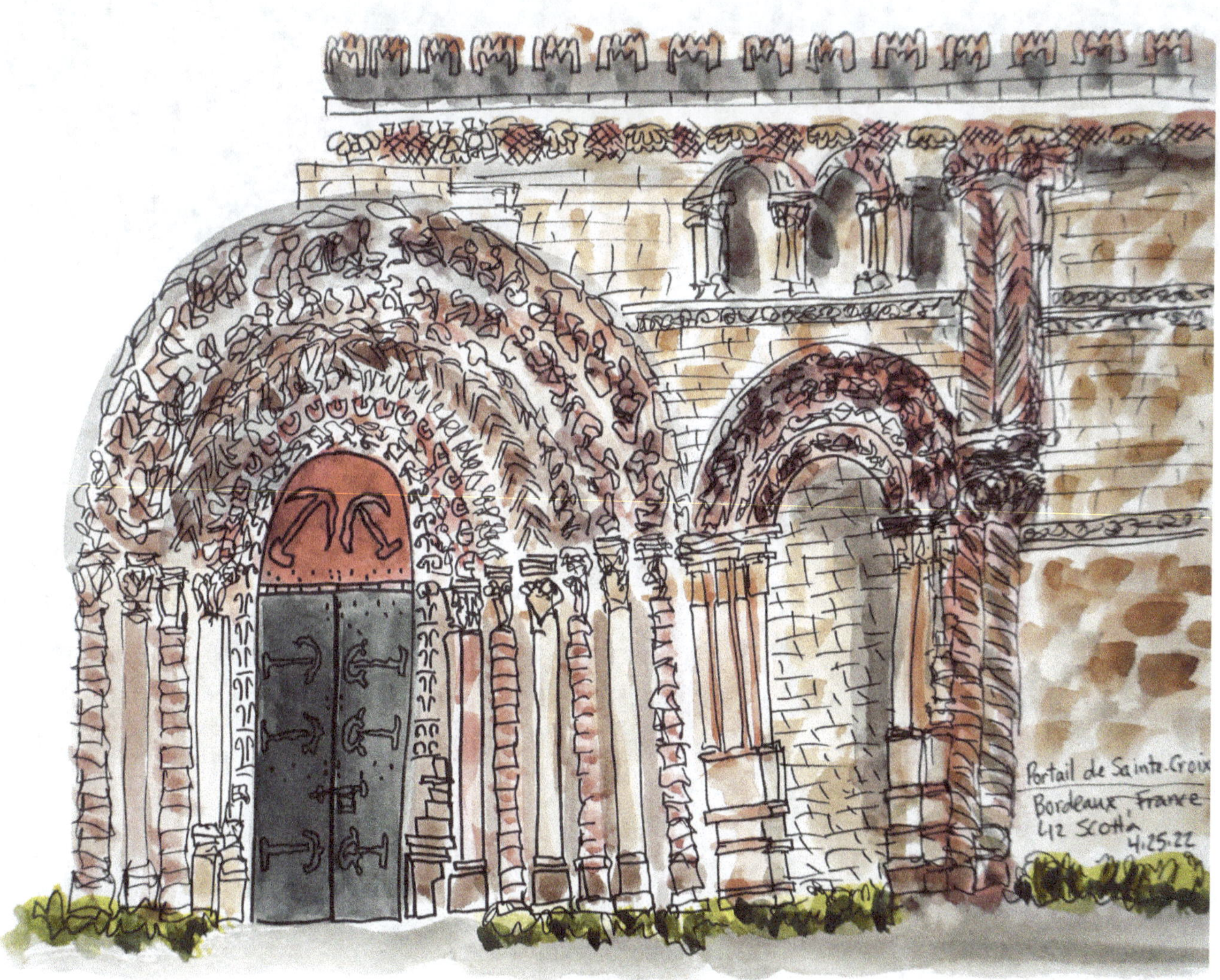

PORTAIL DE SAINTE-CROIX
BORDEAUX

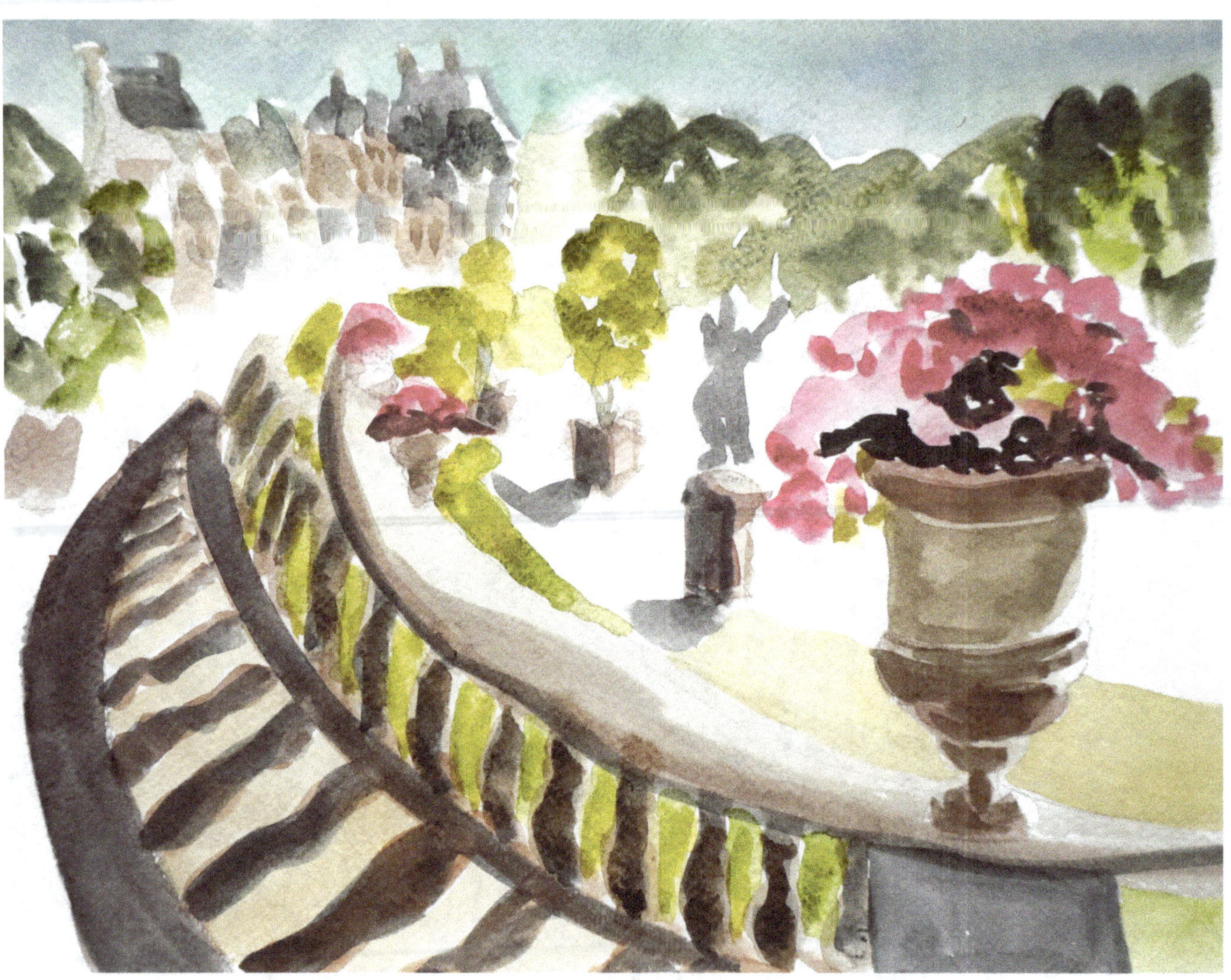

LUXEMBOURG GARDEN
PARIS

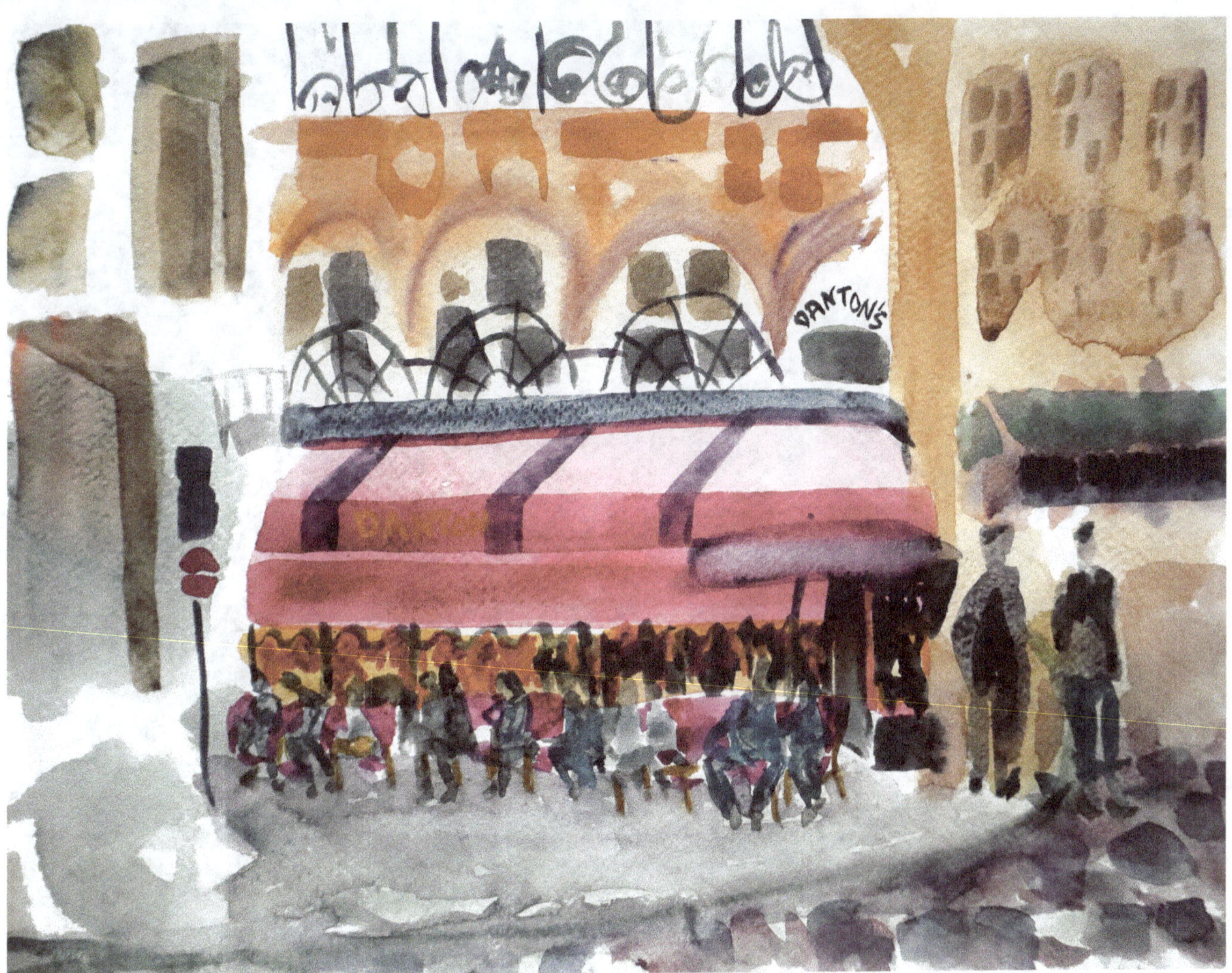

DANTON'S RESTAURANT
PARIS

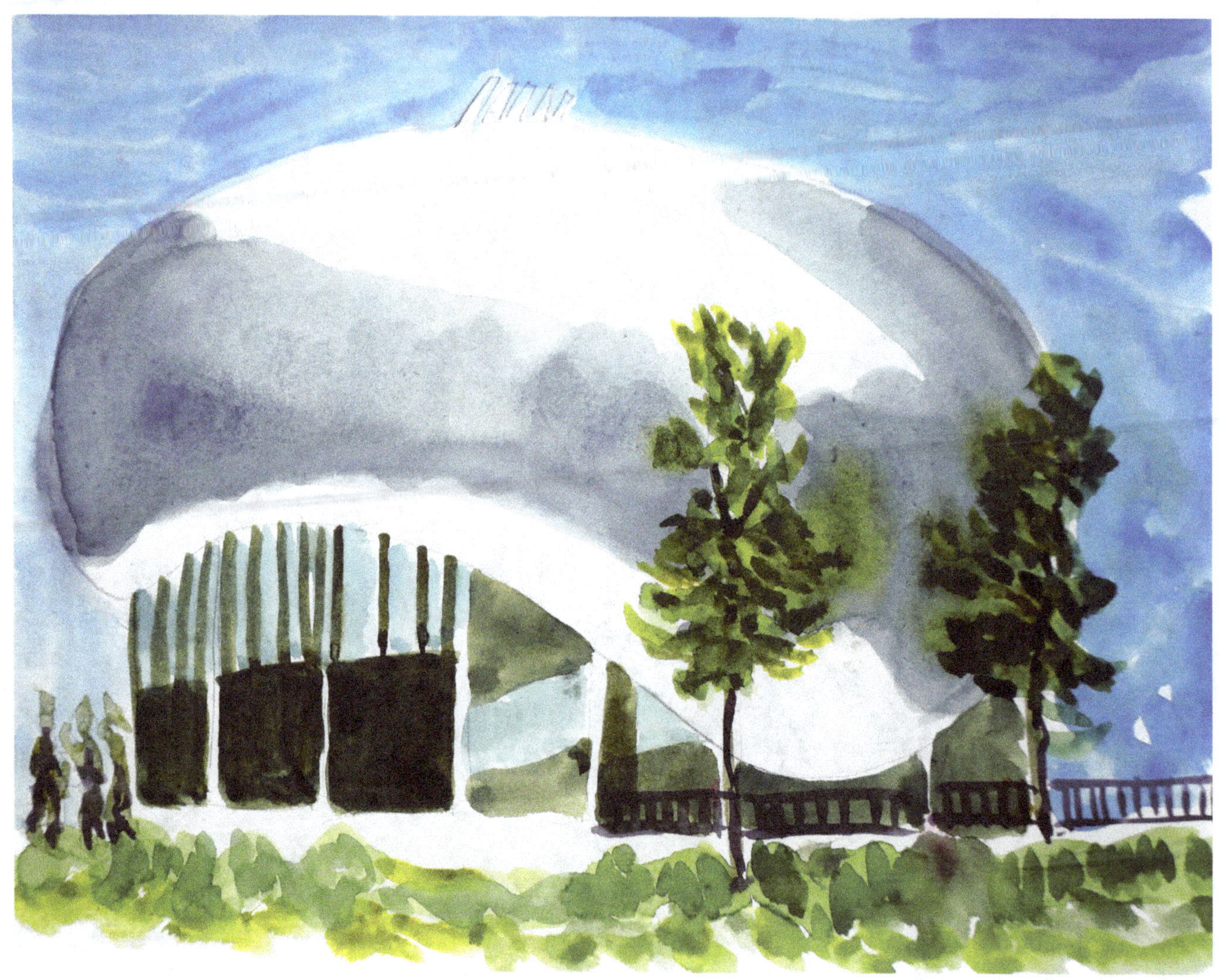

LA CITÉ DU VIN MUSEUM
BORDEAUX

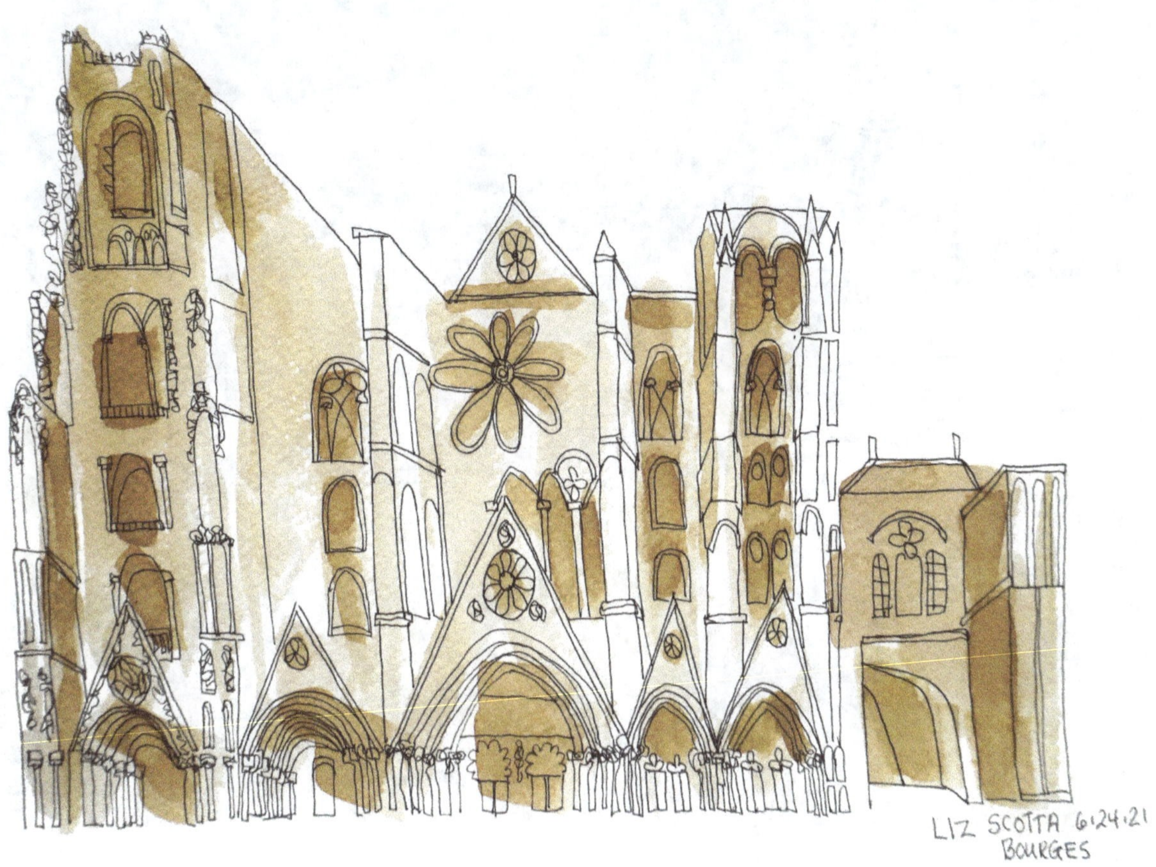

CATHÉDRALE DE BOURGES
BOURGES

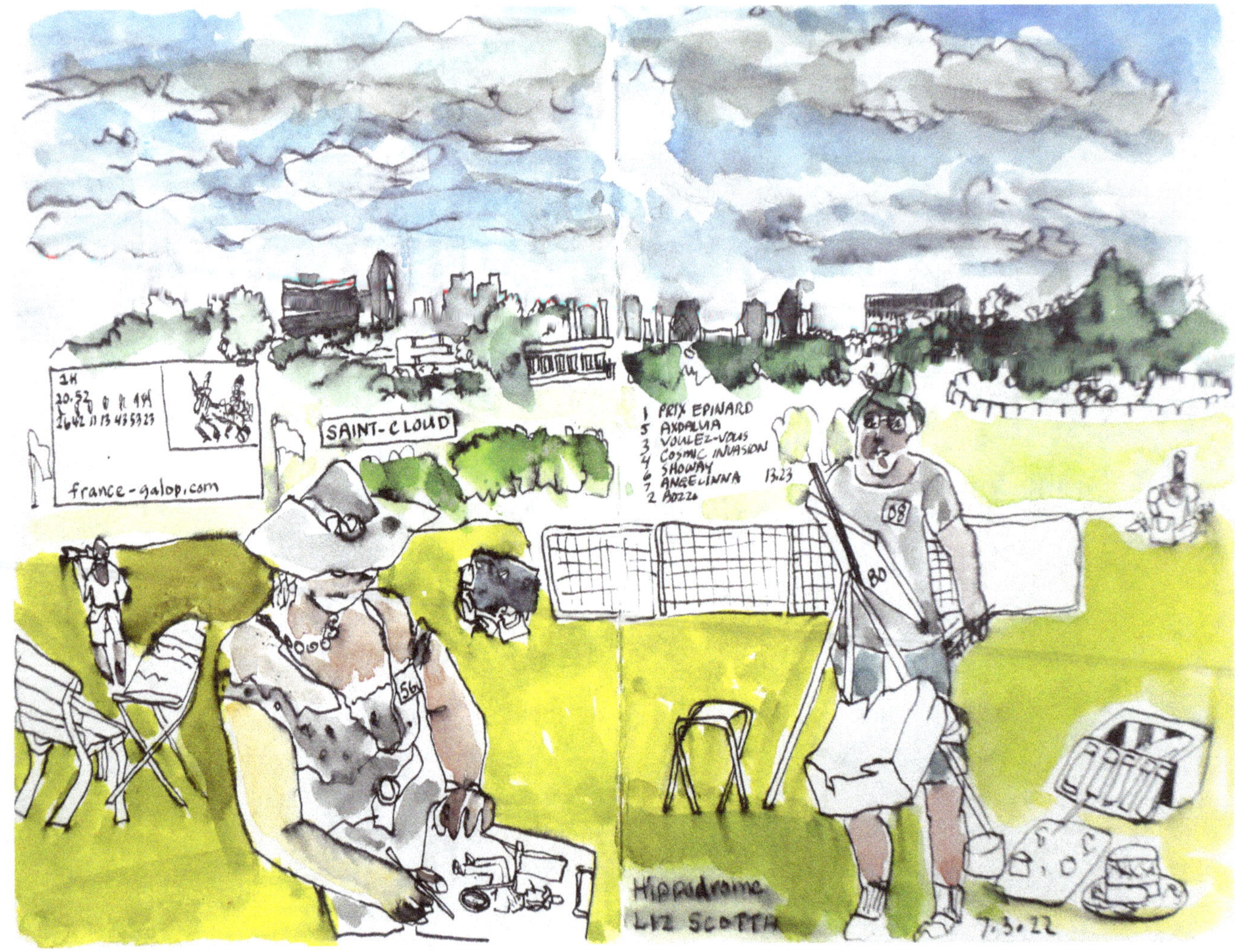

HIPPODROME SAINT-CLOUD
PARIS

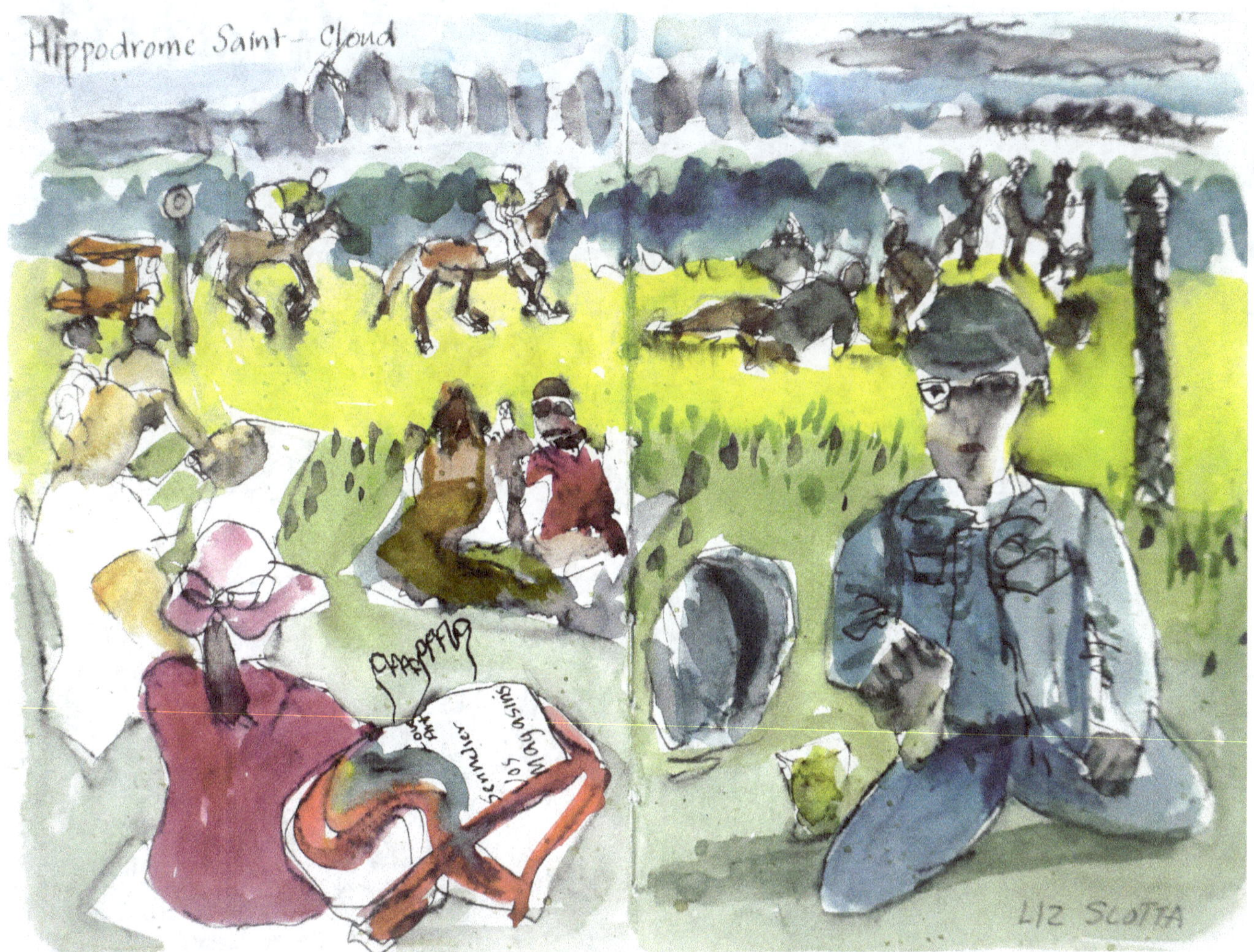

HIPPODROME SAINT-CLOUD
PARIS

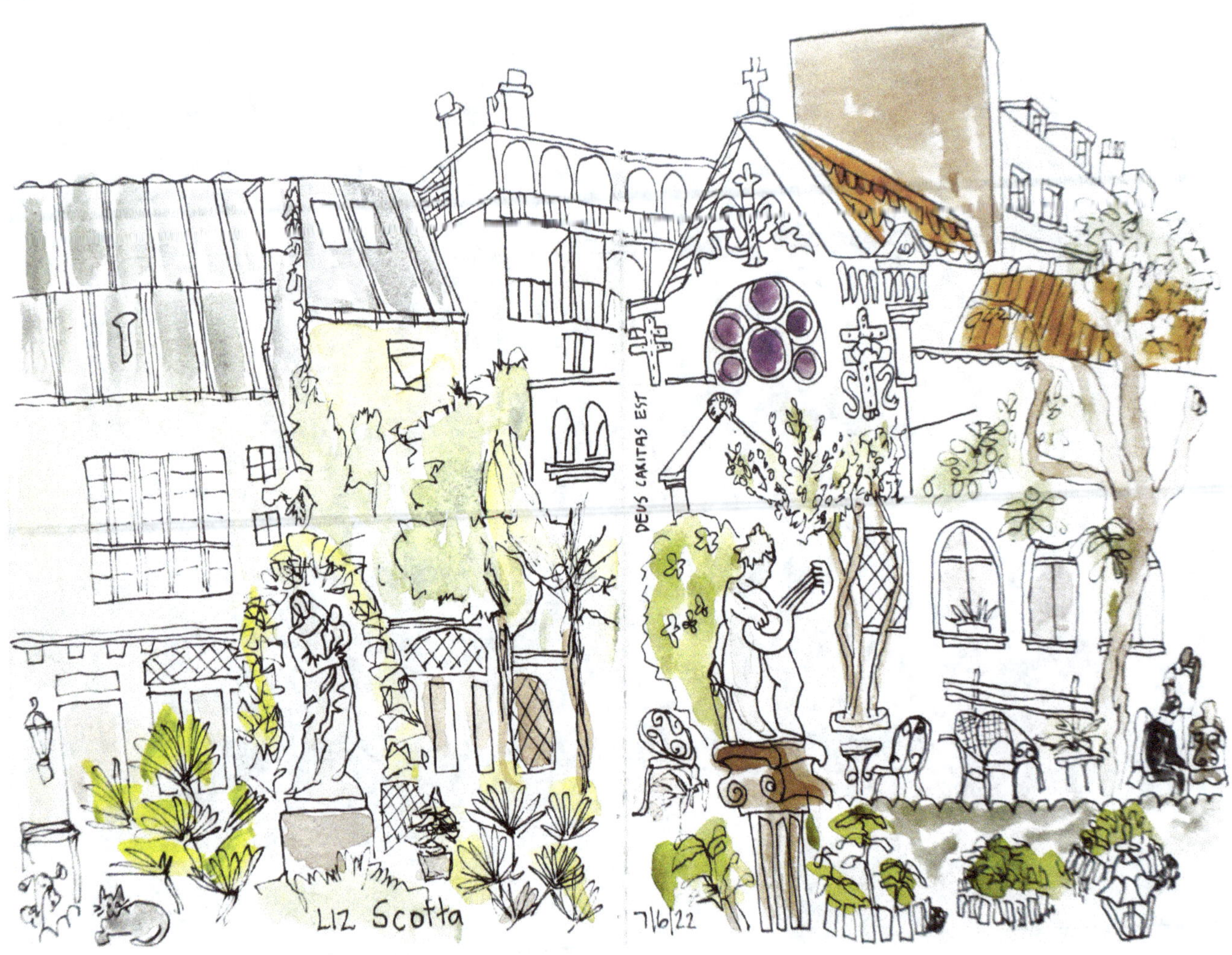

SAINTE-FAMILLE
PARIS

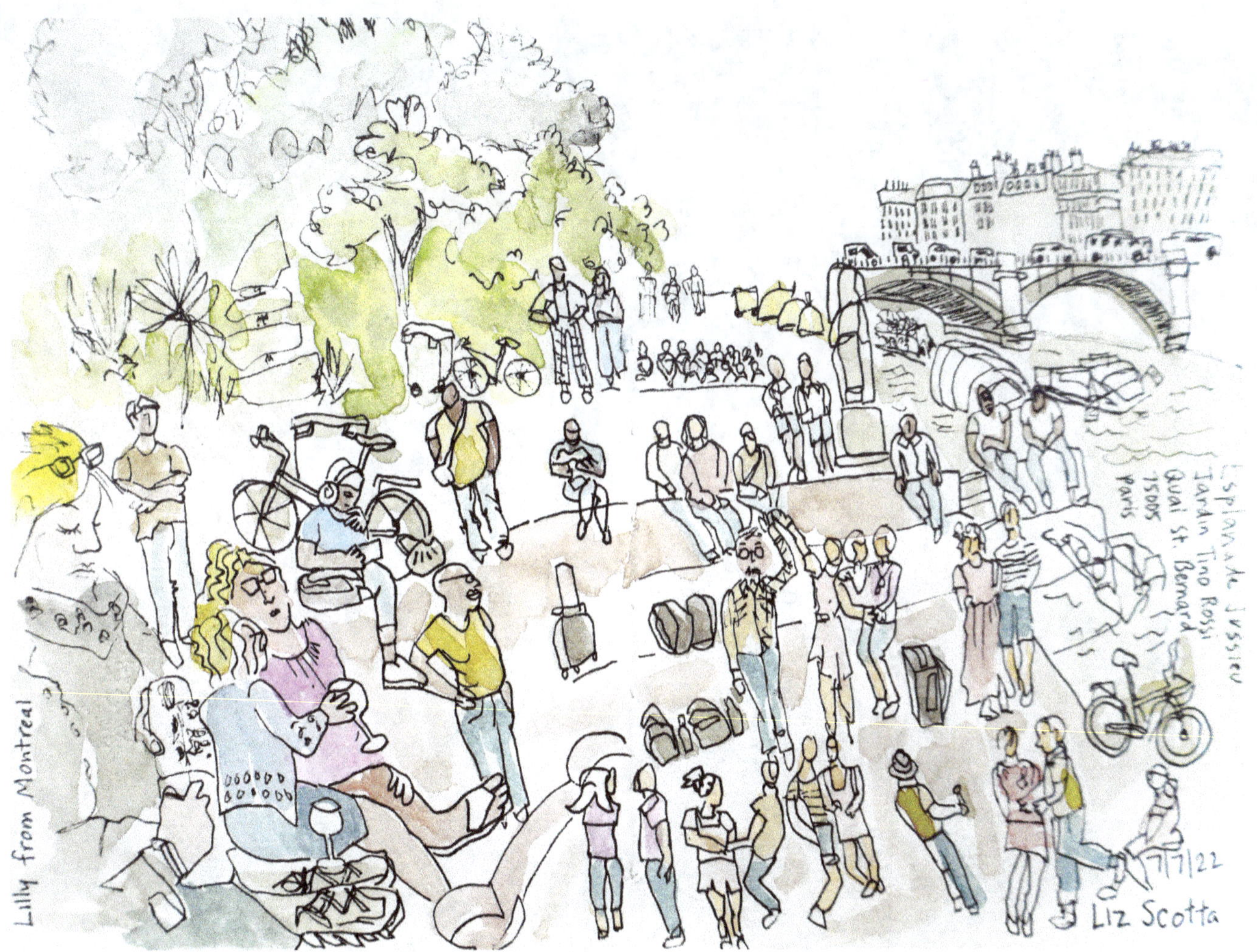

JARDIN TINO ROSSI
PARIS

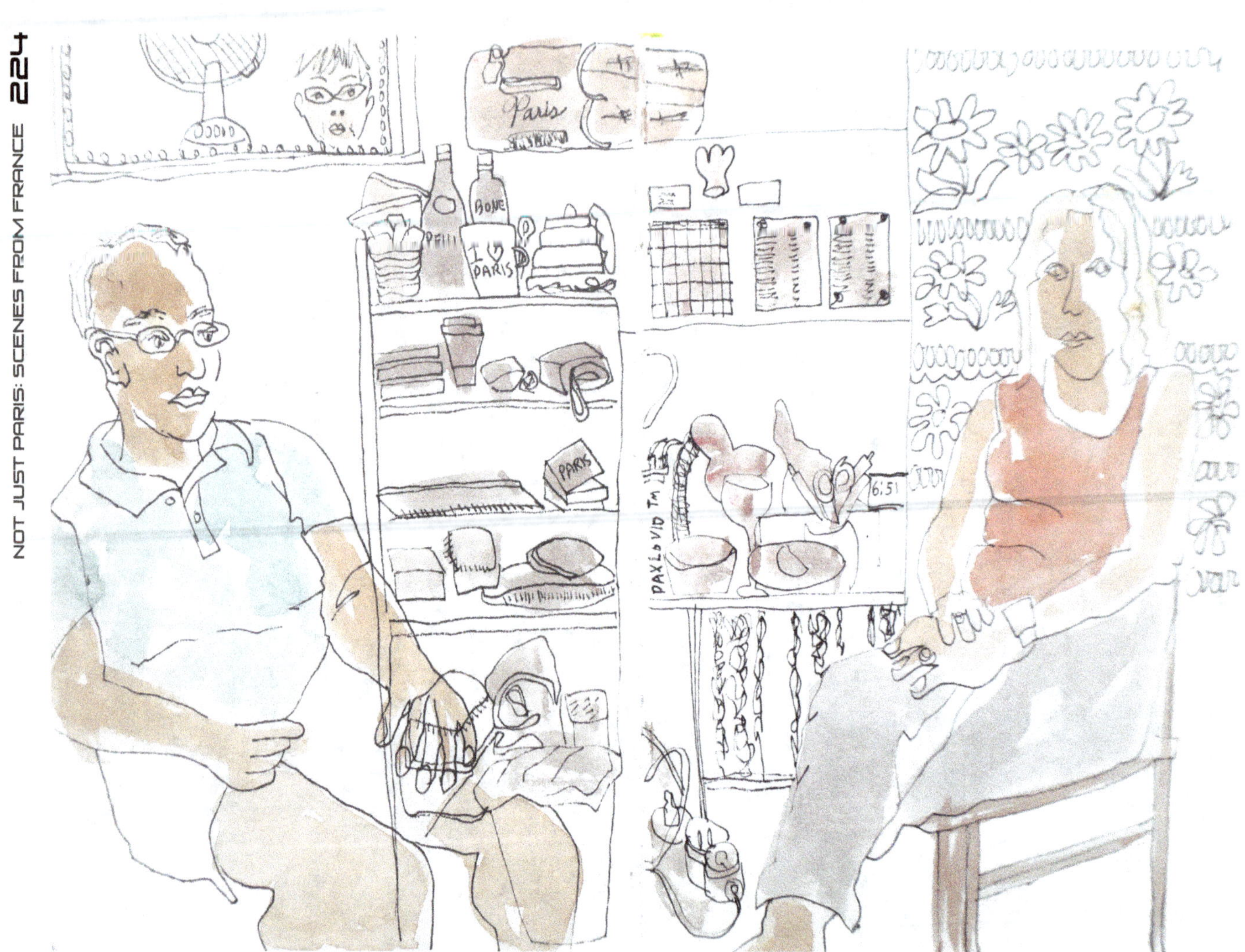

HAPPY HOUR WITH ELTON AND KAREN
PARIS

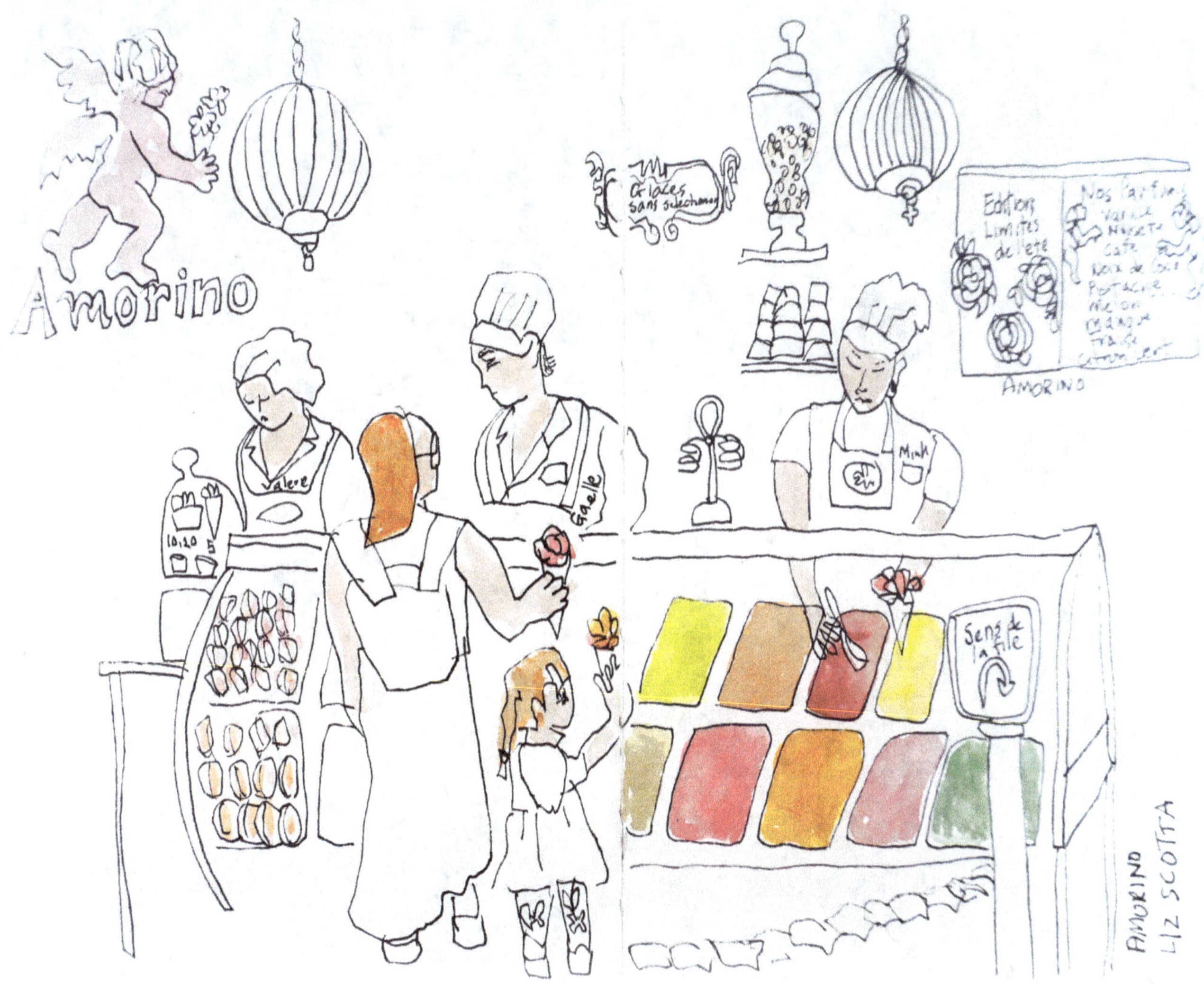

AMORINO ICE CREAM
PARIS

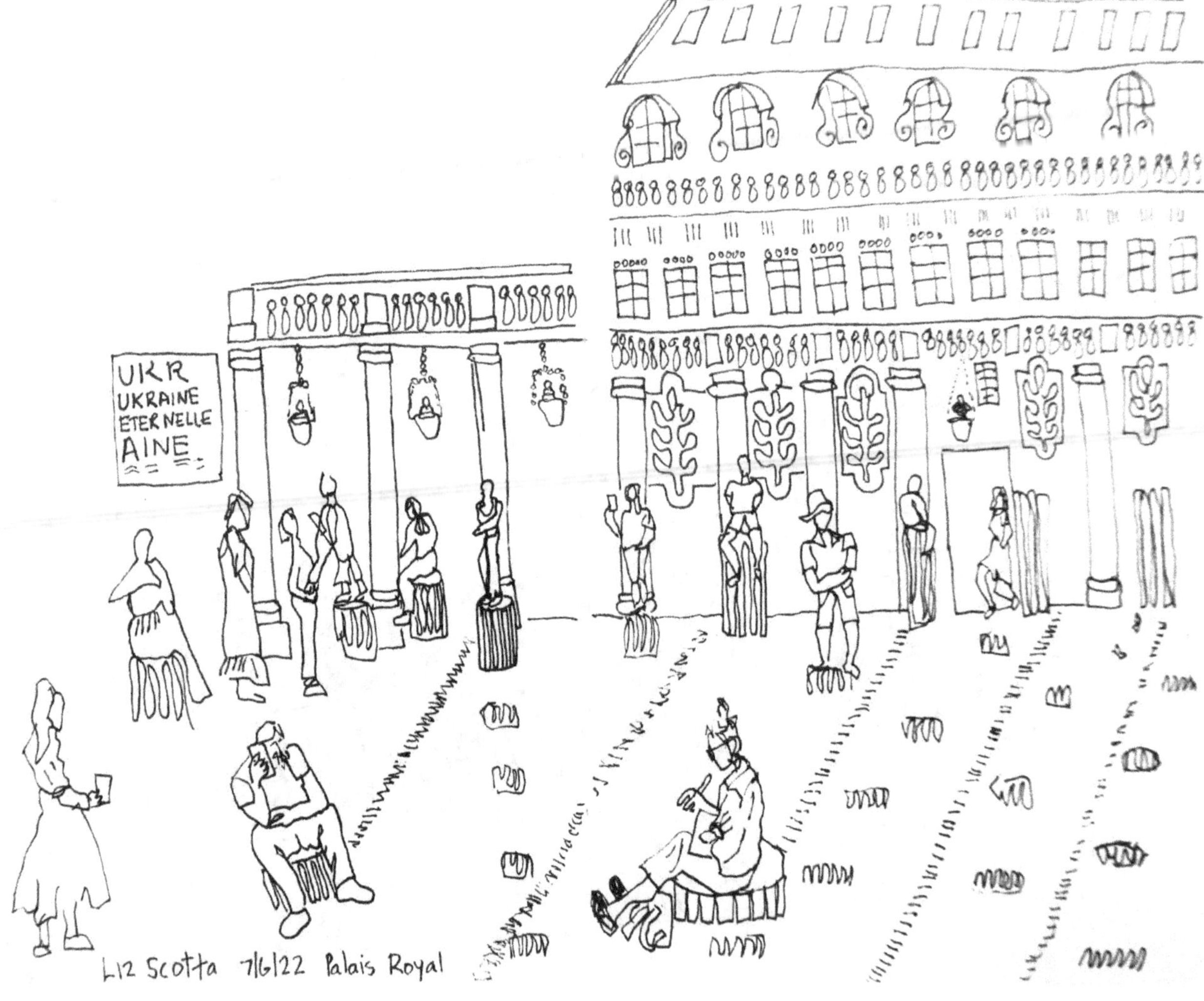

PALAIS ROYAL
PARIS

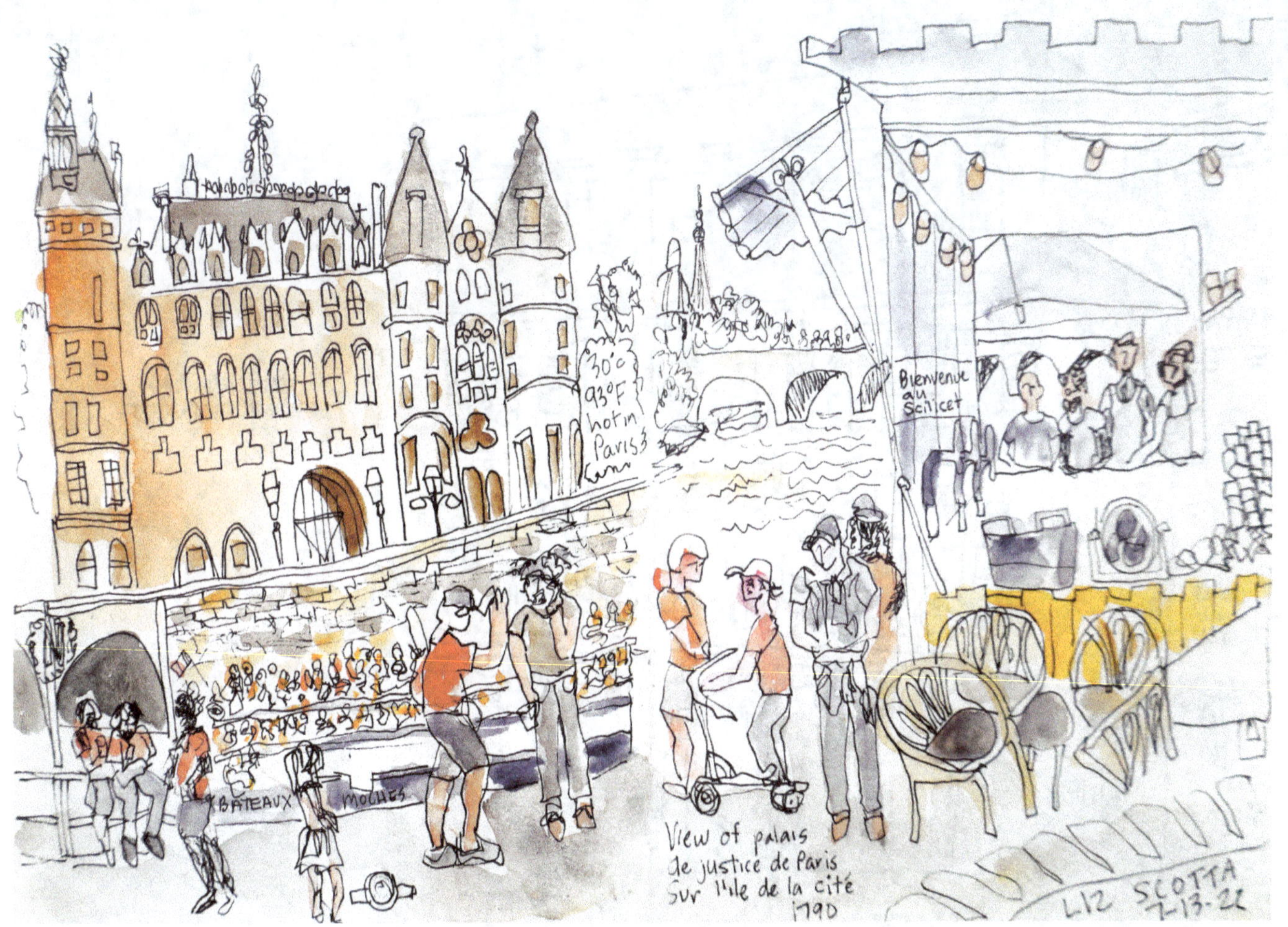

PALAIS DE JUSTICE
PARIS

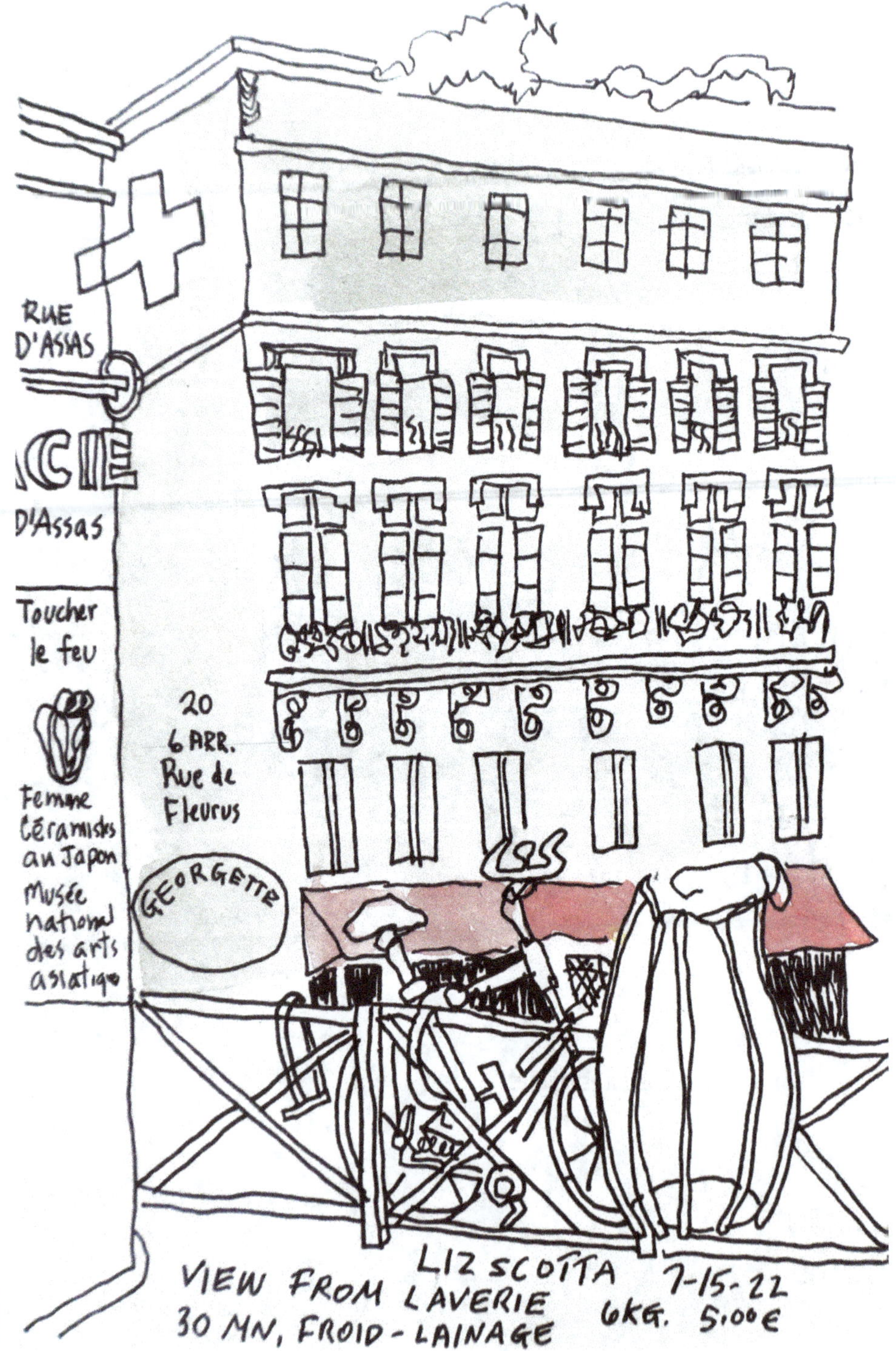

VIEW FROM
LAUNDROMAT
PARIS

MUSÉE DES
ARTS DÉCORATIFS
PARIS

Shocking!

Elsa
Schiaparelli

Liz Scotta 7/15/22

THEATRE DE LA RENAISSANCE
PARIS

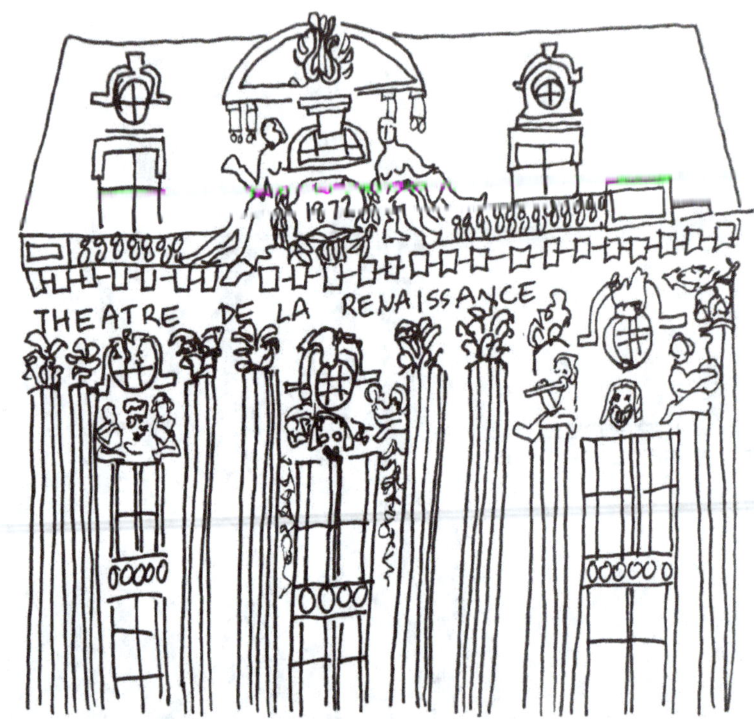

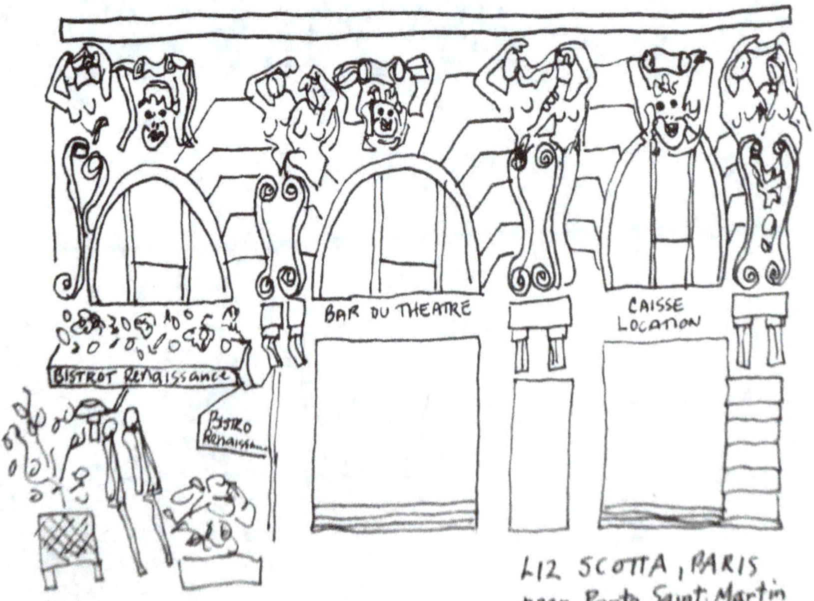

LIZ SCOTTA, PARIS
near Porte Saint-Martin
July 17, 2022

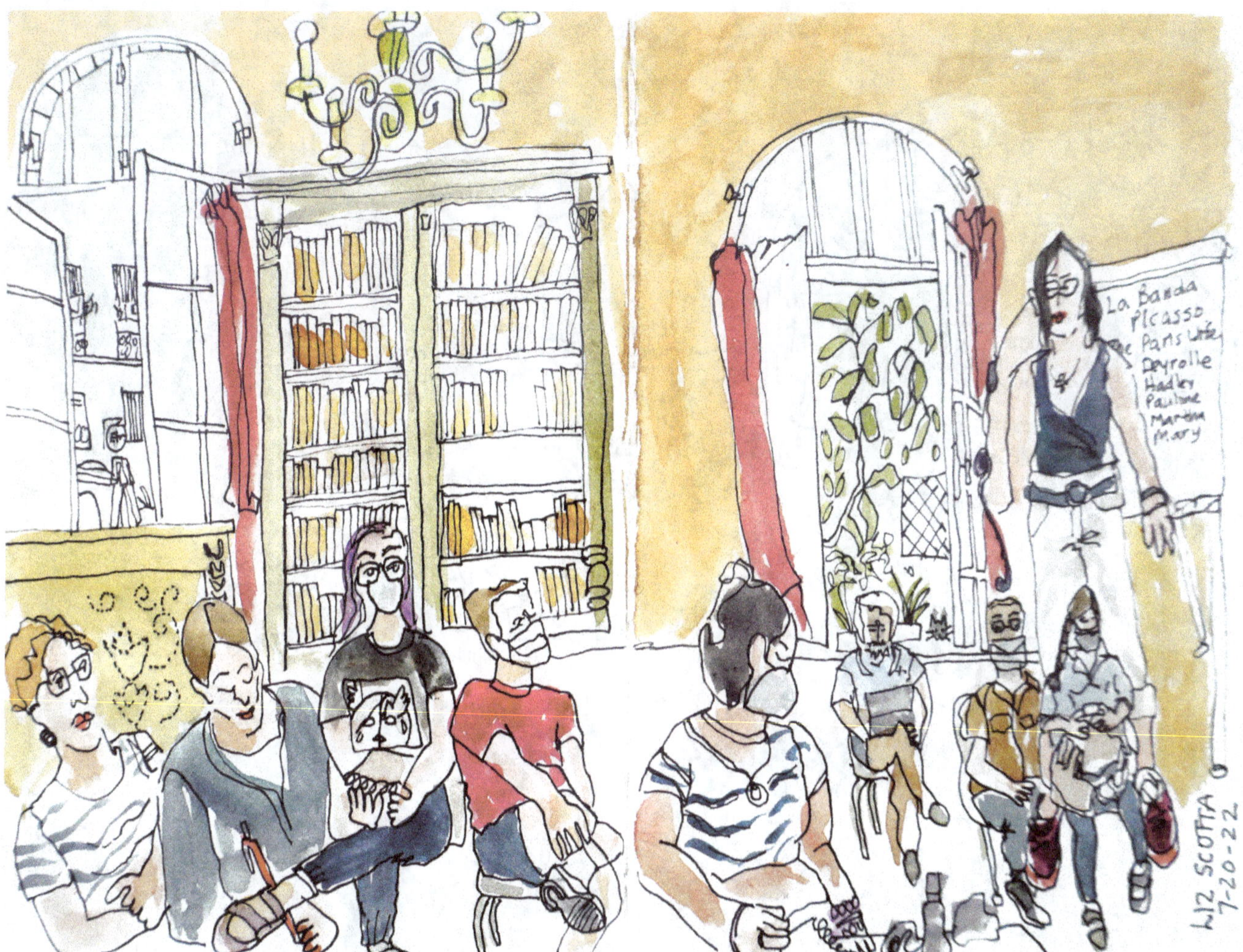

HUMANITIES CLASS
PARIS

21°C
8:23
PORT OBLIGATOIRE DE LA CEINTURE DE SÉCURITÉ
S.v.p, ne pas parler avec le conducteur
Mercedes-Benz
Gilbert James Voyages
ED 327 GR
90 00
Gare Routière
Stationnement Réservé
7·24·22 LIZ SCOTTA · HONFLEUR
MAXED OUT!

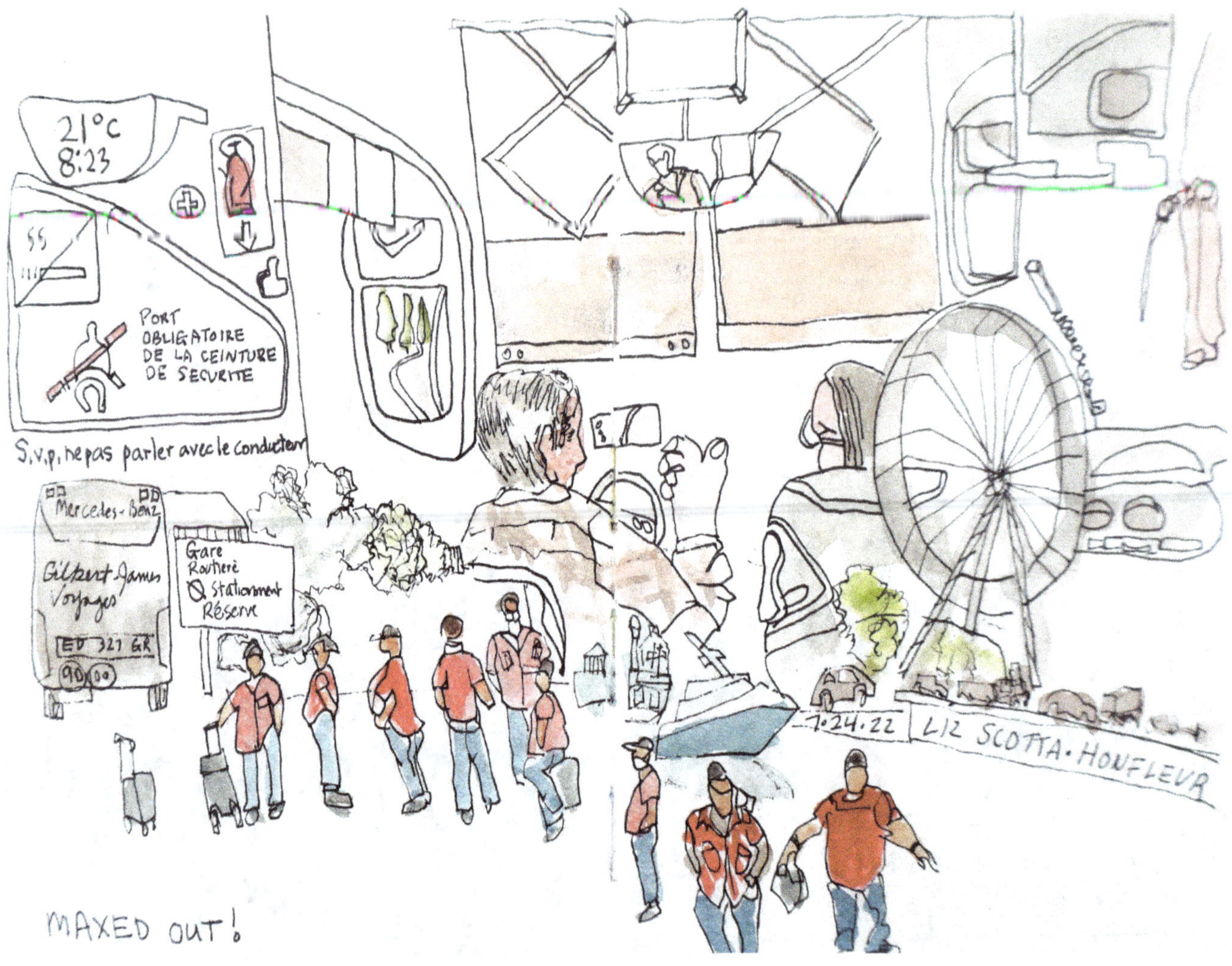

HONFLEUR

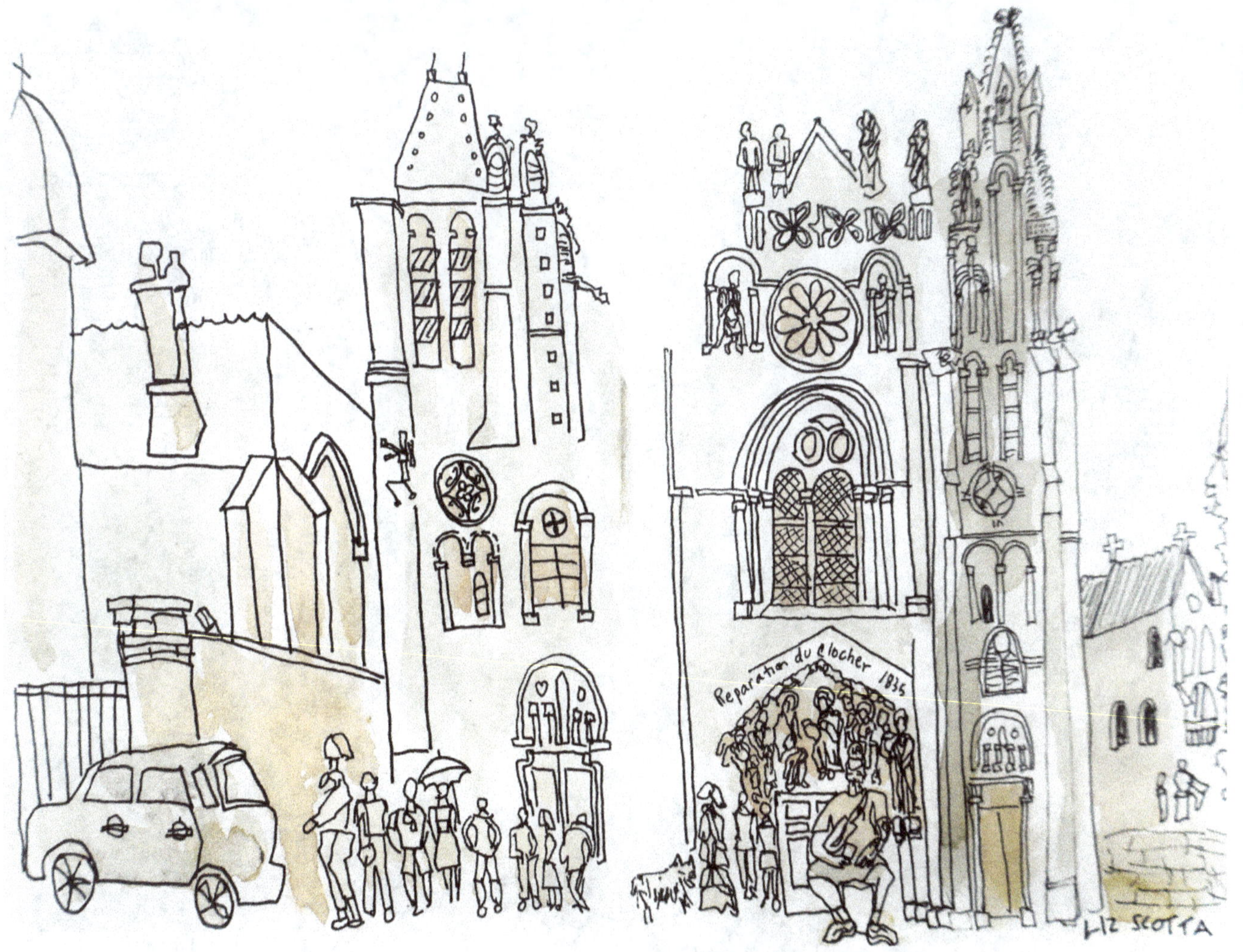

CATHÉDRALE DE SENLIS
SENLIS

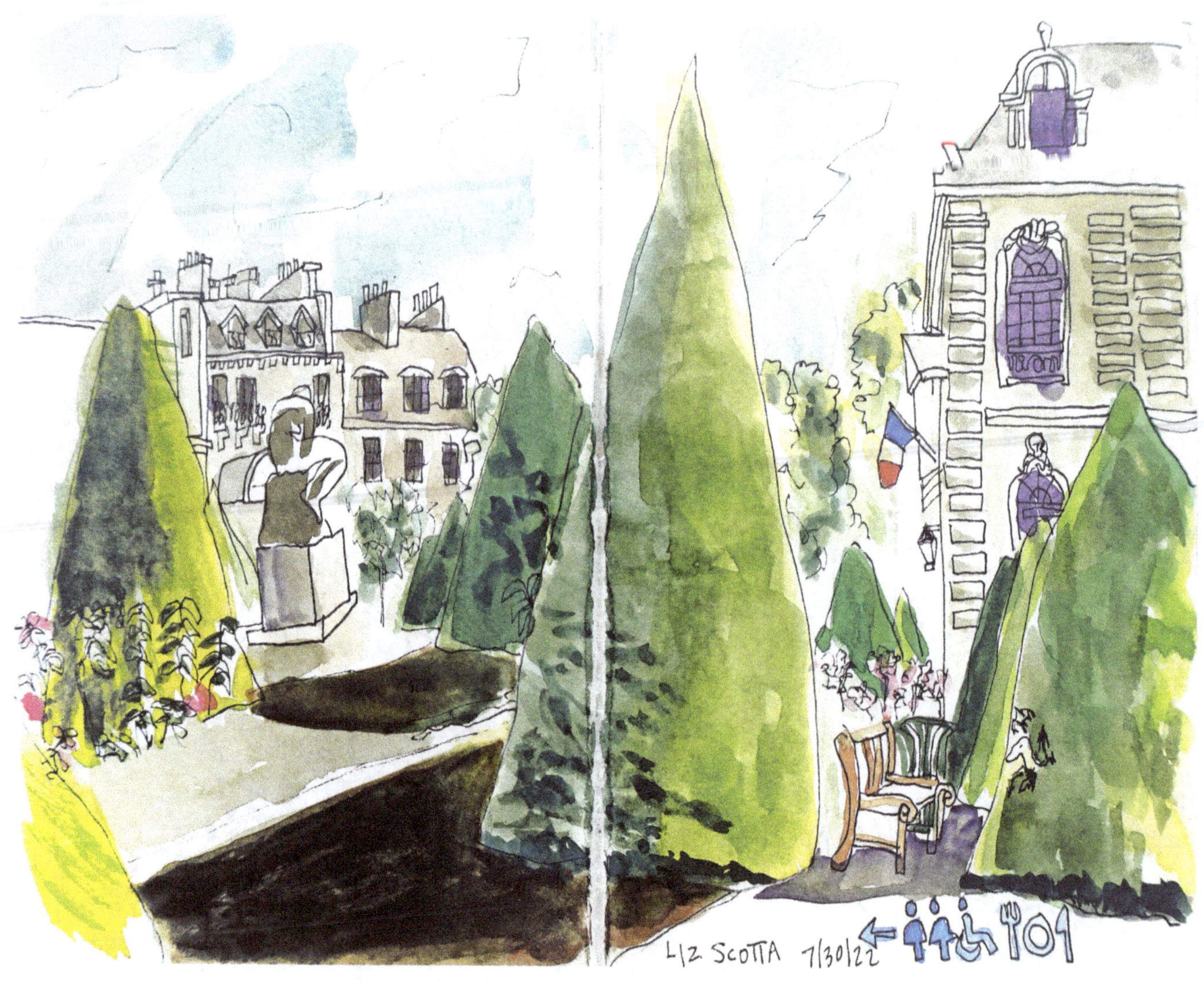

MUSÉE RODIN
PARIS

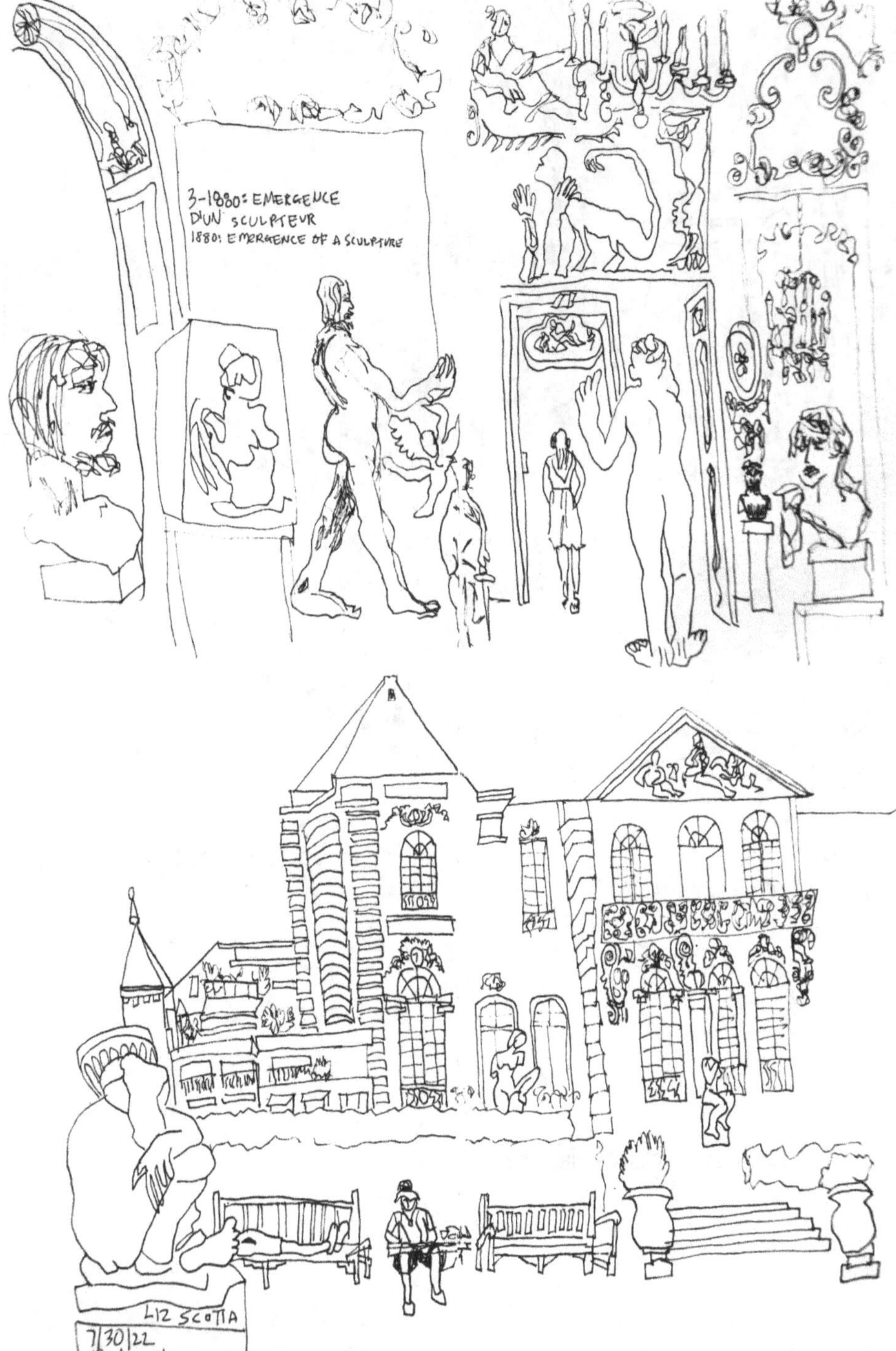

MUSÉE RODIN
PARIS

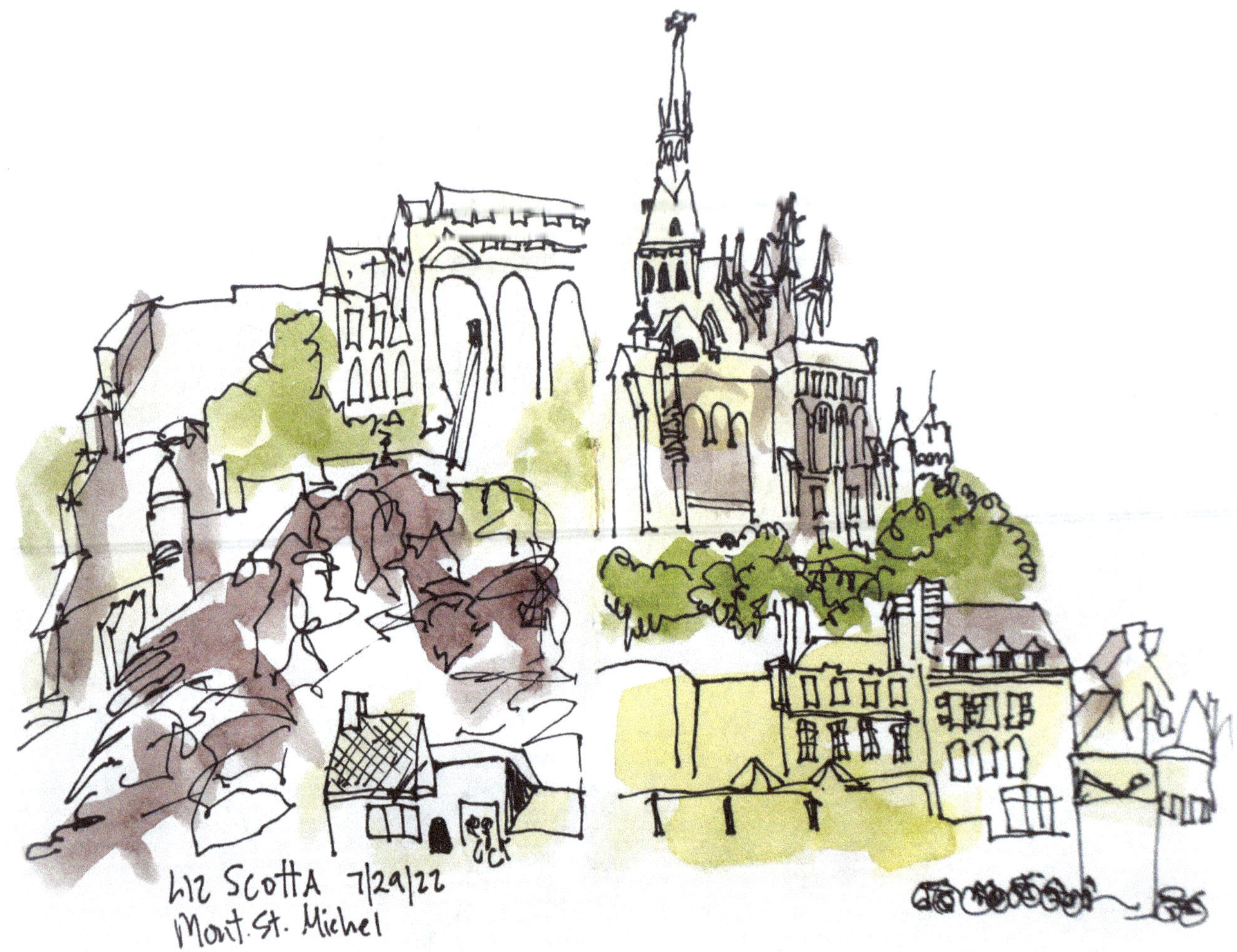

MONT-SAINT-MICHEL

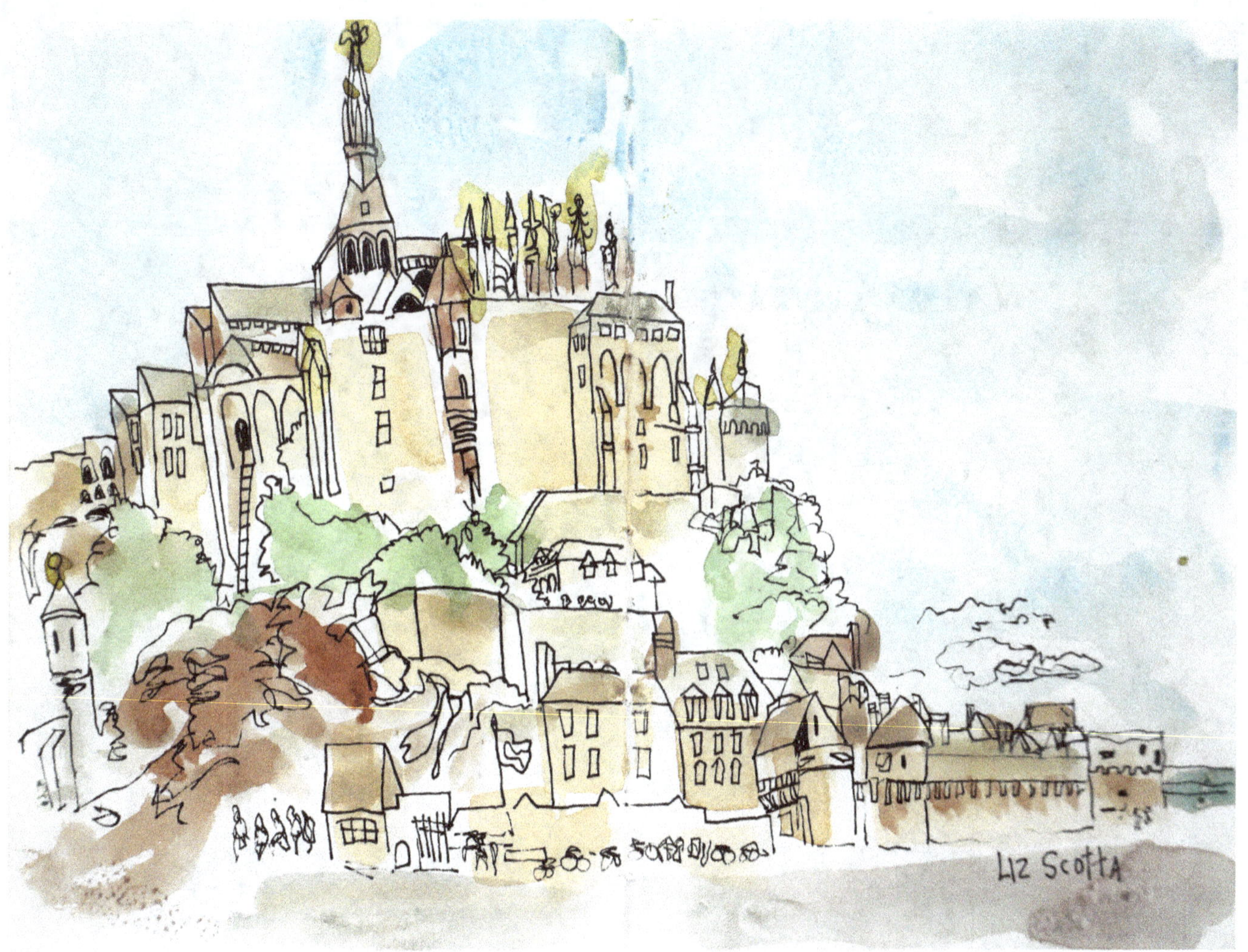

MONT-SAINT-MICHEL

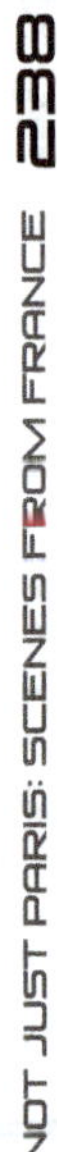

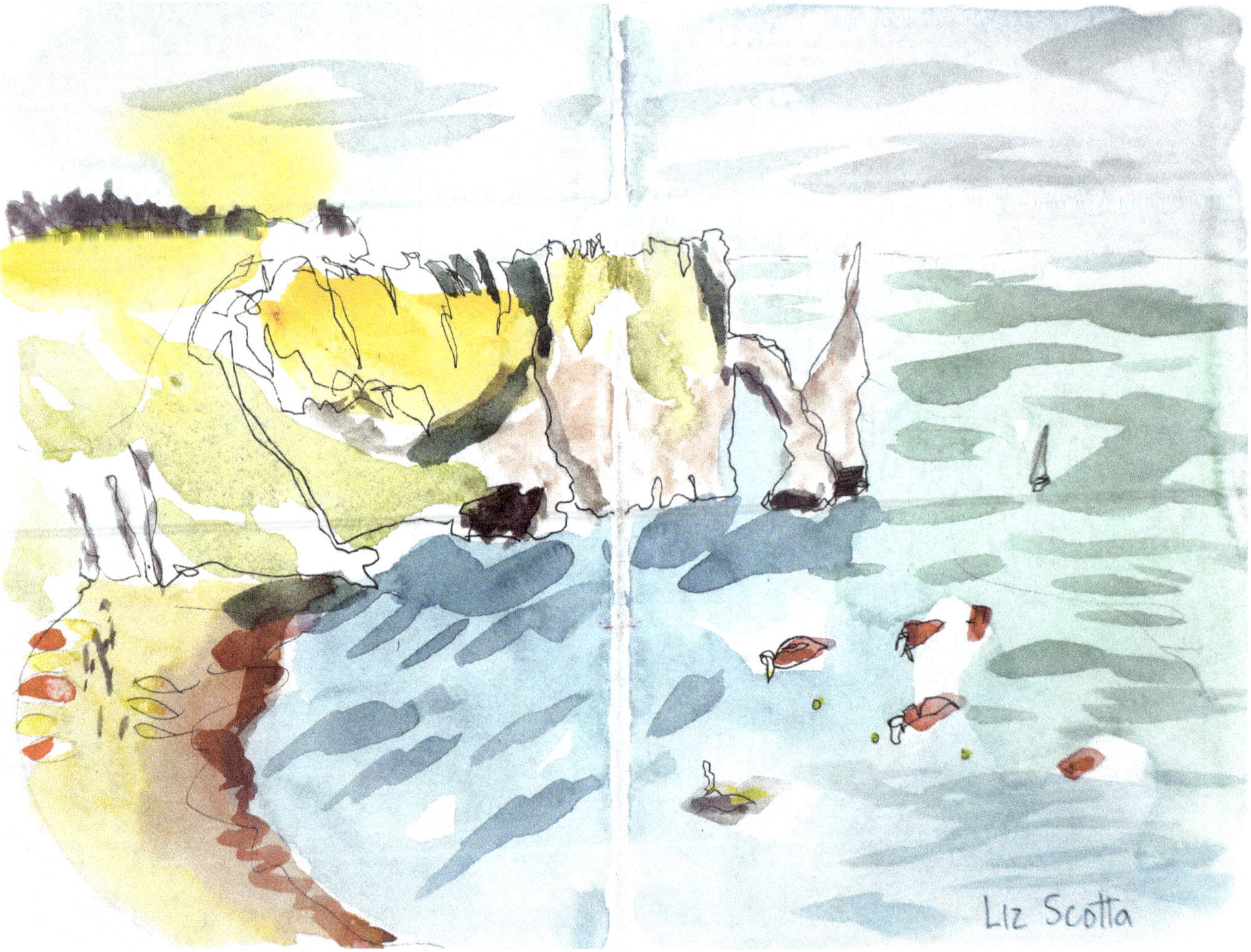

ÉTRETAT

ACKNOWLEDGEMENTS

Ellen Anders, Dr. Tom Blair, Prof. Camilo Bonilla, Roxanne Douc, Eduardo, Gerry Fait, Patricia García, Joan Hoffmann, Terry Linda Hodge, Martin Jennings, Alicia Kartinos, Prof. Philippe Kreiter, Gilet Marco, Cindy Mathieu, Daniel Maxwell, Maria Naoum, Dr. Terri Nelson, Diane Olivier, Kathy Pettibone, Yves Rigutto, Prof. Jennifer Saito, SF Sketchers, Sœur Marie Dolorès, Sœur Marie Catherine, Sœur Marie Goretti, Sœur Marie Estelle, Sœur Mary Joseph, Barbara and Gordon Sizelove, Natalie Smith, Sunset Sketchers, Joseph Toone, Urban Sketchers Paris, Dr. Lynn Vogel-Zuiderweg.

INDEX

INDEX

INDEX

INDEX

www.ingramcontent.com/pod-product-compliance
Lightning Source LLC
Chambersburg PA
CBHW081026060726
47593CB00020B/2898